Learning Maya 7 | The Special Effects Handbook

ACKNOWLEDGEMENTS

Cover design:
Louis Fishauf

Cover image and interior book design:
Ian McFadyen

Production designer:
Mike Barker

Additional production design:
Diane Erlich

Editorial services:
Erica Fyvie

Technical Editor:
Cathy McGinnis

Additional technical review:
Marc Beaudoin, Rick Kogucki, Elliot Grossmann

DVD production:
Roark Andrade and Julio Lopez

Production Coordinator:
Lenni Rodrigues

Project Manager:
Carla Sharkey

Product Manager, Learning Tools and Training:
Danielle Lamothe

Director, Learning Tools and Training:
Michael Stamler

This book would not have been possible without the generous help of Sony Pictures Imageworks. We would like to thank Camille Bingcang, Jerry Schmitz and Sande Scoredos for their tremendous contributions.

Primary author: Marc-André Guindon

Marc-André Guindon is the founder of Realities Studio (www.RealitiesStudio.com), a Montreal-based production facility. An advanced user of both Maya® and Alias® MotionBuilder® softwares, Marc-André and Realities have partnered with Alias on several projects, including *The Art of Maya*, *Learning Maya 6 | MEL® Fundamentals*, and the *Learning Maya 7* series. Realities Studio was also the driving force behind Pipeline Technique DVDs, such as *How to Integrate Quadrupeds into a Production Pipeline* and *Maya and MotionBuilder Pipeline*. Realities also created the Maya Quick Reference Guides and contributed to *Creating Striking Graphics with Maya & Photoshop®* .

Marc-André has established complex pipelines and developed numerous plug-ins and tools for a variety of projects in both the film and games industries. His latest projects include the integration of motion capture for the Outlaw Game Series (*Outlaw Volleyball*, *Outlaw Golf 1* and *2* and *Outlaw Tennis*). He served as Technical Director on *XXX2: State of the Union* (Revolution Studios), *ScoobyDoo 2* (Warner Bros. Pictures) and *Dawn of the Dead* (Universal Pictures).

Marc-André is also an Maya MasterClass™ presenter. Marc-André continues to seek additional challenges for himself, Realities and his crew.

A special thanks goes out to the following authors whose contributions have helped shape this book into what it is today:

Christoph Berndt, Michiel Duvekot, Bill Dwelly, Shawn Dunn, Petre Gheorghian, Lee Graft, Alan Harris, Jill Harrington, Scyalla Magloir, John Patton, Cathy McGinnis, Lorna Saunders.

We would like to thank Carmela Bourassa, Sylvana Chan, Deion Green, John Gross, David Haapalehto, Rachael Jackson, Lorraine McAlpine, Brahm Nathans, James Christopher, Anthony Nehme, Paula Suitor, Jill Ramsay, Shai Hinitz and Olivier Guindon.

We also would like to thank Turbo Squid (www.turbosquid.com) for providing the bonus textures included in this book's DVD-ROM. Thanks to Beau Perschall, Dan Lion and Brian Gaffney.

FOREWARD

Doug Walker | President, Alias

As the President of Alias since 2001, I've had the privilege of watching the development of the 3D graphics industry from a unique perspective. I've been able to visit countless customer sites and to watch the development of those customers' projects over time. While the nature of this collection of work may have varied greatly, they all shared one thing in common - their backbones were built on Alias technology. It's wonderful to see artists, designers, developers and others achieve incredible results and push the boundaries of what our software can do. It's even better to watch them get rewarded for it. And the rewards? They never stop.

I've been thrilled to watch Alias customers accept countless accolades around the world and I'm proud of the role we've played in helping them get there. Because, ultimately, making Maya the world's most powerful 3D modeling and animation tool isn't just about selling software, it's about giving our customers what's necessary to be successful. It's about incorporating your feedback and continuously improving our tools to give you, the artist, the power you need to make your creative vision come alive. This on-going process reaffirms our Corporate Vision – Alias| Imagination's Engine.

The book you hold in your hand is the result of one of the unique partnerships we have with our customers. "For more than a decade, Alias and Sony Pictures Imageworks have partnered with a common purpose - to use technology to create the most spectacular onscreen imagery," says Tim Sarnoff, president of Imageworks. " To continue surprising and surpassing the expectations of our audiences we need to constantly push ourselves. This challenge will never end for us - and that's why our partnership with Alias will continue to be critical to the success of Imageworks."

When we first approached Imageworks to see if they could contribute to this series of books, their enthusiasm was clear and they generously provided assets from their Academy Award® winning short film *The ChubbChubbs!* Within the pages of this book, you'll have the opportunity to build on the models and animations created in *Learning Maya 7 | The Modeling and Animation Handbook*. You'll learn about adding dynamic effects and to render in both Maya and mental ray for Maya.

In any art form, success isn't achieved by creativity alone. Hard work, dedication, long hours and sacrifice are all a part of the recipe for success. Mastering your craft takes time and devotion. It isn't easy, but making your vision reality is the most rewarding work of all. I'm confident this book can help you get there. We provide the engine, you provide the imagination - the possibilities are endless.

Doug Walker
President, Alias

ABOUT *THE CHUBBCHUBBS!*

Sony Pictures Imageworks

The Academy Award® for best animated short film has a long and prestigious history that dates back to the 5th Academy Award ceremonies in 1932. Each year the competition is incredibly intense, and 2002 was no exception. How ironic, then, that the winner would have been a film created in-house at Sony Pictures Imageworks merely as a test of their animation pipeline. "*The ChubbChubbs!* was never even intended for release," explains Imageworks President, Tim Sarnoff. "When it was finished we showed it to people here at the studio and some of the executives in theatrical distribution decided it was worth showing to exhibitors. To our surprise people just kept responding enthusiastically." The decision to test the Imageworks pipeline came about in the fall of 2001 when the company was looking into opening Sony Pictures Animation. While the two companies would share facilities and other resources, the mandate of animation would be geared more towards creating fully CG features while Imageworks would continue to focus on delivering high caliber visual effects. The best way to ascertain if the Imageworks effects pipeline could also support the production of full-length CG films was, of course, to try producing a complete CG film with it.

"We invited staff members to pitch their story ideas," recounts Sarnoff. "Jeff Wolverton, one of our animators pitched a story he called *Attack of the ChubbChubbs*, and we chose it as the best candidate."

The story stars an awkward little alien, Meeper, with a kind heart and big dreams. As the "mop boy" of the intergalactic "Ale-E-Inn" bar he does have some difficulty getting the "respect" he deserves especially as he tries to warn the bar's patrons of an impending invasion by the fearsome ChubbChubbs.

The film's director, Eric Armstrong, worked closely with Wolverton and the Imageworks storyboard department to hone the original story concept into a five minute piece. Meanwhile the film's producer, Jacquie Barnbrook was busy managing the project: finding artists who had time to devote to it, arranging sound and music production and keeping Armstrong – who was busy co-supervising the animation for *Stuart Little II* at the same time – on schedule.

Armstrong believes that, over the course of the project, there were probably about one hundred digital artists who had a hand in *The ChubbChubbs!* The reason for the large number is that animators were brought in as they became available, and left when another more official project came along. The maximum at any one given time were as many as fifteen Maya animators working on modeling, rigging and character/camera animation.

Imageworks has been using Maya for years in its visual effects pipeline. "We did a test a few years ago and found Maya to be the most flexible and powerful 3D package on the market," states Armstrong. "From that point on we've been using it for our modeling and animation needs."

Before winning the Oscar® for best animated short film, *The ChubbChubbs!* took first place at the Los Angeles International Short Film Festival, the London Effects and Animation Festival and the Australia Effects and Animation Festival. Such a plethora of accolades is more than enough proof that *The ChubbChubbs!* animation pipeline test has been – to put it mildly – a success, and that the Imageworks Maya-centered pipeline is capable of producing animated features second to none.

Sony Pictures Imageworks also produced a second "made with Maya" film entitled *Early Bloomer,* which was released in theaters in May 2003. The popular short stars an adorable but awkward tadpole trying to fit in with her mischievous friends. In September 2006, Imageworks expects to launch *Open Season,* Sony Pictures Entertainment's first fully animated feature length film from Sony Pictures Animation, featuring the voices of Martin Lawrence, Ashton Kutcher, Debra Messing and Gary Sinise.

Table of Contents

Introduction

Project01

Project02

Project03

Project04

Project05

Project06

Project07

Project08

HOW TO USE THIS BOOK

Thank you for choosing *Learning Maya 7 | The Special Effects Handbook*. This book builds on the projects begun in *Learning Maya 7 | The Modeling and Animation Handbook*. In some instances, you'll have an opportunity to add detail and effects to the scenes and characters you may have modeled and animated in the first half of this series. *Learning Maya 7 | The Special Effects Handbook* also covers important theories that apply to dynamics and rendering in Maya and mental ray for Maya. Within the pages of this book, you'll both complete the projects begun in the first book, and also to work with and understand a wide variety of other workflows and theories.

How you use this book will depend on your experience with computer graphics and 3D animation. This book moves at a fast pace and is designed to help the intermediate level user improve their rendering and dynamics skills and understand how they relate to one another in a production pipeline. If this is your first experience with 3D software, we suggest that you begin with the *Learning Maya 7 | Foundation* book, as the prerequisite before proceeding through the lessons in this book. If you are already familiar with Maya or another 3D package, you can dive in and complete the lessons as written.

Updates to this book

In an effort to ensure your continued success through the lessons in this book, please visit our web site for the latest updates available: www.alias.com/learningtools_updates/

Windows® and Macintosh®

This book is written to cover Windows and Macintosh platforms. Graphics and text have been modified where applicable. You may notice that your screen varies slightly from the illustrations depending on the platform you are using.

Things to watch for

Window focus may differ. For example, if you are on Windows, you have to click in the panels with your middle mouse button to make it active.

To select multiple attributes in Windows, use the **Ctrl** key. On Macintosh, use the **Command** key. To modify pivot position in Windows, use the **Insert** key. On Macintosh, use the **Home** key.

Alias packaging

This book can be used with either **Maya Complete™**, **Maya Unlimited™**, or **Maya Personal Learning Edition** software, as the lessons included here focus on functionality shared among all three software packages.

Learning Maya DVD-ROM

The Learning Maya DVD-ROM contains several resources to accelerate your learning experience including:

- Lesson support files;
- Instructor-led overviews to guide you through the projects in the book;
- Interview with Alias Certified Instructor Cathy McGinnis;
- Excerpt from the Sony Pictures Imageworks' short *The ChubbChubbs!;*
- Turbo Squid textures – Value $370.00US.

We recommend that you watch the instructor-led overviews before proceeding with the lessons in this book.

Because learning never stops, we've provided you with some great textures from Turbo Squid for your use. Turbo Squid delivers innovative textures from artists around the planet. To access these files, copy the *turboSquid* folder from the DVD-ROM at the back of this book to your computer.

The following textures are located in the turboSquid folder of the DVD-ROM:

People textures provided courtesy of David Silvernell (aka Got3d). Copyright2004.

Material textures provided courtesy of David Silvernell (aka Got3d). Copyright 2004.

Element textures provided courtesy of David Silvernell (aka Got3d). Copyright 2004.

Installing lesson support files – Before beginning the lessons in this book, you will need to install the lesson support files. Copy the project directories found in the *support_files* folder on the DVD disc to the *Maya\projects* directory on your computer. Launch Maya and set the project by going to File > Project > Set... and selecting the appropriate project.

Windows: C:*Documents and Settings\username\My Documents\maya\projects*

Macintosh: *Macintosh HD:Users:username:Documents:maya:projects*

Please note: *Support files require Maya version 7.*

Lessons

Lesson 01 *Materials*

Lesson 02 *Textures*

In Project One, you are going to explore in-depth shading networks. Shading networks are connections between nodes such as surfaces, materials, textures, utilities, etc. and are evaluated when Maya needs to render the scene. You will start by revising the basics of materials, and then explore some common texture nodes and utilities.

By the end of this project, you should feel comfortable creating various shading networks to enhance your scenes.

A material is a set of instructions that describes how the surface of an object will look when rendered. It is not just a collection of attributes you can texture map, but also a mathematical description of how light will behave when it strikes the surface. The Maya attributes allow you to fine-tune the look of a material, whether it is a cartoon effect or photorealism.

In this lesson you will learn the following:

- The definition of an IPR render;

- The basics of materials and shading networks;

- The definition of a specular highlight and how to use it;

- Anisotropic shaders;

- Layered shaders;

- Ramp shaders;

- Shading maps;

- Surface shaders.

IPR

IPR stands for *Interactive Photorealistic Rendering* and is available for both mental ray and Maya renderers. IPR is a type of software rendering that allows you to adjust shading and lighting attributes and see the updates in real time. When you do an IPR render, it writes out a file (deep raster file), that contains all the sample information for each pixel in the image. This file is written to the *iprimages* directory. It will have a name like *_tmp_ipr.iff*. This file is similar to the file that gets written out when you do a normal render in the Render view, in that it gets overwritten every time you do a new IPR Render. As long as the current project stays the same, the file will be overwritten when an IPR Render is started in that user session.

However, IPR does not prefix the camera name on the file like a normal render does. This means if you change cameras and do an IPR Render, the deep raster file will overwrite the same file. A regular render will add the prefix of the camera to the file and generate a new file. If you want to save the Maya IPR file permanently so that it does not get overwritten, you can do a **File → Save IPR File** in the Render View window. This is useful if you are working on a large scene and the IPR file takes several minutes to generate. If this is the case, you can save out the IPR file and work on other things and still return to it at a later time. If you have saved out an IPR file, you can use **fcheck** to view the image component of the file. If you use the mental ray for Maya IPR, the IPR images will be saved in the *Images* directory.

Tip: *IPR files can be quite large and will consume large amounts of disk space. It is a good idea to delete these files if you don't need them.*

1   IPR rendering

- Open the scene file called *01-stage.ma* from the *support_files* directory on the DVD-ROM.

- Press the **IPR Render** button at the top of the main interface or in the Render View.

The scene is rendered, and then a message appears at the bottom of the Render view that says:

        Select a region to begin tuning

- **Click+drag** to draw a region around the portion of the image you want to tune.

You can now begin tuning your lights and materials to see the IPR update automatically.

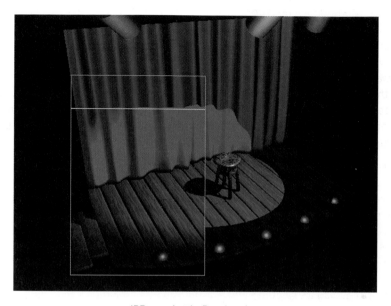

IPR running in Render view

Note: While the IPR is updating, you can add new lights, move lights, modify light attributes and delete lights. You can also create, assign and edit new materials and the render will automatically update.

- Stop IPR with the red stop sign shaped button in the Render View.

Tip: mental ray IPR supports Raytracing attribute updates such as reflections and refractions.

Shading networks

A shading network can be defined as a graph of connected nodes that can be used to shade objects. These networks generally contain what Maya classifies as materials and textures, but they do not have to contain just these nodes.

The idea behind the Maya architecture is to have many simple nodes that can be connected together in a virtually infinite number of combinations, rather than fewer and very complex nodes. For example, you will not find all of the conceivable light attributes on a single node; instead

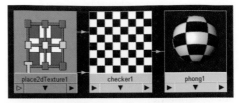

Phong shading network with checker color texture

you will have attributes for the Light on one node, attributes for the Light Fog on another node and attributes for the Light Glow on a third node. While this may seem inconvenient at first, it will become apparent that this is a very powerful method for augmenting a material.

Shading groups

A shading group is a set of objects to be shaded with the shading network. Below is a diagram of a shading group called *Phong1SG* (the *SG* stands for *shading group*). You can see a cone and a sphere connected to the shading group; these objects comprise the *set* that will be shaded by the shading network. In this case, the shading network is a phong material with a checker connected to it:

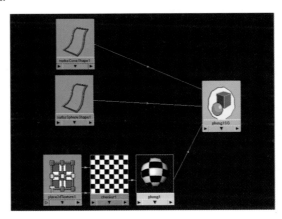

Shading group with attached shading network and surfaces

Note: *At render time, Maya determines which objects will be rendered by going to all of the shading groups and collecting all of the objects contained in each group. If an object is not a member of any shading group, it is not rendered.*

Project One

Connecting shading networks to shading groups

The shading network is connected to a *Port* attribute on the shading group. In a typical workflow, this connection will be made automatically. Below is a view of the Attribute Editor showing the three ports on a shading group:

Surface material

This port is used to shade surfaces such as NURBS, polygons and SubDs.

Volume material

This port is used to shade volumes such as fog and some particle types.

Displacement material

This port is used for displacement mapping surfaces and is used in conjunction with the Surface Material port.

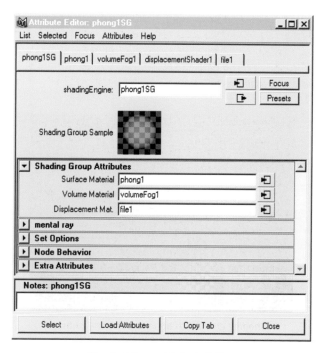

Shading Group Attribute Editor

All shading groups have the same three ports so that any shading group can shade any type of object. Each port has a shading engine associated with it that will evaluate the network attached to it.

Maya Bins

The Hypershade contains a **Bins** tab. Bins allow users to organize their networks into groups under specific headings. For instance, if you have a number of characters in a scene, and each character has a number of different materials assigned to it, then you may want to create a bin for each character and store all associated materials in that particular bin.

1 Create a bin

- Select **Window** → **Rendering Editors** → **Hypershade**.

- Click on the **Bins** tab.

- Click on the **Create Empty Bin** button or **RMB-click** on the **Master Bin** and select **Create** from the pop-up menu.

A dialog box will pop up where you can give your bin a name.

- Select the object to be part of that bin and then **RMB-click** on the name of the bin and select **Add Selected**.

Or

- Select the object to be part of a same bin and then **RMB-click** and choose **Create From Selected**.

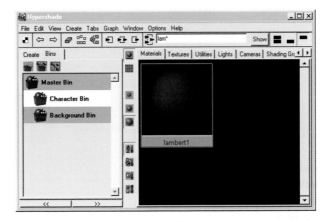

Bins displayed

Tip: *The **Text Filter** will allow you to type in a string or part of a string, and filter the top tabs accordingly. For instance, to see only lambert materials, type in lam*.*

Maya shader library

The shader library is a collection of over 60 shading networks comprised of various example material types. These networks can be used as is or as a basis to create your own materials or shaders. You can preview the library directly in the Hypershade via the **Shader Library** tab located in the bottom panel. To use one of the shaders from the library, simply **MMB-click+drag** it into the Hypershade or **RMB-click → Import Maya file**. Once you have dragged or imported the file, it will appear in the **Materials** tab and can be assigned or manipulated like any other material.

Note: *You cannot assign shader library materials directly from the* **Shader Library** *tab.*

MATERIALS

A material is essentially a shading model that calculates the surface characteristics and determines how a surface will be shaded. The use of the words shader and material are interchangeable and correct for this description. The common industry term for this description is shader, and you will find this term used throughout this book.

Materials and lighting

The single most important thing to do when creating an effective material is to concentrate on how the object's highlight appears. This one factor can dramatically improve the look of the material even before any textures are applied. Look around you and take note of the various ways light falls across surfaces. Notice how shiny objects have a bright small highlight and how a dull surface has barely any highlight at all.

The following will take a closer look at how light reflects off a surface. This diagram illustrates how a portion of incident light is scattered as it reflects, and a portion of the light can be reflected at a more consistent angle. The light reflected at a consistent angle results in an intense bright region called a *specular highlight*. The scattered light is referred to as *diffuse* light.

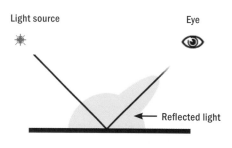

Reflected light

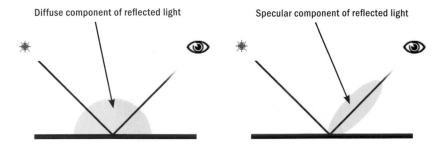

Components of refracted light

In reality, the specular component and the diffuse component of the total reflected light will vary depending on the characteristics of the surface.

In Maya, the diffuse component and the specular component are controlled separately, which gives you the flexibility to simulate virtually any real world surface.

Lambert material

The *lambert* material works well for matte surfaces. It simulates surfaces where most light rays will be absorbed by uneven, tiny surface imperfections. When light rays strike such a surface, they bounce around in the nooks and crannies instead of being reflected back from the surface. Any rays that actually are reflected will be scattered at close to random angles so you won't see a specular highlight. There is very little correlation between the angle of incidence and the angle of the reflected rays.

The extent to which the scattered light is absorbed or reflected is controlled by the **Diffuse** attribute. This attribute exists on all of the basic materials.

Since light reflected from a surface is what gives you the sense of its color, low diffuse values close to **0.0** mean very little light is scattered, so the surface will look dark. A high diffuse value approaching **1.0** means that a lot of light is scattered so the surface will look very saturated.

An example of a lambert surface with a low diffuse value is coal, where most light is absorbed by the surface imperfections. Examples of lambert surfaces with a high diffuse value are things like the surface of the moon or colored chalk. In this case, the surface imperfections cause the light to be scattered and some amount of it is actually reflected, giving these surfaces a strong sense of color.

The following image shows two lambert materials with different diffuse values; otherwise all of their attributes are identical.

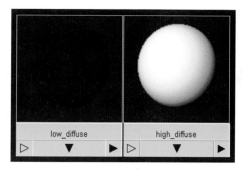

Different diffuse values

Tip: *The lambert shading model is used to compute the diffuse component of surface illumination. All other more complex shading models derive their diffuse component from lambert.*

Phong, phongE and blinn

Very smooth surfaces such as glass, mirrors and chrome will have a very low diffuse value approaching zero. This is because they reflect very little scattered light. The light doesn't get scattered because there are few surface imperfections that would cause it to bounce at random angles. Instead, most of the light rays are reflected off the surface at a similar angle resulting in a *specular highlight*. Because the lambert material does not simulate the specular component of surface illumination, for these types of surfaces you can choose from several other materials: *phong*, *phongE* and *blinn*.

Both phong and blinn shading models approximate the surface physics of incident light reflecting off a smooth surface. They are named after computer scientists Bui Tuong Phong and James Blinn.

The **Specular Shading** attributes on these three material types control how coherent the light rays are as they are reflected off the surface. If the light rays are reflected at close to the same angle, a tight highlight results. If the rays are more scattered, a bigger and softer highlight will result. If the rays were to become scattered enough, you would end up with the look of the lambert shading model.

At the other extreme, these shading models can simulate a mirror's almost perfectly smooth surface where very little light is absorbed and the reflected rays are very coherent.

Unlike the Diffuse attribute, which is common to all of these materials, the attributes that control the specular highlight appearance have different names on each material.

Phong

Cosine Power affects the size of highlights on the surface. This attribute can be thought of as shininess. Low numbers create big highlights while high numbers produce small highlights typically seen on very shiny surfaces.

PhongE

Roughness and **Highlight Size** work together to affect the size and look of the highlight.

Blinn

Eccentricity affects the size of highlights on the surface. Very shiny surfaces will need low values to produce a small and strong highlight, while surfaces like brushed metal will need higher values to produce a large highlight.

Blinn, phong or phongE?

While all three of these materials produce specular highlights, they each provide very different visual results. This visual impact is likely to be the determining factor in terms of which one to use, although it is worth noting that there is a slight increase in rendering time associated with using more complex materials such as blinn.

The order of rendering performance from fastest to slowest:

- PhongE

- Phong

- Blinn

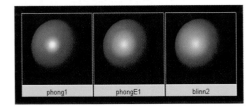

Comparison of materials phong, phongE, and blinn

Phong is less complex than blinn; it doesn't take into account changes in specularity due to the angle at which you are viewing the surface.

Blinn is a more sophisticated and true to life shading model where surfaces appear shinier at more severe angles. This can be controlled by the **Specular**

Roll Off attribute on the blinn material. **Specular Roll Off** also allows surfaces to reflect more of their surroundings when viewed at glancing angles. The following images show the effect of this attribute on reflectivity:

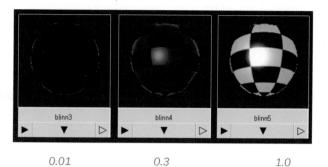

| 0.01 | 0.3 | 1.0 |

Effect of Specular Roll Off on Reflectivity
(reflected color mapped with checker)

Tip: *Use a* **Specular Roll Off** *value of* **0.3** *to simulate a wet surface, such as wet paint.*

You will also see that the Specular Roll Off affects the transition between the Specular Color and the Diffuse Color.

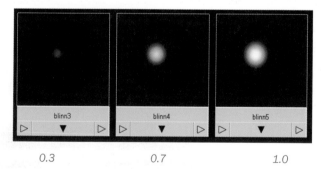

| 0.3 | 0.7 | 1.0 |

Effect of Specular Roll Off on transition from Specular Color to Diffuse Color

---

Tip: *The soft highlights on blinn surfaces are less likely to exhibit roping or flickering than the harder highlights on phong surfaces. Use the blinn material for surfaces with bump or displacement to reduce highlight roping or flickering.*

Specialized surface materials

So far you have looked at the most frequently used materials. There are several other materials in Maya including:

- Anisotropic;
- Layered shader;
- Ramp shader;
- Shading map;
- Surface shader;
- Use background.

Anisotropic

The purpose of the *Anisotropic* shader is to simulate surfaces that have micro-facet grooves when the specular highlight tends to be perpendicular to the direction of the grooves. If an anisotropic surface is spun against the grooves, the shape and location of the highlight will change depending on how the groove direction changes. Examples of uses for this material are satin, silk, nylon, CD's, etc.

In the following exercise, you will create and apply an Anisotropic material to a falling CD, reproducing the rainbow style highlights characteristic of a CDs undersurface. Later in this chapter you will complete the CD using a layered shader.

Anisotropic material (01-satinOrnament.ma)

1 Scene file

- Open the scene file called *01-anisoCD_01.ma*.

This file contains a NURBS disk that was animated as a rigid body colliding with a ground object. The simulation has been baked to allow scrubbing in the Time Slider. The CD geometry is made up of different pieces so different materials can be applied to the various sections. All pieces are parented under one rigid body node.

Project One

2 Layout

- Select **Panels** → **Saved Layouts** → **Hypershade/Render/Persp**.

- In the Perspective view, select **Panels** → **Perspective** → **camera**.

The camera is already animated for this exercise. Make sure when you render that you are rendering using this camera.

3 Create and assign an anisotropic material

- Use the **Create** menu in the Hypershade to create an *anisotropic* material.

- Assign it to *mainCDbody* and *mediumRing*.

4 Tune the anisotropic material

- Set the following values:

> **Diffuse** to **0.05**;
>
> **Angle** to **180**;
>
> **Spread X** to **37**;
>
> **Spread Y** to **0.1**;
>
> **Roughness** to **0.4**;
>
> **Fresnel Index** to **8.4**.

Note: *The Diffuse value should be low because this material is meant to simulate the smooth plastic coating on the underside of a CD. Nearly all reflected light from a very smooth surface will be represented by the specular component. The micro grooves in this coating will produce anisotropic highlights controlled by the following attributes.*

Spread X

Spread X controls how much the grooves spread out in the X-direction. The range is from **0.1** to **100**. (The X-direction is the surface's U-direction, rotated counterclockwise by the **Angle** attribute.) When this value is increased, the specular highlight shrinks in that direction, making the surface appear smoother. When the value is decreased, the highlight spreads out more in that direction, making the surface appear less smooth.

Spread Y

Spread Y controls how much the grooves spread out in the Y-direction. It ranges from **0.1** to **100**. (The Y-direction is perpendicular to the X-direction.) The effect of this attribute is similar to **Spread X**.

Roughness

Roughness controls the overall roughness of the surface. It ranges from **0.01** to **1.0**, with larger values giving a rougher appearance. As this value is increased, the specular highlights are more spread out. This value will also affect the reflectivity of the material if the **Anisotropic Reflectivity** is turned **On**.

Angle

Angle defines the X and Y directions on the surface relative to the surface's intrinsic U and V directions. X is the U direction, rotated counterclockwise by the **Angle** attribute. These X and Y directions are used by the shader to place the microgrooves that control the anisotropic properties of the shader. This value ranges from **0** to **360 degrees**.

Fresnel Refractive Index

Fresnel Refractive Index affects the look of the anisotropic highlight. (If the material is transparent and you are raytracing, it does not affect the way light from other objects bends when passing through the material.) As you increase this attribute, the highlight becomes brighter.

For transparent objects, you may want to set the **Fresnel Index** to match the object's **Refractive Index**. This will give the most physically accurate result for the highlight.

If **Anisotropic Reflectivity** is turned **On**, the reflectivity of the material is calculated directly from its roughness. If this attribute is turned **Off**, the value in reflectivity is used instead.

5   IPR Render

- Go to frame **57**.

- Select **IPR** → **IPR Render** → **camera**.

A variety of highlights will be clearly visible in the render.

- Define a tuning region that encompasses the entire CD.

Note the quality and shape of the specular highlights. They are long and spread out across the surface, not round.

Project One

6 Map Specular Color

The colored highlights that occur on CDs generally run from the inside of the CD to the outer edge and are typically a variety of colors from the visible light spectrum. On real CDs, these rainbow colors appear due to the *diffraction* of light (diffraction is the term for light splitting into its individual wavelengths as it passes through a medium such as a prism). A colored ramp texture will be used to fake the appearance of diffraction.

- In the Hypergraph, show the top and bottom tabs.

- Select the **Textures** tab.

- **MMB-click+drag** the *rainbowSpecRamp* texture onto the *anisotropic1* material and select **Specular Color** from the drop down menu.

7 Adjust the lighting

When working with the anisotropic material, the direction, distribution and intensity of the lighting is vital to the success of the look you are trying to attain. Normally, multiple lights are required at various angles to the surface to see the anisotropic highlights well.

- Increase the **Intensity** of the *spotLight2* to see the impact it has on the brightness of the highlights.

- Move the light to get a feel for the significance of its intensity and position relative to the surface.

8 Save the file

- Save the file, as you will complete the CD in the next exercise.

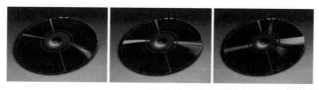

Position and intensity of spotLight2 modified

Note: *A movie file called ansioCD.mov is available to show the final results.*

Lesson 01

Layered shader

The *layered shader* can be used in two different ways. It can be used to layer materials, or it can be used to layer textures. Since there is a node specifically designed for layering textures that will be covered in the Texture lesson, you will experiment here only with the material layering capabilities.

When using the layered shader node, ask yourself if you need to see different material types on different areas of the same surface, or if you need to see different materials at the same time. such as a clear coat over car paint. If all you need is to overlay textures, then you should use a layered texture rather than a layered shader. It is best to avoid using layered shaders unnecessarily because they are very expensive to render.

Layered shader general workflow

In this exercise, you will use the layered shader to combine two different materials together.

1 Create materials to use as layers

Before you can layer anything, you will need some simple materials.

- In the Hypershade, create a *phong* and a *lambert* material.

- Set the *phong* material to *blue* and the *lambert* material to *red*.

- Map a checker to the **Transparency** of the *phong* material.

- Change the **Repeat UV** attribute to **8** and **8** on the *place2Dtexture* node for the *checker* texture.

2 Create a layered shader node

- Create a layered shader node.

- Open the Attribute Editor for the *layeredShader* node.

3 Connect the materials to the layered shader node

- **MMB-click+drag** the red lambert into the **Layered Shader Attributes** section.

- **MMB-click+drag** the blue phong into the **Layered Shader Attributes** section.

You will notice that each time you drag a material into the **Layered Shader Attributes** *section, a new icon appears. These icons represent the layers.*

- Click on the small **x** under the green layer icon to remove it.

The green icon is simply the default layer that you can get rid of once you have added your own layers.

4   Shuffle the layers

You now have a layered shader with two materials in it. However, the swatch for the layered shader will appear to be completely red. This is because the *red lambert* material (without any transparency) is on top of the *blue phong*. You need to change the order of the layers in order to see the phong on top of the lambert.

- In the Attribute Editor for the layered shader, **MMB-click+drag** the *lambert* icon to the right of the *phong* icon.

You should now see both layers in the swatch.

Tip: *The order of the layers from left to right in the Attribute Editor represents the layer order from top to bottom.*

5   IPR render the scene

- Create a sphere.

- Assign the *layeredShader* to the *sphere* and launch an IPR render.

You will notice that the specular highlight falls across both the phong and lambert regions of the surface (because even though the phong is transparent in those regions, its specular highlight is visible). This essentially defeats the purpose of using the layered materials.

Because different parts of the surface show different materials, you will need to change the layers again.

The IPR render

6   Manipulate the layers

- With IPR still running, **break** the connection between the *checker* and *phong* in the Hypershade.

- Create a connection between the *checker* and the *lambert*'s **Transparency** attribute.

- In the Attribute Editor for the layered shader, swap the layers using the **MMB-click** as you did earlier.

Notice how in the IPR render, the specular highlight no longer shows on both the red and blue regions.

Tip: *In more complex layered materials, you may need to apply a Specular Map to control the specular highlights on different layers.*

The shading network would look something like this:

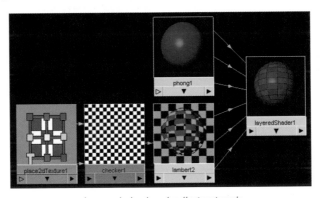

Layered shader shading network

Layered shader example

In this exercise, you will complete the CD that you started earlier in this chapter. You will use a layered shader to add the foil base visible under the clear grooved plastic on the underside of the CD.

1   Scene file

- Use the file you saved earlier.

Or

- Open the file named *01-anisoCD_02.ma*.

2 Layout

- Select **Panels** → **Saved Layouts** → **Hypershade/Render/Persp**.

- In the Perspective view, select **Panels** → **Perspective** → **camera**.

3 Create a layered shader

- Create a layered shader material in the Hypershade.

- Assign the *layeredShader1* to *mainCDbody* and *mediumRing*.

- Open the Attribute Editor for the *layeredShader1*.

- **MMB-click+drag** the *anisotropic1* from the Hypershade into the **Layered Shader Attribute** section in the Attribute Editor for the *layeredShader1*.

- Click on the **X** under the green default layer icon to **remove** it.

4 Launch an IPR

- IPR render frame **57** for test rendering throughout this lesson.

5 Create a blinn for the foil coating

A blinn material will be used to create a silver/gold foil base coating on the CD. This layer will go under the anisotropic clear plastic coating.

- Create a **Blinn** material in the Hypershade.

- **MMB-click+drag** the *blinn* into the **Layered Shader Attribute** section in the Attribute Editor for the *layeredShader1*.

At this point, you will not be able to see the Blinn layer because the anisotropic material has no transparency.

6 Adjust the transparency on the anisotropic material

- Increase the **Transparency** attribute on the *anisotropic* material to a suitable level for clear plastic.

This will reveal the blinn layer.

7 Tune the blinn material

- Adjust the blinn attributes to get a nice silver look.

Tip: *A good metalic material would use very low* **Diffuse**, *high* **Specular Roll Off** *and low* **Eccentricity**.

Lesson 01

8 Add a reflection map

Although the Diffuse, Eccentricity and Specular Roll Off will be the primary attributes you tune on the blinn shader, adding a reflection map will enhance the visual impact of the foil.

- Map the **Reflected Color** attribute on the blinn with an **Env Chrome** from the **Environment Textures** section of the **Create Render Node** window.

This makes the CD appear as though it is reflecting a pseudo-environment.

- Adjust the **Reflectivity** attribute to increase or decrease the brightness of the reflection map.

- Adjust the colors on the *envChrome* texture if you do not want a blue look.

9 Make final adjustments

If you have been test rendering at the same frame, you should check some other frames throughout the animation to make sure the values you are using provide expected results.

The camera angle and lighting position are important parts of the overall effect in this example. Experiment with different lighting to see how it affects the overall image.

The layered shader lets you combine the features of the various shading models together to produce one final result. This extra flexibility does come at the expense of increased render times, but gives you results that may be otherwise difficult to achieve.

10 Save your work

- The final scene file is called *01-anisoCD_03.ma*.

Tip: *The file anisoCDBlendCol.mb demonstrates an alternate method of achieving a similar appearance in the shading, but with the use of a blendColors utility node rather than a layered shader.*

Ramp shader

The *ramp shader* allows extra control over the way color changes with light angle, brightness, or the viewing angle (facing ratio). You can give your objects a flat, toon-like look by using the ramp shader.

This shader shares many attributes with other material attributes. All the color related attributes are controlled by ramps. There are also graphs for defining Specular Roll Off and Reflectivity, improving performance by avoiding complex shading networks and making toon shading easier to achieve.

You will now use a ramp shader to give some bouncing balls a flat, toon-like look.

1 Open the file

- Open the scene file *01-bounce_01.ma.*

This file consists of a number of spheres that use dynamics to bounce on a floor.

Note: *There is also a very large Area Light above the scene, which is why the illumination is so bright.*

2 Create a ramp shader

- Create a **ramp shader** material in the Hypershade.

- Assign the *rampShader* to all the spheres.

- Open the Attribute Editor for the *rampShader.*

You will notice that many of the common material attributes are controlled by ramps.

3 Edit the ramp attributes to create a toon shader

- Under the **Color** section, create another ramp handle in the ramp field by clicking in the field.

- Set the **Selected Position** of this ramp handle to **0.15**.

- Select the first ramp handle, and change its color to a bright blue.

- Select **Interpolation** and change it to **None**.

- Select the second ramp handle and set the following:

    RGB values to **0.4, 0.6, 1.0**;

    Interpolation to **None**.

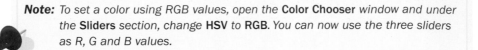

Note: *To set a color using RGB values, open the* **Color Chooser** *window and under the* **Sliders** *section, change* **HSV** *to* **RGB.** *You can now use the three sliders as R, G and B values.*

- Change **Color Input** to **Brightness**.

4   Test render the scene

- Play the scene up to frame **85**.

- Render to see the results.

Notice there are no outlines, just flat bands of color.

Ramp shader so far

5   Edit the Incandescence attribute

- Under the **Incandescence** section, create another ramp handle.

- Set the **Selected Position** of this ramp handle to **0.3**.

- Select the first ramp handle and under **Selected Color**, change the **HSV values** to **-1,-1,-1**.

Ramp shader with outline

Project One

> **Note:** *By setting the incandescence to negative values, you are forcing the light to be absorbed on the outer edge of the geometry rather than being emitted.*

- Change the **Interpolation** to **None**.
- Render the scene.

Notice flat bands of color surrounded by a black outline.

Ramp shader with strong specular highlight

6   Add specular shading

- Under the **Specular Shading** section, change **Specularity** to **1.0** and **Eccentricity** to **0.06**.

This will change the size and brightness of the highlight.

> **Note:** *The rectangular highlight is a result of the area light.*

7   Save your work

- The final scene file is called *01-bounce_02.ma*.

> **Note:** *A movie file called bounce.avi is available to show the final results.*

Shading map

A *shading map* is a node that allows you to remap the output from a material to create custom shading results. Recall that a material is a mathematical formula or set of instructions on how to shade the surface. The purpose of the shading map is to allow you to control the final shaded results to go beyond what is possible with standard materials.

A shading map allows complete control over the transition from the highlight to the shaded area of a surface. For example, you could achieve a cartoon look by mapping a ramp texture to get simple banded shading.

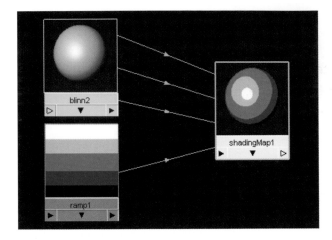

Shading map used with a ramp to produce toon-like blinn shading

Even more complex materials that have a translucent scattering layer can sometimes have a non-lambert falloff in diffuse intensity. This can be roughly simulated using the shading map to help get more natural looking skin, for example.

This can be a very powerful feature in that you can remap the output of any shading model using a shading map. The remapped outputs of different shading models can then be recombined to create a new shading model.

Car paint exercise

Shading maps combined with a layered shader can be used to render realistic metallic paint. This allows for more variation in the look of the paint to avoid surfaces that look flat and monochromatic.

Clear coat and metallic highlight

Car paint can be represented in many ways. The purpose of this exercise is to show the use of a shading map for the control and placement of highlights on a car body.

1 Scene file

- Open the file named *01-car_01.ma*.

2 Create shaders

- In the Hypershade, create the following nodes:

    Layered shader;

    Blinn;

    Shading map.

3 Add the shading map to the layered shader

- Open the Attribute Editor for the *layeredShader1*.

- **MMB-click+drag** the *shadingMap1* material from Hypershade to the **Layered Shader Attributes** section of the *layeredShader1* node.

- Remove the green layer from the *layeredShader1* node.

- Assign the *layeredShader1* material to the car's *bodyGroup*.

4 Tweak the shading map

- Select the *shadingMap1* material and open its Attribute Editor.

In the **Shading Map Attributes** *section, you will notice two attributes called* **Shading Map Color** *and* **Color**.

- **MMB-click+drag** the *blinn1* material from the Hypershade to the **Color** attribute of the **Shading Map Attributes** section of the *shadingMap1* node.

- Set the following for *blinn1*:

    Color to black;

    Diffuse to 0.0;

    Eccentricity to 0.45;

    Specular Roll Off to 0.42;

    Specular Color to white.

    Reflectivity to 0.0.

5 Shading map color

- Map the *shadingMap1*'s **Shading map color** attribute with a **Ramp** texture.

- In the Attribute Editor for the new ramp texture, define four handles as follows:

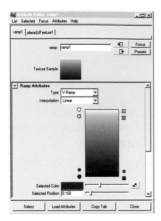

> Handle at **Position 1.0**,
> **RGB 1.0, 1.0, 1.0**;
>
> Handle at **Position 0.9**,
> **RGB 0.71, 0.85, 0.85**;
>
> Handle at **Position 0.1**,
> **RGB 0.22, 0.25, 0.32**;
>
> Handle at **Position 0.0**,
> **RGB 0.0, 0.0, 0.0**.

Ramp attributes

6 Clear coat layer

Just as with a real car, a clear polished shader needs to be layered onto a matte base to create two separate highlight regions.

- In the Hypershade, create a blinn material and set the following:

> **Color** to **black**;
>
> **Transparency** to **white**;
>
> **Diffuse** to **0.0**;
>
> **Eccentricity** to **0.09**;
>
> **Specular Roll Off** to **-10.0**;
>
> **Reflectivity** to **0.0**.

- Rename the new blinn to *clearCoat*.

7 Add the clear coat to the layered shader

- **MMB-click+drag** the clear coat *clearCoat* into the *layeredShader1* node's Attribute Editor.

- Use the **MMB** to reorder layers so the clear coat layer is in front of the base layer.

8 Reflection layer

Although reflections can be added to the clear coat layer, custom reflection effects will be isolated with their own layer.

- Create another blinn shader.

This shader will be used to control reflections.

- Set the **Color** to **black**.

- Increase the **Transparency** to **white**.

- Decrease the **Eccentricity** to **0.01** and increase the **Specular Roll Off** to **0.95**.

This will ensure that the reflection will only be seen on angles oblique to the camera's eye.

- Click in the **Specular Color** attribute and set its **HSV** to **0, 0, 4**.

This will set the specular color to super white, which will allow you to clearly see the reflections caused by the high Specular Roll Off attribute.

- Lower the **Reflectivity** to **0.05** to avoid washed out reflections.

Tip: *You must set **Raytracing** to **On** in the Render Settings to see reflections.*

- Rename the new blinn to *reflectivity*.

9   Add the reflection blinn to the layered shader

- **MMB-click+drag** the reflection *reflectivity* into the *layeredShader1* node's Attribute Editor.

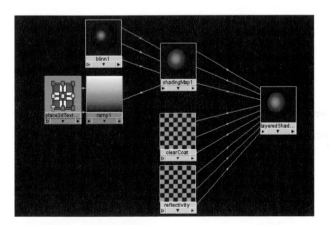

Layered Shader network using a shading map for control of highlights

- Use the **MMB** to reorder layers so the reflection layer is in front of the clear coat layer.

10 Set your render settings for raytracing

- In the **Raytracing Quality** section of the **Render Globals** window, turn **On Raytracing**.

11 Test render the scene

- The final scene file is called *01-car_02.ma*.

Surface shader

Surface shader is a lightweight *pass-through* node that simply allows you to translate the names of any node's outputs to the names required for the shader to be a valid surface material.

What this means is that a node must directly connect to a surface material port of a shading group and have at least one of the following specially named output attributes to be a valid node:

- *outColor*

- *outTransparency*

- *outGlowColor*

If the node connected to the surface material port of a shading group does not have at least one of the above attributes, none of the objects assigned to that shading group will render.

Note: *It does not matter which attribute of a node is connected to the surface material port of a shading group; only the* **outColor**, **outTransparency** *and* **outGlowColor** *attributes of the connected node will be used.*

The surface shader node is simply a means to translate an arbitrary network of Maya or user-written nodes with randomly named output attributes into what the renderer will recognize as a shading network.

Use background shader

The *use background* shader becomes important in workflows involving compositing in the production pipeline. It allows a surface to mask other objects behind it by using the background color. This will be covered in further detail later in this book.

Conclusion

Materials are the foundation for shading your surfaces. A material is a set of instructions that describes how the surface of an object will look when rendered. It is not just a collection of texture maps, but also a description of how light will fall across the surface. Maya provides a number of tools to help you define the materials in your scene.

In the next lesson, you will learn about procedural and file textures that can be used in shading networks.

Alias *Be open-minded. Maya is always evolving and there's no reason not to evolve*
Tip: *with it. By doing so, you might find better and more efficient workflows.*

Tim Wong | Product Specialist QA

Lesson 02 Textures

One of the most important
aspects of a scene is the
look of the textures mapped
to the various objects and
surfaces. These textures give
the objects relevance to their
surroundings, enhancing
the visual quality and
believability of the scene. It
is important to keep in mind
that this is a slower process
than most would think; a
certain amount of tweaking
is involved in designing and
applying textures.

In this lesson you will learn the following:

- How to use textures to build shading networks;

- Texture placement and conversion;

- File texture filtering and the use of BOT files;

- Displacement mapping;

- mental ray Bake Sets.

Layered texture

The layered texture node is designed to composite multiple textures using various blend modes directly inside Maya.

It is important to understand the difference between the layered shader and the layered texture node. The layered texture node allows you to composite textures together using several blending operations, such as add, multiply, subtract, etc., while the layered shader only has one level of transparency to blend textures together.

In the following exercise, a layered texture node will be used to make Diva look dirty and add bandage textures on her nose.

1 Open the file

- Open the scene file called *02-layeredTextureDiva_01.ma*.

2 Interaction and render optimizations

- Hide everything but Diva's skin geometry.

Doing so will speed up the rendering process throughout this exercise.

3 Graph the skin material

- In the Hypershade, graph the material already assigned to Diva.

4 Create a layered texture node

- Create a *layered* texture by selecting **Create → Layered Texture**.

- **MMB-click+drag** the *layeredTexture1* onto Diva's material and connect it to **Color**.

- In the Attribute Editor for the *layeredTexture1*, click inside the **Layered Texture Attributes** section twice to create two new layers.

This results in three layers in total.

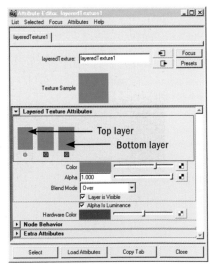

Layered texture attributes

Note: *Just like the layered shader, the top layer is furthest to the left and the bottom layer is on the far right. It is also possible to rearrange the order of the layers at any time by* **MMB-click+dragging** *them in the* **Layered Texture Attributes** *section.*

5   Map the bottom layer

- Click on the bottom layer icon to make it the active layer.

- Make sure the **Blend Mode** is set to **None**.

- Map the **Color** attribute with the file texture that was used to originally texture Diva.

The bottom layer will not be visible yet because the middle and top layers are not set up.

- Temporarily make the top and middle layers invisible by clicking on the layer icon and then turn **Off** the **Layer is Visible** checkbox.

6   Map the middle layer

- In the Attribute Editor for the *layeredTexture1* node, click on the middle layer icon to make it active.

Bottom layer only

- Turn the **Layer is Visible** checkbox to **On** for this layer.
- Map the **Color** attribute with a **Solid Fractal** texture.
- Set the **Blend Mode** to **Multiply**.

*This mode multiplies fractal1 and the skin texture. In areas where the fractal is white, the skin is unchanged because white is equal to **1, 1, 1**. Whichever color is multiplied by 1 gives the original color. Where the fractal is black, the skin becomes black because anything multiplied by **0, 0, 0** gives 0.*

- Set the *solidFractal's* **Threshold** attribute to **0.5**.

The fractal is now more white with black spots of dirt. This will give a nice dirty look to Diva's skin.

Dirt layer multiplied with skin color layer

Note: *The hardware texturing might look very low resolution in the viewport since Maya will trade compositing quality for speed. The texture will be displayed appropriately in renders. To increase the display quality in the viewport, increase the* **Texture Resolution** *for the skin material.*

7 Map the top layer

- In the Attribute Editor for the *layeredTexture1* node, click on the *top* layer icon to make it active.

- Turn the **Layer is Visible** flag back **On** for this layer.

- Set the **Blend Mode** to **Over**.

This mode will add the top layer over the other layers.

- Click the **Map** button for the **Color** attribute of the top layer.

- In the **Create Render Node** window, specify **As projection**, then create a **File Texture**.

- Browse for the file called *bandage.tif* found in the *sourceimages* directory.

- Connect the **Out Alpha** from the *projection1* to the **Input[0].Alpha** attribute of the layered texture node.

- Turn **Off** the **Wrap U** and **Wrap V** placement attributes so the texture doesn't get repeated across the character when placing it.

- Position the *place3dTexture* node to position the bandages on Diva's nose.

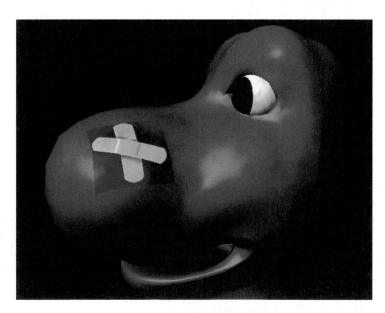

Texture placement for the bandage texture

- Set the **Default Color** attribute to **black** on the *bandage.tif* file texture.

*This step is important because adjusting the **Coverage** attributes on the texture placement in the last step has exposed the **Default Color** surrounding the bandage. Because the **Blend Mode** is **Over**, setting the **Default Color** value to **black** leaves the underneath layers unchanged.*

Lesson 02

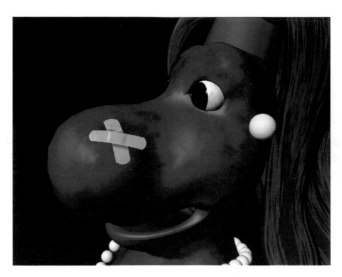

Bandage layer adjusted

8 Save your work

- The final scene file is called *02-layeredTextureDiva_02.ma*.

Using ramps to combine textures

Ramp textures are useful tools for developing textures. A ramp does not only blend colors, it also allows you to combine textures together and control how they blend.

If you look at a ramp in the Attribute Editor, it has position markers that define a specific U or V value along the texture. If you select one of these position markers in the Attribute Editor, there will be a color associated with it. You can then map that position marker's color and, depending on the interpolation settings, the texture will be blended with the other colors of the ramp.

The following example shows some possibilities of using ramps to create texture effects in Maya:

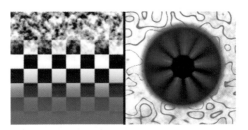

Ramp textures

Note: *The ramp itself will not show the actual texture blend, but the swatch representing the ramp will.*

Rusty flying saucer

You will now build materials for the body of a flying saucer. You will create a shading network using various connected nodes to achieve a rusted and beat-up metal look.

1 Open the file

- Open the file called *02-spaceSaucer_01.ma*.

2 Create a ramp shader

You will start by assigning a shader to the space saucer in order to be able to use the IPR.

- Create a ramp shader and rename it *hullShader*.

- Assign the *hullShader* to the top and bottom part of the flying saucer.

- Set the following for the *hullShader*:

  Color to **black**;

  Color Input to **Facing Angle**;

  Specular Color to **white**.

- Create a new handle in the middle of the **Color** ramp attribute.

- Map it with a layered texture.

- Rename the new layered texture node to *hullLayeredTexture*.

3 Create the base layer

You will now work up the base layer on the layered texture to create dirty painted metal.

Note: *Launch the IPR in order to see your changes.*

- In the Attribute Editor for *hullLayeredTexture*, highlight the layer icon.

This will be the base painted metal layer.

- Map a grid in the Color attribute of the selected layer.

- Set the following for the new *grid* texture:

    Line Color to **black**;

    Fill Color to **white**;

    U Width to **0.0**;

    V Width to **0.04**.

- Set the following for the new *grid*'s *place2dTexture* node:

    Repeat U to **1.0**;

    Repeat V to **10.0**.

The base layer could now use a fractal texture to break up the solid fill color of the grid texture.

- Map a fractal texture in the Fill Color of the grid texture.

- Set the following for the new fractal:

    Amplitude to **0.3**;

    Threshold to **0.4**;

    Color Gain to **orange**.

- Set the following for the new fractal's *place2dTexture* node:

    Repeat U to **0.1**;

    Repeat V to **0.5**.

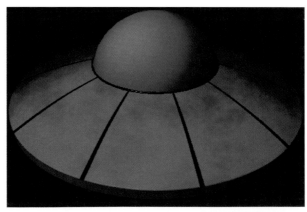

The grid texture and orange fractal on the flying saucer

4 Add a rust layer

You will now add a new layer to the layered texture to create a rusted metal look.

- In the Attribute Editor for the *hullLayeredTexture*, create a new layer.

- **MMB-click+drag** the new layer to the left of the base layer.

- Set the new layer's **Blend Mode** to **Over**.

- Map a granite to the color of the new layer.

5 Define an alpha for the rust layer

At this time, the granite texture covers the entire hull surface, but you will now define an alpha that will make the granite look like rusted patches.

- In the Attribute Editor for the *hullLayeredTexture*, map the Alpha attribute with a ramp.

- Set the ramp's **Type** to **U Ramp**.

- Set the top of the ramp to be **black** and the bottom to be **white**.

- Highlight the middle ramp handle, then set the **Selected Position** to **0.1**.

- Map the selected color with a solid fractal.

- Tweak the new *solidFractal* as follows:

  Threshold to **0.7**;

  Amplitude to **10.0**;

  Depth to **8.0, 8.0**;

  Invert to **On**.

The rust layer

Lesson 02

6   Bump mapping

In order to give a nice bumpy effect to the flying saucer surface, you will map the layered texture to the bump mapping of the ramp shader.

- **MMB-click+drag** the *hullLayeredTexture* on the *hullShader*, then select **bump map** from the pop-up menu.

- Select the newly created *bump2d* node, then set the **Bump Depth** attribute to **0.2**.

7   Light texture

You will now add incandescent light texture on the side of the flying saucer.

- Create a lambert material and assign it to the surface in the middle of the flying saucer.

- Set the **Color** of the lambert to **black**.

- Map the **Incandescence** of the lambert to a file texture.

- Browse for the file called *light.tif*.

- Set the **Repeat V** attribute on the file texture's *place2dTexture* node to **50.0**.

The light texture assigned

Dirty hub

To continue texturing the flying saucer, you will now dirty the hub by adding wiper marks. To do so, you will use another layered texture, and project a file texture onto the surface.

Project One

1 Create a ramp shader

- Create another ramp shader and rename it to *hubShader*.

- Assign the *hubShader* to the flying saucer's hub.

- Set the *hubShader*'s attributes as follows:

    Color to go from **black** to **light blue**;

    Color Input to **Facing Angle**;

    Transparency to go from **black** to **white**;

    Specularity to **1.0**;

    Eccentricity to **0.15**;

    Specular Color to **white**;

Note: *The IPR will not update the transparency correctly; relaunch the IPR in order to see your changes.*

2 Add a layered texure

- Highlight the white handle of the *hubShader*'s **Transparency**, then map a layered texture for it.

- Rename the new layered texture to *hubLayeredTexture*.

- Map a **Solid Fractal** in the **Color** attribute of the *hubLayeredTexture*.

- Set the new *solidFractal*'s **Threshold** to **0.2**.

- Add a layer for the *hubLayeredTexture* and **MMB-click+drag** the new layer in front of the first layer.

- Set the new layer's **Blend Mode** to **Over**.

3 Create a file texture

- Click on the **Map** button for the **Color** attribute of the new layer.

- In the **Create Render Node** window, choose **As Projection** from the 2D Textures' options, then click on **File**.

Doing so will create a 3D placement node in the scene that will allow you to place the projection of the texture easily on the hub. The default setting of projection is **Planar**, *which means that the image is being projected through worldspace just like a slide projector.*

- In the Attribute Editor for the new file texture, browse for the texture called *wipers.tif*.

- Set the *place2dTexure* of the file texture **Wrap U** and **V** to **Off**.

This will prevent the texture from repeating itself to infinity in U and V.

4 Position the texture

- Open the Attribute Editor for the *projection1* node that was created between the *hubLayeredTexture* and the file texture.

- Click on the **Fit To BBox** button.

This will automatically place the file texture to fit the bounding box of the hub surface.

- Translate, rotate and scale the projection so that it looks like the following:

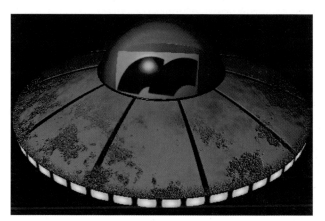

The wiper projection

Tip: *Make sure to put the projection in an angle pointing down. If you don't do so, the projection will also texture the other side of the hub.*

5 Adjust the default color of the texture

- Open the Attribute Editor for the file texture node.

- In the **Color Balance** section, set the **Default Color** to **black**.

By setting the **Default Color,** *you are essentially defining the regions outside of the texture to black.*

Tip: It is possible to texture map the **Default Color** attribute to create
a layered texture look.

6   Connect the projection to the alpha of the layered texture

In order to reveal the base layer of the layered shader, you must define the
alpha layer to have some transparency. In the next steps, you will connect
the alpha of the projection to the alpha of the top layer.

- Open the Attribute Editor for the *hubLayeredTexture* node and highlight the
layer on the left.

- **MMB-click+drag** the *projection1* node from the Hypergraph to the **Alpha**
attribute of the selected *hubLayeredTexture* layer.

Doing so will display the Connection Editor.

- Highlight the **Out Alpha** attribute on the left side and connect it to the
Inputs → **Inputs[0]** → **Inputs[0].Alpha** attribute on the right side.

The wiper projection with alpha

Placement nodes

Because the shading networks created so far are comprised of 3D textures'
placement, *place3dTexture* nodes have been created in the scene. These node can
be manipulated in order to control the placement of the textures on the geometry.

Lesson 02

1 Moving placement nodes

- To adjust a texture placement node, select a *place3dTexture* node in the Hypershade or a green 3D manipulator in a view.

- Move, rotate and scale the 3D manipulator to see its effect on the surfaces.

> **Tip:** When the placement of texture is identical, it may be useful to share one texture placement for all 3D textures to make it easier to adjust them simultaneously. To do so, simply **MMB+drag** a place3dTexture node onto another 3D texture in the Hypershade, and select **Default** from the pop-up menu. This is also true for place2dTexture nodes.

2 Parent 3D placement nodes

Since 3D textures have a *place3dTexture* node in the scene, the texture will slide on its surface when you animate the flying saucer because the model will be moving through the 3D texture. For models that do not deform, it is a good idea to parent 3D texture nodes to the geometry in order to move both at the same time, thus preventing the texture from moving separately from the model.

- Select the *place3dTextures* and parent them to their respective surfaces.

> **Note:** In the case of deforming surfaces, you should use **Texture → Create Texture Reference Object.**

3 Save your work

- Save the final scene as *02-spaceSaucer_02.ma*.

Texture reference objects

When using 3D textures or projections on deforming objects, parenting placement nodes will not fix the crawling or swimming of the textures, so you need to consider using either a *texture reference object* or converting the textures to a 2D file.

A *texture reference object* is a templated copy of the original object which does not deform and is a reference for texture placement on the original object. The idea is that the original object can be deformed and the 3D or projected texture placement information will be based on the non-deforming reference copy.

Some advantages of using this method are:

- It is quick to set up;

- There is no fixed resolution, unlike converting to 2D file textures;

- You have the ability to animate 3D texture attributes;

- It does not require storing texture maps to disk.

Some disadvantages are:

- File size can increase due to extra copies of geometry;

- Noisy 3D textures can sometimes look like they are crawling or shimmering when animated;

- 3D textures can take longer to render than mapped file textures.

Texture reference object for the flying saucer

The following example demonstrates the necessity for special handling of the 3D textures due to deformations applied to the flying saucer. In the following steps, you will create texture reference objects to prevent swimming textures.

1   Scene file

- Open the scene file called *02-spaceSaucerLattice_01.ma*.

Note: *In this file, the place3dTexture nodes are not parented to the geometry. Do not parent the place3dTexture nodes to animated transforms when you are planning to work with texture reference objects.*

2   Create a texture reference object

- Go to frame **1**.

This is the original position of the geometry used when texturing. You are guaranteed that the textures will look good at that position.

- Select the *flyingSaucer* group to select the entire model.

Lesson 02

- Select **Texturing** → **Create Texture Reference Object**.

The texture reference objects are created and templated.

> **Tip:** *It is simpler to always create the texture reference objects after the texturing process and before animating the models.*

- Batch render a small sequence or test render different frames in the animation to see that the textures are now sticking to the surfaces.

Convert to file textures

Another option when dealing with animated or deforming geometry involves converting textures into file texture parametric maps. Once the conversion is done, the file textures are automatically saved to disk and mapped onto the surfaces.

Some advantages of using this technique are:

- It is possible to touch-up or otherwise manipulate a file texture in an Image Editor;

- It is generally much faster to render a file texture than networks of complex procedural textures;

- It is often easier to fix texture problems once the textures are converted to file textures.

Some disadvantages are:

- You can no longer animate texture attributes;

- The resolution is fixed;

- It can require large amounts of disk space to store image files;

- Very high resolution image files can require large amounts of memory during rendering;

- Converting to file textures for many surfaces will produce a separate material for each surface.

How to convert to file textures

- Select the texture, material, or shading group that you wish to convert.

- **Shift-select** the surface you want to create a file texture for.

- In the Hypershade, select **Edit** → **Convert to File Texture**.

The options for this command will allow you to specify the resolution of the new image file, whether or not anti-aliasing will be applied and whether or not to bake the lighting into the resulting texture.

Converting textures on the flying saucer

In this exercise, you will convert the projected and 3D procedural textures to 2D file textures.

1   Scene file

- Open the scene called *02-spaceSaucerLattice_01.ma*.

This is the same scene file that you used to test the texture reference object.

2   Convert the hub texture

- Select the *hub* surface.

- Click on the **Graph Materials on Selected Objects** button in the Hypershade.

This will display the shading network assigned to this surface.

- **Shift-select** the *hubShader* material node.

Both the surface and the material node are selected.

- Select **Edit → Convert to File Texture → □**.

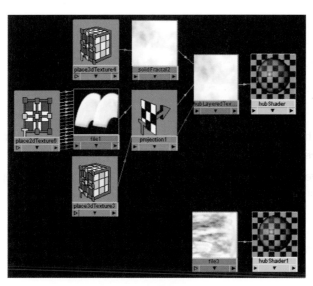

Old and converted shading network

- Set the following:

  Anti-aliasing to **Off**;

  X and **Y resolution** to **1024**.

- Press the **Convert** button.

The command will bake the 3D textures into a file texture. A new material is created and assigned to the surface. The original material remains intact and can be re-assigned if needed.

Note: *This may take a few minutes depending on your system performance.*

Details about converting to file texture

- When you specify the shading node and surface to convert, depending on the shading node's type (i.e. texture, shader, shading group) and depending on how many surfaces are specified, the convert command will run on each surface for each channel in the shading network.

Note: *If a blinn is chosen and there are connections to color and transparency, the command will run twice — once on the node connected to color and once using the node connected to transparency.*

- A discontinuity will be noticeable where the normals are flipped and when the **Double Sided** option is turned **On**. The shading operates using camera normals, so the normal flip will occur around the silhouette of the surface as seen from the active camera. This is turned off by default when converting.

- When the **Bake Shading Group Lighting** option is used, shadows are not included in the computed result. To include the shadow information, turn on the **Bake Shadows** option.

- **Bake Transparency** specifies whether to compute transparency when baking lights. This will sample both the color and transparency of the network.

- The options under **UV Range** specify the surface amount to sample in UV space. For example, if you select one or more faces on a poly object, only the selected faces are sampled rather than the whole surface.

- Bump mapping has the effect of tweaking normals depending on a texture. You may want to convert a bump map, but be aware that the normals cannot be represented as a pixel map.

- When **Anti-alias** is turned **On**, the renderer doubles the resolution of the computed texture and averages four pixels to get the resulting pixel color.

- The active camera is important if sampling needs information from the normal camera. Most rendering nodes (for example, crater or marble) are not sensitive to the camera used but there are others (for example, camera projection and baked lighting) that will be very dependent on the camera used. In these situations you should be aware that the active camera will be used.

- The conversion will name the output by using the sampled node's name with the surface's name. If this file already exists, the version number will be appended to the file. The file will be written to the *sourceimages* folder of the current project.

Limitations

- Depending on how the isoparms are positioned on NURBS surfaces, the samples could all be computed in a very small area of the surface.

- If polygons are used, the surface must have unique normalized UVs. If a polygon has non-unique UVs, or UVs are missing, no error messages are generated and the conversion will fail.

- Fix Texture Wrap is ignored.

Disable initial load of a file texture

To load scenes faster, you can disable the initial loading of a file texture from a disk. To disable the initial loading of a file texture, do the following:

- Select a file texture.

- In the Attribute Editor, under the **File Attributes** section, set the **Disable File Load** attribute to **On**.

When the scene is loaded back into Maya, that file will be prevented from loading into memory, which will load the scene faster.

Test shading networks

The **Test Texture** command allows you to render a preview at any point in a shading network that uses shading nodes (including utility nodes). This will allow you to visualize a rendered result while building complex shading networks.

The following example will show you how to use the **Test Texture** command to perform simple compositing operations using a layered texture:

- Create a layered texture with two layers.
- Map a file texture to the **Color** of the base layer.
- Browse for *meeperBow.tif* from the *sourceimages* directory.
- Map a file texture to the **Color** of a second layer.
- Browse for *roses.0001.tif* from the *sourceimages/roses* directory.

The rose images are a sequence of Sprite particles that have been hardware rendered.

- Set the **Use Image Sequence** to **On**.
- Change the **Blend Mode** of the second layer to **Over**.
- **MMB-click+drag** the *roses* file texture from the Hypergraph to the **Alpha** attribute of the top layer.

If you playback the scene, allowing the hardware rendered roses to fall, you will notice it's difficult to see results in the swatch.

- Select **Edit** → **Test Texture** from the Hypershade menu.

You should now see a rendered result of the current frame in the Render View window. Under normal circumstances you would have to use a compositor to see the results of a hardware rendered image on top of a software rendered image.

Tip: *You can also **RMB-click** on a node in the Hypershade and select* **Test Texture**.

- To render a texture sequence and watch it with fcheck, select **Edit** → **Render Texture Range** → ☐.
- Set the **X** and **Y resolution** to **320** x **240**, then change the frame range to go from **1** to **100**.
- Click on the **Render Texture Range** button.

Quick compositing using Test Texture

Photoshop (.PSD) file texture

You can use PSD file textures in Maya to do compositing based on Photoshop layer sets and alpha information. The following example will use a simple scene to illustrate this functionality.

1 Create a plane

- Create a primitive **NURBS plane**.

2 Assign a lambert material

- Create and assign a lambert material to the NURBS plane.

3 Create a PSD node

- Open the Attribute Editor for the new lambert and click on the **Map** button for the **Color** attribute.

- In the **2D Textures** section of the **Create Render Node** window, create a *psdFile* node.

Tip: *Make sure the* **Create** *option is set to* **Normal***.*

Lesson 02

- In the Attribute Editor for the new *psdFileTex*, browse for the Photoshop file called *PSDFileTex.psd* in the *sourceimages* folder.

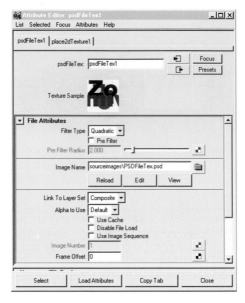

PSD file loaded

 Note: *You will notice that both the* **Color** *and* **Transparency** *attributes of the lambert get mapped with the PSD file. Also notice that once you have loaded the PSD file, the attributes labeled* **Link to LayerSet** *and* **Alpha to Use** *are no longer greyed out.*

4 LayerSet and Alpha to Use

The **Link to LayerSet** and **Alpha to Use** attributes allow adjustment of Photoshop layers and alpha compositing inside Maya.

- Experiment with different settings; use hardware texture shading to interactively see the results.

5 Convert to layered texture

It is possible to convert the PSD file texture to a layered texture network.

- In the Hypershade, **RMB-click** on the PSD file texture node and choose **Convert to Layered Texture**.

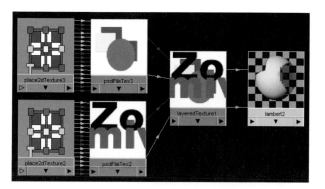

Layered Texture shading network after conversion

Create a PSD shading network

You can also create an entire PSD shading network, which lets you use layer sets in Photoshop to paint a material's channels.

1 Create the PSD file

- Select the object to paint.

- Select **Texturing** →
  Create PSD Texture from
  the **Rendering** menu set.

  The Create PSD Network option window will be displayed.

- In the **Image Name** field, enter a meaningful name.

- At the bottom of the window, highlight and move the attributes you want to paint in Photoshop to the right column.

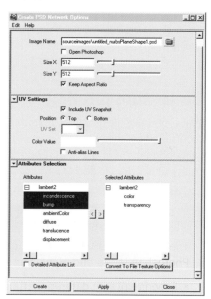

Create PSD Network Options window

Tip: *The **Include UV Snapshot** option can be very useful when you need to see the UVs in Photoshop.*

- Click the **Create** button.

Lesson 02

2   Paint the PSD file in Photoshop

- Open the PSD file in Photoshop and paint the layers as required.

- Save the file.

3   Reload the file in Maya

- Select **Texturing** → **Update PSD Networks**.

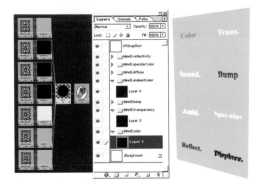

PSD shading network

File texture filtering

When rendering file textures, texture filtering is applied by default. The filtering is controlled by several attributes of file textures and contributes to the overall quality and speed of the final rendered image. Next, you will look at one of the primary filter types called *MipMapping*.

Checker filtering

Project One

Why filter file textures?

In the previous image shown, a single pixel in the final image may correspond to thousands of pixels in the source checker pattern. Determining the final color for a single pixel would require an immense computation. To reduce the amount of work required to compute the final pixel color, a technique called *MipMapping* was developed to produce quicker filtering.

MipMap filtering means that Maya stores multiple resolutions of the same texture. For example, if you have a 512x512 image, Maya stores the 512x512, then 256x256, then 128x128, then 64x64, then 32x32, etc.

Note: *It is most optimal for the MipMap to deal with square resolutions that are a multiple of 2. This is particularly true for bump maps, though close to square resolutions still produce very respectable results. Extreme non-square ratio textures may cause problems.*

The renderer chooses the appropriate level of file texture image to use based on how much screen coverage there is and how obliquely the object is being viewed. The further away or more oblique, the more the renderer tends to use a lower resolution and blurry version of the texture.

How does it affect the image quality?

In terms of quality, the filtering acts like a form of anti-aliasing for textures. By using lower resolution versions of a texture, the resulting pixel colors are more of an average of the surrounding colors on that texture map. This lends to a somewhat blurry look to the receding parts of the textured surface in the rendered image.

However, the upside is that this averaging prevents detectable shifts in color for a single pixel from frame to frame. If the resulting distant pixel colors were precise at all times, you would see noticeable texture crawling or shimmering during animation because the same pixel could have different colors from frame to frame, depending on the viewing angle.

The trick is to strike the right balance between the sharpness of the texture in the final render versus the amount of crawling in the texture during animation.

Tip: *When particular file textured surfaces are crawling, shimmering or flickering, it is best not to play with the anti-aliasing shading samples first. The first choice would be to adjust the file texture's filter attribute values.*

Lesson 02

The **Filter Size** is internally computed by Maya based on how much screen coverage there is and how obliquely the object is being viewed. The **Filter** and **Filter Offset** under the **Effects** section of the Attribute Editor are attributes that can be changed to alter the render.

> **Tip:** *It is not recommend that the **Filter** be set to **0**. Setting the **Filter** to **0** or a very small value will tell the renderer to ignore the internal filter size computation. This will force the renderer to use the highest level of the MipMap.*

As you can see, the purpose of filtering textures has two advantages. Instead of being very accurate about figuring out the color of a pixel far away from the camera, the renderer quickly gets texture values by interpolating between two levels of the MipMap. This makes it quicker to render. The other advantage is more aesthetic, whereby using the filtering structure prevents noisy or shimmering texture problems.

Higher order filter types

In some situations, adjusting the Filter attribute values will not help. When this situation occurs, the more optimal solution would be to employ a higher order filter, such as the *Quadratic Filter*. The Quadratic Filter does more computations in projecting screen pixels to texture space, thus resulting in much cleaner results. This is the default filter type.

Pre-filtering file textures

The **Pre-Filter** and **Pre-Filter Radius** attributes found under the File Attributes section of the Attribute Editor are used to correct file textures that are aliased or contain noise in unwanted areas. When **Pre-Filtering** is **On**, the image file uses a Gaussian type filter to get rid of noise and aliasing, contributing to a better quality image. The **Pre-Filter Radius** will determine the size of the filtering radius. The default value of **2.0** works for most images, but you can increase the radius to provide even smoother results. This can be particularly useful with bump or displacement mapping.

Block ordered textures and caching

In the Attribute Editor for file textures, there is an attribute called **Use Bot**. This attribute can be used as an optimization if you are finding that your renders are running into swap space. Using swap is very slow so you want to avoid this.

By setting **Use Bot** to **On**, you use a lot more disk space but less memory. This is because the renderer does not need to keep whole textures in RAM during the render. Instead, it uses tiles of the texture called *BOT* files as it needs them. BOT stands for Block Order Textures.

BOT are enabled by setting Use Bot to On for a file texture. If this flag is on and the file textures are not already BOT format files, then Maya will automatically create BOT textures from the image files and store them in a temporary directory at render time.

The file textures can be pre-converted to BOT by using the `makebot` MEL command:

```
makebot -i "in_image" -o "out_bot_file";
```

In this case, the resulting BOT files can be stored in a directory you specify. For example:

```
makebot -i "in_image" -o "./sourceimages/out_bot_file";
```

Once the BOT files are created, you need to change the path and name in the file texture's Attribute Editor to point to the BOT files. If the textures are already in BOT format, this saves time at the start of the render. It also allows you to know how much disk space is being taken up by the BOT files on disk before you start rendering.

Technical details

A BOT texture on disk is a compressed MipMap structure with 8x8 **texel** pages. A texel is a texture element derived in much the same way as pixel is a picture element. The textureCache is a 256 texel page cache in memory; that is, it can hold 256 of the 8x8 texel pages. There is only one textureCache for the entire rendering session and the cache is shared between all file textures.

The textureCache is demand loaded. When part of a texture is required, if it is not already in the cache, it is loaded from disk. If the textureCache is full, the least recently accessed pages are removed and replaced with the pages being loaded.

BOT textures have the advantage of reducing the amount of memory required to keep textures in memory. If the image file has already been converted to a BOT texture file, the Maya renderer can use it much more quickly than when it has to convert the file to BOT texture on its own.

Lesson 02

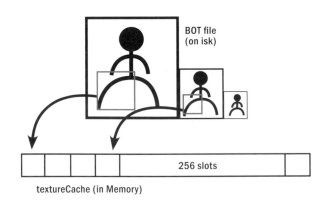

BOT file
(on isk)

256 slots

textureCache (in Memory)

BOT files and texture caching

BOT textures do have some limitations as well. If multiple renderers/processors are using the same BOT file, there can be an I/O bandwidth problem which will cause all the renderers to slow down (having a copy of the BOT texture for each processor is the only work-around). If the image files are not BOT texture files to begin with, then the temporary directory can get full quickly with all of the temporary BOT files.

If different shading networks reference the same file texture image, a single copy of the image is kept in memory and shared by all the shaders.

Tip: Use `maya -optimizeRender -help` *for a list of flags and descriptions to use BOT files.*

Transparency mapping

If you map a file texture containing an Alpha channel to the *Color* channel of a material, you will notice that the *outTransparency* channel is connected to the material automatically. A material's transparency is the opposite of a file texture's Alpha channel, which is generally based on opacity:

alpha opacity (0 = black = transparent; 1 = white = opaque)

material transparency (0 = black = opaque; 1 = white = transparent)

There is no direct way for the Alpha of a file texture to act as a material's transparency. The *outAlpha* of the file texture would have to be sent through a *Reverse* utility node prior to connection to the material's *Transparency* attributes.

Each channel (R,G,B) of the *outTransparency* attribute is the reverse of the node's *outAlpha* attribute. This makes it easier to define the opacity of a material by using only the Alpha channel.

Displacement mapping

Sometimes, rather than modeling the details of a surface, it is more convenient to use *displacement mapping*. Displacement mapping uses a texture to alter the shape of geometry. This is different than a bump map which simply alters the way light hits the surface normals, which creates the illusion of surface relief.

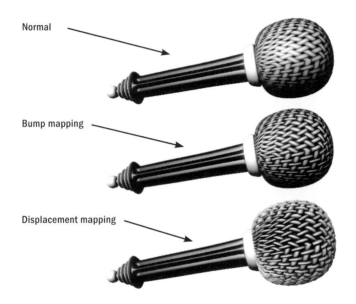

Normal

Bump mapping

Displacement mapping

Displacement and bump mapping

The displacement map is connected to the shading group node instead of the material node. This is because it is applied to the geometry rather than the shading. To see the connections in the Hypershade, select the material node and click on the **Input and Output Connections** button. This will show the displacement map, the material node and all of the geometry that belongs to the shading group.

Displacement mapping adds detail to surfaces at render time in order to capture the small variance in a displacement texture. The renderer then generates high quality displacement tessellation with minimum triangle counts.

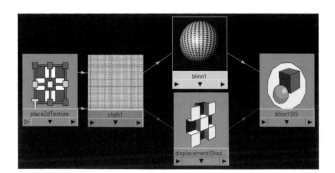

The displacement node is directly connected to the shading group

You will now make use of displacement mapping on Diva's microphone.

1 Scene file

- Open the scene called *02-microphoneDisp_01.ma*.

2 Graph the microphone shading network

- Select the microphone and press the **Graph Materials on the Selected Objects** button in the Hypershade.

At this time, the microphone already has bump mapping assigned. You will use that same texture for the displacement.

3 Connect the displacement

- **MMB-click+drag** the *cloth1* texture onto the *blinn1* material and connect it to displacement map.

This automatically connects the texture to the shading group node.

Tip: *Having both displacement and bump maps will make the geometry shading look more accurate.*

4 Displacement amount

In order to get a general idea of the amount of displacement needed to look good on the microphone, you can change the **Alpha Gain** of the texture used for displacement.

- Test render the microphone.

The default amount of displacement

- Select the *cloth1* texture node.

- In the Attribute Editor, under the **Color Balance** section, set the **Alpha Gain** to **0.2**.

- Test render the microphone again.

The new amount of displacement

Tip: If the displacement appears to be reversed, you can change the **Alpha Gain** to -0.2.

5 Tune the displacement attributes

The displacement attributes are found in the Attribute Editor for the geometry, not the texture map.

If the original tessellation triangle is large and the texture details are fine, then the **Initial Sample Rate** has to be large (from 30 to 50 or even higher). If the triangle is small and the texture details are not that fine, then the **Initial Sample Rate** does not have to be very high (usually the default is sufficient).

Lesson 02

Observe how sharp the texture details are and if there are many clean lines or curved details. The sharper the features and the cleaner the lines, the higher the **Extra Sample Rate** needs to be.

- Select the *microphone* and open its Attribute Editor.

- Under the **Displacement Map** section, make sure the **Feature Displacement** flag is turned **On**.

- If the details in the previous render look too rough, then increase the **Initial Sample Rate**.

- For now, set the **Extra Sample Rate** to 0.

- Test render the microphone to see the results of the displacement.

It is not possible to use IPR to help tune the displacement attributes because the displacement map is applied to the geometry, not the shading. Changes in the shape of the geometry are not supported by IPR.

- If not enough details are captured, increase the Initial Sample Rate some more.

Tip: *Use the lowest acceptable value.*

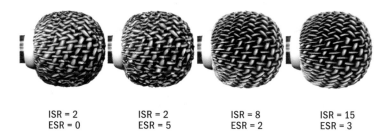

| ISR = 2 | ISR = 2 | ISR = 8 | ISR = 15 |
| ESR = 0 | ESR = 5 | ESR = 2 | ESR = 3 |

ISR = Initial Sample Rate   ESR = Extra Sample Rate

Variations of displacement attributes

- If the features are too jagged, increase the **Extra Sample Rate**.

This attribute refines the displacement results. It is a good idea to try it at 0 and see if the quality is good enough. This will help to keep the triangle count as low as possible. Increase it until the edges of the texture details look acceptable.

6 Using the Displacement to Polygon Tool

The **Modify** → **Convert** menu contains a tool called **Displacement to Polygon**. This tool is very useful because it bakes out the displaced surface as a polygon mesh, providing a great way to visualize the results instead of test rendering. The resulting polygonal object is created in the same location as the original and can be used instead of the original surface (in which case, the displacement map serves as a modeling tool). While the original surface is preserved, there is no history relationship between the original surface and the polygonal object. If changes are made to the original surface or any of its tessellation or displacement attributes, the **Displacement to Polygon Tool** must be used again to see the changes.

Tip: *In general, displacement will result in a very high number of polygons. This creates a very heavy file relative to the original surface. Use at your discretion.*

The following images show an example of the **Displacement to Polygon Tool** results:

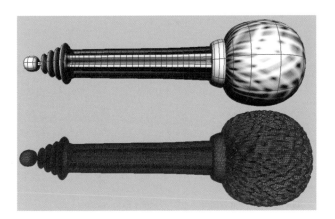

Conversion of displacement to polygons

Displacement mapping in mental ray

mental ray provides the opportunity to optimize a displacement by using the **Displacement Approximation Editor**. By default, mental ray will use the Maya tessellation settings for surface approximations. If you want to override this, use the **Window** → **Rendering Editors** → **mental ray** → **Approximation Editor**.

Note: *The Approximation Editor is discussed in greater detail in Lesson 7.*

mental ray baking

The procedure for baking information (Convert to File Texture) with mental ray is done by using **Bake Sets**. Bake Sets allow users to bake a variety of objects with different baking options such as illumination, shadow, shading and textures. You can also save different baking parameters, making it easier to re-bake when needed.

You can also bake objects that have not been assigned to a Bake Set. If this is the case, the objects are automatically assigned to the initial Bake Set, and the baking proceeds.

To do a simple batch bake using the mental ray renderer:

- Select one or more objects that you want to bake.

- Select **Lighting/Shading** → **Batch Bake (mental ray)** → ❒.

- Set the desired options, then click **Convert**.

To create a mental ray Bake Set:

- Select one or more objects for which you want to create a Bake Set.

- Select **Lighting/Shading** → **Assign New Bake Set** → **Texture Bake Set**.

- Adjust the Bake Sets attributes in the Bake Set Attribute Editor.

When you bake the objects, mental ray will use the Bake Set options they are assigned to.

Tip: *If you want to edit the Bake Set later,* **RMB-click** *on the object and select* **Baking** → **Baking Attributes.**

Memory mapped files

The use of memory mapped texture files is a recommended practice in most scenes as it reduces physical memory usage considerably. Non-memory mapped texture files are read into physical memory and are swapped to disk space in the event of memory running low. This is expensive in terms of memory usage and time-consuming in terms of swapping texture files out to disk. Memory mapped files however, do not use large blocks of memory. Instead, they reside in virtual memory. Memory mapping is particularly beneficial with large textures. However, any scene with more than a few hundred KB of file textures will benefit from memory mapping.

mental ray for Maya has a utility: `imf_copy` that is used for converting textures to memory mapped files.

The syntax is:

```
imf_copy (options) filename.tif filename.map
```

Note: *The `.map` extension does not have to be present; mental ray will recognize memory mapped files regardless. The extension is there as a matter of convention.*

Conclusion

Creating great textures is an important factor in producing a convincing image. Textures help determine the style you are reaching for, from cartoon style to extreme realism. If you have a strong grasp of the tools used to create textures, it opens the door to your artistic freedom.

In the next project, you will learn about lighting and cameras.

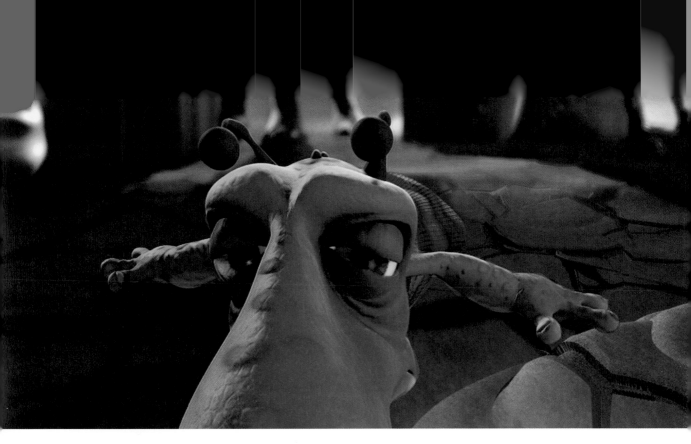

Lessons

In Project Two, you will learn about lights and cameras. Lighting a scene and setting up cameras will give ambience, depth and realism to your renders. The topics outlined in the following lessons are a prerequisite for anyone wishing to create astonishing images.

Once you have read this project, you should feel confident incorporating lights and cameras into your scene.

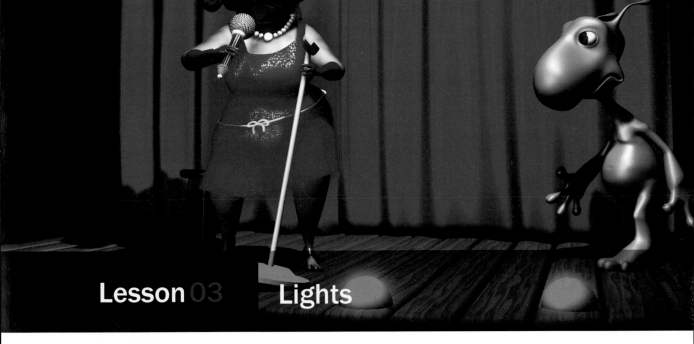

Lesson 03 Lights

Lighting a CG scene is much like lighting for photography, film or theater. As an element of design, light should be considered a basic influence at the beginning of the creative process and not something to be added later. This is especially true in computer graphics where lighting is based on mathematical algorithms, and creating real world lighting effects requires a solid understanding of the software application.

In this lesson you will learn the following:

- Lighting basics;

- How to use decay rates and intensity curves;

- How to use color curves and color mapping;

- How to do light linking;

- How to create mental ray area lights.

Lighting concepts

The basic premise of good lighting is that when done right, objects and characters look like they fit and live in their surroundings. The design potential of light is inherent in its physical characteristics. By controlling its intensity, color and direction, light becomes a key factor in creating a scene. Lighter and darker areas help to compose the frame and guide the eye toward certain objects and actions.

Choosing light types

Once you have determined the direction and distribution of lights in a scene, you will also need to consider the type of light source.

Maya provides a selection of different light types that all have attributes that can be edited and animated to simulate real world lighting. These lights can produce a range of qualities from soft and diffuse to harsh and intense because they each have different characteristics. While it is likely that your combination of lights and techniques will vary with each production, the design principles of combining sharp and soft edged light, different angles, intensities and shadows remain the same.

Directional lights

Directional light

You will notice that the **directional light** icon depicts several parallel rays. This is because its purpose is to simulate a distant light source, such as the sun, where the light rays are coherent and parallel.

This type of light will typically produce a harsher, more intense quality of light with harder edges and no subtle changes in surface shading because of its

Project Two

parallel rays with no decay. Directional lights are not very expensive to render because the angle is constant for all rays and decay is not computed.

Point lights

Point light

The **point light** icon depicts light rays emanating from a single point outwards in all directions. Its purpose is to simulate an omni-directional local light source, such as a light bulb or candle. This type of light does have decay and will typically produce a more subtle, yet richer shading on surfaces.

Ambient lights

Ambient light

Lesson 03

An **ambient light** is normally used as a non-directional light to simulate the diffused scattered or reflected light you see in real life.

However, you can adjust the **Ambient Shade** attribute, which, gives directionality to the light. If set to 0.0, it acts like an RGB multiplier, allowing you to control the overall contrast levels in the scene. However, it is very difficult to determine the edges of objects at this setting with no other light source. The default is set to **0.45** to give a slight hint of shading on surfaces. If **Ambient Shade** is set to **1.0**, it is fully directional, i.e. the location of the light is the source of the rays.

Ambient lights are quick to render because they have no decay and create no specular highlights. Often they are used as a secondary light source, supporting a stronger light source. Be aware that using only an ambient light for illumination has limitations. For example, bump maps will not show up.

Spot lights

Spot light

A **spot light** has a cone of influence in a specific direction. This is controlled by the **Cone Angle** attribute, which is measured in degrees from edge to edge. The spot light also has **Decay**, **Dropoff** and **Penumbra**, which will be covered later in the lesson.

Area lights

Point, directional and spot lights are all abstract lighting models in the sense that they are zero-size lights that exist at a single point.

Because all lights in the natural world occupy some amount of space, area lights can help to produce a more realistic lighting distribution; an area light computation reflects the size and orientation of the light.

Area light

There are three effects that are difficult to achieve using light sources other than area lights:

- Straight, long, specular highlights (like those created by neons);

- Soft lighting distribution;

- Realistic shadows that vary from hard to soft.

Specular highlight size and orientation

Simply position and scale the light using IPR to see the specular highlight interactively.

Soft lighting distribution

The size, orientation and position of the area light's manipulator in a view controls the lighting distribution.

- If you have a large area light, more light is emitted. The light can be non-proportionally scaled to modulate the distribution.

A real world analogy would be a window with a shade that pulls down; as you lower the shade, the size of the window opening gets smaller and the amount of light is reduced.

- The farther away the object is from the light, the less light is cast onto the object. Quadratic is the default decay.

Lesson 03
Area lights

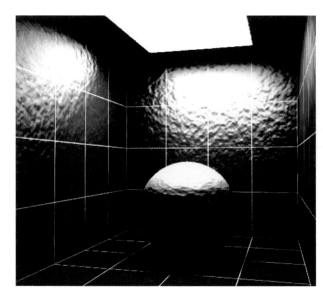

Highlight size and soft light distribution

Realistic shadows

The size and shape of an area light can help to achieve realistic raytraced shadows that dissipate as the receiving surface gets more illuminated by the area light. This normally requires a relatively high number of shadow rays and can be expensive to render.

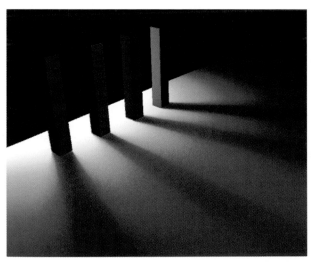

Realistic shadows using raytracing

Note: *Shadows will be discussed in greater detail in the next lesson.*

Optical effects

Any light that is visible to the camera lens has the potential to produce an optical effect, such as light glow or flare. Optical effects for an area light reflect the shape of its manipulator.

Optical light glow on an area light

Note: *Optical effects will be covered in more detail in Lesson 8.*

Area light limitations

- Depth map shadows do not reflect the size and orientation of the area light.

- The specular highlight produced by an area light on an anisotropic shader is poorly defined.

- The specular highlight produced by an area light on plug-in shaders will not reflect the size and orientation of the area light. Enhancements have to be made to the architecture to support a proper specular direction.

Volume lights

Volume light

The **volume light** illuminates objects within a given volume. Volumes can be spherical, cylindrical, box, or cone shaped. The advantage of using this type of light is that you have a visual representation as to the extent of the light. In addition to the common attributes found in all lights, volume lights have attributes that allow greater control over the color of the volume. The **Color Range** section in the Attribute Editor allows the user to select one color or blend between colors within the volume. You can control the direction of a light within the volume by using the **Volume Light Direction** attributes.

Default lights

If there are no lights in a scene, Maya will create a directional light when the scene is rendered. This light is parented to the rendered camera and illuminates the scene regardless of where the camera is facing. After the render is complete, Maya removes the default light from the scene.

That same default light is used to shade models in the views except when Use All Light (**7**) or High Quality Rendering mode is turned On.

Light intensity

Light intensity can be defined as the actual or comparative brightness of light. Like most other render attributes, it can be modified either by using the slider or by mapping a texture to the channel.

> **Tip:** It is possible to enter negative values for intensity. This will subtract
> light in the scene and can produce dark spots instead of hot spots on
> specular shading models.

The **Emit Diffuse** and **Emit Specular** flags are **On** by default and will control the
diffuse or specular shading results for the light. Ambient lights do not have
these attributes.

Decay rates

Decay refers to how light diminishes with distance. It is possible to alter the
rate of decay for point and spot lights by adjusting the **Decay Rate** in the light's
Attribute Editor. The default is **No Decay**. The other settings are **Linear**, **Quadratic**
and **Cubic**.

> **Note:** For computer animated characters or other elements that must match
> live action shots, it is very important to consider the decay rate. For
> example, if your character is moving towards or away from a light source,
> the intensity of the light cast onto the character must appear to increase
> or decrease as it would in real life, or it will not be believable when it is later
> added to the live shot. This is especially true if the character is placed next
> to a live actor who is also moving towards or away from the light source.
> For this reason you may choose to work with **Quadratic** decay for realism.

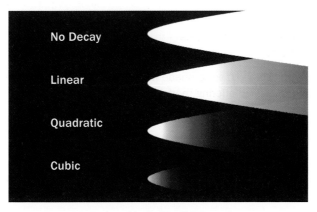

Light decay

Lesson 03

No Decay - Light reaches everything.

Linear - Light intensity decreases in direct proportion to distance (I=1/d).

Quadratic - This is how light decays in real life (I=1/d*d)

Cubic - Light decays faster than real life (I=1/d*d*d)

> **Note:** *The decay factor occurs only after a distance larger than 1 unit. Otherwise, the decay factor can result in over-exposure in lighting with distances less than 1 unit.*

Precision lighting

While decay rates offer a mathematically accurate way to have light fall-off over distance, they do not allow for any control in precision lighting.

Being able to do precision lighting is crucial to working on special effects, i.e. being able to interactively clamp lighting at an exact spot, or easily specifying the light intensity at an exact distance, etc. Currently, spot lights have all the tools to perform precision lighting.

> **Tip:** *When beginning to work with decay on spot lights, it is best to use either the decay approach or the precision lighting approach, as mixing both may yield unexpected results.*

Decay regions

The primary purpose of decay regions is to allow regions to be lit or non-lit within the same cone of light. The decay regions can be used in conjunction with the decay rates to control effects, such as table lamps or car headlights, where the visible light beam emanates from a broad region rather than a single point in space.

The following steps show how to set-up decay regions on a spot light:

- Create a spot light.

- In the Attribute Editor, click on the **Map** button for the **Light Fog** attribute.

- In the Attribute Editor for the *spotLight*, turn **On** the **Use Decay Regions** under **Light Effects** → **Decay Regions**.

- Display the Decay Region manipulators by selecting **Display** → **Camera/ Light Manipulator** → **Decay Regions**.

You can interactively move the manipulator's rings in the views to define the regions of illumination.

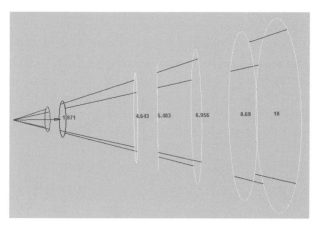

The Decay Regions Tool

- Test render the light.

You should see the different regions because of the light fog.

Tip: *An alternate way to adjust the regions is to open the **Region** subsections of the **Decay Regions** section in the Attribute Editor and enter values in the **Distance** fields. This tool can also be very useful as an interactive measuring tool to determine distances from the light.*

Intensity curve

At times it is important to be able to control the exact intensity of a light at a given distance from the light source. Intensity curves allow precise control over this effect.

- In the Attribute Editor for the *spotLight*, click on **Light Effects** → **Intensity Curve** → **Create**.

A curve is created and connected to the light's intensity channel.

- With the light still selected, select **Window** → **Animation Editors** → **Graph Editor...**

- Press **a** to frame all in the view or use **View** → **Frame All**.

There will be a number of keyframes on the curve.

Notice that the vertical and horizontal axes represent **Intensity** *and* **Distance** *for this curve.*

You can edit this curve as you would edit any other animation curve in Maya by moving keyframes, adding or deleting keyframes, changing tangents, etc.

 Tip: *To try this with a point light, create a spot light and set up the intensity curve, then convert the spot light to a point light through the Attribute Editor.*

Color curves

Similar to intensity curves, *color curves* allow you to individually control the red, green and blue values of the light over distance.

- To create **Color Curves**, open the *spotLight's* Attribute Editor, then click on **Light Effects** → **Color Curve** → **Create**.

 Tip: *Don't delete any of the color curves because this can give unexpected results. Instead, if you want to take out all of the green component, for example, delete the middle keys and set the remaining two keys to an intensity value of* **0.0.**

Color mapping lights

Another way to specify light color is to map a texture onto the color channel. This essentially allows the light to act like a movie projector, projecting the texture onto the objects in the scene.

 Tip: *Mapping the color channel of a spot light with a water texture can create realistic looking caustic patterns, especially when the texture is animated.*

In the following example, you will project colored stars on to Meeper by mapping a texture in a spot light Color attribute.

1 Scene file

- Open the scene file called *03-lights_01.ma*.

2 Create a spot light and place it

- Select **Create** → **Lights** → **Spot Light**.

- Select **Panels** → **Look Through Selected**.

You are now looking through the spotLight in order to help its placement.

- Dolly and tumble in this view to make any adjustments to the position of the *spotLight*.

Make sure to place Meeper in the view circle, which defines the borders of the spot light.

3 Map to the spot light

- Open the Attribute Editor for the *spotLight*, then click on the **Map** button to the right of the **Color** attribute.

- In the **Create Render Node** window, create a file texture.

- In the Attribute Editor for the new file texture, browse for the image called *stars.tif* from the *sourceimages* directory.

Tip: *You can position an image in the spot light by changing* **Coverage,** **Translate Frame** *and* **Rotate Frame** *on the file texture's place2Dtexture node to position the image in the spot light.*

4 Add another light source

Since the spot light is now black with colored stars, you need another light source in your scene in order to see Meeper and the stage.

- Create and place another spot light in front of the stage.

Colored stars mapped into spot light color

5 Test render

Dropoff

Spot lights also have a **Dropoff** attribute. Dropoff is similar to decay except that its function is to cause the light to diminish in intensity perpendicular to the light axis, instead of along the light axis.

- Select a spot light and open the Attribute Editor.

- In the **Spot Light Attributes** section, adjust the **Dropoff** attribute.

  You can watch the effect in the spot light swatch in the Attribute Editor or in the IPR window.

Spot light dropoff effect

Note: *The results are computed as follows: cosine raised to the power of dropoff (where Cos is the dot product of the light axis and the lighting direction vector).*

Penumbra angle

The **penumbra** is an area of diminishing intensity rimming the edge of the cone of light. The intensity of the light falls off linearly between the cone angle and cone angle + penumbra angle.

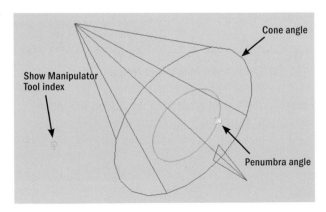

Cone angle

Show Manipulator Tool index

Penumbra angle

Spot light penumbra manipulator

Note: *It is possible to enter negative numbers for* **Penumbra Angle.** *This will create a softening effect inwards from the edge of the cone of influence.*

Light linking

Often when trying to solve specific lighting tasks, you will need to control which lights shine on which objects in your scene. This can be accomplished easily by using several different methods. All of these methods will accomplish the same results, so it is really just a case of which one is the easier workflow for what you are trying to set up.

Relationship Editor light centric

This method is the easiest to use when you are learning to use light linking, but it is not the fastest approach.

- Select **Window** → **Relationship Editor** → **Light Linking** → **Light Centric**.

The Relationship Editor is automatically configured for a **Light Centric Light Linking** *task, and shows all of the light sets and individual lights in the scene on the left column. On the right column, it shows all of the geometry and shading groups in the scene.*

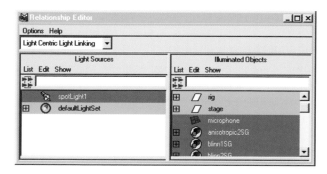

Light centric light linking

- Click to select a light or light set from the list on the left.

Geometry illuminated by the selected lights is highlighted on the right.

- Toggle the highlight on the right side to specify the geometry to be illuminated by the selected light(s).

Unhighlighted geometry will not be illuminated by the selected light(s).

Lesson 03

Relationship Editor object centric

- Change the Relationship Editor configuration to **Object Centric Light Linking** or select **Window** → **Relationship Editors** → **Light Linking** → **Object Centric**.

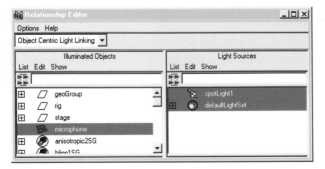

Object centric light linking

- Click to select an object or set of objects from the list on the left.

Lights illuminating the selected objects are highlighted on the right.

- Click on the right side to choose which lights will illuminate the selected objects.

Unhighlighted lights will not illuminate the selected objects.

Lighting/Shading menu

This workflow is the fastest method for setting up light linking. By default, a new light added to a scene illuminates all objects in the scene. This means that there is a link between the light and each piece of geometry to start with. The **Lighting/Shading** menu provides a simple way to break or make any of these links without needing to bring up the Relationship Editor.

- Select light(s), then **Shift-select** the object(s) you do not want illuminated.
- Select **Lighting/Shading** → **Break Light Links** from the **Rendering** menu set to break the link(s) between the selected nodes.

Now the selected lights will not illuminate the selected geometry.

- Use the same workflow outlined above to recreate light links using **Lighting/Shading** → **Make Light Links**.

Note: *It does not matter whether you select the lights first or the objects first.*

Illuminates By Default

This workflow uses the menu actions described on the previous page and the **Illuminates By Default** feature. This method is recommended when adding a light that needs to shine on only one or a few specific objects in a scene, where there are many other objects and lights already set.

Using the Relationship Editor method would be time-consuming to turn off all the objects you do not want illuminated by the new light(s). Using the **Lighting/Shading** menu would also be time-consuming because again, you would need to select all the geometry you do not want illuminated in order to break all the links to the new light(s).

In this case, it is better to start out by telling the light(s) not to illuminate any geometry initially. Then it is just a matter of selecting the geometry you intend to illuminate with the new light(s) and making a link with the **Make Light Link** menu.

- Open the Attribute Editor for a light.

- Turn **Off** the **Illuminates by Default** checkbox.

- **Make Light Links** between the light and geometry.

Lights in mental ray

All of the Maya lights will render using mental ray. As added features, some light types have extra mental ray attributes and support photon emission. Photon emission is necessary for effects such as *Caustics* and *Global Illumination*, which will be discussed later in this book. Lights that are capable of this include *directional*, *point*, *spot* and *mental ray area lights*. The other light types, *ambient*, *volume* and *Maya area lights*, are supported but do not have mental ray attributes or support photon emission.

mental ray area light

The mental ray area light is slightly different than a Maya area light. The Maya area light is only capable of being rectangular, whereas mental ray lights have a few more shape options.

Create a mental ray area light

- Create a point light or a spot light.

- Open the Attribute Editor for the light, then scroll down to the **mental ray** → **Area Light Editor** section.

- Set the **Area Light** checkbox to **On**.

- Adjust the area light as desired.

The icon will let you know the direction the light will be emitted.

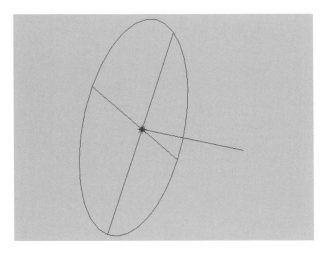

A disc-shaped mental ray area light

Type

Type refers to the shape of the area light source. Shapes available from the drop-down list include **Rectangle**, **Disc**, **Sphere** and **Cylinder**.

Sampling

Sampling represents the number of sample points emitted from the light (X and Y). The default values are **3** and **3**. Increasing these values will reduce graininess, but will increase render time.

Low Level

If this value is greater than **1**, the light source will use the **Low Sampling** values as long as their sum is greater than the **Low Level** value. This affects reflection and refraction. The default is **0**.

Project

Low Sampling

The defaults are **2** and **2**. Increasing this value may help where a lit edge looks grainy. This value will then be used as the minimum sampling value while the **Low Level** value is greater than **1**.

Visible

If you want the light object to be visible during a render, turn this on.

Conclusion

Lighting is an important aspect of the rendering process and having a good understanding of it can help you establish mood and atmosphere in your scenes. Understanding the technical aspects of lighting can help you create impressive renders.

In the next lesson, you will learn to create and control shadows.

Lesson 04   Shadows

Some cinematographers say that the most important thing in lighting is what you don't light. They are referring to the relative effects of light and shadow. Shadows are involved in creating atmosphere and mood in a scene and help to define the look and feel of a scene.

In this lesson you will learn the following:

- How to use depth map shadows;

- The different light types and their shadows;

- How to create volumetric lighting effects;

- How to use raytraced shadows;

- How to use mental ray shadow maps;

- How to motion blur shadow maps;

- How to use mental ray raytrace shadows.

Shadows

When working on lighting a scene you need to take into consideration the type of shadows you want. For example, the elevation and direction of a light are important influences on the amount and shape of the shadow areas in the frame. Generally, shadows become more dominant as the angle of light incidence increases and as the lighting moves from front to back positions. This, in turn, affects the overall mood of the image; if you want a dark and gloomy scene you want the lights behind your objects so the shadows are being cast into the frame.

Shadows also play an important role in rendering texture. To maximize texture you use side lighting, also known as cross lighting. Side lighting creates long shadows that interact with the lit parts of the subject to yield good texture patterns. To minimize texture, you use frontal light as it will create a very flat look because there will be fewer shadows.

By default, all objects have the ability to cast shadows as well as receive shadows. Each are controlled separately from the **Render Stats** section of an object in the Attribute Editor.

Note: *The* **Receive Shadows** *attribute is ignored when IPR rendering.*

When rendering shadows in Maya, you have the option to either **Raytrace Shadows** or to use **Depth Map Shadows**.

When using depth map shadows, the depth maps are computed as a first pass before rendering, while raytraced shadows are computed during the rendering phase.

Note: *Use* Lighting → **Shadows** *to preview the position of your shadows when displaying hardware textures. This function is only possible with depth map shadows and only with certain graphics cards and drivers. See the Maya documentation for more information.*

Depth map shadows

The shadow depth map computation is done by rendering a depth image from the point of view of the light source, and later used during the rendering phase to determine if that light illuminates a given point. Point, directional, volume, spot and area lights are the light types that can produce depth map shadows.

How Dmaps work

Similar to a topographical
map, a Dmap is used to
record distances between
the light and objects in
the scene. The Dmap is
a square grid of pixels in
front of the light. This grid
of pixels is projected over
the scene from the light's
point of view, dividing the
scene into sections.

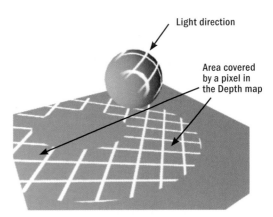

Dmap grid example

A ray is cast through the center of each pixel in the Dmap. When the ray
intersects the nearest shadow casting surface, Maya records the distance from
the light to that surface. These depth measurements make up the Dmap's pixel
values. The Dmap can be viewed with **fcheck** by hitting the **Z** key. In this example
it would look like the following image:

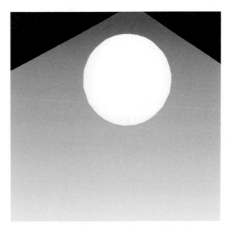

Dmap viewed with fcheck

This process takes place at the beginning of the render process. The renderer later uses this depth information when creating the final image from the camera view. This process is described below.

In the diagram below, the shading is computed for points on the ground plane because the ground plane is visible to the camera. During this process, one of the necessary pieces of information is whether or not a point is in shadow.

In order to determine whether the point on the ground plane is in shadow or not, the renderer makes a comparison - it checks with all of the shadow casting lights to see if the point being shaded is closer or further from the light than the point stored in the Dmap.

If the distance from the point being shaded (on the ground plane) to the light is greater than the stored depth value, then some other surface is closer to the light. This means that the point being shaded must be in shadow.

In this diagram, many points being shaded on the ground plane fall within the coverage region of a single pixel on the Dmap. This means that all of these points would be compared to the same stored depth value and hence, would be considered to be in shadow. Obviously, some of the points do not look as though they should be in shadow. The next section of this chapter looks at ways to resolve this type of inaccuracy.

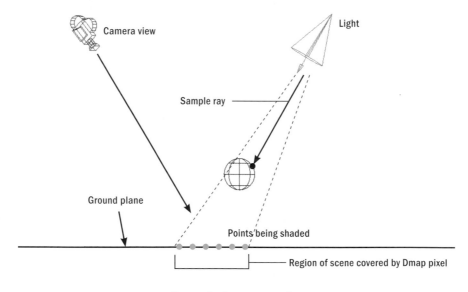

Dmap shadow computation

Self-shadowing

Self-shadowing refers to a surface shadowing itself.

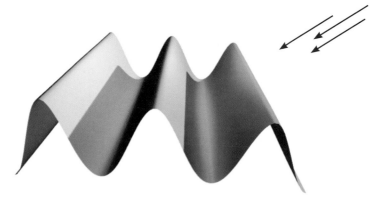

Self-shadowing

Dmap can cause self-shadowing artifacts simply due to the finite resolution of the Dmap - not necessarily due to the shape of the surface. Because only one depth value is stored per pixel, if you happen to be shading a point on a surface that lies between samples in the Dmap, there is the possibility that the averaged depth from the Dmap will incorrectly shadow the point being shaded. This self-shadowing will result in an undesirable moire pattern or banding on surfaces facing towards the light.

The self-shadowing from Dmap shadows can be somewhat puzzling at first because it can happen even when logic would suggest that it is not possible because there is nothing to cast a shadow.

The following rendered image shows self-shadowing artifacts on a single ground plane:

Banding caused by self-shadowing

The diagram below explains how this happens in the case of the plane shown on the previous page:

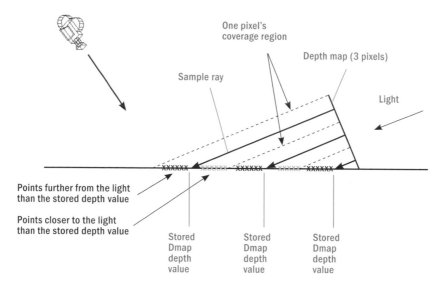

Diagram of self-shadowing computation

Even with a simple plane, self-shadowing can occur due to the limited number of depth samples stored in the Dmap. Each pixel on the Dmap covers a large region of the ground plane. As the image is rendered from the camera, any points on the plane that are further from the light than the stored depth value on the Dmap will be incorrectly thought to be in shadow from the plane itself.

The image below shows the moire pattern that is also typical of self-shadowing:

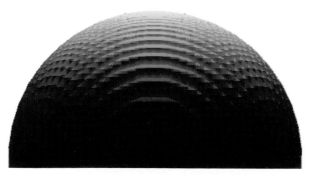

Moire pattern caused by self-shadowing

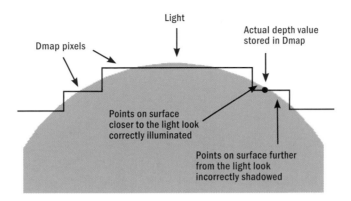

Self-shadowing problem on a curved surface

In the examples shown above, the resolution of the Dmap is intentionally low to exaggerate the self-shadowing artifacts. Increasing the resolution will not get rid of the artifacts, it will just make them smaller, sometimes giving a dull, dirty looking appearance to a surface.

Correcting self-shadowing with Dmap Bias

There are two shadow attributes available to help correct self-shadowing:

- **Use Mid Dist Dmap** which will be discussed later. This feature is turned **On** by default and in many cases will prevent the self-shadowing artifacts shown above.

- **Dmap Bias** is another important Dmap shadow attribute that is used to correct self-shadowing.

The **Dmap Bias** attribute is very important when dealing with self-shadowing artifacts. The *bias* is a value by which the camera ray's intersection point

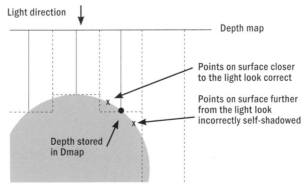

Typical self-shadowing situation

is moved closer to the light source to avoid incorrect self-shadowing. In other words, it is a value that can be thought of as a *fudge factor* for shadow purposes, to move the point being shaded closer to the light to bring it out of self-shadow.

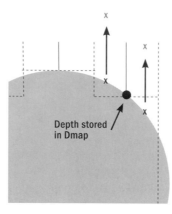

All points being shaded (x) are biased towards the light. This makes them (x) closer to the light than the stored depth value. This corrects the self-shadow problem.

Dmap Bias moves the points to escape self-shadowing

While adjusting the **Dmap Bias**, care must be taken to find the right value. Using too small a value may result in self-shadowing artifacts on the surface as the previous images have shown. Using too large a value may lead to surfaces that should be in shadow not being in shadow. A large value might also lead to shadows that are detached from the casting objects causing the object to appear to be floating as shown below:

The object appears to float above the ground surface

> **Note:** The **Dmap Bias** *is not in world units. Here is how it is applied:* **Dmap Bias**
> *current Z-depth = bias value. The farther away the point is from the light*
> *source, the bigger the bias value. But, it multiplies with the perspective Z-*
> *depth, so consider the user-entered* **Dmap Bias** *as a normalized bias value.*
> *Directional lights are the same, except it does not multiply it with the Z-depth.*

Correcting self-shadowing with Mid Distance

Use Mid Dist Dmap is turned **On** by default to help prevent self-shadowing
artifacts. It stands for *Use Middle Distance Depth Map*, which is a variation on the
Dmap algorithm.

> **Note:** *If the Dmap is to be used for purposes other than shadowing, it is*
> *best to turn this option* **Off**.

Use Mid Dist Dmap attempts to eliminate the need for the Dmap Bias attribute
by storing the midpoint between the first and second surface visible to the light
source rather than simply storing the distance to the nearest surface. Because
this midpoint is normally further from the light than any of the points on the
surface itself, self-shadowing is less likely to occur. The diagram below shows
how this works:

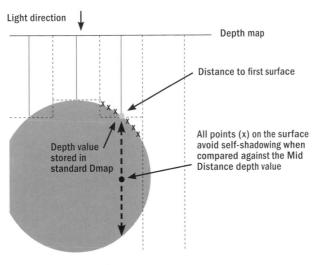

Mid Distance computation

Lesson 04

Because **Use Mid Dist Dmap** is turned **On** by default, surfaces such as ground planes are not as susceptible to self-shadowing. The question often arises of what happens when there is only one surface that uses the *Mid Distance* algorithm? Answer - since there is only one surface, Maya uses the farthest bounding box of the receiving shadow surfaces.

> **Tip:** When **Use Mid Dist Dmap** *is turned* **On,** *there are actually two Dmaps created - the standard Dmap that stores the distances to the first surfaces and another one that stores the distances to the second surfaces. To see the difference, write the Dmaps to disk and* **fcheck** *them viewing the Z-buffer. The Dmaps are stored in the depth directory of your current project.*

Using Both Dmap Bias and Use Mid Dist Dmap

The **Use Mid Dist Dmap** can prevent some self-shadowing artifacts. However, depending on the model and the angle of the lights, a small **Dmap Bias** is normally required as well (the default is 0.001). The reason for this is that when surfaces are modeled close together, the Mid Distance is not significantly far enough from the first surface to allow the first surface to escape self-shadowing.

The following diagram shows the previous example of the plane. This time, a second plane is added slightly below the original. Because the planes are close together, the mid distance does very little to reduce the self-shadowing.

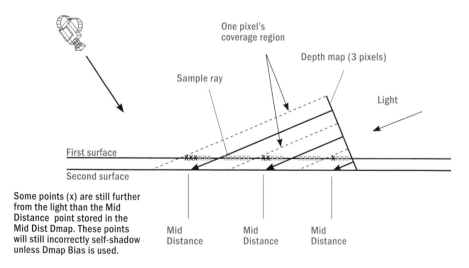

Using both Dmap Bias and Use Mid Dist Dmap

The following rendered images show the real effect of both **Use Mid Dist Dmap** and **Dmap Bias** working together to effectively remove all self-shadowing artifacts.

Mid Dist Dmap Off
Dmap Bias = 0.0

Mid Dist Dmap On
Dmap Bias = 0.0

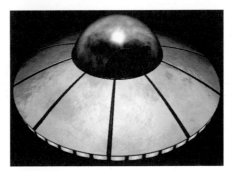

Mid Dist Dmap On
Dmap Bias = 0.01

Lesson 04

Angle of light and self-shadowing

The following diagram illustrates how the angle of light directly affects the likelihood of self-shadowing on a surface. Surfaces that are at an angle to the light are most likely to show self-shadowing because a single pixel's depth value is forced to approximate the shadows for a much larger region, which results in greater self-shadowing error.

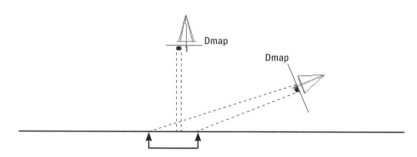

Angle of light impacts self-shadowing

Depth Map Resolution

Dmap Resolution defines the size of the Dmap rendered from a shadow casting light. If it is set at 512, which is the default, the Dmap will be 512 x 512 pixels. As mentioned earlier, from the light point of view the map is a square grid of pixels in front of the light. This grid is projected over the scene, dividing it into sections. As a result, each section of the scene is represented by one pixel on the Dmap.

For example, let's say you have a scene that is 100 grid units by 100 grid units. There is a light casting shadows in your scene and the **Dmap Resolution** is set to **100**. Since the **Dmap Resolution** is set at **100**, one pixel from the Dmap will cover approximately one grid square of the scene. If there is a sphere that is 1 grid unit in size, the shadow for it will be calculated with the depth value

Low Dmap resolution

of as little as one pixel in the Dmap. As you can see in the image above, there isn't enough information in the Dmap to create a decent shadow.

In the following image, the **Dmap Resolution** has been increased, resulting in enough information in the Dmap to create an accurate shadow.

To automatically get the most detailed and accurate shadows out of a Dmap, there is an attribute called **Use Dmap Auto Focus** in the **Depth Map Shadow Attributes** section of the Attribute Editor. When this attribute's value is true, the renderer automatically computes the bounding volume for the shadow casting objects in the view from the light source

High Dmap resolution

and uses the smallest possible field of view to render the shadow map. However, this can create artifacts over an animation if the bounding volume of the objects in your scene changes, possibly creating aliasing artifacts in your shadows, or unwanted softening or noise in the shadows.

Depth Map Filter Size

Dmap Filter Size helps control the softness of shadow edges. The softness of the shadow edge is a combination of the size of the shadow, the **Dmap Resolution** and the **Dmap Filter Size**. If you have an object casting a shadow and the shadow is a little rough around the edges, increase the **Dmap Filter Size** to soften the edge. The following image shows the effect of **Dmap Filter Size**. Increasing **Dmap Filter Size** will increase render time, especially in conjunction with an increase in **Dmap Resolution**. For really soft and fuzzy shadows, try lowering the resolution and using a medium **Dmap Filter Size**. Be aware that the lower the resolution, the lower the accuracy of the shadow; using too low a resolution can result in flickering shadows in animation.

Dmap Resolution 64
Dmap Filter Size 1

Dmap Resolution 1024
Dmap Filter Size 10

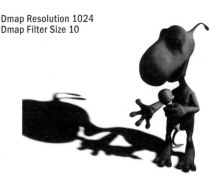

Effect of filter size with various Dmap resolution

Shadow color

A phenomenon of color vision is the tendency of the eye to perceive the shadows cast from a colored light source to be the complementary color. It is not there in reality, but it is an optical illusion or color impression within the eye.

Lightening the shadow color also increases the transparency of the shadow. The following rendered images show this effect:

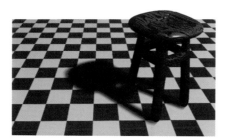 

Blue lighting with a black and blue shadow color

Dmap Auto Focus

To avoid using very high resolution Dmaps wherever possible, it is important to keep the Dmap focused tightly on the shadow casting objects. The **Use Dmap Auto Focus** feature allows the light to automatically determine the most optimal coverage region for the Dmap. The behavior of Auto Focus is shown in the examples below. The workflow when turning off auto focus is described in the directional light example following the spot light example. In all examples below, the **Casts Shadows** flag is turned off on the ground plane to help optimize Auto Focus.

For spot lights, the **Cone Angle** limits the size of the Dmap coverage when the light covers an area smaller than the shadow casting objects. When the cone angle covers an area larger than the objects, Auto Focus keeps the Dmap tightly focused on the shadow casting objects. When **Use Dmap Auto Focus** is turned off, you need to set a specific angle to focus the Dmap. Care must be taken when setting this angle because if you set the **Dmap Focus** too small, the shadow may be cut off or may not appear at all.

When the **Cone Angle** covers an area larger than the objects, **Auto Focus** keeps the Dmap coverage focused on the shadow casting objects.

Large spot light coverage, but Dmap is focused

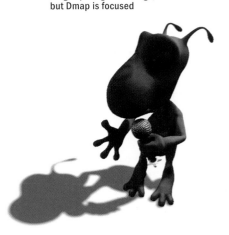

Light view

Resulting Dmap

Use Dmap Auto Focus On

For directional lights, if **Use Dmap Auto Focus** is on, Maya will compute the vector for the light and the world bounding box based on all shadow casting objects. The Dmap coverage will be fit to the width of the world bounding box looking through the light's Orthographic view. If you have a scene that scales a lot up or down or an object that crosses a large distance perpendicular to the light, the auto focus can cause flickering in animation. This is because the Dmap Resolution remains constant but the coverage will keep changing, affecting the quality of the shadows. To avoid this, turn **Off** the **Use Dmap Auto Focus** option and manually set the **Dmap Width Focus**.

To determine the value to use as the **Dmap Width Focus**, look through the selected light and track and zoom until the shadow casting objects are closely bounded by the view. Select **View → Camera Attribute Editor**, and under the **Orthographic Views** section, the **Orthographic Width** is the value you should use as the **Dmap Width Focus** on the light.

Tracking and dollying the view of the light changes the position of the light. Normally, the position of a directional light is not important, however, when turning **Use Dmap Auto Focus** off, you need to turn **On Use Light Position** on the light so that Maya knows the location from which you positioned the Dmap. Forgetting to turn on **Use Light Position** results in the default behavior where the Dmap is positioned at the origin. This may result in incorrect or offset shadows.

Lesson 04

Directional light shadows

Directional lights have two possible behaviors when using Dmap shadows. Since directional lights are assumed to be at an infinite distance from the scene (hence the parallel light rays), by default, they will cast shadows on the entire scene. The bounding box of the scene is taken and an orthogonal Dmap region is created, which contains the entire scene. This can result in shadow Dmap resolution problems if the scene is very large, but only if a small section of the scene is being viewed, or if the scene changes size dramatically over an animation.

Use Light Position is provided to limit the number of objects that are involved in a directional light's Dmap. Setting this attribute to true makes the directional light take its position (the location of the directional light icon in the view) into account. Objects in the half space defined by the light's position and direction are illuminated by the directional light and are used in the creation of the shadow Dmap. Any objects *behind* the directional light are not lit and do not participate in the generation of the shadow Dmap. The **Use Light Position** attribute is not on by default and can only be accessed when the **Use Dmap Auto Focus** is turned off.

The following explains how to create nice looking shadows with a directional light:

1 Set the Dmap options

- Select the directional light that you are using to cast Dmap shadows.

- In the Attribute Editor, go to the **Dmap Shadows** section and set **Use Dmap Auto Focus** to **Off**.

- Set the **Use Light Position** to **On**.

2 Look through the light

- Make sure the directional light is selected, then select **Panels → Look Through Selected**.

- Place this view until all shadow casting objects are closely bounded by the view.

When you **Look Through Selected** *on a light, a camera node underneath the light's transform node is temporarily created. When you change the panel's view back to an Orthographic or Perspective view, the extra camera node is removed.*

3 Note the Orthographic values

- While looking through the directional light, select the **Camera** by going to **View → Camera Attribute Editor...**

- Open the **Orthographic Views** section and note the **Orthographic Width** value.

The Orthographic Width value is the distance across the camera view. If you navigate around the scene until all the objects that will be casting shadows are contained within the view, the Orthographic Width will be the distance across the scene.

4 Set the Dmap Width Focus

- Select the light.

- Enter the value recorded from above into the **Dmap Width Focus**.

Tips for good directional light shadows

- Render out the scene with **Disk Based Dmap** on **Overwrite Existing Dmaps** and **fcheck** the Dmap for the light. It will be in the *depth* directory of the current project. This will help troubleshooting. There is a *midmap* and the standard Dmap. You will need to press the **Z** key to see the depth information in these files.

- To help set up accurate detailed shadows without using huge Dmap resolutions, background geometry or ground planes may be able to have the **Casts Shadows** flag in the **Render Stats** section of the Attribute Editor turned **Off** so they will not be included in the auto focus. Another option is to use **Auto Focus Off** and **Use Light Position On** to manually tighten the shot.

- In the case where you have a problematic scene (where the world bounding box changes size dramatically or an object crosses a large distance perpendicular to the light), you may have to sacrifice speed and use a very high resolution Dmap and manually set the **Dmap Width Focus** to avoid flickering shadows.

Point light shadows

Point lights produce shadows by casting up to 12 Dmaps; a standard Dmap and a midmap are created in each of the cardinal axes directions (+X, -X, +Y, -Y, +Z, and -Z) from the point light's position in space. If there is no shadow casting object in a particular cardinal axis direction, no Dmap for that direction is created. Be aware that if you specify a large shadow Dmap resolution, there can be 12 Dmaps of that large resolution generated. Maya does try to compact the Dmaps as much as possible, but large Dmaps can still occupy a great deal of memory and take valuable time to render. To further optimize your shadow Dmaps from point lights, you can turn individual directions off. For example, if there is nothing of interest to cast shadows on the ceiling of your room, you could disable the +Y Dmap by turning **Off** the **Use Y+ Dmap** attribute in the **Dmap Shadow Attributes** section of the point light's Attribute Editor.

Project Two

Spot light shadows

Spot lights by default use only one Dmap. Using only one Dmap has limitations when the angle of the spot light exceeds 90 degrees; the resolution of the Dmap must be increased dramatically to keep the shadow quality high. You can use up to six Dmaps for spot lights by turning **Off** the **Use Only Single Dmap** in the Attribute Editor. When this attribute is turned off, and the cone angle of the spot light exceeds 90 degrees, five or six Dmaps are created around the spot light, tiling the faces of an axis-aligned cube with faces in each of the axis directions – much the same as for a point light. The only difference is that a spot light will only cast five Dmaps if the spot light does not shine onto one of the six faces. Just as cubic reflection maps avoid aliasing at the boundaries between faces of the cube, the cubic shadow map is also filtered to avoid artifacts.

Motion blurred shadows

Shadows themselves do not motion blur. To work around this limitation, render a shadow pass separately and process it to add blur before compositing. The other option is to use the mental ray shadow maps.

Dmap shadows in IPR

There are some **Dmap Shadow** attributes that will update automatically in an IPR region, while others can only be previewed by selecting in the **Render View** window **IPR → Update Shadow Maps**. The shadow attributes are arranged in the light's Attribute Editor so that these attributes are grouped together.

Casting Dmap shadows example

In this exercise, you will experiment with casting Dmap shadows using Diva on the stage. The *stageLight* is the only light source in the scene so it should definitely cast shadows.

1   Turn On Dmap shadows

- Select *stageLight* and set **Use Dmap Shadows** to **On**.

- IPR render the scene and select a section that will allow you to see updates to the shadow.

You will notice that the shadows do not look very good. They look blockish and the image contains many self-shadowing artifacts.

2 Turn Off shadow casting

In this scene, the shadows are looking pixelated because the scene is large and the **Resolution** of the Dmap is at the default of 512. Before increasing the resolution of the Dmap, remember that the large ground plane and the back wall do not cast shadows on anything so you can turn their **Cast Shadows** render attribute to **Off**. This allows **Dmap Auto Focus** to reduce the area that the Dmap covers, which improves the shadows from *stageLight*.

- Select the *floor1* and open its Attribute Editor.

- In the **Render Stats** section, set the **Casts Shadows** flag to **Off**.

The floor1 geometry will not be taken into consideration when computing the world bounding box.

- Repeat for the *wall* geometry.

Tip: *If you need to do this for many objects, use* **Window** → **General Editors** → **Attribute Spreadsheet...** *and look under the* **Render** *tab.*

- In the Render view window, use **IPR** → **Update Shadow Maps** to see the change in the shadows.

The shadows will have tightened up a little bit.

Diva casting shadows

Lesson 04

3 Increase the resolution

You can see that the shadow quality is still blockish. The default resolution of 512 is not sufficient for this light shadowing the entire scene. You could just increase the **Dmap Filter Size** and have very soft shadows. However, some shadows from thin objects would become very faint and could flicker in animation with such a low resolution shadow map.

- In the Attribute Editor for *stageLight,* increase the **Dmap Resolution** until the blocky appearance is reduced and the level of shadow detail is to your satisfaction.

 Tip: *Remember to use the* **Update Shadow Maps** *to see the results in IPR.*

Shadows with high resolution 2048 Dmap

4 Adjust the Dmap Bias

At this point, the shadows are looking much better. However, you might notice self-shadowing artifacts. This can be solved using the **Dmap Bias** attribute.

- With IPR running, adjust **Dmap Bias** very slightly to values that are greater than **0.001**.

The Dmap Bias will update in IPR automatically.

Project TWO

Note: *Too large a value may result in surfaces coming out of shadow that should be in shadow.*

5   Adjust the Dmap Filter Size

The final step is to smooth the rough edges of the shadows.

- Increase the **Dmap Filter Size** until the shadows have a nice soft look.

A value of **5** *should be enough to give nice smooth edges on the shadows. The higher you set this attribute, the softer the edges will look, but you will pay a significant price in the length of time it takes to render.*

Shadows with Dmap Filter Size of 5

Tip: *For very soft and fuzzy shadows, sometimes it is better to use a low resolution Dmap with some amount of filtering rather than very high resolution Dmaps with very high filter sizes.*

Lesson 04

Optimizing Disk Based Dmaps

The **Dmap Shadow** section contains settings to allow you to **Overwrite Existing Dmap(s)/Reuse Existing Dmap(s)**. These settings cause the Dmaps to be written to or read from disk and should be enabled when doing iterative render tests on a scene with shadows that are finalized, or when there is only a camera fly-by/fly-through of the scene. Be aware that if you set these flags with animated moving objects, it will cause your shadows to remain stationary while the objects move.

To help lower render times with **Disk Based Dmaps**, set **Disk Based Dmaps** to **Reuse Existing Dmap(s)**. The Dmap will be calculated the first time you render and save to disk. During each subsequent render, the same Dmaps will be read from disk and the mid-distance between them calculated.

Volumetric lighting effects

Another feature of Dmap shadows is the ability to cast volume shadows through fog. This is a very popular effect in movies and television. This effect is referred to as **Volumetric Lighting**.

In the support files, there is a scene called *04-volumetricLight_01.ma* that contains an example of volumetric lighting. Watch the movie *fogLightMoth.mov* for a rendered example of this effect.

Shadowing the fog is done by examining the shadow map a number of times across the fog volume.

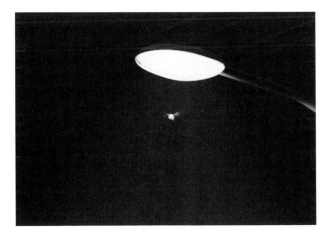

The shadows are cast within the light fog

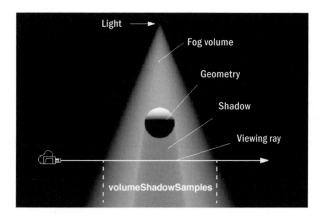

Side view of a ray penetrating a shadow volume

The number of times the fog is sampled is controlled by the attribute **Fog Shadow Samples**. The higher the number of samples, the higher the quality of the shadows in the fog. Keep in mind, though, that this will increase render times. Also note that, internally, Maya does not use **Mid Distance** when fog shadows are being rendered.

To darken the shadows in the fog, the **Fog Shadow Intensity** can be increased. The effect of increasing the **Fog Shadow Intensity** and the **Fog Shadow Samples** is shown in the following images:

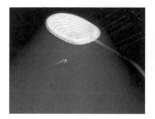
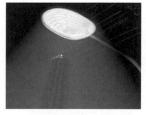

Samples: 20
Intensity: 1
Faint and grainy
shadows

Samples: 20
Intensity: 3
More dramatic
shadows – still grainy

Samples: 60
Intensity: 3
Dramatic and
smooth shadows

Various fog shadow intensity and samples' values

Light fog texture

Light fog is usually caused by small particles that scatter the light, giving an impression of volume. In order to recreate this effect, you can map a 3D texture in the fog and even animate the texture. It is very easy to add light fog texture to a scene, but it will cost some time to the renderer to calculate this effect.

In order to add a fog texture to a light, simply click on the **Map** button of the **Light Fog** attribute under the **Light Effects** section of the Attribute Editor. Doing so will create the nodes and connections required to render a homogeneous volumetric light fog. Map a 3D texture, such as a solid fractal, in the **Light Fog Color** attribute. Animate the texture to give the impression of fluidity.

In the support files, the scene called *04-volumetricLight_02.ma* contains the following Meeper scene that uses volumetric textured fog.

Light fog with 3D texture

Raytraced shadows

Raytraced shadows are slower to render than Dmap shadows and generally have quite a different look than Dmaps. However, there are several reasons you would need to use raytraced shadows:

- To render transparency mapped shadow casting objects where you want to see the details of the texture map in the shadow;

- To have colored transparent shadows from objects with a material that has color on the transparency channel;

- To have shadow attenuation where the shadow dissipates as it gets further away from the shadow casting object and for transparent objects, a shadow's tendency to be brighter in the center;

- To have shadows from ambient lights because they have no Dmap shadows.

Detailed shadow through
transparency mapped surface

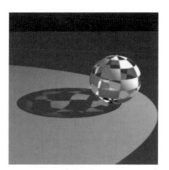

Shadow attenuation

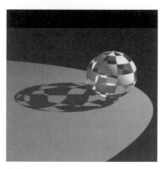

Colored shadows from colored
transparent surface

Shadow from ambient light type

Various raytraced shadow effects

How to get soft attenuated shadows

The raytraced shadow attributes **Light Radius** and **Shadow Rays** help control the final look of the shadow. Increasing the Light Radius to a non-zero value will cause the shadow to begin to dissipate as it gets further from the shadow casting object. To achieve a smooth appearance of raytraced shadows, the number of Shadow Rays will usually need to be increased. This can be seen in the following images:

Lesson 04
Raytraced shadows

Light radius: 0
Shadow rays: 1

Light radius: 3
Shadow rays: 1

Light radius: 3
Shadow rays: 10

Attenuated raytraced shadow variations

Tip: The shadow of transparent objects tends to be brighter in the center, simulating a light's focus. On the material node of that object under the **Raytrace Options**, there is a **Shadow Attenuation** control to simulate this property. A setting of 0 results in a constant intensity of the shadow, whereas a setting of 1 results in brighter shadows focused in the center.

Self-shadowing raytraced shadows - Terminator Effect

To calculate raytraced shadows, the renderer sends a ray from the camera and when this ray hits a surface, it spawns a secondary ray towards the light. This is a shadow ray which reports whether or not it hits any shadow-casting objects on its way to the light. If it does hit a shadow-casting object, then the point from which the shadow ray originated is in shadow. Because there is a shadow ray for each camera ray, raytraced shadows are very accurate, leading to their characteristic sharp edges. This also explains why they take longer to render.

There is a common limitation when working with raytraced shadows that leads to a self-shadowing error known as the **Terminator Effect**. Terminator is the term for the transition point at which the illumination on a surface ends and the shadowed region begins. When raytraced shadows are used, artifacts may appear at this terminator point on the surface; thus, the name Terminator Effect.

This type of artifact results from the fact that the renderer uses flat polygonal triangles at render time to approximate curved surfaces (in the case of NURBS). If the raytraced shadows were computed using the real position of the curved surface, there would not be any self-shadowing. However, because part of the polygon lies slightly below the actual surface, the shadow ray can intersect the surface itself on the way to the light, causing the self-shadowing artifact.

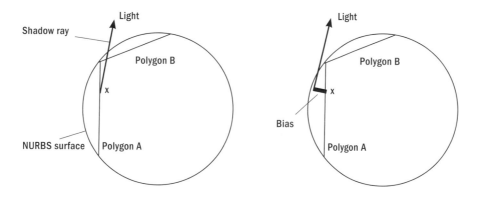

Terminator Effect explanations

There are two ways to correct this type of artifact:

- One way is to increase the tessellation on the surface. This results in triangles that more closely approximate the real position of the curved surface, thereby reducing or eliminating the self-shadowing artifact.

- The other way to correct these artifacts is to use the **Bias** attribute in the **Raytracing Quality** section of **Render Settings**. The bias amount will offset any secondary ray from the surface generating the secondary ray so that it does not self-intersect.

The following images show the effect of increasing the tessellation or using the bias:

 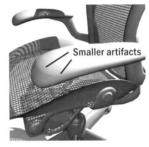 

Terminator artifacts

Increased tessellation
Some artifacts remain

Bias: 01.
Artifacts eliminated

No tessellation increase

Terminator Effect examples

Note: *Raytraced shadows may not render properly with motion blur.*

mental ray shadow maps

The shadow map computation in mental ray is similar to the Dmap shadow computation. Like Dmap shadows, this type of shadow can be imprecise, yet it is faster to compute than raytraced shadows.

In mental ray, point, directional, spot and area lights are the light types that can produce shadow maps. To enable this option, select a light and turn **On** the **Shadow Maps** option in the light's mental ray section of the Attribute Editor.

Dmap resolution

Resolution under mental ray **Shadow Maps Attributes** is the same as the Maya **Dmap Resolution** attribute. It defines the size of the shadow map rendered from a shadow casting light. The larger this value, the more accurate the shadow map, resulting in more precise shadows. However, increasing this value will increase your render time.

Samples

Samples represent the number of samples the renderer will take to alleviate artifacting. The higher the samples, the longer the render will take. In the following examples, you can see how increasing the samples' value gets rid of any artifacts. Note that increasing this value also increases render time.

Softness

Softness works the same as the Maya **Dmap Filter** attributes in that it controls the softness of the shadow edge. This often works best when used with a low resolution value.

Softness: 0   Softness: 0.3   Softness: 0.3
Samples: 0   Samples: 0   Samples: 30

mental ray shadow variations

Lesson 04

> **Note:** *The mental ray Shadow Map algorithm attempts to resolve self-shadowing artifacts without user interaction. Therefore, parameters such as* **Use Mid Dist Dmap** *and* **Dmap Bias** *are not necessary and will not be used when the* **Take Settings from Maya** *button is used.*

Auto Focus shadow maps

The mental ray shadow map algorithm employs a similar **Auto Focus** feature to keep the shadow map focused tightly on the shadow-casting objects. Unlike Maya, however, a user cannot edit the placement of these maps.

Reusing shadow maps

You can re-use shadow maps to help speed up render times. Normally, mental ray will compute one shadow map per frame for an animation. If the light or shadow does not change over the course of an animation, you can reuse the same shadow map over and over, saving computation time and speeding up the render process. To reuse a shadow map, do the following:

- Open up the mental ray **Render Settings** and under the **Shadows** section, make sure the **Rebuild Shadow Maps** flag is **Off**.

- Open the **Shadow Map Attributes** section under the **mental ray** section of the light's Attribute Editor, and type a name for the shadow in the **Shadow Map File Name** field.

This will be the name of the shadow map that is saved to disk.

> **Tip:** *You can also specify to add the* **Light Name**, **Scene Name** *and* **Frame Extension** *to the shadow map name.*

- Do a render to generate that shadow map.

The file will be saved in the mentalRay sub-directory of your current project directory under shadowMap.

- Leave the name in the field and mental ray will automatically re-use this map for every frame of an animation.

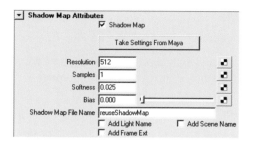

Shadow Map Attributes

Motion blur shadow maps

In the real world, a photographer selects a camera with specific properties, adjusts the camera's settings (for example, the shutter speed), positions the camera to compose the shot and then photographs the three-dimensional real world to produce a two-dimensional photograph. One of the properties the 3D camera will attempt to reproduce is motion blur - the phenomenon of an object to look blurred as it moves quickly across a frame. With mental ray, if an object has motion blur, its shadows can also exhibit motion blur.

The following will take you through setting up motion blurred shadow maps:

1   Scene file

- Open the file called *04-motionBlurredShadows_01.ma*.

  The file consists of a plane of light and an animated sphere.

2   Turn On Dmap shadows

- Select *shadowLight* and turn **Shadow Maps** to **On**.

- Do a render at frame **15** and click on the **Keep Image** button in the Render View window.

3   Turn On motion blur

- Open *the* **mental ray Render Settings** and under **Motion Blur**, choose **Linear** from the **Motion Blur** pull-down menu.

- Make sure the **Motion Blur By** is set to **3** to increase the amount of blur.

- Make sure that **Motion Blur Shadow Maps** under the **Shadows** section of the **Render Settings** is **On**.

Lesson 04

4 Render a frame

- Do another render at frame **15** in the Render View window.

- Keep this image and compare the shadows from the first image, which have no motion blur on them, to the current image.

5 Edit the motion blurred shadow

- If you find that your shadow exhibits artifacting or that the shadow itself is not soft/blurred enough, you may want to go to the shadow map settings under the light's Attribute Editor and increase the **Samples** and **Softness** parameters.

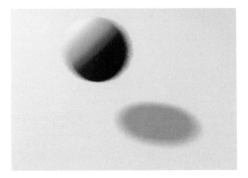

Motion blurred shadows

Tip: *If the blur on the object is relatively small, you may want to use only the softness attribute to give the illusion of a motion blurred shadow.*

Volumetric shadow maps

In order to cast shadows through a fog volume, you can use either shadow maps or raytrace shadows. If you use raytrace shadows, you will be able to cast transparent information through the shadow volume. Capturing transparent information through a volume is something that is not available when using the Maya shadow options.

The following example shows how to create volumetric shadow maps.

1 Scene file

- Open the file called *04-volumeShadows_01.ma*.

The file is very simple, consisting of a spot light and a sphere.

2   Turn on shadows and fog

- Select *fogLight* and set **Use Dmap Shadows** to **On** and **Shadow Maps** to **On**.

- Select the Map button next to **Light Fog** under the **Light Effects** section.

3   Edit the shadows

You may find that you either cannot see your shadows or there may be some artifacting. To get rid of this, do the following:

- Increase the **Samples** attribute under the **mental ray** section of the Attribute Editor to **2**.

- Slowly increase the value for the **Volume Samples Override** in the **Render Stats** section of the light's *coneShape1* node.

- To further alleviate artifacting, set the **Depth Jitter** option to **On**.

This will randomize the samples of the volume by replacing banding artifacts with noise.

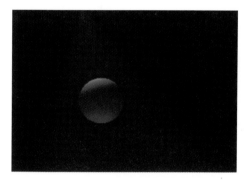

Volumetric shadows

mental ray raytraced shadows

Raytraced shadows in mental ray are the same to set up and use as in Maya. If you are using the mental ray renderer with raytrace shadows, you will need to make sure **Raytracing** is turned **On** in the **mental ray Render Settings**. Other reasons to use mental ray raytrace shadows include:

- Capturing transparency mapped detail in a shadow that is cast through a volume.

- Rendering motion blurred shadows.

Lesson 04

> **Note:** *As you have seen earlier, you can also use mental ray shadow maps to get motion blurred shadows.*

Raytraced shadow methods

mental ray has three global shadow overrides. These modes affect all raytraced shadows in a scene. They can be useful for globally refining and adjusting the amount of information that is considered in the calculation of raytraced shadows. The controls are found in the mental ray **Render Settings** → **Shadows** section.

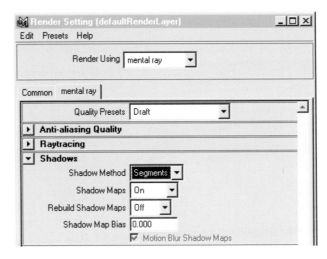

Shadow methods

Simple method

The distinctive feature associated with this shadow calculation mode is that the searching order for objects occluding illumination rays from a light source is unpredictable. This mode makes for faster shadow calculation.

Sorted method

This shadow mode is similar to simple mode with the exception that occluding objects are first listed and then sorted. Objects that occlude light rays from the light source are evaluated first.

Segmented method

This is the default. With this mode shadow rays are sent from the illuminated point backwards towards the light source. This is the reverse of what happens with simple and sorted shadows. When a shadow ray hits an occluding object, its shadow shader is *called*. The occluding objects shadow shader then sends another shadow ray off towards the light source. This shadow mode allows volumetric raytraced shadows.

Off

This is a handy global switch or override that turns all shadow calculations in a scene off.

Conclusion

Shadows are an important part of creating mood and atmosphere in a scene. There are a number of important concepts to understand in order to achieve the best shadows possible without compromising your render times.

In the next lesson, you will learn about cameras.

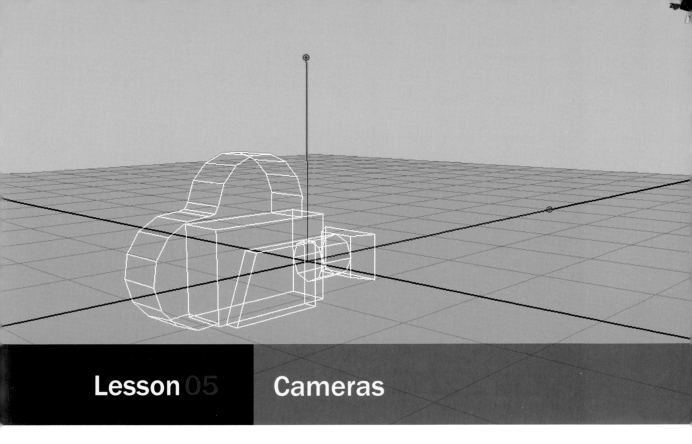

Lesson 05 Cameras

A 3D camera is very similar
to a motion picture or still
camera. It mimics real world
settings to allow you to
match images captured by
real cameras.

In this lesson you will learn the following:

- How to work with cameras;

- How to work with film gates and film backs;

- Aspect ratios;

- How to do rotoscoping using D1 images;

- mental ray camera attributes.

Camera basics

The vast majority of your renderings will make use of the *Perspective* camera. While there is nothing technically wrong with using this camera for all of your animation and rendering, it is advisable to create a new camera to work with.

Note: *The Perspective camera is treated differently because it is a static node. It is invisible to start with to discourage you from using it for your animation and rendering.*

There are two ways to create a new camera in your scene:

Creating a new camera

- In any view, go to **Panels** → **Perspective** → **New**.

Or

- Go to **Create** → **Camera**.

The **Create** *menu method will place the camera at the origin while the* **Panels** *menu method will place it away from the origin like the default Perspective camera. Other than the location at which it is created, there is no difference between these two methods.*

Renaming the camera

- With the new camera selected, use the name field at the top of the Channel Box to give the camera a new name.

This method of renaming will name both the transform node and the shape node.

Working with cameras

Once you have created a new camera or several new cameras, it is very easy to switch between them or change a view.

Switch between cameras

- In any view, select **Panels** → **Perspective** and choose from the list of cameras.

Positioning a camera

The main workflow for positioning cameras is to use the following combinations:

Alt + **LMB** to tumble the camera;

Alt + **MMB** to track the camera;

Alt + **LMB** + **MMB** or **Alt** + **RMB** to dolly the camera.

Additionally, Maya has a suite of camera tools that can be used to achieve precise control over your camera's position and behavior.

In the modeling window, select **View** → **Camera Tools**.

Tip: *For more information on camera tools, see the Maya online documentation.*

Stepping back and forth between camera views

It is possible to step back and forth between your present and past camera views.

- Use the] key to go forwards and the [key to go backwards though your recent camera views.

Undo camera movements

The camera views are intentionally not included in the **Undo** feature. If you would prefer them to be included, do one of the following:

- Enable **Camera Attribute Editor** → **Movement Options** → **Undoable Movements**.

Or

- Select **View** → **Camera Settings** → **Undoable Movements**.

Camera bookmarks

Camera bookmarks can be very helpful when you need to return to a specific camera view. To create a bookmark, do the following:

- In the camera view, go to **View** → **Bookmarks** → **Edit Bookmarks...**

Selection and frame selection

To quickly dolly in on a selected object or group of selected objects, there are several methods.

- Use **View** → **Look at selection** to have the object centered in the window.
- Use **View** → **Frame Selection** to have the object centered in the window and close up to the camera.

These camera commands will also establish a new point of interest that the camera will orbit around. If you find that you cannot zoom in close enough on an object, try framing it with **Frame Selection** first.

Tip: *You can do* **Frame Selection** *with the* **f** *hotkey to frame the selected objects. To frame all objects in the scene press the* **a** *hotkey.*

Box dolly feature

To quickly dolly in on an area of the scene, you can use the box dolly feature.

- **Alt+Ctrl** and draw a marquee around the objects you wish to dolly in on.

    Left to *right* dollies **in**.

    Right to *left* dollies **out**.

Dolly vs. zoom

The difference between *dolly* and *zoom* is that when you dolly, you are physically moving the camera in space while zoom refers to changing the camera's focal length.

What is the difference between moving the camera and changing the focal length? Why would you choose one over the other? The answer is that when you move the camera, the perspective changes. Objects far from the camera change in relative size at a slower rate than objects close to the camera. This is essentially what you see through your human eyes; as you walk around your perspective changes.

When you zoom, you are changing the focal length of the lens; perspective does not change. This is something that your eyes cannot achieve, which creates an unsettling quality when used for heightened effect.

Perspective could be thought of as the rate that objects change in size in the frame as their distance from the camera changes.

Tip: *In the camera's Attribute Editor, you can adjust the* **Focal Length** *in the* **Camera Attributes** *section to adjust the zoom, or use the* **Zoom Tool** *in the Camera Tools.*

If you look at a camera icon, you will see that the length of the lens is changing but the camera is not moving.

*Notice how this also changes the **Angle of View** attribute. It is not possible to animate the **Angle of View**, but it is possible to animate the **Focal Length** attribute.*

Hitchcock's Vertigo effect

Anyone who has seen the Alfred Hitchcock movie *Vertigo* may be familiar with the eerie camera effect where some objects appear to move further away while others appear to move closer to the camera.

This is achieved by zooming in while dollying out or by dollying in while zooming out.

Cameras for batch rendering

For batch rendering, you will need to specify which camera you wish to render from.

- For most purposes, use **Render Settings** → **Image File Output**.

- Select the camera from the **Camera** pop-up list.

Tip: For more advanced users who need to render more than one camera at the same time, it is possible to use the **Camera Attribute Editor** → **Output Settings** → **Renderable** flag. In this case, the Render Settings will show more than one camera marked as renderable in the **Camera** pop-up list.

ADVANCED CAMERA ATTRIBUTES

Display options

When you are trying to frame a shot to render, you need to be able to see what area will actually be rendered. Cameras have some display mechanisms that allow you to see the rendering area very clearly.

Lesson 05

Resolution Gate

- Within the camera view panel, enable **View** → **Camera Settings** → **Resolution Gate**.

Doing so will display a green rectangle surrounding the renderable area in the camera view.

Overscan

- While in the Attribute Editor for the camera, go to the **Display Options** section.

- Increase the **Overscan** attribute.

The **Overscan** *value does not change the rendered image. It is just a display feature to allow you to see parts of the scene outside of the region that will be rendered.*

Tip: *You can also modify the* **Overscan** *attribute for the camera to a value less than* **1** *to get a close-up of your scene without disturbing your camera position.*

Film gates and film backs

The following is a fairly extensive description of what *film gates* and *film backs* are in real life and in Maya. If you are creating an entire shot in Maya and have complete artistic license over the view from the camera, there is no reason to be concerned with film backs. As you have already seen above, the default settings will ensure that everything inside of the resolution gate will be rendered. If you are trying to match the look of a real shot, film backs become important.

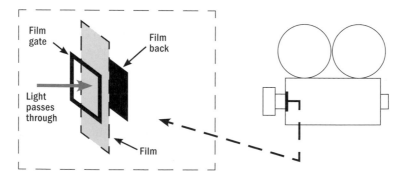

Film back, film gate and film relationship

Project Two

In real cameras, the film negative is passed between two plates called the *film back* and the *film gate*. The film negative sits against the film back and is held in place by the film gate.

The *film back* corresponds to the size of the film negatives and is measured in millimeters. Because of this, when people talk about a 35mm camera for instance, they are referring to the size of the film back and the film negative.

The *film gate* is a metal plate that sits in front of the film negative to hold it in place. The plate overlaps some portion of the film so only the region inside the gate is actually exposed to light. It is this region that you are simulating in Maya in order to match the real footage. It is expressed as the **Camera Aperture** attribute.

Note: *There is no attribute to specify the entire size of the film back separately as this would just represent unexposed wasted portions of the film in real life.*

The **Film Gate** attribute in Maya is presented as a list of presets. In the list you will see five different settings for 35mm. This is because for all 35mm cameras the film back and film negative sizes will be the same. However, the size of the region inside the film gate will differ depending on how big the opening is in the gate. Keep in mind that it is the exposed region of the film that you are simulating when you render an image in Maya.

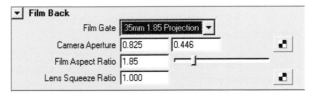

Film Back attributes

Another attribute that is used to describe this region inside the film gate is the **Film Aspect Ratio**. The following diagram shows the meaning of **Film Aspect Ratio**. It is simply the **Camera Aperture** attribute represented as a ratio.

Film aspect ratio

Film back with focal length and angle of view

The following explains the relationship between the film back, focal length and angle of view.

Change the film gate presets

- Use the pop-up list of presets to switch between various film gates.

Notice that the angle of view changes but the focal length does not.

Adjust the focal length

- Adjust the **focal length** and notice that the **angle of view** changes.

As you extend the focal length, the angle of view gets narrower. As you shorten the focal length, the angle of view gets larger.

The following diagrams illustrate these relationships:

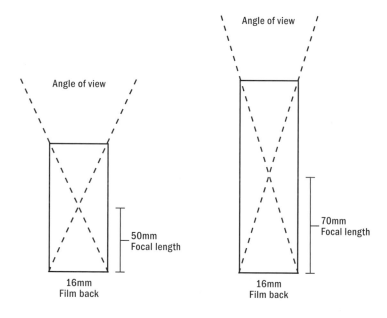

Effect of changing focal length without changing film back

> **Tip:** *The focal length of a lens is defined as the distance from the lens to the film plane. Lenses are identified by their focal length expressed in millimeters. By this you can see that a 50mm lens has a focal length of 50mm.*

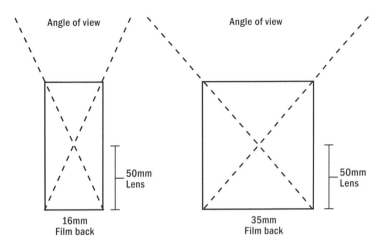

Angle of view   Angle of view

50mm Lens   50mm Lens

16mm Film back   35mm Film back

Effect of changing film back without changing focal length

Most people are familiar with the effect of changing the focal length in real cameras. This amounts to switching to different lenses or adjusting the zoom to lengthen or shorten the lens you are using. You can see how this affects the angle of view in the first diagram above.

The second diagram above illustrates what will happen if you keep the same lens, but switch to a different size camera.

The process of switching to a different size camera while keeping the same size lens is exactly what you are doing when you switch the **Film Back** in Maya. The result is that the angle of view changes but the focal length does not.

Now you can see why changing to different film backs without changing the focal length seems to cause the camera to zoom in and out.

Note: *The camera aperture relates to the focal length in that different film backs have different normal lenses. A normal lens focal length is not telephoto or wide-angle. It closely approximates normal vision. As the size of the camera aperture increases, a longer focal length is required to achieve normal perspective. That is why a 35mm camera uses a 50mm lens as a normal lens. On a 16mm camera, the same 50mm lens would appear to be telephoto in nature. A normal focal length for a camera is a focal length that equals the diagonal measurement of the camera aperture in millimeters, which means you have to find the hypotenuse.*

Film gate and resolution gate

Now that you have looked at the meaning of film backs and film gates, you need to understand how this relates to the **Resolution Gate** for rendering.

1 Create a new file

2 Turn on the Resolution Gate

- Set both the **Resolution Gate** and **Film Gate** checkboxes to **On** in the camera's **Display Options** in the Attribute Editor.

Notice that at this point the gates do not match. This is because they do not have the same aspect ratio.

3 Change the Overscan

- Set the **Overscan** value to **1.3**.

You will now see the gates properly.

4 Fit Resolution Gate

The **Fit Resolution Gate** attribute controls how Maya fits the film gate to the resolution gate. By default, the **Fit Resolution Gate** attribute is set to **Horizontal**.

- In the camera's Attribute Editor, change the **Fit Resolution Gate** attribute in the **Film Back** section to **Vertical**.

Notice how the film gate is drawn differently relative to the resolution gate.

Horizontal Fit

Vertical Fit

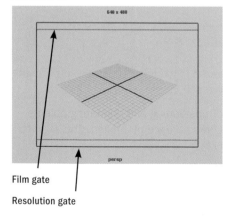
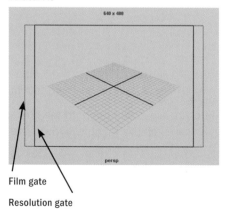

Film gate

Resolution gate

Film gate

Resolution gate

Fit/resolution gate difference

Because the two gates have a different aspect ratio, Maya can only match them in one dimension - either horizontally or vertically, but not both.

In the case of **Horizontal Fit**, the horizontal width of the film gate is matched to the resolution gate's horizontal dimension. This means that the gates will not match vertically.

In the case of **Vertical Fit**, this ensures that the vertical height of the film gate is matched to the resolution gate's vertical dimension. In this case, the horizontal width of the gates will not match.

Match the resolution gate and film gate

If you are working with film gates, chances are you are trying to match a real camera, so you want your rendered images to match the real film gate exactly.

The only way that the film gate and resolution gate can match exactly in both dimensions is if they share the same aspect ratio.

Note: *Again, this matching of aspect ratios is only required when aiming for the look of a specific real camera. Otherwise film backs do not need to be considered at all.*

MATCHING LIVE ACTION

Image planes

Image planes are 2D texture mapped planes connected to a camera, perpendicular to the lens axis. They can be used for several things such as creating environments or tracing concept sketches in the early phases of modeling. In this lesson, you are going to look at how to use them to match live action.

Matching live action refers to the process of positioning and animating objects in a scene relative to a background live action sequence of images. The specific case that will be covered involves working with NTSC digital video footage.

Note: *NTSC is the only example that will be covered. Other examples, like PAL, will not be covered but the workflow itself is the same; only the specific numbers differ.*

Non-Square pixels

Using **NTSC Digital Video**, or **D1**, as it is commonly referred to in the industry, poses a unique challenge that is often misunderstood. The challenge surrounds the fact that digital video is generated by devices that typically use **Non-Square pixels**. However, computer monitors display only square pixels. To compensate for this, Maya has a workflow to allow your objects to match-up correctly with the background plates.

Aspect ratios

The key to successfully matching live action is to understand the meaning of several different aspect ratios.

Image aspect ratio

This is the aspect ratio of the image you will render and is represented by the **Resolution Gate**. Image aspect simply represents the resolution of an image as a ratio.

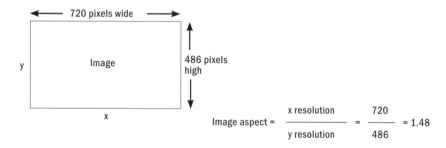

$$\text{Image aspect} = \frac{\text{x resolution}}{\text{y resolution}} = \frac{720}{486} = 1.48$$

Image aspect ratio

The above diagram illustrates how a digital video image does not satisfy the 1.33 aspect desired for television viewing, unless you take into account the **pixel aspect ratio** as described in the next section. This is the special case of image aspect differences you encounter when working with digital video that needs to match computer generated imagery.

Pixel aspect ratio

Each image is made up of pixels. The pixels themselves also have an aspect ratio called **pixel aspect ratio**.

When you are dealing with digital video, the pixels have an **aspect ratio** of **0.9**. They are slightly taller than they are wide.

Project Two

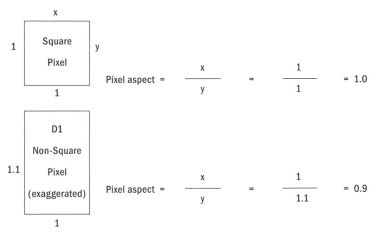

Pixel aspect ratio

Device aspect ratio

Up until now, all of the aspect ratios you have looked at have followed the same equation of *x* divided by *y* equals *aspect ratio*. The device aspect ratio is calculated differently:

Device Aspect = Image Aspect x Pixel Aspect

$$= 1.48 \times 0.9$$

$$= 1.33$$

Device aspect ratio

Film aspect ratio

Another attribute that is used to describe the region defined by the film gate is the **film aspect ratio**. It is simply the **Camera Aperture** attribute represented as a ratio.

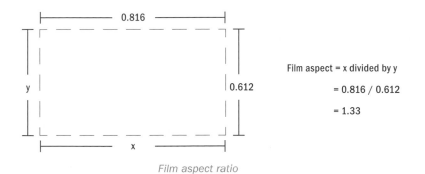

Film aspect ratio

You will see where these aspect ratios fit in as you go through the workflow.

Lesson 05

Workflow to match live action digital video

1   Open a new scene

- Start with a new scene by selecting **File** → **New**.

2   Set the resolution

- Open **Render Settings** and set **Image Size** → **Presets** to **CCIR 601/Quantel NTSC**.

3   Set the camera attributes

- Open the **Display Options** in the Camera Attribute Editor and set the **Resolution** and **Film Gates** to **On**.

- In the **Film Back** section, set the **Overscan** to **1.3**.

Recall that this is only a display mechanism that will allow you to see the gates entirely.

- While in the **Film Back** section, chose the preset **Film Gate** → **35mm TV Projection** which has a **Film Aspect** of **1.33**.

You would need to be given the information about which real camera the video footage was shot on in order to know which film gate to choose for an accurate match.

Tip: *The important thing here is that the **Film Aspect** is **1.33**, which matches the device aspect of **D1** video. As long as these two aspect ratios match, the resolution gate and the film gate will match precisely.*

4   Create the image plane

- In the **Environment** section of the camera's Attribute Editor, click on the **Create** button to create an **Image Plane**.

This will build the nodes and the connections required for the image plane.

5   Bring in D1sphere.iff

For this workflow example, bring in the D1 image of a sphere. The sphere makes it very obvious that you are seeing a distorted image due to the non-square pixels.

- In the **Image Plane** attributes, browse the **Image Name** and select *D1sphere.iff*.

The image comes in looking slightly stretched horizontally.

- In the **Placement** section of the Attribute Editor, set the **Fit** to **To Size.**

*The **To Size** fit method on the image plane will alter the original aspect ratio of the D1sphere.iff image to make it fit the aspect ratio of the film gate (by default, the image plane is fit to the film gate).*

You will notice that as soon as you fit to size, the sphere looks correct.

6 Animate the D1 sequence

If you had a sequence of images, you would need to animate them on the image plane. The easiest way to do this is to select the **Use Image Sequence** attribute in the file node's Attribute Editor.

7 Match the live action

At this point, you can go ahead and model, position and animate your objects using the image plane as your guide.

8 Turn Off the display of the image planes

- Once the animation is done, set the **Display Mode** to **None** in the **Image Plane Attributes** section.

This ensures that the image plane will not be rendered in your final images.

9 Render the sequence

- In the **Render Settings**, set the **Frame/Animation Ext** pop-up list to one of the settings that has a **#** in it.

This will enable the rendering of an animation.

- Set the **Start** and **End** frame numbers.

- Batch Render the sequence using **Render** → **Batch Render...**

10 Composite the images

Once the images are rendered, you will be able to composite them with the D1 footage and everything will match perfectly.

Clipping planes

Clipping Planes are used to determine which objects will be rendered in your scene. There is a *near clipping plane* and a *far clipping plane* and all visible objects between these clipping planes will be rendered. The position of these clipping planes is found under **Camera Attributes** in the Attribute Editor. The clipping planes are viewable in the modeling views if they are turned On.

- To turn **On** clipping planes in the view, use **Display** → **Camera/Light Manipulators** → **Clipping Planes**.

- Adjust them interactively in the view or from the Attribute Editor.

Maya outputs a **Z-depth buffer** which can be used to determine at which depth a pixel makes first contact with geometry in a scene. The Z-depth values will be between **-1** and **0** depending on how far the geometry is from the near and far clipping planes. Those intersections clipped by the near or far plane will be given a depth of 0. If the clipping planes have a fairly large separation distance in units, precision will be lost when comparing depths that are similar or close to one another.

For example, if your clipping planes are set far apart and you have a number of objects clustered together, each object will have a depth value that is very similar to the others. If these depth numbers are rounded-off, the values can become identical, resulting in *artifacts*.

These rendering artifacts will look like background objects appearing to be showing through foreground objects.

Auto Render Clip Plane

If you select a camera and open the Attribute Editor you will notice that **Auto Render Clip Plane** is **On** by default. This allows Maya to automatically set the near and far clipping planes most optimally depending on where objects are in the scene. This tries to minimize the likelihood of the artifacts mentioned above.

With **Auto Render Clip Plane** turned **On**, the clipping planes can change from frame to frame in an animation. So, if you are outputting Z-depth information for some other purpose, you may wish to turn the Auto clipping **Off**.

If you turn **Off** the **Auto Render Clip Plane**, the values shown in the camera's Attribute Editor will be used in the render.

Optimize renders using clipping planes

- To see the camera's **Frustum** use **Display** → **Camera /Light Manipulator** → **Clipping Planes** or **Display** → **Show** → **Camera Manipulators**.

- Geometry that penetrates the **near** clipping plane will be clipped to the near clipping plane. Any part of the geometry nearer to the camera than the near clipping plane will not be rendered.

- If a piece of geometry spans the **far** clipping plane, it will be rendered in its entirety.

- If a piece of geometry is beyond the far clipping plane, it will not be rendered at all.

The type of clipping occurring at the far clipping plane is at the object level, not at the triangle level.

The following diagram shows this clipping relationship. Geometry 01 will be cut by the near clipping plane so that only the portion beyond the near clipping plane is rendered. Geometry 02 will be completely rendered because part of it is nearer to the camera than the far clipping plane. Geometry 03 will not be rendered since it is beyond the far clipping plane.

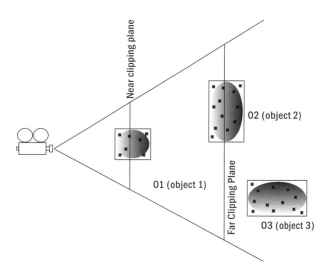

Near and far plane clipping: 01 is partially rendered, 02 is rendered, 03 is not rendered

Camera output settings

The camera's Attribute Editor contains a section related to what the selected camera will output at render time. Switches can be found here that control whether the camera is a renderable camera and whether or not it will output mask, depth, or color (image).

You can also select how the camera will derive depth information for use in post-process rendering effects such as Maya Paint Effects and depth of field.

The default setting for camera depth lookup is **Furthest Visible Depth**. This is the setting necessary for proper handling of camera to object depth sorting when working with Maya Paint Effects' element rendering.

The **Furthest Visible Depth** setting can have a detrimental effect on other depth based effects such as depth of field. If you find this to be the case, set this attribute to **Closest Visible Depth**.

mental ray cameras

Output shader

Allow post-processing of a file prior to it being written. These are plug-ins written in C/C++ that allow custom compositing, motion blurring, depth of field, halo, color correction and file grain. These custom effects may be preferable to what is in the base package.

Volume shader

In the simplest case, this is a uniform fog that fades objects in the distance to white. It can also be used for smoke, clouds and fur items that normally would be difficult to model. For Global Illumination, use the photon volume shader.

Lens shader

By allowing modification of the ray direction and origin, more realistic paths through the camera can be achieved instead of passing through a precise path. It can be used to achieve custom depth of field effects.

Environment shader

This option attaches an environment shader to the camera and maps a texture on an infinite theoretical shape.

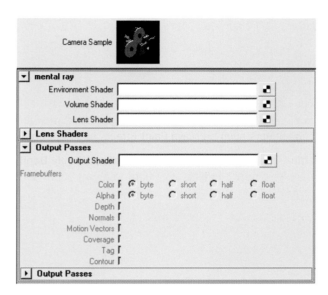

mental ray section of Attribute Editor

Conclusion

Camera attributes are important for understanding the rendering process.
In order to be able to use them effectively, it is essential to have a complete understanding of the topics covered in this lesson.

In the next lesson, you will learn about raytracing features.

Lesson 06   Raytracing

Raytracing is a method of rendering in which rays originate from the camera/eye and are sent out into the scene. Depending on what they encounter, they can spawn other rays. For instance, if a ray hits a reflective surface it will spawn another ray that will bounce off the surface, and if it encounters another object, you will get a reflection.

In this lesson you will learn the following:

- How raytracing works;

- Reflection, refraction and shadow limits;

- Memory requirements.

Raytracing

Raytracing enables you to cast accurate shadows through partially transparent surfaces and allows you to see real reflections. If you don't raytrace, you can still get the look of reflections through the use of texture maps on the reflected color attribute. However, this can amount to a lot of work and still cannot produce important self-reflections. Raytracing also enables your scene to have refractive surfaces.

The Maya rendering architecture is a hybrid renderer. It uses an **EAS (Exact Area Sampling)** or **A-buffer algorithm** for primary visibility from the eye, and then raytraces any secondary rays.

When an object is encountered that requires raytracing to compute some component of its shading (raytraced shadows, reflections and refractions), the raytracer is invoked. An important distinction to make here is that not all objects in a scene will need to be raytraced. If you had a transparent surface with a **Refract Index** of **1.0** (meaning no bending of light will occur), you would simply leave the **Refractions Flag** turned **Off** for that material. In order to use raytracing in Maya, you will need to enable it through the **Render Settings** window.

Note: *Keep in mind that raytracing is memory intensive and will increase rendering time.*

1   Enable Raytracing

- Select **Window** → **Rendering Editors** → **Render Settings** and open the **Raytracing Quality** section.

- Click the **Raytracing** checkbox to turn it **On**.

You have now enabled raytracing for the entire scene.

2   Set which objects will not be raytraced

There is a further level of control in choosing which objects you want raytraced in a scene. By default, all objects have raytracing turned On. You will want to turn off raytracing for objects that do not need to be raytraced to cut down on rendering time.

- Select an object you do not want raytraced and open the **Attribute Editor.**

- Open the **Render Stats** section.

- Turn **Visible in Reflections** to **Off.**

- Turn **Visible in Refractions** to **Off.**

3 Start rendering

You can now render into a view or batch render the scene file.

Reflections, refractions and shadows

Once you have turned **Raytracing** to **On** in the **Render Settings** and the appropriate **Render Stats** are set, when you render a scene it will have reflections and refractions depending on the materials assigned to the surfaces. If you have turned **Raytrace Shadows** to **On** for the lights in your scene, then you will also get raytraced shadows. Notice when you turned Raytracing on in the Render Settings that there are three sliders: **Reflections, Refractions** and **Shadows.** These sliders correspond to limits that are associated with the rays being used in raytracing. Because shooting many reflection, refraction or shadow rays increases rendering time, there is a way to limit the number of such rays being shot. There are two locations where these limits are available. The first is available in the Render Settings, which affect everything. The other is in the material's Attribute Editor for reflections and refractions and in the lights' Attribute Editor for raytraced shadows. The lower of the two sets of values will determine the limit for each surface. If you have your limits set too low, you won't get the desired results.

For example, if you have light passing through a transparent sphere, then on a plane and back again through the sphere, you need to make sure that you have enough reflection rays to pass through all those surfaces. The same goes for shadows. If you have the shadow limit set at 1 and you want to cast a shadow through a transparent surface, you will not see a shadow. You would need to increase the shadow limit on the light.

Reflectivity

In the case of transparent surfaces such as glass, the level of reflectivity depends on the angle at which the glass is viewed. Standing in front of a storefront window looking straight in, you will see a very faint reflection. However, if the viewer is to look at the window from an angle, the reflections will be more pronounced. This is controlled by the **Specular Roll Off** attribute on the blinn material.

There is a physical property called *Total Internal Reflection*. This is when light tries to pass from a dense medium to a less dense medium at too shallow an angle and the light bounces off the boundary of the two mediums. This effect is the basic mechanism behind optical fibers. Light bounces along the inside of the optical fiber, unable to escape because whenever it tries to leave, total internal reflection occurs.

Refractions

There is an additional control for refractions called **Refraction Index.** This can be defined as the ratio of the speed at which light is traveling in the object versus in a vacuum. If the index of refraction is 1.0, then there is no distortion or bending of the light as it travels through the surface. For example, water (20 degrees celsius) has a refraction index of 1.33.

> **Tip:** *To make objects viewed through a refracting surface less jagged, try increasing the shading samples on the refracting object. If it is just a single object that causes you trouble, you should increase the shading samples on a per object level.*

An important feature to be aware of with reflections and raytracing is the ability to map the **Reflected Color** of a material and also get reflections from objects in the scene. This means reflection maps and raytraced reflections can be used together. Basically, if a reflection ray coming off a surface strikes an object, it will reflect that object, and if the ray goes off to infinity, it will use the reflection map. This can be used to get the environment to show up on a reflective surface.

Reflection specularity

This helps control the contribution of the specular highlights in reflections. Sometimes you can encounter some artifacts in the reflections of highlights.

Light absorbance

This will describe how light-absorbing a material is. Transparent materials usually absorb an amount of light that passes through them. The thicker the material, the less light gets through.

Surface thickness

This simulates a surface thickness in world space of transparent objects created from a single surface. This works well when the edges of the surface aren't visible (i.e. a car windshield).

Chromatic aberration

Different wavelengths of light refract at different angles when passing through a transparent surface during raytracing. Chromatic aberration only affects light rays as they pass through the second surface of a transparent object.

1 Create a reflective material

- Create a blinn material.
- Set **Reflectivity** to **1.0**.
- Assign the blinn to a sphere.

2 Create an image plane

- Select the camera and open the Attribute Editor.
- Go to the **Environment** section and click **Create** beside **Image Plane**.
- Under **Image Plane Attributes** → **Type**, change **Image File** to **Texture** and map a **Granite** texture.
- Change **Color1**, **Color2** and **Filler Color** to **black**.
- Change **Color3** to **white**.

3 Position camera and render

- Make sure you have turned **On** the **Raytrace** in the **Render Settings**.
- Add a light to your scene.
- Render the scene.

You will notice that none of the stars are reflecting off the sphere.

4 Map the starfield onto the shader

- Select the blinn material and open the Attribute Editor.
- Drag the granite texture onto the **Reflected Color** of the *blinn* material.

Lesson 06

5 Render the scene

You should now see stars reflected in the sphere.

6 Add other objects

- Create a cone.

- Render your scene.

- Notice that the other objects will be reflected in the sphere as well
  as the stars.

Note: *If you have a number of objects in your scene that need to reflect the
environment, you will need to map the environment texture onto each
one. Another work around for this issue is to create a large sphere
and map your environment texture onto it. Then place all your objects
inside of it. When you raytrace, the reflections of the environment will
come from the large sphere.*

Memory and performance options

In the Render Settings, if you open the **Memory and Performance Options**
tab, you will find a **Raytracing** section. This section has several controls that
the renderer uses to define what will happen when you start a render with
Raytracing enabled.

The first thing you need to know is when a raytrace is invoked, it breaks the
bounding box of the scene into cubes that are called *voxels*. The **Recursion
Depth**, **Leaf Primitives** and **Subdivision Power** attributes are used to determine
the size and number of the voxels used. If there are too many objects in a
voxel, the renderer subdivides the voxel into smaller voxels all contained in
the big voxel.

Why does the renderer *voxelize* the space? One of the primary performance
problems in raytracing is *surface intersection*. If the renderer can limit the
number of objects participating in the calculation, it can speed up the
algorithm. As a ray is traced through the scene, the renderer can immediately
and efficiently know which voxels are intersected and which ones are not.
The renderer can safely ignore those objects contained in voxels that *don't*
intersect the ray. That way, the renderer has limited the number of objects
participating in surface intersection.

Recursion depth

With a fixed resolution for voxels, it is possible that a voxel may contain many triangles, causing raytracing to be very slow if this voxel is hit because the ray will need to intersect against many triangles. When there are many triangles, the renderer can further subdivide the voxel into another 3D array of voxels occupying the space of the parent voxel. Thus, each of those voxels should contain pointers to fewer triangles, reducing the amount of work for the raytracing. The **Recursion Depth** attribute determines the number of levels that this occurs on. It is recommend that this stay at **2**, because there is a trade-off of voxel *traversal time* vs. *triangle intersection time*. Larger does not mean better. Larger also means more memory used by the voxels.

Tip: *In cases where the raytrace is running out of memory to the point where it cannot complete the render, it is possible to lower the* **Recursion Depth** *to* **1**. *This will take much longer to render but will use less memory.*

Leaf primitives

This attribute determines the number of triangles in a voxel before you recursively create voxels.

Subdivision power

Subdivision power determines the *X,Y and Z* resolutions of the voxels. So, when it is determined that a voxel needs to be subdivided, the **Subdivision Power** is used to determine how many voxels will be created.

A problem that arises when raytracing is that of the *big floor*. If you have a large plane in a scene with a small concentration of detailed surfaces in one area, it will be slow to render with raytracing. The problem here is that the entire bounding box of the scene will be used to create evenly sized voxels. What you get is a bunch of voxels that are empty or have only one surface in them and you get one voxel with the bulk of the geometry. Even if the voxels are recursively subdivided, you still end up with lots of geometry in few voxels. This will slow down the renderer. One way around this is to turn **Raytracing Off** for the big floor. With the big floor out of the way, the bounding box for raytracing is centered around the concentrated geometry and you get a much better voxel/geometry distribution.

mental ray rendering

mental ray is a raytrace renderer. To determine pixel colors, the raytracing algorithm sends rays into the scene from the position of the render camera. These rays will either hit an object or go through empty space. If a ray hits an object, the corresponding material shader is referenced or *called*. If the material shader is reflective or refractive, secondary rays will subsequently be sent into the scene. These secondary rays are used to calculate reflections and refractions.

Shooting rays into a scene can become expensive in terms of rendering efficiency. mental ray ensures render efficiencies through the initial use of the scanline rendering algorithm. The initial scanline rendering phase entails sorting of the scene elements with respect to their relation to the camera.

Note: *It is important to note that the scanline algorithm is not used if distorting lens shaders are used. An example would be the physical _lens_dof shader.*

If a scanline ray encounters a material shader that requires reflections or refraction, secondary raytraced rays are then sent out from the sampled point. The ray then continues until it encounters either a diffusive surface or infinity.

Note: *Infrasampling is a term used to describe the condition where there are fewer samples than pixels in the rendered image. Oversampling implies more samples than pixels.*

Shadow method calculation is a function of which rendering algorithm is used. The scanline renderer calculates shadow information using pre-computed depth maps. These shadow depth maps describe whether a given point is in shadow. This scanline shadow calculation is fast, but has limitations in the area of shadows from transparent objects. The raytrace algorithm does support transparent shadows.

Conclusion

Some interesting effects can be achieved using a raytracing renderer. With a general understanding of limits and memory requirements, you will be able to optimize raytracing and achieve great results.

In the next project, you will learn about the different integrated Maya renderers.

Project Three

Lessons

In Project Three, you will learn about renderers and rendering tasks. At the end of this project, you will understand what rendering involves and should be comfortable launching and controlling rendering processes. You will also experiment with creating different non-realistic renders, such as cartoon style images and web style images. As well, you will also work through some Maya Paint Effects tasks.

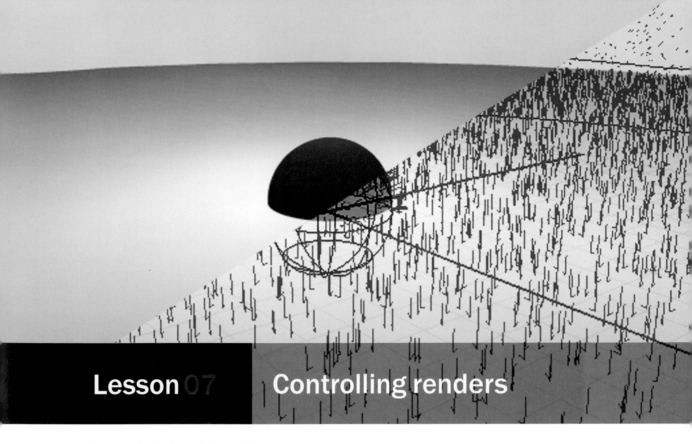

Lesson 07   Controlling renders

An important consideration when rendering in production is the amount of time it takes to render a frame. Fortunately, there are a number of options that allow you to get the best performance from the Maya renderer. This chapter will focus on how to set up renders to get the best quality and shorter render times.

In this lesson you will learn the following:

- Anti-aliasing;

- Tessellation and how to control it;

- Memory requirements and optimizations;

- Render diagnostics;

- mental ray sampling quality;

- mental ray Approximation Editor.

Anti-aliasing

Part of the philosophy of a renderer is to attempt to solve each part of the rendering process independently, using the best method for each rendering problem. For this reason, when it comes to anti-aliasing, geometric edge anti-aliasing is solved completely before the shading is solved. The following takes a closer look at what this means.

Note: *Anti-aliasing is the smoothing of jagged, stair or step effects in images by adjusting pixel intensities so there is a more gradual transition between the color of a line and the background color.*

In some renderers, both the edge anti-aliasing and the shading anti-aliasing are affected by the same controls. In the Maya software renderer, these two processes are controlled separately. There is a significant benefit to separating the anti-aliasing controls, which will become clearer as they are defined.

Separate controls for edge anti-aliasing and shading samples

Edge Anti-aliasing

When the renderer goes to render a pixel, one of the things it needs to know is what geometry is visible in that pixel. When the renderer determines what geometry is visible in a pixel, it subdivides a pixel in a grid much denser than the pixel, then checks if a triangle is visible in any section of the pixel. This gives very accurate information about the visibility of objects within the pixel. The renderer uses this information to compute edge anti-aliasing. The algorithm used to determine edge anti-aliasing is called *Exact Area Sampling*, or *EAS* for short.

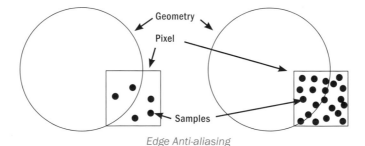

Edge Anti-aliasing

As you can see in the previous diagram, a small number of visibility samples will not provide very much information about the edge of the geometry in the pixel. However, if there are many visibility samples, there is a lot more information and the renderer can more accurately determine the object's edge in a pixel. The appearance of the edge becomes much cleaner and smoother in the rendered image as the number of visibility samples increases.

The number of visibility samples the renderer looks at in a pixel is controlled by the **Edge Anti-aliasing** attribute in the **Render Settings**.

1 Scene file

- Open the scene file called *07-antialiasing_01.ma*.

This is a very simple scene with a NURBS plane in it.

2 Adjust the Edge Anti-aliasing

- Open the **Render Settings** and in the **Anti-aliasing Quality** section, set the **Edge Anti-aliasing** to **Low Quality** and render the scene.

Notice how the edges of the plane look rough and jagged.

Close-up of the rendered image

Tip: *You can dolly and track in the Render View just like in any other editor.*

- Use the **Keep Image** feature in the Render View.

- Repeat the above steps with the **Edge Anti-aliasing** set to **Medium** and **High Quality**, keeping the image after each render.

3 Compare the results

- Use the arrows on the far sides of the slider at the bottom of the Render View to step through the images for comparison.

Notice how the edges of the NURBS plane get smoother as the quality is increased.

The actual number of visibility samples used at each quality level is as follows:

- **Low Quality** - Fastest anti-aliasing setting. For each pixel being rendered, **2 samples** are analyzed, producing low quality Edge Anti-aliasing. This setting is mostly used for quick test renders of complex scenes as it produces very low quality anti-aliased edges.

- **Medium Quality** - For each pixel being rendered, **8 samples** are analyzed, producing medium quality Edge Anti-aliasing. This quality is a little slower and gives moderately good edge anti-aliasing.

- **High Quality** - For each pixel being rendered, **32 samples** are analyzed, producing high quality Edge Anti-aliasing.

- **Highest Quality** - This quality setting also uses **32 samples** per pixel. However, it also enables something called *adaptive shading,* which leads to the discussion of shading anti-aliasing covered later in this lesson.

Small geometry Edge Anti-aliasing

Often in animation, the silhouette edges of very small objects will appear to flicker due to inaccuracy of visibility determination. In this scenario, the 32 samples used on **High** or **Highest Quality** is not sufficient to prevent this flickering. However, there is a way to solve this problem.

1   Increase Edge Anti-aliasing

- In the **Render Settings**, set the **Edge Anti-aliasing** to **High** or **Highest**.

The geometry **Anti-aliasing Override** *does not take effect unless the* **Edge Anti-aliasing** *is set to* **High** *or* **Highest Quality**.

2   Turn On Geometry Anti-aliasing Override

- Select the flickering geometry.

- Open the Attribute Editor and go to the **Render Stats** section.

- Turn **On** the **Geometry Anti-aliasing Override** flag.

You will notice that the **Anti-aliasing Level** *attribute becomes un-greyed.*

Note: *The* **Geometry Anti-aliasing Override** *switch and the* **Anti-aliasing
Level** *are also available from the* **Rendering Flags** *window and
from the attribute spreadsheet.*

3 Set the Anti-aliasing Level

- Set the **Anti-aliasing Level** to **2**.

- Render to see if the flickering has stopped.

- If the flickering remains, increase the **Anti-aliasing Level** to **3** and render.

- Keep increasing the level until you are happy with the results.

There are currently five different anti-aliasing levels defined with **1** being the
default (highest quality **Edge Anti-aliasing** in the Render Settings), and **5** being
the **best** anti-aliasing quality. A higher anti-aliasing level setting will take longer to
render the object. Anti-aliasing level 2 or 3 should be sufficient for most problems.

The following are **Geometry Anti-aliasing Override** level settings:

Level 1 *takes* **32 visibility samples** *per pixel;*

Level 2 *takes* **96 visibility samples** *per pixel;*

Level 3 *takes* **288 visibility samples** *per pixel;*

Level 4 *takes* **512 visibility samples** *per pixel;*

Level 5 *takes* **800 visibility samples** *per pixel.*

One important thing to note, the cost to render the rest of the image does not
change. It is only more expensive to render the geometry with the **Geometry
Anti-aliasing Override** turned **On** and with higher anti-aliasing levels. So it
is important to switch on the **Geometry Anti-aliasing Override** for only the
flickering geometry.

This feature is useful only for non-3D motion blurred objects. If 3D motion blur
is enabled and there is no camera animation, a non-moving object's anti-aliasing
level can be overridden and set to some higher value. A moving object's anti-
aliasing level setting will be ignored. If moving an object's Edge Anti-aliasing is
a problem, try increasing the **Max 3D Blur Visibility** samples in **Render Settings**
when rendering on **Highest Quality** mode.

Lesson 07

Tip: *If the flickering is caused by small geometry that is a few pixels in size, it is best to switch on multi-pixel filtering. Sometimes it is theoretically impossible to fix the flickering problem without multi-pixel filtering. This is because without the filtering, the Edge Anti-aliasing is done with respect to **1** pixel and roping artifacts will appear even if the most accurate answer for that pixel's Edge Anti-aliasing is given. When multipixel filtering is used, it filters more than **1** pixel's results (the ideal pixel width being **2**). Also note that sharp television cameras have the same problem — even though each pixel is resolved completely, thin, high contrast lines (such as the white lines on sports fields) can exhibit the same artifacts, so the problem is not isolated to computer graphics. The best multi-pixel filtering options can be one of the default 3x3-width gaussian filters or a 3x3-width quadratic, but if it's too soft, try a 2x2-width triangular filter.*

Shading Anti-aliasing

As you may have noticed, working with the Edge Anti-aliasing has allowed you to clean up the edges of the example plane, but what about the rough looking circle of light on the plane? The *jaggies* at the edge of the circle of light are affected by **Shading Anti-aliasing**.

When it comes to shading, the renderer tries to shade each object only once per pixel. However, this is not always a high enough sampling frequency to properly anti-alias some shading events like thin specular highlights, shadow edges, or complex textures.

In the **Render Settings**, there is a section that deals with **Number of Samples**. This allows you to control the shading anti-aliasing.

Notice that when the **Edge Anti-aliasing** is set to **High Quality**, the **Max Shading** attribute is greyed-out. This means that whatever value the **Shading** attribute is set to will determine the number of shading samples per object per pixel. The **default** is **1**. This means only one shading sample per object per pixel.

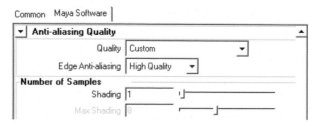

Anti-aliasing Quality section

You will now look at how changing the shading samples will affect your image. Focus on the region illuminated by the spot light on the plane.

1 Scene file

- Continue working with the scene file called *07-antialiasing_01.ma*.

2 Increase edge anti-aliasing

- Render the file with the **Edge Anti-aliasing** set to **High Quality** and the **Shading** set to **1**.

- Keep the image.

- Change the **Shading** value to **8**.

- Render the image again.

Notice how this time the image takes a lot longer to render.

- Compare the images.

The images should look like this:

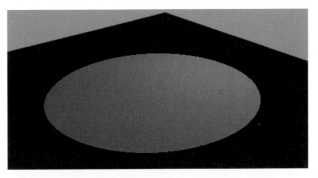

Edge Anti-aliasing set to High Quality — Shading samples set to 1

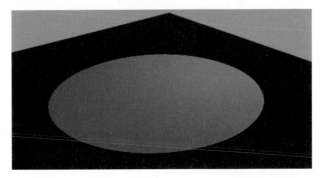

Edge Anti-aliasing set to High Quality — Shading samples set to 8

By setting the **Shading Samples** to **8**, the edge of the lighting on the surface had been smoothed, but rendering time increased significantly. For this reason, increasing this value is not recommended because it will increase the number of shading samples globally for *every* pixel, whether it needs it or not. This can amount to a lot of wasted render time.

A more efficient approach to improving Shading Anti-aliasing is to use **Adaptive Shading**. This adaptive feature is enabled by setting the **Edge Anti-aliasing** to **Highest Quality**. Notice that the **Max Shading** attribute becomes un-greyed.

Note: *As discussed earlier, the* **Edge Anti-aliasing** *is resolved separately and ahead of the Shading Anti-aliasing. Setting the* **Edge Anti-aliasing** *to* **Highest Quality** *is the switch that enables the adaptive shading capabilities.*

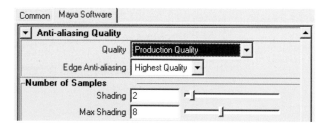

Adaptive shading enabled

Both **High** and **Highest Quality** will use **32** visibility samples to compute the edge anti-aliasing so the edges of the plane will anti-alias the same whether on **High** or **Highest**.

3 Set Edge Anti-aliasing to Highest Quality

- Set the **Edge Anti-aliasing** to **Highest Quality**.

- Set the **Shading** attribute back to a value of **1**, and the **Max Shading** attribute to a value of **8**.

- Render the scene again.

  You should notice that this time the circle of light is looking very smooth, but the render time did not increase as much as before.

The reason why the shading quality looks much better but did not take longer to render is that the renderer only used more shading samples on the pixels where it needed it around the edge of the circle of light. Because the renderer was able to adapt to the needs of the shading, it is called *adaptive shading*.

Adaptive shading

To do this adaptive process, the renderer examines the contrast between a pixel and its five already computed neighboring pixels (the next scanline in a tile is not yet rendered so all eight neighboring pixels cannot be examined). The following diagram shows the five neighboring pixels involved in the contrast computation:

Once the renderer knows how much contrast there is between a pixel and its five neighbors, it compares this value to a **threshold** value specified in the **Render Settings**.

If the contrast between the current pixel being shaded and any of its neighbors exceeds the **Contrast Threshold** in the **Render Settings**, additional shading samples are used.

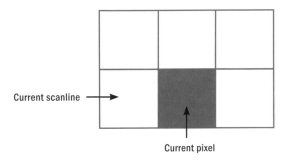

The five neighboring pixels used to compute contrast

The number of additional shading samples used is determined by a simple linear function. The following diagram shows a chart of how this mechanism works:

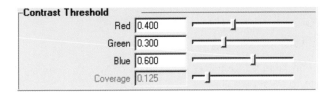

Render Settings Contrast Threshold

The number of samples starts at the **Shading Samples** value (SS) and remains at that number until the Contrast Threshold is exceeded. At this point, as the distance above the threshold increases, so does the number of shading samples taken until the full contrast of **1.0** is reached and **Max Shading** samples are taken.

There are several examples of how you can use this mechanism to your advantage:

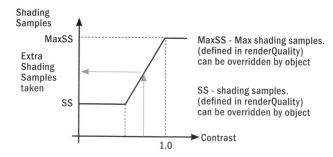

The number of extra shading samples for highest quality is computed

Low contrast scene

Suppose there is a low contrast scene — either all lowlighting or all evenly brightly lit. When the renderer looks at the difference between two pixels, it will likely find very little contrast. When this difference is compared against the threshold in Render Settings, it is very likely to slip under the threshold (i.e. the contrast between the two pixels is less than the **Contrast Threshold**).

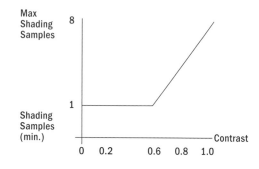

Shading Samples vs. Contrast Threshold

The result is that the minimum number of shading samples will be used to shade the current pixel.

If you look at the default **Contrast Threshold** settings in the **Render Settings**, you will see that they are:

> **Red** to **0.4**;
>
> **Green** to **0.3**;
>
> **Blue** to **0.6**.

These settings were chosen because they roughly correspond to the human eye's responsiveness to these wavelengths of light.

Note: *The human eye is very sensitive to changes in green, but not very sensitive to changes in blue.*

Shading samples override

In cases where there is a particular object that requires a very high number of shading samples, it is possible to override the adaptive shading range set in the Render Settings.

Overriding shading samples

- Select the object.

- Open the Attribute Editor and go to the **Render Stats** section.

- Turn **On** the **Shading Samples Override** flag.

- Enter the required **Min** and **Max** shading samples for that object in the **Shading Samples** and **Max Shading Samples** fields.

- Render the scene.

This is much more efficient than increasing the shading samples in the Render Settings.

Image plane aliasing

If your image plane appears aliased, increasing the **Global Shading Samples** will not help. The only way to improve the anti-aliasing of the image planes would be to increase the values of the **Shading Samples** and **Max Shading Samples** in the Attribute Editor of the image plane. If the image of the image plane matches the resolution of the rendering, additional anti-aliasing will not be required.

Tessellation

Tessellation is the process of approximating a NURBS surface with triangles. Tessellation is a required step because the renderer only knows how to render triangles and volumes, not NURBS surfaces. Tessellation generally applies only to NURBS surfaces, but in the case of displacement mapping, it can also apply to poly meshes.

You need to be aware of tessellation since it determines how smooth an object will look when you start getting close to it. When objects are poorly tessellated and close to the camera they will look faceted (image below on the following page). If an object in your scene never approaches the camera then you could probably leave the tessellation controls at a lower setting. In the following diagram, there are three images of the same object at different positions. The tessellation settings are the same for each image and you can see that the closer you get, the more it is a factor in the smoothness of your object.

Lesson 07

If the object never gets any closer then the small image on the left, you can leave the tessellation at its default setting. As it comes closer to the camera, you need to start increasing the amount of tessellation to smooth out the surface. At its closest position, the tessellation controls need to be set quite high to ensure that the surface is smooth.

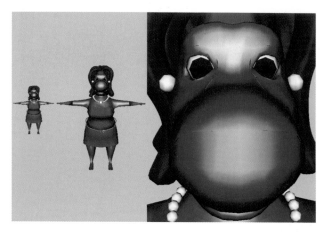

Object approaching camera

In the pre-production phase of a project, the models needed in the scene will be decided upon. Based on storyboards, you will know their positions in the scene and distance to the camera. You need to determine which objects will never get close to the camera and which ones will. Once that information is determined, it is easy to define how the tessellation controls need to be set. If an object is far from the camera at all times, leave it at the default. If an object is mid-distance to the camera, increase the tessellation slightly. If the object gets very close to the camera, increase the tessellation more.

The only way to determine how much tessellation is needed is to do some test renderings. These test renderings can be done very early in the process, since tessellation has nothing to do with the material that is assigned to the surface (unless the surface has a displacement map). As soon as an object is modeled, you can set the tessellation attributes.

Note: *If you are tessellating a surface that will have a displacement map, you need to have the displacement map assigned to the surface to determine good tessellation levels.*

The next image has the same objects as the previous image, but the tessellation has been improved so the surfaces appear nice and smooth.

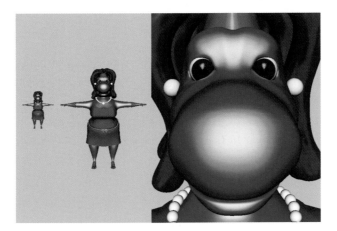

Improved tessellation

Tessellation methods

There are two ways to set tessellation in Maya. One way is to select the object and look in its Attribute Editor under the **Tessellation** section to find the attributes for tessellating that particular object. Another way to set tessellation is by going to **Render** → **Set NURBS Tessellation**.

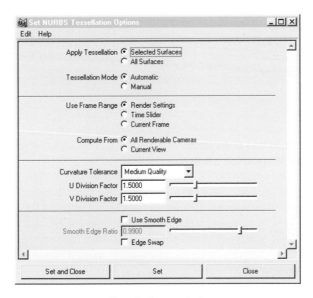

Tessellation controls

You can apply tessellation on a per surface basis or set a number of attributes and apply those to all objects. If you choose **Automatic**, Maya will evaluate the tessellation based on coverage and distance of the surface from the camera. Because of the manner in which this is evaluated, if the surface or camera is animated, this relationship will change over time. When the surface is closest to the camera, you will require the best tessellation. Maya will compute this for you for a specified frame range set under **Use Frame Range**. The tessellation will be evaluated at each frame, and the tessellation attributes will be adjusted to provide optimal tessellation.

If you choose **Manual Mode**, you can use a number of controls that will allow you to evaluate the best tessellation. There are two levels of tessellation control. The first level is **Basic**.

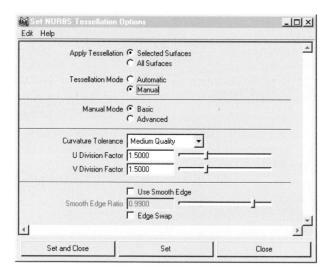

Basic tessellation controls

This first level of tessellation control is a good starting point in determining the tessellation of your surfaces. It allows you to change the tessellation of your surfaces from a pull-down menu. The first thing you should do is go to the object's Attribute Editor and set **Display Render Tessellation** to **On**. This is an invaluable tool in helping you to determine tessellation. If you are in wireframe mode and enable this feature, it will put you in shaded mode so you will be able to visually see how the surface will be tessellated when it is selected.

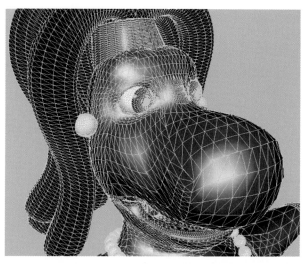

Surfaces with Display Render Tessellation set to On

Curvature Tolerance has a pull-down menu that allows you to change tessellation criteria from **No Curvature Check** up to **Highest Quality**. When you are changing these values, the software is actually changing the **Explicit Tessellation Attributes** for you. Maya is trying to give you one menu where you can control a number of different settings that affect tessellation.

The **Curvature Tolerance** setting in the top part of the **Tessellation** section has several settings. These settings correspond to the **Primary** and **Secondary** **Tessellation** attributes. For the **Primary Tessellation** attributes, modes U and V are set to **Per Surf # of Isoparms in 3D**. The **Secondary Tessellation** attributes are affected by **Chord Height Ratio**. They correspond to the following:

- **Curvature Tolerance - Low Quality** = Chord Height Ratio of **0.987**;

- **Curvature Tolerance - Medium Quality** = **0.990**;

- **Curvature Tolerance - High Quality** = **0.994**;

- **Curvature Tolerance - Highest Quality** = **0.995**.

U Divisions Factor and **V Divisions Factor** allow you to further increase the surface tessellation. These numbers act as a multiplier on the **Per Surf # of Isoparms in 3D** as per the following equation:

```
Number U/V = U/V Divisions Factor* ((#spans U/V) + 1)
```

Where the #spans information can be found at the top of the NURBS shape's Attribute Editor.

Lesson 07

Display Render Tessellation

1 Create a NURBS plane

- Set **2** spans in **U direction** and **2** spans in **V direction**.

2 Display Render Tessellation

- In the Attribute Editor for the plane, open the **Tessellation** section and set **Display Render Tessellation** to **On**.

3 Change U and V Divisions Factor

- Set **U Divisions Factor** to **1**.

- Set **V Divisions Factor** to **2**.

According to the above equation, the surface should have 6 isoparms in the V direction and 3 in the U direction.

number U = 1 * (2 + 1) = 3;

number V = 2 * (2+1) = 6.

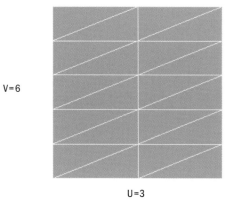

V=6

U=3

Plane with Display Render Tessellation On

Smooth Edge

Depending on the surface you are tessellating, you will often have sections that are over-tessellated. This happens when you are trying to increase the tessellation to improve the smoothness of one area and the control causes another area to be over-tessellated. One way to control the tessellation of edges without affecting the surface is to use Smooth Edge. It allows you to increase the tessellation along the edge of a surface without having to add extra tessellation over the entire surface. This can help keep tessellation values down for a surface when extra tessellation is only needed along the edge. For example, you might trim a hole out of a plane. When you render the object you might need to use Smooth Edge in order to increase the tessellation along the trim edge. By using Smooth Edge, you avoid having to increase the tessellation for the entire surface. In the following images, the surface is a plane with one corner pulled up. The image on the left has Smooth Edge off and the image on the right has Smooth Edge on. You can see that along the curved edge there is more tessellation on the image on the right, but the flat areas of the surface have the same tessellation.

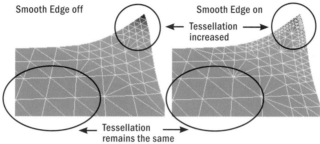

Smooth Edge

The Smooth Edge option lets you increase the tessellation quality (number of triangles) only along the boundary of an object to avoid faceting artifacts along the edges, without incurring the high rendering time cost of increasing the tessellation level uniformly across the entire object.

To control **Smooth Edge** and how finely it tessellates a boundary, there is an attribute called **Smooth Edge Ratio**. It is a ratio between the length of the tessellated triangle and the curve of the boundary. The closer this value approaches **1**, the more triangles will be tessellated along the boundary.

There are some situations when the Smooth Edge attribute should not be used. In the following diagram, when **Smooth Edge** is turned **On**, you will notice some artifacts in the highlights along the curved parts of the surface. What has happened is the surface was tessellated normally everywhere except the edge, where more triangles were used to get a smooth edge. This caused the curvature in the surface to be slightly different closer to the edge.

Smooth Edge on — causing artifacts

To correct the above problem, you need to turn Smooth Edge off and rely on tessellating the entire surface. This ensures the same number of triangles are used along the entire curved section. This will give you an even highlight.

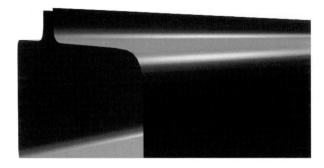

Smooth Edge Off with Explicit Tessellation attributes

Note: *When using* **Smooth Edge**, *it is important to notice that when you increase tessellation along the edge, it can also increase tessellation further into the surface to prevent cracking and T-junctions within the surface.*

Explicit Tessellation Attributes

If you have set **Curvature Tolerance** to its highest setting and are still not satisfied with the smoothness of your surfaces, then you need to turn **On** the **Explicit Tessellation** attributes. The explicit tessellation attributes are broken down into **Primary Tessellation** attributes and **Secondary Tessellation** attributes.

The Primary Tessellation attributes describe how the overall surface will be tessellated. **Mode U** and **Mode V** tell Maya how to tessellate the surface. The U and V values represent the U and V parametric dimensions of the NURBS surface. These values can be set differently so you could have different tessellation for each direction of your surface.

There are four settings for Modes U and V:

- **Per Surf # of Isoparms** lets you specify the number of isoparms you want to create on your surface, ignoring the surfaces' isoparms. This lets you get a sparser number of isoparms on your surface than there are spans on your surface.

- **Per Surf # of Isoparms in 3D** also lets you specify the number of isoparms you want on your surface, but attempts to space the isoparms equally in 3D space (as opposed to parametric space). Good for converting NURBS to polygons. This mode produces more evenly distributed triangles than other modes.

- **Per Span # of Isoparms** lets you specify the number of subdivisions that will occur between each span, no matter how large or small. Therefore, very small spans are divided into the same number of subdivisions as very large spans. This is the most common mode. The default setting is **3**. The per span settings are important as they can help in avoiding cracks between joined surfaces where the spans match. This is particularly important for character building with multiple surfaces.

- **Best Guess Based on Screen Size** creates a bounding box around the NURBS surface, projects it into screen space and calculates the number of pixels in the space. Maya uses this number to guess at the per surface # of isoparms. The maximum value is **40**. The more screen space the object uses, the higher the number that is set by using this mode. This mode would not be ideal for animation if the camera or the object is moving, since the bounding box would be changing constantly. If the bounding box changes, so does the tessellation and this will cause textures to jitter. You may also experience problems with specular highlights.

> **Note:** Be careful when using **Best Guess Based on Screen Size** when **Display Render Tessellation** is On. If you have a complicated NURBS surface it can take some time to update the display.

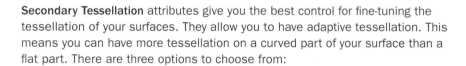

Secondary Tessellation attributes give you the best control for fine-tuning the tessellation of your surfaces. They allow you to have adaptive tessellation. This means you can have more tessellation on a curved part of your surface than a flat part. There are three options to choose from:

- **Use Chord Height** is the first option and it is a physical measurement based on units. A surface curve will have triangles that will try to approximate the curve. The chord height is the perpendicular distance at the center of a triangle edge to the curve that defines the surface. If the actual distance measured is greater than the chord height value, then the triangle is subdivided again. Once it is subdivided, it will be checked against the same criteria again and if it still doesn't meet the criteria, it will continue to be subdivided until it does. Since chord height is based on a default unit, it doesn't always work well for very small models as the chord height values on a small model will be smaller still.

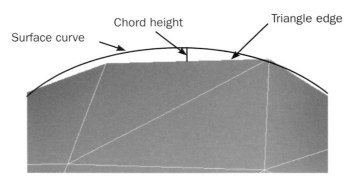

Chord height

- **Use Chord Height Ratio** is the second option and is the option used by the **Curvature Tolerance**. It is a ratio based on the chord height divided by the triangle edge length and subtracted from 1.

  Chord Height Ratio = 1 – (Chord Height / Triangle Edge Length)

  If you look at the chord height diagram above you can see what the chord height is. The triangle edge length is the length of the edge defined by the two points on the triangle that intersect with the surface curve. The default value is **0.983**, which means the chord height is very small compared to the triangle edge length. The closer this control is to 1, the tighter the fit of the triangle to the surface.

- **Use Min Screen** is the third option. It bases the tessellation on a minimum screen size for which the default value is 14 pixels. All triangles created during tessellation must fit within this screen size. If they don't, they are further subdivided until they do. This option is good for still images with a setting of **11.0** for **Min Screen**. It will render out nice and smooth surfaces. It is not recommended for animations, because the tessellation will constantly be changing when an object is moving. This will cause textures to jitter or jump, because the shading for a particular pixel will have different tessellations to deal with on each frame.

Note: *Be careful when* **Display Render Tessellation** *is* **On** *and you are using* **Min Screen***, as the display can take a few seconds to update.*

It is possible in the Secondary Tessellation attributes to turn on more than one option. Do not turn on more than one option as the renderer will go through each option and check the tessellation of the surface. This will cause the renderer to slow down with no gain in visual appearance.

Tessellation and displacements

Displacement maps are a special case since the surface does not know how the displacement map will displace it. It is very difficult to effectively detect curvature changes based on the displacement, so a higher initial tessellation is needed. By default, when you add a displacement map to a surface the tessellation is increased by a factor of **6**. You should also avoid using the Secondary Tessellation attributes as you want to make sure the surface is evenly tessellated all over for the displacement map.

Note: *It is possible that you will have a surface that is hard to smooth out using the tessellation controls. One possibility is to rebuild the surface with more isoparms and use the setting* **Per Span # of Isoparms.**

Scene optimization

To help optimize your scene, there are two commands you can run. In the Hypershade window, select **Edit → Delete Unused Nodes,** or from the main window select **File → Optimize Scene Size**. These commands can help optimize the size of your scene by cleaning up unused nodes and other things.

Edit → Delete Unused Nodes will delete any unused nodes in the Hypershade window, such as duplicate shading groups that are not being used, extra placement nodes, extra utility nodes, etc.

File → Optimize Scene Size will clean up the following:

- Invalid NURBS surfaces and curves;

- Empty sets, partitions and transforms;

- Unused nodes;

- Duplicate shading networks.

It is recommended that you make a habit of optimizing your scene size before you save. Optimizing your scene size before saving can:

- Improve overall performance of renderers;

- Improve use of memory;

- Reduce unnecessary waste of disk space.

Lesson 07

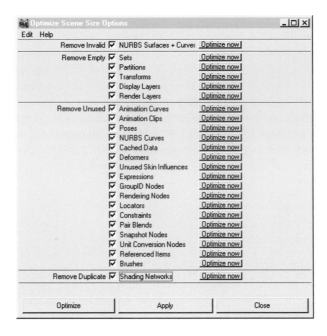

Optimize Scene Size Options

Use the following steps to optimize scene size:

1 Optimize scene

- Select **File** → **Optimize Scene Size** → ❒.

The Optimize Scene Size Options window opens.

- Select the items you want optimized.
- Click **Optimize**.

2 Save settings

- Click **Save** in the window to save the settings.
- When you select **File** → **Optimize Scene Size**, the saved settings are used.

3 Save your work

Pre-render optimization

Pre-render optimization is a command you can run that will create a smaller and more efficient Maya binary (*.mb*) file reserved for rendering. By deleting information not relevant to the renderer, the new *leaner* file can help reduce overall memory usage and decrease render times. When the command is invoked, your file is run through **Optimize Scene Size** with all flags checked **On**, and then additional information is deleted (history, UI settings, datablocks, static actions and animation caching). BOT files are also created and relinked to existing textures. It is a good idea when using file referencing to **Export All** first, otherwise some optimizations may be missed. The usage for this pre-render setup is straightforward. See the `maya -optimizeRender -help` message for a list of flags to use with this.

> **Note:** *You will get optimal results when using BOT files for large resolution textures. When using the* `-botRes` *flag, you will specify the resolutions that will be relinked with BOT files. If you specified* `-botRes 1024`, *all textures bigger than 1024x1024 will be relinked to use BOT files.*

This script searches for the following scenarios:

- Motion blur limitations;
- Output image file format restrictions;
- By frame of 0 causing hang;
- Fractional by frame requiring modify ext.;
- No renderable cameras;
- Ortho camera rendering artifacts.

The following warnings may be issued:

- No lights warning;
- Composite rendering warning.

Warnings for the following scenarios which affect performance:

- Suggestion of using 2D motion blur instead of 3D motion blur;
- RT warning and RT limits;
- High shading sample warning.

mental ray sampling

Sampling in mental ray is adaptive, meaning that the algorithm attempts to use the fewest number of samples to achieve the best quality image. mental ray will only take extra samples or oversample when appropriate to compute high resolution, anti-aliased details. Sampling performance and quality is controlled by the **Anti-aliasing Quality** section in the mental ray Render Settings.

Anti-aliasing Quality section

Contrast

Contrast is an important tuning factor. Starting with the minimum level of sampling specified, an image is broken into blocks and sampled at its corners. The resulting samples are then compared with neighboring blocks. If the contrast between the sampled blocks is higher than the RGBA threshold values, further subdivisions are made. The process is repeated until either the contrast between each block is lower than the threshold values or the maximum sampling value has been reached.

For best results, in terms of render time, use the high threshold values with lowest possible sampling levels. The default values for RGBA are 0.1. Most usable values are in the range of 0.2 and 0.05. The A (alpha) value is an average of the R, G and B contrast values. If alpha is not necessary, it's recommended to set that value to 1.0.

Time Contrast

Time Contrast controls temporal contrast. This is similar to contrast but is used solely with moving geometry's motion blur.

Note: *Motion blur may need higher sampling limits.*

Samples

Control the minimum amount of samples that will be taken as well as the maximum. If the sample limit is less than 0, there will be fewer samples taken than there are pixels. This is called *infrasampling* and is useful because of edge following. If the sample limit is greater than 0, there are more samples taken than there are pixels. This is called *oversampling* and occurs on an adaptive basis based on the minimum and maximum sampling values.

The sampling limits are specified in powers of 2. The sampling levels determine the size of the blocks:

- -2: block will contain 4x4 pixels with 1 sample;
- -1: block will contain 2x2 pixels with 1 sample;
- 0: block will contain 1 pixel with 1 sample;
- 1: pixel will contain 4 blocks with 1 sample for each block;
- 2: pixel will contain 16 blocks with 1 sample for each block.

The useful sample limit range lies between -3 and 4. Typical sample values:

- -2, 0: low quality preview render;
- -1, 1: medium quality render;
- 0, 2: high quality render;
- 0, 3: highest quality render.

Jitter

Jitter slightly randomizes sample points which alters underlying sample point clustering. This can be used to reduce regular sampling artifacts such as *mach* banding, without having to increase sample rates. Jitter is more effective with raytracing.

Note: *If aliasing occurs, lower the* **Contrast Threshold** *values before increasing the sample limits. Lowering these threshold values will cause more samples to be taken in the problem areas while the rest of the image will be sampled at the lower rate. Sometimes values below* **0.05** *will be necessary to avoid artifacts. If this doesn't help, add jitter before increasing sample rates.*

Lesson 07

Filters

Once block samples are calculated, they are combined into pixels using a filter. Large filter sizes tend to blur the image and can slightly increase render times.

Alias *When rendering with mental ray, get comfortable with the Approximation*
Tip: *Editor. The defaults that are interpolated from Maya are not optimal. Any large scene pretty much requires that each surface be given its own values in the Approximation Editor. There is huge room here to speed up your renders.*

Martin Crawford | Product Specialist

mental ray tessellation

In mental ray, *approximation nodes* are used to control how finely the renderer tessellates surfaces into triangles for rendering.

Approximation nodes can be used to specify separate tessellation settings for surfaces, trim curves and displacement maps. The different kinds of approximation nodes give users control over all aspects of the tessellation process, allowing them to produce tessellations that capture the important aspects of their surfaces without over-tessellating and slowing down the renderer. For example, consider a simple, flat NURBS surface with a complex trim curve. For such a case, users would specify a low quality surface approximation in conjunction with a high quality trim curve approximation. mental ray would then ensure that the surface is approximated with only a few triangles except around the trim curves, where many triangles would be used to ensure a smooth edge.

The same analogy applies to a simple surface with a complex displacement map. For that case, users might apply a low quality regular surface approximation in conjunction with a high quality displacement approximation, to ensure that triangles are added only to areas where they are needed to capture the complexity of the displacement map.

Note: *Currently, there is no equivalent to* **Display Render Tessellation** *in mental ray.*

The Approximation Editor

The **Approximation Editor** provides users with the ability to create approximation nodes that can be assigned to geometry on a per object basis. Approximation nodes contain information on how that surface will be tessellated at render time. Depending on the surface topology, certain geometry may require various forms of tessellation.

The Approximation Editor is found under **Window** → **Rendering Editors** → **mental ray** → **Approximation Editor**. The default approximation settings are **DeriveFromMaya**.

- **Surface Approximation** calculates the tessellation of a NURBS surface;

- **Trim Curve Approximation** calculates the tessellation of a trimmed NURBS surface;

- **Displacement Approximation** calculates the tessellation of a NURBS or poly surface that is influenced by displacement maps. If the Displacement Approximation is set to **DeriveFromMaya**, mental ray will use the **Fine** setting and triangles will be placed only in areas where they are needed. If a Displacement Approximation is created with the Fine tessellation method, the user will have access to the Fine attributes, enabling greater control;

- **Subdivision Approximation** controls render time smoothing of poly mesh surfaces.

There are three options at the top of the editor:

- **Single** will create one approximation node that can be used for more than one object. For instance, if you have a number of objects selected with this option On, then each object will use that one approximation node;

- **Multi** will create an approximation node for each object that was selected when you select the **Create** option. This will allow each object to have its own individual tessellation control;

- **Show in Hypergraph** is useful when you have many objects selected and are using the **Multi** option. The Hypershade will open automatically when you select the **Create** option, which will allow you to see which object is assigned to which approximation node.

With certain surfaces selected, the three options to the right of the editor may become active.

- **Create** will generate a new approximation node. Any geometry that is selected will use this approximation node.

- **Assign** will assign a new approximation node on the selected geometry. Assigning an approximation node to a surface is done automatically at creation time.

- **Edit** will open the Attribute Editor for the selected approximation node.

Approximation Presets

The **Presets** drop-down menu provides some useful tessellation settings. Selecting an entry from this list will load the preset values for the approximation node's attributes. These settings can be used as is, or taken as useful starting points for tweaking.

- **Regular Grid** means the user has control over all approximation attributes. This is the default. Regular Grid subdivides the surface as a whole into a fixed number of triangles. This method will ensure equal triangulation over a surface even if the spacing of the isoparms is uneven.

- **Parametric Grid** subdivides each span into a fixed number of triangles. Use this when triangles are distributed roughly according to the spacing of isoparms on the surface, with closer isoparms producing a higher number of triangles.

Tip: *The Parametric Grid setting is good for patch models.*

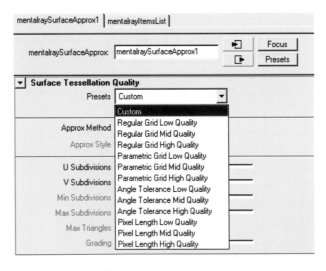

Presets drop-down menu

- **Angle Detailed** is an adaptive form of tessellation where more triangles are placed in areas of high curvature. This method is good for capturing sharp features, while still using as few triangles as possible to describe a large, flat area.

- **Pixel Area** tessellates surfaces based on their size in pixels in the final rendered image. Surfaces that are close to the camera will receive more triangles, whereas surfaces that are farther away will receive fewer.

Approximation method

The **Approx Method** drop-down menu determines the criteria the tessellator uses for determining when to subdivide a part of the surface. Some methods will place a fixed number of triangles evenly over a surface, while others are more adaptive and place triangles over a surface where needed, based on a set condition.

- **Parametric** subdivides a surface based on U and V. Each patch is subdivided into N triangles, where:

      N = (U Subdivisions) * (V Subdivisions) * degree^2 * 2

Thus, with U subdivisions set to 1.333 and V subdivisions set to 4 on a degree-3 NURBS surface, each patch will be subdivided into 1.333*4*3*3*2 = 96 triangles.

- **Regular Parametric** also subdivides a surface based on U and V except when the entire surface is subdivided into N triangles, where:

      N = (U Subdivisions) * (V Subdivisions)

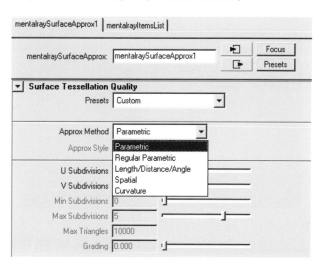

Approx method drop-down menu

Lesson 07

Unlike the Parametric method, which tessellates each patch independently, the number of triangles will be constant over the entire surface.

- **Length/Distance/Angle** are adaptive, which means the surface is tessellated until certain criteria are met. The three criteria are:

   Length where a triangle is subdivided until no triangle has an edge longer than a certain length. If **View Dependent** is **On**, the value is specified in pixels.

   Distance will subdivide triangles until they are not further than a certain distance from the NURBS surface. If **View Dependent** is **On**, the distance is expressed in pixels.

   Angle will subdivide until the normals of neighboring triangles form an angle of less than a certain tolerance. Small values can cause the number of triangles to increase. A recommended value is 45 degrees. 0 is ignored by the tessellator.

   The **Any Satisfied** flag will determine when subdivision stops. It will stop when any one of the criteria is satisfied (i.e. triangles are smaller than a certain size **or** distance from the surface is less than a certain amount).

- **Spatial** is the same as the **Length** criteria described above.

- **Curvature** is the same as the **Distance** and **Angle** criteria mentioned above. This method is included for backwards compatibility only.

The following images were created using a default NURBS plane.

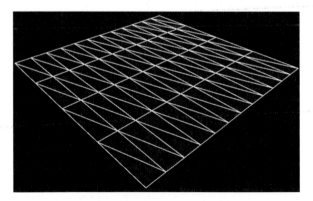

Parametric approximation mode
U subdivisions = 1.33, V subdivisions = 4, total triangles = 96

Project Three

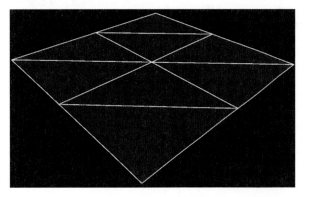

Regular Parametric approximation mode
U subdivisions = 2, V subdivisions = 2, total triangles = 8

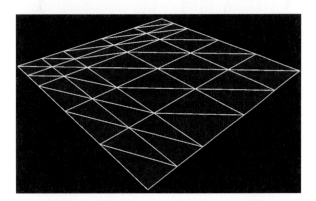

Length, Distance, Angle approximation modes
Min subdivisions = 0, Max subdivisions = 5, Length = 0.5

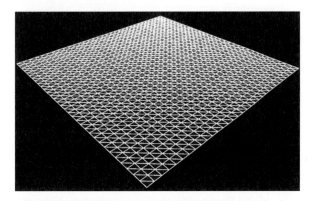

Length, Distance, Angle approximation modes - View Dependent enabled
Min subdivisions = 0, Max subdivisions = 5, Length = 0.5

Approximation styles

The **Approx Style** drop-down menu determines the general framework the tessellator uses to subdivide the surface into triangles.

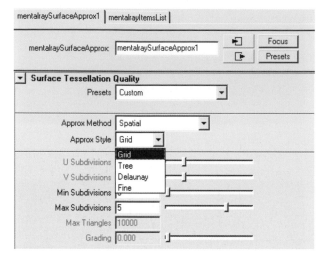

Approx Style drop-down menu

- **Grid** works on a grid of isolines that allows subdivisions by adding more isolines. This produces regular triangle meshes that can sometimes contain more triangles than necessary.

- **Tree** uses a hierarchical subdivision style that allows local subdivisions without affecting other areas.

- **Delaunay** attempts to maximize triangle compactness and avoid thin triangles. This style is supported only for NURBS surfaces. The **Max Triangles** and **Grading** attributes can be used to fine-tune tessellations using the Delaunay style.

- **Fine** subdivides surfaces into a large number of uniformly-sized small triangles in order to guarantee a smooth result. To deal with the large amount of triangles, mental ray breaks the surface up into independent sub-objects that are each tessellated and cached separately. This allows the tessellator to generate a large number of triangles without a huge memory cost.

U and V Subdivisions

These values are used by **Parametric** and **Regular Parametric** methods. They specify how many times each span (Parametric) or surface (Regular Parametric) will be subdivided in the U and V directions.

Min and Max Subdivisions

When using the **Length/Distance/Angle** method, these attributes can control the minimum and maximum number of times that triangles are subdivided. You can get good results with a maximum value as low as **3**. As a rule, each subdivision level can increase the triangle count by a factor of **4**. Therefore, raising the maximum subdivisions from 3 to 4 can produce four times as many triangles.

Grading

Setting this value to non-zero enables a smoother transition from the surface's interior triangle density to its edges. Values less than **20** are recommended.

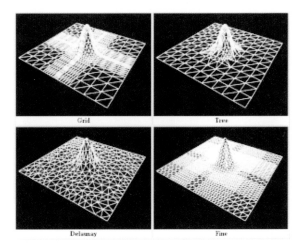

Approximation styles in mental ray for Maya

Sharp

Will use the surface normal to create the impression of a sharp edge (Sharp = 1) or a rounder edge (Sharp = 0). Use a high value when trying to capture sharp details in a displacement.

Render diagnostics

mental ray diagnostics is a set of tools that is used to troubleshoot and refine render efficiency. These software renders provide visual, statistical information in the form of dots and lines, etc. that can be used for render debugging and optimizing. This functionality is located in **Render Settings** and includes: **Sampling**, **BSP** (**Depth** and **Size**), **Grid** (**Object**, **World** and **Camera**) and **Photons** (**Density** and **Irradiance**) options.

Lesson 07

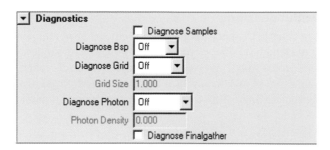

mental ray render diagnostics

Diagnose samples

This mode will result in a grayscale representation of sample density. Black areas indicate no samples, while white pixels indicate maximum samples as described in **Render Settings → Min and Max Sample Levels**. Task boundary size or image task is indicated with a grid of red lines. Turn On the **Diagnose Samples** checkbox to enable this diagnostic.

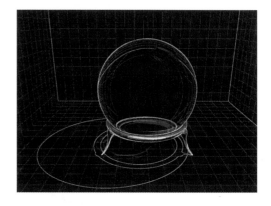

mental ray diagnostics — samples enabled

Diagnose BSP

This mode gives a visual of the *BSP* (Binary Space Partition) tree. It is possible to review the tree depth and size. Colors range from blue (low recursion level in the BSP tree) through cyan, green, yellow and red. Red indicates that the attendant geometry is at the maximum of the BSP tree. This would specify an increase to the BSP depth for optimal performance.

mental ray diagnostics — BSP depth enabled

Diagnose Grid

With this mode, the X, Y and Z-axes are depicted with red, green and blue lines in **Object**, **World** and **Camera** orientations. This mode provides distance and size information between objects and is used for debugging.

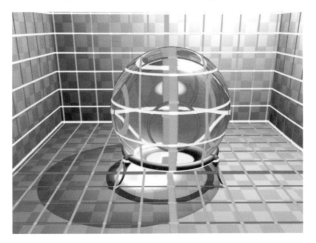

mental ray diagnostics — Grid World enabled

Diagnose Photon

This mode is used to optimize the number of photons to be used. There are two modes: **Density** and **Irradiance**. The photon density is the average of the red, green and blue irradiance components. The photon irradiance is the total incoming illumination.

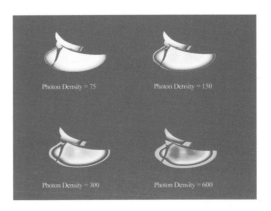

mental ray diagnostics — Photon Caustic Density enabled

The photon density and irradiance option provides a visual indication of the number of photons per unit surface area, or in the case of irradiance, total incoming illumination. Once rendered, areas that are blue indicate no photon density (irradiance), while areas that are red indicate photon density (irradiance) values entered. The range in color values in increasing order of photon density (irradiance) is blue (none), cyan, green, yellow, red and white. White areas indicate photon densities that exceed the entered photon density (irradiance) value.

Lesson 07

Render Settings overrides

This section of Render Settings allows for overall scene *switches* that can be used to turn features on or off, allowing for overall scene control of tessellation and photon mapping parameters. This can be a timesaver.

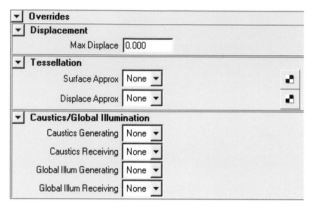

mental ray Render Settings - overrides

Overrides - Tessellation

The **Surface** and **Displacement Approximation Overrides** allow for overall scene tessellation using one approximation node. This can be of particular use when you have a scene that has several approximation nodes in it with a variety of settings. Turning tessellation override on ensures that all geometry in the scene will be tessellated using the same approximation node.

Overrides - Caustics/Global Illumination

Use these attributes to turn all **Caustics** and **Global Illumination** in a scene off.

Memory and performance

There are two raytracing acceleration algorithms that can be used when rendering with mental ray. The default is the **BSP** algorithm. The **Grid Acceleration Method** may be used where memory limits have been reached with the BSP method.

BSP acceleration algorithm

This algorithm breaks down the 3D space of a scene geometry into an organized structure of recursively arranged voxels or volume elements. These voxels are placed by the algorithm into a *nested* or recursive pattern. From a conceptual standpoint, this recursive structure resembles a tree with a main trunk (the initial voxel) and the many branches as the geometry recursively placed into voxels. This adaptive approach results in voxels only where they are needed. Each one of these voxels contains geometry triangles that are limited in size by the **BSP Size** attribute. This method of geometry organization lends itself to most scene arrangements.

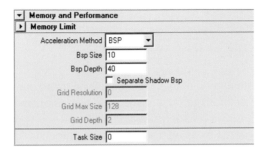

mental ray - memory and performance

BSP Size

The **BSP Size** attribute defaults at **10** triangles and determines the maximum number of triangles that can reside in a voxel. Once the maximum BSP size has been reached, the voxel is subdivided into another voxel until the **BSP Depth** value has been reached. This makes for very efficient sorting of scene geometry.

BSP Depth

For fine-tuning a scene's rendering efficiency, adjusting the **BSP Depth** attribute can be beneficial. Average scenes should be adequately accelerated using the default value of **40**. Starting points for smaller scenes would be **25** and for larger scenes **50**. Values higher than **60** are uncommon.

Grid acceleration algorithm

For scenes where the geometry is not evenly placed throughout 3D space, the grid acceleration method may be used. This acceleration method also breaks down the scene geometry into voxels, but not in an adaptive fashion. This method lends itself to large cityscape-type scenes with uniformly complex geometry throughout 3D space. In such a situation, the adaptive, recursive breakdown of the BSP algorithm may not be as efficient as the grid algorithm. The grid method can result in lower and more predictable memory usage.

Grid Resolution

Determines the number of grid voxels in X, Y and Z. The default value of **0** allows mental ray to compute an appropriate value upon render startup.

Grid Max Size

This attribute determines the maximum allowed number of triangles in a voxel. The default is **128**.

Grid Depth

This is the maximum number of times voxels can be subdivided. The default value of **2** indicates that a subdivided voxel cannot be subdivided further.

Task Size

The **Task Size** attribute can be of use when balancing loads during parallel rendering. Task Size defines the rectangular tiles size as an image is rendered. If a value is not entered, an appropriate value for the scene is calculated. This attribute can be visualized by using the **Diagnostics Sampling** functionality. The task size will be displayed using red lined boundaries.

Memory Limit

This is the maximum allowable cache size in MB that mental ray will use.

mental ray framebuffer attributes

The framebuffer is that part of memory that has been allocated and reserved for saving out the output from rendering. The mental ray framebuffers are found under **Render Settings** → **Framebuffer Attributes**.

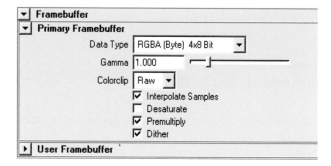

mental ray - framebuffer attributes

Data Type

This is the level or depth of binary information at which the rendered image will be output. Greater bit depths allow for greater color ranges and larger file sizes.

Gamma

When rendering for specific output device requirements, use **Gamma** to adjust for non-linear color response curves.

Colorclip

When outputting to a non-floating point framebuffer, **Raw**, **Alpha** and **RGB** control how colors are clipped into a valid range.

Desaturate

mental ray clips colors to a range (0 to max as specified by the **Colorclip** mode), when required RGB components are outside the precision as specified by the **Data Type** structure.

Premultiply

When on, rendered objects are not anti-aliased against the background. This generates unassociated alpha.

Dither

When outputting to lower precision values (8 bits per pixel), banding can occur where material shader pixel values exceed 8 bit image picture precision as specified by the data type. In such a case, the pixel values are rounded off. **Dither** ensures that rounded values are smoothed, thereby reducing banding.

Map Visualizer

The mental ray **Map Visualizer** is a useful visual cue for understanding and refining the output of Global Illumination Photon Mapping and Final Gather. This information is available to users interactively in a 3D view.

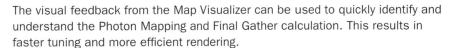

Note: *Global Illumination and Final Gather will be covered in Lessons 12 and 13.*

The visual feedback from the Map Visualizer can be used to quickly identify and understand the Photon Mapping and Final Gather calculation. This results in faster tuning and more efficient rendering.

The Map Visualizer interface is available from **Window** → **Rendering Editors** → **mental ray** → **Map Visualizer...** When the window is initially launched, a *mapVizShape* node is created.

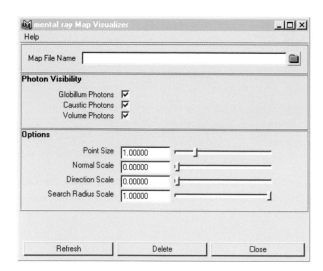

mental ray Map Visualizer window

Visualize a Final Gather map

1 Scene file

- Open the file *07-mapVisualizer_FG_01.ma*.

This file will be used to interactively view Final Gather rays.

2 Set the renderer

- In the **Render Settings**, make sure that **Render Using** is set to **mental ray**.

3 Create a Final Gather map

- Still in the **Render Settings**, scroll down to the **Final Gather** section and turn it **On**.

- Set the number of **Final Gather Rays** to **100**.

- Enter a file name in the **Final Gather File** field such as *FGmap*.

The Map Visualizer needs a file name to create the interactive map.

- Set **Rebuild Final Gather** to **Off**.

4 Render the scene

- Render the scene.

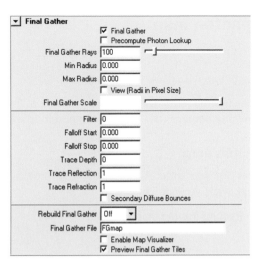

Final Gather render settings

The Final Gather map file will be created and placed into the current project mentalRay\finalgMap directory. This is the file that will be used to interactively view the Final Gather rays.

5   Open the Map Visualizer

- Go to **Window** → **Rendering Editors** → **mental ray** → **Map Visualizer...**

- Browse and load the *FGmap* file into the **Map File Name** field.

The interactive view will update with a graphic representation of the Final Gather map.

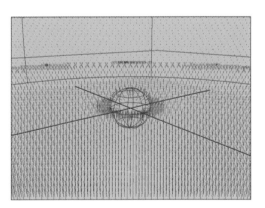

Final Gather map

Tip: The **Point Size** and **Normal Scale** are attributes that can be used to adjust the interactive display of Final Gather points.

Visualize a photon map

1 Scene file

- Open the file *07-mapVisualizer_Photon_01.ma*.

This file will be used to interactively view a Photon Map. The file has one point light that is emitting photons and **Global Illumination** *is enabled.*

2 Create a photon map

- In the **Render Settings**, enter a file name in the **Photon Map File** field, such as *PhotonMap*.

- Turn **Off** the **Rebuild Photon Map** checkbox.

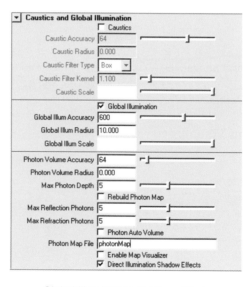

Global Illumination render settings

3 Render the scene

- Render the scene.

The Photon Map file will be created and placed into the current project mentalRay\photonMap directory. This is the file that will be used to interactively view the Photon Map.

4 Open the Map Visualizer

- Go to **Window** → **Rendering Editors** → **mental ray** → **Map Visualizer...**

- Browse and load the *PhotonMap* file into the **Map File Name** field.

The view will update with a graphic representation of the Photon Map.

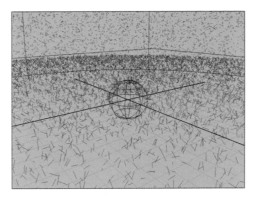

Photon map

Tip:	The **Point Size** and **Normal Scale**, **Direction Scale** and **Search Radius Scale** can be used to adjust the interactive display of a Photon map. The three checkboxes in the Photon Visibility section are used to edit what will be visible in the view.

5 Delete the maps

- When the interactive display is no longer needed, click on the **Delete** button in the Map Visualizer to remove the maps.

Conclusion

When everything else is completed in a scene and you are ready to render, you need to be aware of how to control the render. This means paying attention to image quality, memory requirements and render times. This lesson has given you the tools to be prepared for your next render.

In the next lesson, you will look at special effects' rendering and compositing.

Lesson 08   SFX and compositing

Once you have modeled, textured and added lights to your scene, there are a number of effects you can include to enhance the quality of your render.

In this lesson you will learn the following:

- How to control glow;

- How to use motion blur;

- How to use mental ray motion blur;

- How to use depth of field;

- How to render for compositing.

Special effects

OpticalFX lets you add glows, halos and lens flares to lights. Those effects can be used to simply brighten up a light source or to create explosions, rocket thrusters, and other special effects. Shader glow can be used to brighten up a material with a luminous radiance. It can be used to create lava, neon lights and other glow effects.

Light glow

In the real world, when light shines directly into an observer's eye or into a camera's lens, the light source may appear to glow. If the light passes through a mesh (for example, a star filter on a camera) or through hair or eyelashes, the light will refract, producing a star-like glow. In some cases, the light may reflect off the surface of a camera's compound lens and produce a lens flare. These are all examples of optical light effects.

When lights appear to glow, it is purely a retinal effect in the eye. To see this, look up at a light source such as a street light and squint. You will see a glow around the light. Now use your finger to block only the light source; the glow disappears. Notice also that if you cover only part of the light source, the glow is still visible and will in fact appear in front of your finger. The light glow in Maya simulates this real world effect and the effect of blocking the light source is called *occlusion*.

Light glow occlusion

The most common issue that arises when working with light glow in Maya is the need to control the **Light Source Occlusion**. Often people will animate the position of objects that pass in front of glowing lights and will find that the glow shows right through the objects. This is because the light needs you to specify how big or small the light source actually is in order to know when it is completely covered by an object.

Note: *The light glow feature is only supported by the Maya software renderer.*

1   Create a light glow

- Open a point light's Attribute Editor.

- In the **Light Effects** section, click on the **Map** button beside the **Light Glow**.

An opticalFX node is automatically created, connected to the light node, and displayed in the Attribute Editor. Also, a new icon has appeared surrounding the light source in the views.

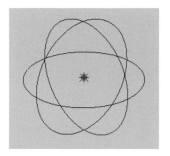

Point light OpticalFX icon

2   Set the size of the light source

Now that you have created a glow effect, you need to consider how you want this glow to behave. Recall that the light glow is only going to shut off completely if the entire light source is occluded. If the light is going to pass behind an object, the size of this *sphereShape* icon, relative to the size of the object, will determine whether you see the glow though the object or not.

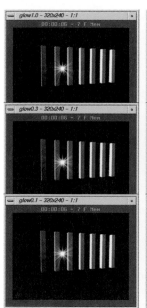
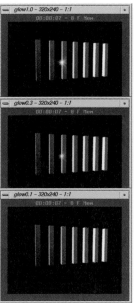
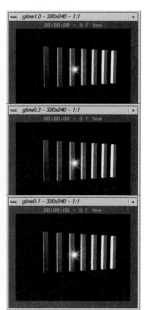

Comparison of different radius values

- Select the light glow icon in one of the views.

Notice that a new tab appears in the Attribute Editor called sphereShape.

- Click on the *sphereShape* tab.

- Select **Render Sphere Attributes** → **Radius**.

- Use this **Radius** attribute to adjust the size of the icon in the scene.

Note: *Adjusting the **Radius** attribute will not affect the appearance of the light glow. It is only used to determine occlusion.*

In the images shown on the previous page, a glowing point light moves from left to right behind the columns. In the middle images, the glow is partially dimmed with a radius of **1.0**, increasingly dimmed with a radius of **0.3**, and fully occluded with a radius of **0.1**.

Shader glow

Unlike light glow, shader glow in a scene is controlled by a single *shaderGlow* node. This node can be found in the Hypershade window, under the **Materials** tab.

Glowing surfaces

The following example shows how to apply glow to surfaces on a ZyZak head.

1 Scene file

- Open the scene called *08-glow_01.ma*.

2 Add glow effect to the eyes

- In the Hypershade, select the *eyePhong* material.

- In the Attribute Editor, scroll to the **Special Effects** section and set **Glow Intensity** to **1.0**.

- Render the head.

You should see a red glow in the eyes of the character. The glow is red because of the color of the eyePhong material. Notice the glow is more intense at the specular highlight of the phong material.

Project Three

3 Increase the ambient color

- In the Attribute Editor for the *eyePhong* material, increase the **Ambient Color**.

- Render the head.

By increasing the ambient color, you increase the luminosity of the eye surfaces, thus causing a stronger glow.

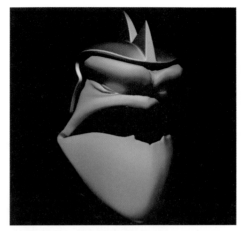

Eye glow

4 Mouth glow

- Assign a new **Lambert** material to the surface in the mouth of the character.

- Set the **Color** of the *lambert* to a bright red.

- Increase the **Ambient Color**.

- Open the **Special Effects** section and set **Hide Source** to **On**.

The **Hide Source** *attribute will render the glow without the geometry, giving an interesting effect.*

- Set **Glow Intensity** to **1.0**.

- Render the head.

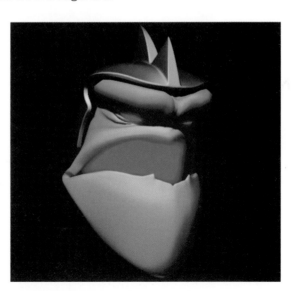

Mouth glow

Lesson 08

Creating neon effect

Neon tubes are the quintessential shader glow example. Try this to create a realistic neon effect.

1 Create the shader

- Create a **Surface Shader** material and assign it to an object.
- Set the **Out Color** attribute to a bright color.
- Set the **Out Glow Color** to a darker complementary color.

Notice how you are able to set the glow color directly.

2 Render the effect

Surface shader glow

With other material types, there is no attribute to control the shader glow color directly. It is derived from the glow color on the *shaderGlow* node and the color of the material. With the surface shader material, it is possible to experiment with different combinations of glow color and surface color. Also, because the surface shader has no sense of a shading model, it renders as though it is self-illuminating perfect for neon tubes, L.E.D. displays, etc.

Motion blur

Motion blur simulates how a real camera works if some objects are moving while the camera's shutter is still open. This technique is very common in the entertainment industry to create photorealistic images and animation involving quick motions.

With the Maya software renderer, there are two different types of motion blur: **2D** and **3D**. The shutter angle determines the blur length, but this can be overriden in the Render Settings. This matter will be discussed later in the lesson.

Understand the shutter angle

Whether using 2D or 3D motion blur, it is important to understand the shutter angle. The motion blur algorithm uses a **shutter open**, **shutter mid** and **shutter close** sample for every frame to determine the change in position of a given triangle.

Note: *Triangle refers to a tessellation triangle on a surface.*

The shutter angle that you specify for motion blur will determine the resulting amount of blur to be calculated. Following is how the motion blur is calculated, taking into account the shutter angle:

> Take the **Shutter Angle** value (the default is **144**), and divide it by **360** degrees. For example, 144 / 360 = 0.4.

> **0.4** represents the interval in time between the shutter open and shutter close samples. Shutter mid is always the frame time itself. For example, for motion blur at frame **1**, shutter open would be at frame **0.8** and shutter closed would be at frame **1.2**. However, when we calculate motion blur for mental ray, we calculate forward only.

By this, you can see that a shutter angle of 360 degrees would give shutter open and close samples that are exactly one frame apart, i.e. 360/360= 1.

You will notice that by setting the shutter angle to 360, the amount of motion blur increases. This is because the longer the shutter is open (i.e. the further apart the shutter open and shutter close samples are taken), the blurrier a moving object will appear to be.

How to change the shutter angle

- Open the Attribute Editor for the camera.

- Open the **Special Effects** section.

- Adjust the **Shutter Angle** attribute.

Lesson 08

mental ray motion blur

In mental ray, there are two different types of motion blur: **Linear (transformation)** and **Exact (deformation)**. Motion blur in mental ray blurs everything: shaders, textures, lights, shadows, reflections, refractions and Caustics. The shutter angle determines the blur path length, but this can be adjusted by the mental ray motion blur attributes in the Render Settings.

To turn on motion blur in mental ray, you need to go to the mental ray Render Settings and open up the **Motion Blur** section. From there, you can select one of the options from the calculation drop-down menu.

Blurred shadows and reflections using mental ray

Note: *Motion blur in mental ray is calculated forward only.*

Linear vs. Exact motion blur

Like the software rendered's motion blur, the decision to use linear (2D) or exact (3D) motion blur depends on the type of motion of your object, as well as the time available to render the animation. Linear motion blur is faster to calculate than exact motion blur.

Linear motion blur only takes into account an object's transformation, rotation and scale. The object's deformation will not be considered. For example, if you have blend shapes or a skeleton that deforms a piece of geometry, the resulting motion wouldn't be considered when calculating this type of motion blur.

Exact takes into account all the transformations, as well as the object's deformations. This type of blur is more expensive to render.

Note: *An object's motion blur can be turned off in its* **Render Stats** *section of the Attribute Editor.*

Editing mental ray motion blur

Motion Blur By is a multiplier for the **Shutter Angle**. The larger this value, the longer the shutter remains open, resulting in more blur.

Shutter represents the length of time the camera's shutter is open. As stated earlier, the longer a shutter is open, the more blurry an object will be. However, unlike a real camera, the shutter value does not affect the brightness of an image. If the shutter is set to 0, there will be no motion blur. Larger values increase the length of the blur.

Shutter Delay represents the normalized time that a shutter remains closed before opening. For instance, if the shutter delay is set to 0, the shutter opens at the beginning of the frame. If the shutter delay is set to .5, then it opens halfway through the frame.

There are four separate controls for **Time Contrast: Red, Green, Blue** and **Alpha**. If you have a fast moving object, these values can usually be set high. Motion blur tends to make sampling artifacts less noticeable, so you can get away with higher contrast values (in other words, lower quality settings). However, if you find that your motion blur is grainy, you can smooth it by decreasing your time contrast values. The lower the time contrast values, the greater your render times.

Tip: *Always try fixing the quality of motion blur by decreasing* **Time Contrast** *values first and* **Number of Samples** *last. This way, you could increase render performance while not compromising non-blurred anti-aliasing.*

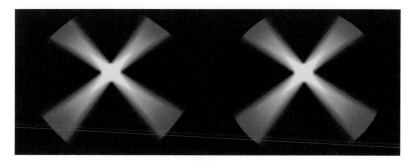

Different amount of motion steps

Motion Steps can create motion paths from motion transforms. The image on the previous page represents a value of **1** for motion steps. The image on the right represents a value of **8** for motion steps.

Note: *Notice the rounder blur on the edge of the blade on the right.*

2D vs. 3D motion blur

The decision to use 3D or 2D motion blur is really a matter of determining which one is more appropriate for a given scene and the time available to render the animation. 3D motion blur is usually slower and memory intensive. However, there will be times where 3D motion blur is required due to some limitations of 2D blur. In general, it is recommended that you try to use 2D motion blur because it is very fast and produces excellent results in most cases. All of the motion blur attributes, other than **Shutter Angle**, are found in the Render Settings under the **Motion Blur** section. If it is desirable for motion blur to be off for some objects, open the Attribute Editor for those objects and toggle **Off** the motion blur in the **Render Stats** section.

The following image shows some examples that compare the results of 2D vs. 3D motion blur.

Comparison between 2D and 3D motion blur

There was quite a difference in rendering time for the previous image. The 3D motion blur image took about four times the time the 2D motion blur image took to render.

> **Note:** *The motion vector files can be used by other programs to generate blur.*

Limitations of 2D motion blur

The 2D motion blur does not work well in these situations:

Moving transparent objects with a background

The background will also be blurred in this case. The solution is to blur the transparent object separately and composite with the rest of the scene.

Detailed background behind moving objects

Some details might be lost since the renderer has to make assumptions on the background area occluded by the moving objects. The solution is to blur the moving objects without the background and then composite the results.

Object rotating with 2D motion blur

Lesson 08

Fast rotating objects

The following image shows a case where the 2D motion blur breaks down with rotation.

The microphone is rotating quickly in this scene. The motion vector thinks the movement is linear because it does not know about the position of the geometry in-between the first and last positions.

Objects entering from outside the image or leaving the image

The renderer does not know the object color outside of the image and has to make assumptions. The solution is to render a slightly larger image, which covers the original image, and then crop it to the desired size.

Volume objects (particles, fog) and image planes

Motion vectors are only calculated for moving triangles (tessellated NURBS and poly meshes).

Note: *The rendered results from 3D and 2D are quite different. It is not a good idea to mix the rendered images from these two different kinds of blurring operations.*

Depth of Field

Depth of Field is a photographic effect, where objects, within a certain range of distance, remain sharply focused. Objects outside this range appear out of focus. We can simulate this using the camera's Depth of Field attribute. This is not a post-process effect in mental ray, but true depth of field.

1 Setting up the camera for depth of field

- Open the file 08-depthOfField_01.ma.

- In a four-view layout, set *camera1* to replace the Perspective view.

- In the top view, select *camera1* and press **t** to show the camera's **Manipulators.** Place the **Center of Interest** to the location you want to remain in focus.

- Select **Window** → **General Editors** → **Connection Editor**.

- Open the Hypershade and select the camera you are using from the **Cameras** tab.

Image rendered with depth of field

- Reload this camera into both sides of the **Connection Editor**.

- Connect the **Center of Interest** to the **Focus Distance**.

> **Note:** *Another alternate but equally useful workflow in setting up depth of field is to use the* **Distance Tool**. *This can be found under* **Create → Measure Tools → Distance Tool**. *This will allow you to measure the distance between the camera and the point in your scene that you want to use as the focus distance.*

2 Enable Depth of Field

- In the Attribute Editor for the camera, open the **Depth of Field** section.

- Set the **Depth of Field** flag to **On**.

- Adjust the **F Stop** to control the amount of depth of field.

The **F Stop** *value represents the distance in front of and behind the focus distance that will remain in focus. A low value represents a short distance that will be in focus; a very high value Fstop will result in very little blur due to the deeper range in focus. In essence, the lower the Fstop value, the smaller the in focused region will be.*

Lesson 08

Tip: *It is possible to use Render Region to test render depth of field.*

Limitations of depth of field

Transparent surfaces can cause problems with depth of field. The technical reason for this limitation is that the transparent surface is at a certain depth from the camera. The renderer only stores one depth per pixel, and it chooses to store the nearest point to the eye. For transparent surfaces, the depth of the transparent surface will determine the blur, so the background will show through, un-blurred. The background, when seen through the transparent object, will be blurred at the same depth as the transparent surface. This limitation is not limited to Maya and has led to the industry accepted practice of rendering components separately and compositing.

Reasons to render for compositing

Compositing is the process of merging multiple layers of image information into one image to create a final look. A common misconception is that compositing is for large productions with many artists. However, smaller production facilities and individual artists can also benefit from the opportunities and advantages offered by compositing. For example, with compositing you can:

- Have the flexibility to re-render or color correct individual elements without having to re-render the whole scene.

- Increase creative potential and achieve effects with the 2D compositing package that are not possible with the renderer.

- Take advantage of effects that are faster and more flexible in 2D, such as depth of field and glow, rather than rendering them in 3D.

- Combine different looks from different renderers, such as hardware and software particle effects.

- Combine 3D rendered elements with 2D live action footage.

- Save time when rendering scenes where the camera does not move; you only need to render one frame of the background to be used behind the whole animation sequence.

- Successfully render large complex scenes in layers so that you don't exceed your hardware and software memory capabilities.

Set up a render for compositing

Rendering in layers refers to the process of separating scene elements so that different objects or sets of objects can be rendered as separate images. The first step is to determine how to divide the scene into layers. This may be very simple or incredibly complex and will depend entirely on your needs for any given project. Once you have decided how you want to separate your scene elements, there are several workflow approaches you can use to render them separately.

Rendering with render layers

A typical approach to separating your scene elements is to use **Render Layers**. You can assign objects to render layers using the same workflow as you would when working with display layers.

Display / Render layers

The render layers allow you to organize the objects in your scene specifically to meet your rendering needs. The most basic approach might be to separate objects into foreground, midground and background layers. Or, you may decide to divide the scene elements by specific objects or sets of objects.

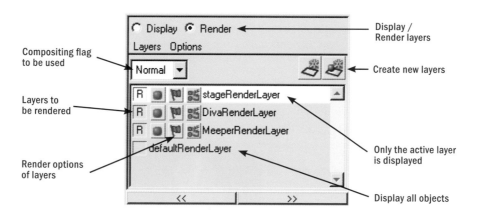

Render Layer Editor

If you need to have very precise control over the color of your rendered objects separate from the shadows on them, you can further breakdown your shot by rendering separate passes within any render layer. The term render passes generally refers to the process of rendering various attributes separately, such as color, shadows, specular highlights, etc. The Render Layers Editor allows you to set this up.

The following image shows Diva was rendered with different render passes: specular highlights and diffuse. The last image to the right shows the resulting composited image.

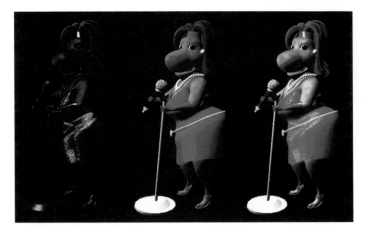

Specular and color rendered as separate render passes and composited

Tip: *Render passes are not limited to the example above. You can easily render beauty, shadow, specular, color and diffuse by setting simple checkboxes to on.*

The alpha channel

When rendering objects for compositing, one of the most important requirements is an *alpha channel*. The alpha channel, sometimes called a *mask* or *matte*, contains information about the coverage and opacity of objects in an image. This information is later used by the compositing application to combine the images.

Alpha and RGB channels

Project Three

In the alpha channel, opaque regions of objects are white, while fully transparent objects or empty spaces are black. The grayscale regions in the alpha channel represent semi-transparent objects.

The image on the previous page shows the RGB channel and the alpha channel for Diva.

Matte Opacity

There are many cases where compositing the separate elements of even a simple scene can be tricky and require careful planning.

The following image depicts the compositing of two separately rendered objects. A problem exists where, for example, the microphone stand goes behind Diva's left hand, but in front of her right arm. This is because the alpha channel does not contain any information about what part of what object goes in front or behind other objects. For this reason, the compositing application doesn't know this information either.

The **Matte Opacity** feature provides one way to resolve this dilemma.

Stand in front
of Diva layer

Stand behind
Diva layer

Stand is not
behind the hand

Stand is now
in front of arm

Separately rendered objects that will be difficult to composite correctly

Note: *In some cases, it is also possible to affect the alpha channels later in the compositing application to allow images to composite correctly. A third possible approach is to render the images with a depth channel for use in compositing packages with depth compositing capabilities. However, there are limitations to depth compositing techniques so it is a good idea to learn these other methods as well.*

Lesson 08

To ensure that the objects composite properly, you can use an attribute called **Matte Opacity,** found in the Attribute Editor for all materials. This allows you to manipulate the rendered alpha value on a per-material basis.

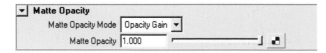

Matte Opacity found in any materials' Attribute Editor

The **Matte Opacity** feature has three modes:

Black Hole

To solve this particular compositing problem, the **Black Hole** mode is useful. This mode will set the RGBA values to exactly (0,0,0,0), resulting in images with cutout regions that allow the objects to fit together correctly. The image below shows the alpha of the microphone stand once Diva's materials are set to black hole.

Black Hole used to hide parts of the objects

Opacity Gain

This is the default mode for **Matte Opacity**. Alpha values are calculated in the normal way, then multiplied by the **Matte Opacity** value. Because the **Matte Opacity** attribute has a default value of **1.0**, the rendered alpha values remain unchanged (1.0 * x = x). However, you can adjust the Matte Opacity value for the following scenerios:

- Animate the Matte Opacity value from 0-1 or vice versa to create fade-in or fade-out effects when composited.

- Texture map the Matte Opacity attribute to create interesting compositing effects, especially if you use an animated texture or sequence of images.

Solid Matte

When Matte Opacity is in **Solid Matte** mode, the normally calculated alpha values are ignored in favor of the Matte Opacity setting. The entire matte for the object is set to the value of the Matte Opacity attribute. This can be useful if you need an object to have a specific alpha value. For example, if you have a transparent object, the normal alpha value calculated by the renderer will be 0. Solid Matte can be used to set a non-zero value for the alpha on the transparent object. If you were rendering a view through a window and wanted to composite this into another scene, setting the Matte Opacity value to 1.0 (in Solid Matte mode) on the window's material would help you achieve this.

> **Note:** *Opacity gain and solid matte modes will not change the RGB component of your image. They will only change the alpha value generated by the shader.*

Altering the mattes in compositing application

Depending on what effects will be used at the compositing stage, it is sometimes important to render the whole object rather than having parts cut away with Black Hole. This gives you greater flexibility for effects such as blur, or overcoming moire patterns on edges. Under these circumstances, you would need to use some techniques in the compositing application in order to composite the elements correctly. This can involve manipulating a combination of the alpha values themselves, or creating custom masks to reveal/conceal objects as they are layered together.

Rendering shadows and reflections separately

Maya also provides a way to create custom reflection and shadow passes. You may need to do this, for example, if you want to blur the reflections or adjust the shadow color in a compositing package. Setting this up involves the **Use Background Shader,** which acts as a shadow and reflection catcher.

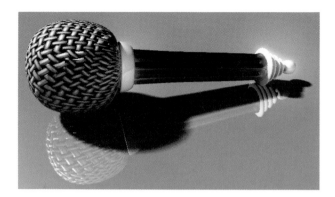

Image rendered normally

Following is an example of how you could render the reflection and shadow in separate passes.

1 Scene file

- Open the file called 08-passes_01.ma.

2 Assign a Use Background material

- Assign a **Use Background Shader** to the ground plane.

The ground plane is the reflection-catching object in this case.

3 Turn Off Primary Visibility

- Select the microphone geometry.

- In the Attribute Editor under the **Render Stats** section, set the **Primary Visibility** checkbox to **Off**.

Turning off Primary Visibility will ensure that the microphone is not visible but will still appear in the reflections on the ground plane.

4 Tweak the Use Background material

- Disable shadows temporarily by turning the **Shadow Mask** option in the *useBackground1* material to **0.0**.

- Set the **Reflectivity** to the desired value between **0.0** an **1.0**.

*This value should be set to the same value as the **Reflectivity** on the original material assigned to the ground plane.*

- Render the scene.

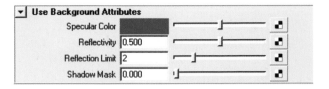

Use Background Attributes

This rendered reflection pass shows the reflections in the RGB channels and a white mask in the alpha channel. In some cases, the alpha channel would not be used in the final composite because reflections are normally added to the background image. However, if the background image is a light or white color, adding the reflections will not be visible; in this case, the alpha is needed.

RGB channels' reflections only

Alpha channel reflections mask

To render only shadows

- In the Attribute Editor for the *useBackground1* material, set the **Shadow Mask** to **1.0**.

- Set the **Reflection Limit** to **0**.

Lesson 08

This will ensure that no reflections are visible in the rendered results.

Shadow alpha mask

mental ray blurred reflections and refractions

Typically, raytraced reflections and refractions exhibit very sharp definition. In reality, there are always inaccuracies in surface finishes and impurities in material structures that cause light rays to be reflected and refracted slightly off the original ray direction.

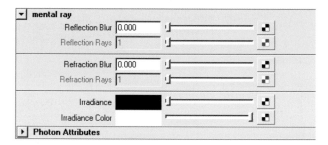

mental ray reflection and refraction blur of a material

Adjustments for mental ray reflection and refraction blur are located in the **mental ray** section of the material node.

Reflection and Refraction Blur

These attributes determine the amount of reflection and refraction blur. A good starting point is between 0.1 and 0.3.

Reflection and Refraction Rays

When reflection and refraction blur has been enabled, ray direction is not exactly determined by the raytracing algorithm. **Reflection** and **Refraction Rays** will randomly deviate as specified by the blur attributes. This attribute is used to control the amount of *supersampling* required by the random deviation of the ray direction. Generally, higher reflection and refraction rays are required with more blur.

Use Background Shader

You can also use the **Use Background Shader** to make 3D geometry look like it is part of a real image. For example, if you want to place Meeper over a background shot of a desert, you will need his shadows to be on the sand. Doing so would greatly help to incorporate the CG elements to the background image.

1 Scene file

- Open the file called 08-desert_01.ma.

2 Image plane

- Create an **Image Plane** for the *camera1*.

- Browse for the image called *dune.tif* from the *sourceImages* directory.

3 Ground plane

- Model a surface that approximately matches the perspective and shape of the background image where Meeper is standing.

- Assign a **Use Background Shader** to the stand-in geometry.

This will make the stand-in geometry disappear seamlessly into the background image.

- Place the camera and models on the stand-in geometry.

4 Lights

- Create lighting similar to the one in the background image.

Stand-in geometry receives shadows

- Turn **On** shadows on the lights.

- Render the scene.

The stand-in geometry will receive shadows, creating the illusion that Meeper is actually part of the image.

Tip: *The same approach can be used to make a 2D image on an image plane look like it is part of a 3D scene. Use the same technique for modeling stand-in geometry: (1) Assign a Use Background Shader to the stand-ins; (2) With the stand-in geometry casting shadows and raytraced reflections of other geometry in the 3D scene, it is very convincing.*

Camera projection

The Use Background technique described above reaches its limit in a case where, for example, you decide you want to be able to animate something that is getting its color from part of a 2D image plane. This might be a case of making a dog talk or a cat's eyes bulging open where the dog and cat exist in a live shot behind stand-in geometry. In this case, you can use a **Camera Projection** method of texture mapping to project the 2D image onto the stand-in geometry instead of using an image plane. Then you would do a **Convert Solid Texture** to create parametric texture maps on the surfaces. Once this is done, you can animate the stand-in geometry and render it so that it can be composited with the original images.

Composite rendering

If you find yourself in a situation where you are rendering an object over a background that is any color other than completely black (0,0,0), you should set **Premultiply** to **Off** in the Render Settings under the **Render Options** section.

What this feature does is prevent the edges of geometry from being anti-aliased against the background color. For this reason, the RGB component of the image will look badly aliased. However, the mask channel is perfectly anti-aliased. The mask channel is what is used to blend the rendered element into the background of choice at the compositing stage. Because the composite rendering flag prevented the edges from including any of the rendering background color, you will not get an unsightly rim showing in the rendering background color after compositing.

Premultiply Threshold is mainly a games feature. This is a normalized [0,1] alpha threshold; the foreground is registered only if the alpha value is above the composite threshold.

Conclusion

Adding effects enhances a scene's quality and produces some interesting results. Compositing involves rendering a scene in separate components and then merging those components together.

In the next lesson, you will review hardware rendering.

Lesson 09   Hardware rendering

In the past, the Hardware Render Buffer was used to create fast, low quality previews of animations or to output hardware rendered particles. However, modern graphic cards have become more sophisticated and are able to support more advanced features. You can now use the Hardware Renderer to get fast, good quality images and more features than the Hardware Render Buffer.

In this lesson you will learn the following:

- Hardware Renderer basics;

- How to use the Hardware Renderer;

- How to hardware render particles;

- How to adjust and optimize hardware renders.

Hardware rendering vs. Hardware Render Buffer

There are two ways to do a hardware render in Maya. One is to use the **Hardware Render Buffer** and the other is to use the **Hardware Renderer**. Both methods use the power of graphic cards to create bitmap images, but the Hardware Renderer delivers much more in terms of quality and features.

The Hardware Render Buffer uses the graphics buffer and graphics memory of your computer to draw an image to the display and then take a snapshot of it. The snapshot is then written to a file as a rendered image. This technique has the advantage of being very fast, but also the limitation of few rendering perks like shadows, reflections and post-process effects such as motion blur.

To access the Hardware Render Buffer go to **Window** → **Rendering Editors** → **Hardware Render Buffer**. The Hardware Render Buffer has its own render settings, and the window will assume the size of the selected resolution format.

Note: *It is important to note that since the Hardware Render Buffer is taking screen grabs of the image on your monitor, you'll need to make sure that there are now other windows visible in front of this window when you are rendering. It is also advisable to turn off your screensaver for renders that may take a while.*

Unlike the Hardware Render Buffer, the Hardware Renderer will allow you to output features like shadows, per-pixel specular highlights, bump maps and reflections for materials. The quality of particles is much better than when using the Hardware Render Buffer. The other advantage to using the Hardware Renderer is the user can output images in batch mode. This means you can create images in the background or offline and work in Maya or other applications at the same time. For a full list of supported hardware render features, check the documentation of the current release.

Note: *To see which graphic cards are qualified to use with Maya, see the qualification charts on the Alias website at www.alias.com*

Using the Hardware Renderer

The speed and quality of the hardware rendered image is scene dependent. When you first start up your render, it may take a while for the first frame to render. The reason for this is that the Hardware Renderer must translate the scene into a data structure that is optimized for the graphics' hardware. This is done in the software by the CPU and includes the translation of geometry into a format optimized for drawing, loading file textures and evaluating and baking shading networks, if necessary. If the data doesn't change, it's cached for subsequent frames, which is probably the reason why the first frame seems to take longer to compute than other frames.

You can control image quality and optimize your scene by:

• Using lambert and phong materials.

Other shading models will work, but lambert and phong are the best because their appearance in the Hardware Renderer is similar to that of the Software Renderer. Note that this won't actually speed things up but will make tweaking easier.

• Using polygons.

Try to model with polygons or tessellate NURBS surfaces by using **Modify** → **Convert** → **NURBS to Polygons***. Something to keep in mind is that the Hardware Renderer uses the same tessellation settings as the Software Renderer.*

• Be aware of the UV mapping of your polygon.

For example, you may notice that the quality of your specular highlight is poor. A reason for this can be the spacing between UVs. Try to avoid overlapping triangles, thin triangles or triangles that cover small UV areas. These could impact image quality. Note that if UV coordinates are not specified, the Hardware Renderer will create them on the fly for specular highlights and bump mapping. It will take some time to compute this, although it's usually quite small.

• When possible, bake your textures.

Use the **Edit** → **Convert to File Texture** *command in the* **Edit** *menu of the Hypershade or the* **Lighting/Shading** → **Batch Bake** *command in the* **Render** *menu to bake your textures to files.*

Hardware Render Settings

There are several ways to access the Hardware Renderer. One way is to go in the Render Settings and set **Render Using** → **Maya Hardware**. Another way is to select **Render** → **Render Using** → **Maya Hardware**.

Following is information about the Hardware Render Settings. You will notice two sections in the **Maya Hardware** tab: **Quality** and **Render Options**.

Quality settings

Presets

These presets will change the quality of the hardware rendering.

Number Of Samples

Defines the number of samples per pixel. This attribute influences the render time dramatically. The higher the value, the better the anti-aliasing, but the longer it takes to calculate.

Transparency sorting

This attribute defines two different ways to detect and draw transparent objects:

Per object

Objects are sorted from farthest to closest in depth relation to the camera. The object's bounding box is used to determine its position related to the camera position. If an object has different shaders assigned to it, each part of the object gets its own bounding box with respect to the assigned shader. This option provides faster results, but may not render complex transparent objects correctly because each object's polygons are drawn in arbitrary order. However, in most cases this option gives you a proper result.

Per polygon

Each object's polygons are sorted and drawn from farthest to closest in distance from the camera. This option provides more accurate transparency representation, but takes longer to process. Only use this option if **Per object** delivers incorrect results.

Color and Bump Resolution

The Hardware Renderer automatically bakes 3D textures into 2D textures, and you can define the resolution of the resulting files with the **Color** and **Bump** attributes. This process is comparable to the Hypershade command **Edit → Convert to File Texture**, but processed automatically. The baked channels may include color, diffuse, bump, incandescence, specular color, cosine power and ambient color.

Render options

Culling

This option controls how the rendered polygon is rendered, dependent on its normal direction to the camera.

Per Object

The setting in the Attribute Editor **Render Stats** section of each individual object is used by the Hardware Renderer.

All Double-sided

Both sides of the polygons in the scene are rendered. This is a global effect.

All Single-sided

Only polygons with normals facing to the camera are rendered. This is a global effect.

Motion Blur

The Hardware Renderer supports motion blur if this option is On. If you render particles with motion blur, it is recommended to create a particle disk cache for proper calculation and to bake simulations before rendering. Failure to do so will result in incorrect particle positions. Motion blur requires the scene to be evaluated both forward and backwards in time; if there is no disk cache for dynamics, the image will be rendered with the wrong particle positions when the scene is evaluated backwards in time.

Motion Blur By Frame

The Hardware Renderer calculates the motion blur by evaluating the object at different positions and blending them. With the **Motion Blur by Frame** option, you can modify the start and end point of the motion blur calculation. This attribute is related to **Number of Exposures** and the **Shutter Angle** attribute in the camera's Attribute Editor.

Number of Exposures

This attribute defines how many samples are calculated to create a smooth motion blur. It divides the given time range into specific frames. The final image is the accumulated average of all the exposures.

Geometry Mask

This option is typically used when rendering hardware particles. It renders the geometry of the scene just like if there was a **Use Background Shader** assigned to all the geometry, with the alpha channel of the geometry set to black. This allows you to easily composite the particle images right on top of the normal color render of the scene.

Hardware render

In this exercise, you will learn some methods to manipulate the output settings and general look of your hardware rendering.

1 Changing the output filename

- Open the file *09-divaFire_01.ma*.

- Go to the **Render Settings** window and make sure the option **Render Using** is set to **Maya Hardware**.

- Rewind to frame **1**, then **play** the animation and stop where you see the fire emitting from Diva's arm.

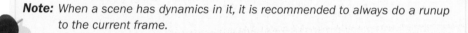

Note: *When a scene has dynamics in it, it is recommended to always do a runup to the current frame.*

- Render the scene.

2 Light linking

You will notice that all objects in the scene cast shadows, including the particles. To avoid this, break the light link for the particles.

- Select the *spotLight* casting the shadows, then **Shift-select** the smoke and fire particle objects and select **Lighting/Shading** → **Break Light Link** from the **Rendering** menu set.

By default, particles cast shadows

- Render the scene.

The fire no longer casts shadows.

Hardware render without shadows on particles

3 Performing a batch command

You can use the Render View window to see single frame hardware rendered results. To render an animation, define the frame range in the **Render Settings** as usual, and then choose **Render → Batch Render**.

To batch render outside Maya, you have to run Maya from the command window. The command is:

```
maya -prompt -file filename -command hwRender
```

In this case, you can type:

```
maya -prompt -file 09-divaFire_01.ma -command hwRender
```

If you need to specify additional options, such as frame range, use the `setAttr` command to set attributes on the Hardware Render Settings node before running the `hwRender` command. Multiple commands can be specified in the `-command` flag by enclosing the commands in quotes and separating the individual commands by semicolons.

1 Rendering with motion blur

- Open the scene *09-podCrash_01.ma*.

This scene contains an animation with dynamics.

- Render *camera1* at frame **78**.

You will notice that the motion blur looks blocky and incorrect. The problem is that, for the speed of motion, there are not enough motion exposures to create the blur.

Motion blur artifacts are noticeable

2 Motion blur length and exposures

- Go to the **Render Options** section of the **Hardware Render Settings**.

- Reduce the length of the motion blur by lowering the value for **Motion Blur by Frame** to **0.2**.

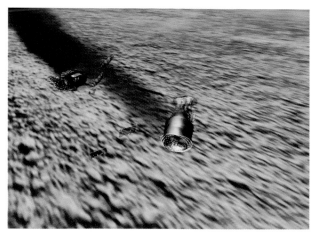

Blur by Frame reduces the length of the motion blur

- Gradually increase the **Number of Exposures** until you get an acceptable motion blur quality.

Increasing this attribute will give more definition to the motion blur, but it will also increase the render time.

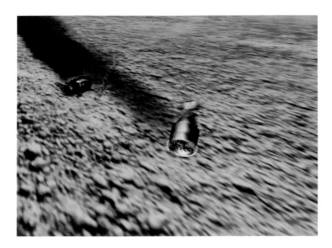

Number of exposures set to 6

3   Caching particles

If you like to render with motion blur and your scene contains particles, it can be necessary to create a particle cache before rendering the entire scene. To do so go to **Solvers** → **Create Particle Disk Cache** from the Dynamics menu set.

Note: *Dynamics will be covered later in this book.*

Conclusion

The Hardware Renderer and Hardware Render Buffer both use the power of the graphic card to render images. Despite the fact that they offer a lower image quality, they are very fast and efficient for rendering geometry and particles.

In the next lesson, you will look at the Maya Vector Renderer.

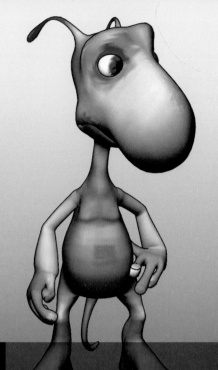

Lesson 10 Vector rendering

In computer graphics, there are two principal ways of storing graphic elements: bitmap images and vector images. Both techniques satisfy different needs and have their own advantages and disadvantages. In this lesson, you will render vector images using the Maya Vector Renderer.

In this lesson you will learn the following:

- The difference between bitmap and vector images;

- How to render vector images;

- How to change the Vector Renderer options;

- How to view a vector image or animation.

Bitmap images

Bitmap images are largely used to display photographs, textures or computer generated images. A bitmap image has two main characteristics that define the quality: *resolution* and the *number of bits per pixel*. The resolution is defined by the number of pixels in the X and Y directions. The number of bits per pixel defines how much information can be stored per pixel. Both attributes together define the file size of an image. The advantage of bitmaps is their ability to carry the necessary information to display photorealistic content. The biggest disadvantage is that the resolution directly affects image quality. Scaling a bitmap image always has an impact on the image quality, and high quality bitmaps need a lot of disk space and memory. These are some of the drawbacks that limit the use of bitmaps.

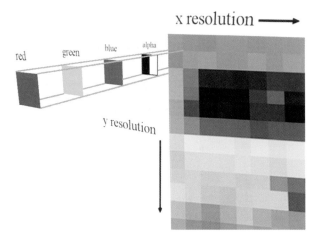

A bitmap image

The most common type of image format output by a renderer is 32 bit (24 bits for the color information (red, green, blue) and 8 bits for the alpha channel (RGBA)). This means you have 24 bits of color information per pixel = 2 to the exponent 24 = 16,777,216 colors. The alpha channel contains an additional 8 bits of information that are used for compositing.

Vector images

Vector formats are chiefly used for print publishing, especially diagrams, logos and typography. Web vector formats are also very common because they have a relatively small file size and are scalable. Vector images handle curves and closed shapes that can be filled with solid colors or color ramps.

Project Three

A vector graphic is described by two color properties: *outline* and *fill*. These two properties are a mathematical description for the shape and color and because of this, the quality of a vector image is independent of the resolution. That means you can scale a vector graphic to any size you choose without losing quality or detail. As well, vector graphic formats don't take up as much disk space as bitmap images.

Also, the individual elements can be easily animated and used for interaction with the user. The disadvantage is that it is hard to get realistic results with a vector graphic.

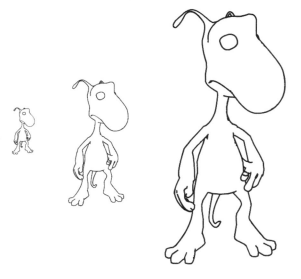

A scaled vector graphic of Meeper

The above vector render was viewed through a web browser. It illustrates a vector graphic in three different scales.

The Vector Renderer is based on RAViX Technology (Rapid Visibility Extension). This technology detects the lines and vertices that make up a 3D model and converts 3D models into 2D vector-based imagery. Because of this, animated objects like menu icons or characters can easily be done in Maya. Animation can also be rendered in vector format and later reused and edited in software packages like Macromedia® Flash® or Adobe® Illustrator® .

The Vector Renderer supports the most common vector formats: Macromedia Flash (.swf), Swift 3D Importer (.swft), encapsulated postscript (.eps), Adobe Illustrator (.ai), and scalable vector graphics SVG (.svg).

You can use software like FlashMX® , GoLive, Freehand, Illustrator, or CorelDraw® to edit these formats, or you can simply view them in a web browser.

In addition to the vector formats, the Vector Renderer can output from the vector graphic the bitmap file format commonly used. By using these image formats, you can create nonrealistic effects and compose them with any other rendered images.

The Vector Renderer is not designed to create a vectorized copy of the software rendering. Because of this, the vector doesn't support all features that are available with a traditional renderer, like the Software Renderer or mental ray.

Tip: *It is recommended you work with polygonal objects when using the Vector Render, but you are not limited to them. NURBS and subdivision surfaces are supported as well.*

Render settings

This section describes the options in the **Render Settings** window and their impact on the output image. It is important to understand these attributes as they effect render time, file size and image quality.

To see the Vector Renderer options, open the Render Settings window and under **Render Using** select **Maya Vector**.

Note: *If you don't see this option, you will need to go to* **Window** → **Settings/ Preferences** → **Plug-in Manager** *and load VectorRender.mll.*

Tip: *You can experiment with the different options on the scene file called 10-meeperVector_01.ma.*

Image format options (swf)

Under the **Common** tab in the **Image File Output** section, notice the default **Image Format** is **Macromedia SWF** (**.swf**) format. If you choose the **Maya Vector** tab, you will get attributes that accompany that format.

Frame Rate

The frame rate measured in frames per second for the output animation.

Flash Version

The version of the rendered Flash Player file.

Open in Browser

If enabled, the vector image or animation is displayed in your default browser after it is rendered. The browser gives you information about the image name, location, file size and the time it took for rendering.

Combine Fills and Edges

When **Combine Fills and Edges** is **On**, outlines and fills for a surface become a single object. When **Combine Fills** and **Edges** is **Off**, outlines and fills for a surface become separate objects. The size of the rendered file will be smaller when **Combine Fills and Edges** is **Off**.

This option can usually remain disabled. The optimization of the file size typically happens in Flash. When using Flash, it is important to have easy access to all parts of the vector graphics. This option only includes fills and outlines. If you add highlights and reflections, these effects are treated as separate objects in Flash.

Image format options (svg)

Under the **Common** tab in the **Image File Output** section, if you choose the SVG format, the **Maya Vector** tab will show attributes that accompany that format.

Frame Rate

The frame rate measured in frames per second for the output animation.

Svg Animation

If **Svg Animation** is **Native**, the renderer creates one svg file containing the frames of your animation and the scripting that drives it. If **Svg Animation** is **Script**, the renderer creates an svg file containing the frames of your animation and an HTML file containing the JavaScript that drives it.

If your animation is long, file size increases when **Svg Animation** is **Native**.

Compress

Only use this option if you plan to publish the rendered svg file directly to the Web. If you plan to import the svg file into another application like GoLive or Illustrator, the **Compress** attribute must be disabled, because you can't edit a compressed svg file.

Appearance options

Curve Tolerance

A value from **0** to **15** determines how object outlines are represented. When Curve Tolerance is **0**, object outlines are drawn by a series of straight line segments (one segment for each polygon edge). This produces an outline that exactly matches the outline of polygons, but also produces larger file sizes.

When Curve Tolerance is **15**, object outlines are represented by curved lines. This produces an outline that may appear slightly distorted compared to the original object's outline, but also produces smaller file sizes.

Secondary Curve Fitting

This option provides more control over the conversion of line segments into curves by adding a second pass. Typically, this results in more linear segments converted to curves. While this option increases render time, it can help produce better results and smaller files.

Detail Level Preset

Predefined settings for the **Detail Level** attribute.

Detail Level

Determines the level of detail in the rendered image. High values produce more detailed images and more accurate renders than low values, but takes longer to render and increases file size.

A value of **0** sets **Detail Level** to **Automatic** to allow the renderer to choose the appropriate level of detail for your scene.

With a higher detail level, the Vector Renderer generates more edit points for the single objects. The best way to see this is to compare the vector images in vector editing software.

Low Detail Level   High Detail Level

Detail level comparison

The Meeper image on the left was rendered with a **Curve Tolerance** of **10** and a **Detail Level** of **1**. The file size is 2 KB and took 1 second to render. The Meeper image on the right was rendered with a **Curve Tolerance** of **10** and a **Detail Level** of **50**. The file size is 5 KB and took 20 seconds to render. As you can see in the images above, there are additional details in specific areas when the detail level is high, but the influence to the overall look for this object is not so dramatic.

Fill options

Choosing to use the **Fill Object** attribute has a main impact on file size, as well as render time. Keep in mind that if you really need a photorealistic rendering, a bitmap format is the better choice.

All fill styles, except single color, respond to point lights and get the final color from the color attribute in the assigned material of the object. All other light types and most of the material attributes are ignored by the Vector Renderer. If your scene does not contain point lights, a default point light is automatically created, which is located at the camera and will be deleted after rendering. Also, light linking and all attributes except primary visibility in the **Render Stats** section of the objects are ignored by the Vector Renderer.

In the following description of the attributes, the terms *face*, *surface* and *triangle* are used. Face is used to describe a polygonal face. Surface represents a single NURBS surface. The term triangle is used to describe the triangulated version of a polygonal face or a NURBS surface.

Single Color

If **Single Color** is selected, the fill color behaves similarly to a surface shader. The objects appear flat-shaded and independent from lighting. They get the color from the **Color** attribute of the assigned shader. Internally, an ambient light is calculated to shade the surfaces, so the final color may vary slightly from the material **Color** attribute.

Single Color fill

Two Colors

This attribute uses two solid colors to achieve a shaded, 3D-like look on the surface. This doesn't mean that the final image only contains two tones of a color. An object with a blue material can have various tones of blue, depending on the view angle and lighting.

Four Colors

Works like the attribute Two Colors, but uses four solid colors to shade a surface.

Two Color fill

Four Color fill

Project Three

Full Color

Shades each triangle with a solid color. You can achieve a similar look when using **Shading** → **Flat Shading All** in the panel menu of a view. This option creates a big file and takes a long time to render because the color must be calculated for each triangle. This means that the tessellation for NURBS objects is also taken into account.

Full Color fill with different model resolution

Average Color

When selecting Average Color, each face and surface is shaded with one solid color. The definition of a face is driven by the smoothing angle between them. By making edges hard with **Edit Polygon** → **Normals** → **Soften/Harden**, you can influence the look of the shaded object.

Average Color fill

Lesson 10

Area Gradient

This attribute fills each face and surface with one radial gradient. This attribute can create a nice 3D effect with a small increase of the file size. Flat faces and surfaces get a more even fill, smooth surfaces and faces a gradient fill. These attributes are only available if swf or svg as the output formats are selected.

Area Gradient Color fill

Mesh Gradient

This is the most expensive option available in this section and creates the biggest files. However, it gives you a vectorized look that is the closest to a regular software rendering. These attributes are only available if swf or svg as the output formats are selected.

Mesh gradient fills each triangle with a linear gradient based on the material color and lighting. A similar look can be achieved inside Maya when selecting **Shading** → **Smooth Shade All** from a view menu.

Mesh Gradient Color fill

Show Back Faces

If this option is enabled, the Vector Renderer also renders faces whose normals are facing away from the camera. This option is equivalent to the attribute **Double sided** in the **Render Stats** section of an object. Disabling this attribute reduces the file size in some cases.

SWF options

The next three options are only available with Macromedia SWF, or a bitmap format, as the selected output format. Shadows, highlights and reflections have a global influence to the scene. As mentioned above, the **Render Stats** in the Attribute Editor are ignored. You can only control the shadows, highlights, and reflections for the whole scene, not on a per object basis.

If you render with these attributes enabled, each feature appears as one part in the vector graphic. If you import it into vector editing software, you will get the whole image on one layer. But, each part is separate and you can select it as one piece, making it easier to apply each feature to one layer.

Shadows

If selected, it enables all objects to cast and receive shadows. Both Dmap and raytrace shadows will work. When raytraced shadows are used, the **Light Radius** attribute in the light's Attribute Editor is also ignored. Only shadow-casting point lights are rendered.

> **Tip:** There are two other restrictions when rendering shadows with the Vector Renderer — transparent objects cannot receive shadows and the shadow color is ignored.

Four Color fill and shadows

Highlights

This option is only available when **Fill Style** is **Single Color**, **Average Color** or **Area Gradient**. With this attribute, a highlight is calculated. The highlight appears as a number of concentric solid color regions. The number of rings is driven by the **Highlight Level** attribute. The highlight is a separate, semi-transparent layer that lies above the fill and edges. Therefore, objects appear brighter than without the highlights.

The following material attributes influence the look of the highlight:

Anisotropic	**Roughness;**
Blinn	**Eccentricity;**
Phong	**Cosine Power;**
PhongE	**Roughness.**

Single Color fill and Highlights

If the **Specular Color** is mapped with a texture, the materials' default color is used to compute the color of the highlight.

Reflections

This attribute enables the Vector Renderer to render reflections. If you select this option, all objects show up in reflections. The attribute **Reflection Depth** controls how often a reflection is *traced*. This attribute is comparable to the Reflection Depth attribute for a material.

Single Color fill and Reflections

Project Three

Edge options

Enable this option to render your objects with an outline.

> **Note:** *To better see the character, edge outlines were used in all the images in this lesson.*

Edge Weight

This option lets you control the thickness of the outline. It is measured in points. If you render to a vector format, you can modify the line thickness later in vector editing software. The option **Edge Weight Presets** provides you with some presets.

Edge Color

Controls the overall color of the outline.

Edge Style

Controls the placement of the outline. If set to **Outlines**, the object's contour is rendered as an outline. If set to **Entire Mesh**, the object's triangulation is vectorized.

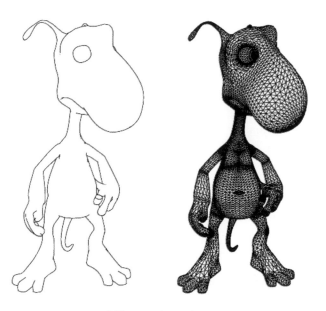

Different edge styles

Lesson 10

Hidden Edge

If this option is enabled, the Vector Renderer displays all edges. This creates a wireframe-like look.

Hidden Edges   *Outlines and Edge Detail*

Edge Detail

If this option is enabled, sharp edges between polygon edges are rendered as outline. The **Min Edge Angle** attribute acts as a threshold and gives you global control where a line is drawn in the inside of the object. It decides at which angle an edge is drawn or not. The appearance of a line is also influenced by the smoothing angle. This means you can force the renderer to add and delete lines with **Polygon** → **Normals** → **Soften/Harden**. This workflow allows local control and works for single parts of an object.

Render layers

Objects on different render layers are rendered to different files. To compose them, these files can be imported in the vector graphics software.

Tip: *Remember that when working with render layer passes, features such as shadows and reflections are calculated only for objects on the same layer.*

Project Three

Create render layers

- In the Layer Editor, switch to **Render Layers**.

- Create new layers and assign objects to them.

- If you select **Render** → **Batch Render,** the renderer will output each layer to a specific vector file.

Command Line to vector render

You can also render your scene through the Command Line. Open a command window and type:

```
mayaVectorRender -help
```

This command will show you the options to use the Vector Renderer via the Command Line. To render a scene, go to the directory that your scene file is in and type:

```
mayaVectorRender —file   filename
```

This command launches a vector render with the Render Settings that were saved in the scene file.

Conclusion

In this lesson, you explored the various outputs of the Vector Renderer. By using vector rendering, you will be able to render cartoon style images and animation, or fulfill tasks like generating vector content for a web site. In the next lesson, you will learn about some Maya Paint Effects and Toon features.

Lesson 11   Maya Paint Effects

Maya Paint Effects offers a wide variety of brushes that let you add real-time effects to a scene. With this toolset, you can work on either a 2D canvas or in a typical 3D scene. This makes it possible to create either bitmap images or integrated brush strokes that can be viewed and animated in 3D. Paint Effects' vast library of pre-sets makes it easy to add effects to your scene with a few brush strokes. As you learn more, you can also enhance the existing brushes and even add your own to the library.

In this lesson you will learn the following:

- Maya Paint Effects;

- How to paint brush strokes;

- How to render Maya Paint Effects;

- How to convert Maya Paint Effects;

- How to use Toon.

Paint Effects brushes

When you create Paint Effects, you first need to select a *brush* and then paint strokes either in your 3D scene or on a 2D canvas. A brush defines how the Paint Effects spawn and look from a stroke. A stroke is usually user drawn, defining a path along which the Paint Effects will be assigned.

Paint Effects works by creating a series of dots along a curve, which can take basically any shape with any color. When you paint, the closer the dots are together, the smoother the brush stroke will look. Brushes can be almost anything you want. Included in Maya is a group of default brushes such as grass, trees, lightings, fur and much more.

Alias *I love painting plants and greenery with Maya Paint Effects. Because even a*
Tip: *developer can make something that looks good :-)*

Mike Taylor | Software Architect

Rendering Paint Effects

Rendering Paint Effects involves a post-process in the Maya Software Renderer. This means that you cannot render Paint Effects with another renderer. The way to work around this is either to render a separate pass with only the Paint Effects that will be composited with your other layers, or you can convert the Paint Effects to NURBS or polygons.

When you convert Paint Effects to geometry, the history of the brush and stroke is maintained. By doing so, you can render fully animated brushes in any other renderer.

In the following example, you will see how to use Paint Effects and convert it so it can be rendered into the Vector Renderer.

1 Scene file

- Open a new scene.

2 Paint strokes

- In the **Rendering** menu set, select **Paint Effects** → **Get Brush**...

- In the Visor, select the *flowers* directory, then click on the *sunflower.mel* brush preset.

Doing so will automatically load the brush preset, and will activate the Paint Effects Tool.

- Paint directly on the grid in your scene.

Sunflowers will spawn at your stroke path.

3 Share one brush

Each time you click and draw a line in the viewport, a stroke and brush are created. This lets you customize each stroke individually, but doing so also makes it difficult to change the look of all the strokes at the same time. Fortunately, you can specify that all the strokes share the same brush, which will allow you to tweak only a single brush for all your strokes.

Sunflowers painted directly in the view

- Open the Outliner.

You should see all the different strokes you have just drawn.

- Select all the strokes.

- Select **Paint Effects** → **Share One Brush**.

Now all the strokes use the same brush. Modifying this brush will change all the strokes at the same time.

4 Render

- Render the scene using the Maya Software Renderer.

Maya Software Render

Convert Paint Effects

In order to be able to render Paint Effects into another renderer, you must convert the strokes to geometry. Doing so will conserve the history of the strokes, so you will still be able to tweak the look of the strokes, modify their animation and change the conversion resolution.

1 Scene file

- Continue using the scene created in the last exercise.

2 Convert to polygons

- Select all the strokes.

- Select **Modify** → **Convert** → **Paint Effects to Polygons**.

The strokes are now converted to polygons.

3 Change the resolution of the geometry

- Select the geometry and open the Attribute Editor.

- Select the *sunflower1* tab.

This is the original brush used to paint the sunflowers.

- Tweak the brush attributes and see how the polygonal geometry gets updated.

Note: *Any attributes controlling the shaded look of the strokes will not get updated. This is because materials were created to shade the geometry and these materials are not connected to the strokes.*

Alias *My favorite tool is Artisan. The brush paradigm is so natural for users.*
Tip: *Having the ability to select, paint, edit and animate attributes as well as add, remove and sculpt geometry with a brush is a powerful high-level interface to what would otherwise require tedious and error prone manipulation of many individual elements.*

Shai Hinitz | Sr. Product Manager

4 Playback the scene

▪ Playback the scene.

Notice the original Paint Effects stroke is animated, so the geometry is also animated because of construction history.

5 Render using the Vector Renderer

▪ Render the scene using the Maya Vector Renderer.

Paint Effects is now renderable with other renderers

Toon

The **Toon** menu under the **Rendering** menu set allows you to give a cartoon look to your geometry. Through this menu, you can control the fill color of the geometry along with its outline. As you will see in this exercise, you can assign Paint Effects strokes to the outlines, thus giving a more refined cartoon look.

1 Scene file

▪ Open the scene file called *11-meeperCartoon_01.ma*.

2 Assign an outline

▪ Select all the *Meeper* geometry.

▪ Select **Toon** → **Assign Outline** → **Add New Toon outline**.

A new pfxToon node is created, allowing you to customize the outline of the geometry.

Tip: *To speed up the view, toggle* **Show** → **Strokes**.

3 Change the camera background color

- Select **Toon** → **Set Camera Background Color** → **Persp**.

- In the displayed **Color Chooser**, select white as the background color.

4 Assign a Paint Effects brush

- Select the *pfxToon1* node from the Outliner.

- Select **Paint Effects** → **Get Brush...**

- In the Visor, select the *pencils* directory, then click on the *pencilScribbleDark.mel* brush preset.

- Select **Toon** → **Assign Paint Effects Brush to Toon Lines**.

The Toon outline is now composed by the selected Paint Effects brush.

5 Tweak the Toon outline

- Select the *pfxToon1* node from the Outliner and open its Attribute Editor.

- Under the *pfxToonShape1* tab, open the **Screenspace Width Control** and set the following:

    Screenspace Width to **On**;

    Distance Scaling to **0.8**.

- Render the scene.

Enabling the **Screenspace Width** *option sets the width of the Paint Effects strokes relative to the rendered image size rather than scene size. This means that the size of the strokes will stay the same even if Meeper walks away or comes close to the camera.*

Project Three

Meeper with Toon outline

6 Change the fill color

As you can see in the previous render, you have only specified the outlines of the geometry, and not the fill color of Meeper.

- Select all the *Meeper* geometry.
- Select **Toon** → **Assign Fill Shader** → **Solid Color**.

A new white surface shader will be created and assigned to the Meeper geometry.

Note: *You could create various fill shaders. Experiment with them if you so wish.*

- Render the scene.

Meeper with Toon outline and white fill color

Lesson 11

7 Tweak the outlines

There are several options you can tweak to customize the Toon outlines.

- Select the *pfxToon* node.

- Open the Attribute Editor.

- Change the various settings that control the different line types.

- Change the fill color if wanted.

- Render your scene to see the effects of your changes.

Meeper with Toon outline and two color fill

8 Save your work

- The final scene file is named *11-meeperCartoon_02.ma*.

> **Alias** *Maya Paint Effects is still the coolest thing going for me. It continues to blow*
> **Tip:** *my mind how I can create such realistic looking natural scenes with so little*
> *effort (and artistic talent, but that's another story). I saw the beginnings of this*
> *demo'd long before it found its way into the product, and it was something*
> *that made me think, "Now *this* is why I got into computer graphics.*
>
> *Kevin Picott | Principal Engineer*

Conclusion

In this lesson, you experimented with some simple Paint Effects and Toon features. Maya Paint Effects enables you to create good-looking scene content very quickly. On top of the extensive library of brush presets already included with Maya, you can edit presets to create new customized brushes. You also learned how to render Paint Effects into other renderers by converting Paint Effects to geometry. Lastly, you used the Toon features, along with Paint Effects, to quickly give a full cartoon style to your geometry.

In the next project, you will learn how to create photorealistic images by using the mental ray renderer.

Project Four

Lessons

In Project Four, you will overview some advanced features of the mental ray renderer. Some of the features you will experience here can greatly improve your renders and add that certain quality that makes photorealistic CG images believable.

Caustics & Global Illumination

Caustics are light patterns formed by focused light. They are created when light from a source illuminates a diffuse surface by way of one or more specular reflections or transmissions. Examples of Caustic effects include the hot spots seen on surfaces when light is focused through a refractive glass or reflected off metal, or the patterns created on the bottom of a swimming pool from light shining through the water.

In this lesson you will learn the following:

- How to use Caustics;

- How to fine-tune Caustics;

- How to use Global Illumination;

- How to fine-tune Global Illumination.

Direct illumination

Direct illumination occurs when a light source directly illuminates an object or objects in a scene. Indirect illumination occurs if light illuminates objects by reflection or transmission by other objects. Global Illumination is the technique used to describe indirect illumination. Indirect illumination includes Global Illumination, Final Gather and effects such as Caustics.

Since Global Illumination and Caustics cannot be simulated efficiently using standard raytracing methods, mental ray uses a mechanism based on photon maps. Light is emitted from the source in the form of energy, called photons. Photons are followed as they bounce around a scene until they are either absorbed or escape to infinity. The absorbed photons are then stored in a Photon Map and used at render time to calculate illumination in a scene. Photons can be emitted from standard light sources, as well as from user defined photon emitting shaders.

Caustics

In this exercise, you will learn to enable Caustics and fine-tune the effects.

1 Scene file

- Open the scene file called *12-cognacGlass_01.ma*.

- Render the scene to see the initial results using software rendering.

This is a simple scene consisting of a glass and a spot light. The glass and its contents have refractive materials, and the spot light casts raytraced shadows. You can see that the shadows cast by the glass are properly colored and transparent, but the image lacks the hot spots usually seen when light shines through glass.

Initial software render

2   Enable Caustics

- Open the **Render Settings** window and change **Render Using** to **mental ray**.

- In the **mental ray** tab, go to the **Quality Presets** setting and select the **PreviewCaustics** preset.

- Scroll to the **Raytracing** section and increase the settings as follows:

    Refractions to **6**;

    Max Trace Depth to **8**.

The Refractions value is the number of times the ray must go through a transparent surface before it stops. The Max Trace Depth value should be equal to the reflection rays + refraction rays.

- Scroll to the **Caustics and Global Illumination** section.

*Note that the **Caustics** option is now enabled.*

- Increase **Max Photon Depth** and **Max Refraction Photons** to **6**.

*The photon goes through six transparent surfaces and then stops, hitting a diffuse surface, in this case the wall. Therefore, the default value of **5** would not produce proper results.*

Tip: *In the* **Translation** *section, you can set* **Export Verbosity** *to* **Progress Messages** *in order to check rendering progress messages in the Output Window.*

---

3   Enable photon emission

In order to use Caustics, at least one of the light sources in your scene must emit photons. Each photon emitted by the light source is traced through the scene until it either hits a diffuse surface or until it has been reflected or transmitted a maximum number of times as indicated by **Photon Trace Depth**. The Caustic Photon Map holds just those photons that have been specularly reflected or refracted, before hitting a diffuse surface where they are stored.

Note: *It is also possible to use custom mental ray shaders as photon emitters.*

- In the Hypershade, select the **Lights** tab.

- Select *spotLightShape1* and open its Attribute Editor.

- Scroll to the **mental ray** → **Caustics and Global Illumination** section and set **Emit Photons** to **On**.

- Make sure **Photon Intensity** is set to **8000**.

Photon Intensity *is the amount of light distributed by the light source. Each photon will carry a fraction of the light source energy and distribute it into the scene.*

- Make sure **Caustic Photons** is set to **10000**.

*The number of **Caustic Photons** emitted by the light source will determine the quality of the generated Caustics. More photons produce higher quality results, but also increase memory usage. A suggested workflow is to use the default number of photons or less while tuning your image to produce quick, low quality Caustics. You can increase the number of photons to produce higher quality images.*

- Make sure **Exponent** is set to **2**.

*This attribute acts like decay; the intensity increases as the value decreases. The default value of **2** simulates quadratic (realistic) decay.*

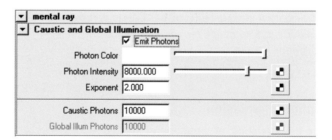

Caustic and Global Illumination light attributes

4   Test render the scene

You should now see Caustic effects around the glass, but the brightness and quality will not be very good; the Caustic effects will be spotty. Further tuning is needed to improve the appearance of Caustics.

Initial results of render with Caustics

5 Fine-tuning Caustics

You may find that the Caustic effects are not bright enough. Raising or lowering the **Photon Intensity** of your light source will increase or decrease the brightness of your Caustics.

- Open the **Attribute Editor** for the light and scroll to the **Caustics and Global Illumination** section.

- Make sure the **Photon Intensity** value is set to **8000**.

- In the **mental ray** tab of the **Render Settings**, scroll to the **Caustics and Global Illumination** section.

The appearance of Caustics can be fine-tuned using the Caustic Accuracy and Radius settings.

- Increase **Caustic Radius** to **1.5** or **2** by small increments and test render to see its results.

Caustic Radius *controls the maximum distance at which mental ray considers photons. For example, to specify that only photons within 1 scene unit away should be used, set* **Caustic Radius** *to* **1**. *When* **Caustic Radius** *is left at the default value of* **0**, *the renderer will itself calculate an appropriate radius based on your scene size. However, this default result is not always acceptable, as in this case. Increasing the* **Caustic Radius** *will generally decrease noise but give a more blurred result. To decrease noise without blurring details, it would be necessary to increase the number of Caustic photons emitted by your light source.*

- Increase **Caustic Accuracy** to **100** by small increments and **test render** to see its results.

Lesson 12

Caustic Accuracy *controls how many photons are considered during rendering. The default is 64; larger numbers make the Caustics smoother. For example, to specify that at most 100 photons should be used to compute the Caustic brightness, set* **Caustic Accuracy** *to* **100***. You can also use greater values for more accuracy.*

Caustic Radius 2.000, Accuracy 100, Photon Intensity 25000

- In the **Caustics and Global Illumination** section of the **Render Settings**, change **Caustic Filter** to **Cone**.

Changing the **Caustic Filter Type** *to* **Cone** *can produce smoother results.*

Results using Cone filter

- In the **Caustics and Global Illumination** attributes for the light, increase **Caustic Photons** to **20000**.

In order to further increase the quality of Caustic effects, you can increase the amount of emitted photons. This will slow down your rendering time, but improve image quality.

- Further improvements to Caustics generally require experimentation with the light's **Intensity**, **Caustic Photons** and **Exponent** values, as well as the Render Settings' **Caustic Accuracy** and **Caustic Radius** values.

20000 Caustic Photons, Caustic Accuracy 200, Caustic Radius 1.5

6   Save your work

- The final scene file is called *12-cognacGlass_02.ma*.

Global Illumination

In this exercise, you will enable Global Illumination and fine-tune the results.

1   Scene file

- Open the scene file called *12-global_01.ma*.

This scene consists of Meeper's flying saucer in a garage. The garage door is animated open, allowing indirect light to spill into the scene and illuminate its contents.

- Go to the last frame of the animation, where the illumination will be at its fullest.

- Render the scene to see the initial results using software rendering.

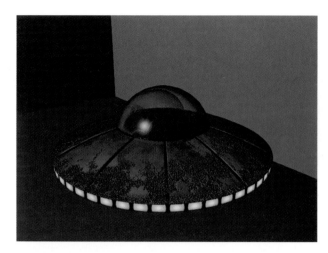

Software render

2   Enable Global Illumination

- Open the **Render Settings** window and change your selected renderer to **mental ray**.

- Go to the **Quality Presets** and select **PreviewGlobalIllum**.

Note that if you scroll to the **Caustics and Global Illumination** *section, the* **Global Illumination** *is now enabled.*

3   Enable photon emission

As with Caustics, at least one of the light sources in your scene must emit photons.

- From the Outliner, select the *spotLight* and open the Attribute Editor.

- Under the **Spot Light Attributes** section, set **Intensity** to **0.3**.

This means that most of the illumination in the scene will come from photons.

- Scroll to the **mental ray → Caustics and Global Illumination** section and set **Emit Photons** to **On**.

- Leave **Photon Intensity** at the default **8000**.

- Leave **Exponent** at its default value of **2** for now.

- Leave **Global Illum Photons** at the default number **10000**.

4   Test render the scene

There is very little, if any, illumination in the scene. Further tuning is needed.

Note: *If you get a message stating "no photons stored after emitting 10000 photons," it means that photons emitted by the source don't hit any energy storing object. One reason this can happen is the photon emitting source is emitting photons in the wrong direction.*

5   Change the Exponent value

As mentioned in the previous exercise, the **Exponent** attribute represents decay.

- To increase the chances of photons reaching the back of the garage, decrease the **Exponent** attribute to **1**.

- Render the scene.

6   Change the Photon Intensity values

You can now see the effect of the Global Illumination at the back of the garage and on the floor a little more clearly but you may find that overall the scene is still not bright enough.

- Change the **Photon Intensity** value to **15000**.

- Render the scene.

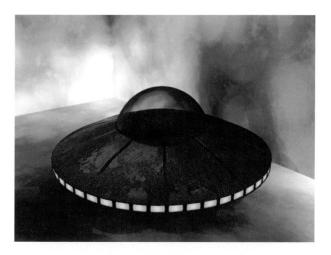

Exponent 1, Photon Intensity 15000

Lesson 12

7 Change the Global Illumination radius

The scene is bright enough, but now we need to further fine-tune
the photons.

- In the **mental ray** tab of the **Render Settings**, open the **Caustics and Global Illumination** section.

- Set the **Global Illum Radius** to **1** and test render the scene.

Increasing this value will help smooth out the photons and reduce blotchiness.

- If you still find that your photons are not smooth enough, increase the **Global Illum Radius** to **2**.

Tip: *Using the* **Keep Image** *button in the Render View window menu bar will allow you to compare current renders to previous renders.*

- Continue increasing the radius until you see little or no change in image quality.

When you reach the point where changing the **Global Illum Radius** *has little effect on the image, start increasing your* **Global Illum Accuracy** *value.*

8 Increase the accuracy

- Increase the **Global Illumination Accuracy** values.

This will further refine your photons, helping to smooth them.

Radius 2, Global Illumination Accuracy 900

Global Illumination and Shadows

9   Further refinements

Most illumination in this scene comes solely from photons. You may find that the shadow information created this way is either weak or absent. The following image was rendered using soft raytraced shadows. This helps add depth to the scene and separate the ship from the background.

10 Save your work

- The final scene file is called *12-global_02.ma*.

Conclusion

Adding Caustics and Global Illumination to your scenes can help create more subtle and realistic light effects.

In the next lesson, you will learn about Final Gather and HDRI, which can also be used to bump up shadow information.

Final Gather in mental ray is a process that can be used with Global Illumination to obtain a finer level of diffuse detail resolve, and it can also be used by itself as an independent rendering alternative.

In this lesson you will learn the following:

- Final Gather;

- How to set up Final Gather rendering;

- How to combine Final Gather with Global Illumination;

- How to use HDRI;

- How to use image based lighting.

Final Gather

With Final Gather (FG), mental ray calculates the scene irradiance or total incoming illumination in the scene. Every object in your scene is, in effect, a light source. It is possible, therefore, to render a scene without any lights. This can be a very useful technique.

It is important to note that one ray generation is used in the Final Gather process. This differs from Global Illumination Photon Mapping, where photons bounce around many times. Final Gather allows for one Final Gather ray emission and then contact with a surface to determine if there is a diffuse light contribution to the emitting surface points color value. Final Gather does not allow for multiple diffuse light bounces. It will calculate color bleeding and diffuse contributions from the first surface, but not from a secondary surface.

With Final Gather, a semi-hemispherical area above the point to be shaded is sampled to determine the indirect and direct illumination. This semi-hemispherical area is defined by the **Min Radius** and **Max Radius** values found in the **Final Gather** section of the Render Settings.

Not all points are sampled with this approach. Rather, an averaging of nearby points is calculated, and this value is used for the sampled point. This technique is used, as Final Gather ray generation is too expensive to calculate for all sampled points.

The final result of the FG process is a value for how much light is incident upon each point in the scene.

Final Gather is useful in the following situations:

- In very diffuse scenes where indirect illumination changes slowly;

- In the elimination of low frequency noise when using Global Illumination, as well as low photon emission values;

- With finer detail resolution;

- When combined with Global Illumination, a more physically accurate solution is possible;

- For convincing soft shadow techniques;

- To help eliminate dark corners.

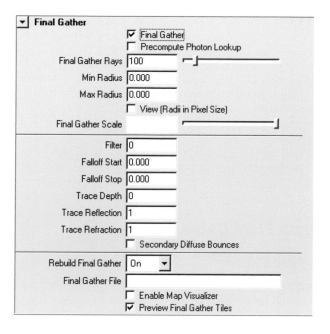

Final Gather default Render Settings

Final Gather Rays

This is the number of rays that are sent out from each sampled point. The default value is **100**. When rendering out for production, more **Final Gather Rays** will be required.

Min Radius and Max Radius

The **Min Radius** and **Max Radius** attributes control the size of the sampling region within which the Final Gather rays search for irradiance information from other surfaces.

With the default **0.0** values, mental ray will calculate values that seem appropriate based on scene dimensions. This will speed things up. However, using the default values does not allow for a specific scene's individual geometry complexity. Ultimately, you will want to enter your own scene specific Min Radius and Max Radius values for optimal Final Gather results.

Typically, a good rule is to take 10% of your scene's overall dimension in units for the Max Radius, and then take 10% of that value for the Min Radius. Again, this is a starting point, as a particular scene may contain geometry that requires lesser or greater values for proper detail resolution.

Min Radius and Max Radius are functions of scene geometry detail level and how it is arranged in the scene. Every scene will be different and will require some initial adjusting for optimum results.

> **Note:** *In the section on combining Global Illumination and Final Gather, the interior architectural scene benefits from adjusting the default Min Radius and Max Radius values. This adjustment creates better diffuse detailing between the duct work and ceiling and along the stairs.*

Speeding up Final Gather

Rebuild Final Gather

This is the default setting and will ignore any Final Gather map that has been generated previously. Turning this off will force Final Gather to use the results from a previous Final Gather render if an FG map was created. Use of this toggle will speed the Final Gather considerably.

It is important to note that if the number of rays is changed, the Final Gather map will be ignored and new Final Gather rays will be emitted. A glance into the Output window will reveal the following message in such an event:

```
RCFG 0.2  info : finalgMap/test1: final gather options differ from
ones currently used, content ignored
```

```
RCFG 0.2  info : overwriting final gather file "finalgMap/test1"
```

If you are rendering out a still image and are not changing the Final Gather settings, turning the **Rebuild Final Gather** off can save considerable time.

When rendering out a camera animation sequence, it may be possible to get away with the Final Gather calculations of the previous frames. This will depend on how the irradiance changes during the course of the camera animation. In such an event, considerable time can be saved if the **Rebuild Final Gather** is disabled. However, if there are objects in the scene that are moving, the irradiance values for the scene will have to be re-computed for each subsequent frame.

Final Gather File

Final Gather File allows Final Gather results to be stored in a file. This allows later frames to reuse Final Gather results from a frame rendered earlier. The file is saved into the current project's *mentalRay\finalgMap* directory.

Project Four

To create a Final Gather map, do the following:

- Set **Rebuild Final Gather** to **On**;

- Enter a file name in the **Final Gather File** field;

- Render the scene.

Irradiance

Irradiance can most easily be defined as total incoming illumination. It is an environmental lighting parameter that determines the amount of light that is incident upon a surface. The following attributes are found on each material's Attribute Editor, under the **mental ray** section.

Irradiance attribute

This attribute is used to map an incoming *illumination map*, such as one created using **Convert to File Texture**, mental ray, or other texture map that may have been created. With this shader attribute mapped, the Final Gather solution takes the irradiance information from the texture map and not from surrounding surfaces.

Irradiance Color attribute

This attribute controls the effects of photon mapping and Final Gather on a surface. For example, if a red ball is sitting on a white diffuse plane, the plane will acquire a red tinge from the ball. Irradiance Color allows for the control of this color bleeding effect.

Using Final Gather

With this series of workflows, you will discover that Final Gather can be affected and adjusted in several ways. The Final Gather solution can be affected by:

- The number of Final Gather rays;

- The Min Radius and Max Radius;

- The camera background color;

- Colored incandescence in the scene;

- Ambient color in the scene;

- Irradiance contributions from shaders;

- Irradiance color mapping contributions from shaders;

- Whether there are lights in the scene and their locations.

Lesson 13

Another technique for overall illumination, when doing a Final Gather render, includes the use of *HDRI* or *High Dynamic Range Image*, or using an out of camera view dummy surface (light card) with an Incandescence value.

1   Scene file

- Open the scene file called *13-finalGather_01.ma*.

The scene file consists of a flying saucer sitting on a ground plane. There is one directional light in the scene. The dome shader has a slight incandescence value. This is the illumination or irradiance contribution in the scene.

Note: **Incandescence** *could be supplanted with* **Ambient Color** *to get the same effect.*

2   Disable Illuminates by Default

It is important to turn off the directional lights' **Illuminates by Default**, since all illumination will come from Final Gather rays.

- Go to the *directionalLight*'s Attribute Editor and under the **Directional Lights Attributes**, set the **Illuminates by Default** attribute to **Off**.

Note: *It is important to note that color bleed will not occur in your scene if there are no lights, colored incandescence, or ambient color.*

3   Final Gather rendering

- In the Render Settings, change the **Render Using** to **mental ray**.
- Scroll down to the **Final Gather** section and set **Final Gather** to **On**.
- Make sure the number of **Final Gather Rays** is set to **100**.

This will speed the render time up considerably. This is a good starting point for test renders.

- Keep the **Min Radius** and **Max Radius** values at **0.0**.
- Render the scene.

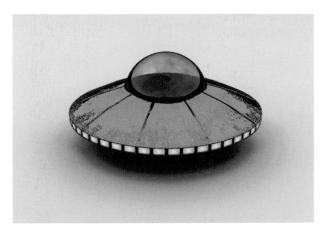

Final Gather render - no lights - no color bleed

Notice the soft shadows on the underside of the flying saucer. The points being shaded under the ship are hidden from the scene irradiance, and from the illumination contribution from the incandescence on the dome shader. This results in a soft shadow effect.

Note: *The scene will render out black if there are no lights or irradiance contribution from other surfaces in the scene. Try increasing and decreasing the dome shader's incandescence value. With a low value, the scene will render out dark because there is little irradiance in the scene from any source. With a high value, the scene will render brighter because there is more irradiance in the scene.*

4   Color bleed

Now, you will look at some techniques for introducing and adjusting color bleed when using the Final Gather process.

- Set the **Illuminates by Default** checkbox for the *directionalLight* to **On**.

- Render out the scene.

Notice the color bleed from the orange ship onto the white floor. This is caused by the directional light.

Lesson 13

Final Gather color bleed

- Go to the **mental ray** section of the floor shader's **Attribute Editor**.

- Decrease the **Irradiance Color** very slightly.

- Render out the scene.

Notice the decrease in color bleed and the darkening of the floor.

Tip: *Another technique that can be useful is mapping the* **Irradiance Color** *attribute of a shader with a file texture.*

5 Color bleed with no lights

With no lights in the scene, it is still possible to achieve the color bleed effect.

- Set the **Illuminates by Default** checkbox for the *directionalLight* to **Off**.

- Adjust the **Ambient Color** or add colored incandescence to the ship's ramp shader.

- Render again.

Notice the color bleed, which is now everywhere underneath the ship.

Note: *With this scene, the default Final Gather Min Radius and Max Radius values of 0 are sufficient for good image quality. With the interior architecture scene, adjusting these values will give better image quality.*

Final Gather color bleed - no lights

Note: *Another technique for contributing lighting levels in a Final Gather rendered scene is changing the camera's background color to a value other than black. Go to the camera's Attribute Editor to change the Environment Background Color to gray and render the scene.*

Final Gather and Global Illumination example

Using Final Gather and Global Illumination together results in very fine diffuse detail resolution. The technique is particularly useful for interior architectural shots where lighting definition is a function of light contribution from interior and exterior sources.

In this exercise, you will set up daylight lighting in a loft and then set up Global Illumination. Once the scene is correctly illuminated using photon mapping, you will add Final Gather.

1 Scene file

- Open the scene file called *13-FgGi_01.ma*.

The scene contains an interior architectural shot with attendant lights and shaders. There are pre-positioned lights in the scene: three linked spot lights for the translucent panels over the kitchen area, one linked directional light for exterior lighting, one spot light on the outside for interior direct illumination and shadows, and two spot lights for the lampshade over the dining area.

Lesson 13

2 Set up the exterior light

- Select *spotLight5* and change the **Decay Rate** to **Quadratic** and the **Intensity** to **2500**.

This light is used for direct illumination and primary shadow generation.

- Enable **Raytrace Shadows**.

Note: *When setting up Global Illumination and Final Gather, use the quadratic decay rate. This ensures that light levels in the scene decrease in intensity based on the inverse square law.*

3 The translucent panels

The three translucent panels in the kitchen generate warm light effects. The three spot lights overhead need to be linked to the translucent panels.

- Select **Window** → **Relationship Editor** → **Light Linking** → **Light Centric**.
- Link the three spot lights to the translucent panels as follows:

  spotLight1 linked to *panel1*.

  spotLight2 linked to *panel2*;

  spotLight3 linked to *panel3*;

4 Exterior lighting

- Link *directionalLight1* to the exterior *wall1* geometry.

5 The lamp shade

There are two spots lights in this lampshade arrangement. The top spot light needs to be linked to the lampshade geometry. The bottom spot light that fits just inside the lampshade is used for direct illumination, shadow generation and photon emission.

- Link *spotlight6* to the *lamp1* geometry.

Doing so allows for controlled illumination of the warm light effect on the lampshade geometry.

- Select *spotLight4* and change the **Intensity** to **45** and **Decay Rate** to **Quadratic**.

The intensity of spotLight4 will be increased later, when Global Illumination and Final Gather are enabled.

6 Render set up

- Open the **Render Settings** and make sure to render using mental ray.

- Render the scene.

Because there is no Global Illumination occurring in the scene, the render is only using the direct illumination from the lights in the scene for illumination. If you render this scene out using the Software Renderer, the result will be almost the same.

No Global Illumination - no Final Gather

Global Illumination

You will now enable Global Illumination in the scene.

1 Enable Global Illumination

- Open the **Render Settings** and set **Global Illumination** to **On**.

- Set the following:

  Global Illumination Accuracy to **450**;

  Global Illumination Radius to **6.0**.

2 Photon emission

- Select *spotLight4* and set **Emit Photons** to **On**.

- Set the following:

  Photon Intensity to **2000**;

  Exponent to **2.0**;

  Global Illumination Photons to **25000**.

3 Render

- Render the scene.

Notice how the scene gets a warm tone from the yellow lighting.

Global Illumination - no Final Gather

Final Gather

1 Disable Global Illumination

- Set **Emit Photons** to **Off** in the Attribute Editor of *spotLight4*.

- Set **Global Illumination** to **Off** in the **Render Settings**.

2 Enable Final Gather

- Set **Final Gather** to **On** in the **Render Settings**.

3 Adjust Final Gather Rays

- In the **Final Gather** section of **Render Settings**, change the number of **Final Gather Rays** to **125**.

*This is a good value for test rendering. For a higher quality render, **400 - 600** rays will give very fine detailing.*

4 Adjust the Min Radius and Max Radius

The Min Radius and Max Radius define the search area, within which Final Gather Rays will look for irradiance information from neighboring surfaces. The areas above the ducting, in the far corner, and along the wall on the left, are good examples of where the default 0 and 0 Min Radius and Max Radius values are not sufficient for optimum image quality.

- Set **Min Radius** and **Max Radius** to **8** and **20** respectively.

- Render the scene.

Final Gather - no Global Illumination

Note: *Results may vary from the image shown here.*

Tip: *If your render is too bright, try adjusting the intensity of your lights. If you notice splotchy areas, enabling **Jitter** will sometimes further assist with the removal of these areas.*

Final Gather and Global Illumination

You will now render the interior architectural scene out using Global Illumination and Final Gather.

1 Enable Global Illumination

- In the **Global Illumination and Caustics** section of **Render Settings**, set **Global Illumination** back **On**.

2 Pre-compute Photon Lookup

The **Pre-compute Photon Lookup** toggle arranges irradiance to be stored with the photon map when Global Illumination is enabled. This toggle is only used if Global Illumination is turned on, i.e. photon emission is occurring in the scene. Fewer Final Gather points are required with this option, as the photon map will carry a good approximation of the irradiance in the scene. This is because irradiance can be estimated with a single lookup instead of using a large number of photons. Enabling this feature will slow the Photon Mapping phase but will speed the Final Gather process. Ultimately, the render will be faster with this feature enabled.

- Go to the **Final Gather** section of **Render Settings** and turn **Pre-compute Photon Lookup** On.

- Turn back on the *spotlight4*'s **Emit Photons** attribute.

3 Render the scene

Notice the areas under the table are now correctly illuminated. With the Quadratic Decay, light interacts with surfaces based on real world physics. The scene is now correctly illuminated.

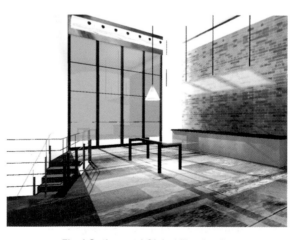

Final Gather and Global Illumination

> **Tip:** To increase or decrease the overall lighting levels, adjust the **Photon Intensity** value of spotlight4.

High Dynamic Range Image

The Final Gather process can also make use of a *High Dynamic Range Image* (HDRI), as the basis for illumination information in a scene. This is known as *image based lighting*.

High Dynamic Range Image nappaValley.tif

An HDRI has an extra floating point value that is used to describe the exponent or persistence of light at any given pixel. This overall illumination information is used in the Final Gather process. Low Dynamic Range Image (LDRI), the kind of image that everyone is familiar with, has limitations when it comes to describing the range of colors necessary to correctly describe light values precisely. Think of a dark cathedral with strong light spilling through a stained glass window - the range from dark to bright is too broad for a conventional LDRI. Such an LDRI will have overexposed and very black areas.

Pixels that have a high floating point value (exponential value), are not affected very much by a darkening of the overall image. Pixels that have a lower persistence of light would be affected more by this same darkening operation.

Creating your own HDRI involves taking several shots of the same subject matter with bracketed f stops and then assembling the images into a floating point tiff HDRI. There are applications available for this purpose.

Lesson 13

HRDI example

In this exercise, you will use the HDRI *nappaValley.tif* as the source of illumination and reflection for the flying saucer.

1 Scene file

- Open the scene file called *13-HDRI_01.ma*.

The scene contains the flying saucer, a ground and a giant dome surface.

2 Create and apply the HDRI shading network

- In the Hypershade, select the dome shader.

- Map a **File** texture to the dome's **Ambient Color**.

- Browse for the *nappaValley.tif* file found in the *sourceImages* directory.

Note: *When loading an HDRI into Maya, a warning message will be generated specifying that Maya cannot read the HDRI. Ignore this message since mental ray can handle that type of file just fine.*

3 Render Settings

- In the **Render Settings**, set **Final Gather** to **On**.

- Make sure the number of **Final Gather Rays** is set to **100**.

This is sufficient for testing purposes. Leave the other settings' attributes at their default settings.

4 Render

- Render the scene.

Notice the yellow highlight on the left of the ship while the other side is more blueish. These colors are coming from the HDRI.

HDRI used as background and illumination source

> **Tip:** You may need to increase the Final Gather Rays to obtain good shadow quality.

5 Adjust the effect

- To adjust the effect of the HDRI irradiance contribution, go to the **Color Balance** section of the HDRI's file texture node and change the values to your needs.

Increasing the brightness of the image will increase the amount of light contribution in the scene.

6 Save your work

- Save the scene as *13-HDRI_02.ma.*

Image based lighting

In the previous HDRI exercise, you enclosed scenes using a dome surface and mapped it with an HDRI texture. While this workflow is appropriate if a finite distance to the environment is required, it can have several issues when environment is infinitely distant. Because the sphere is geometry, mental ray processes it as such (i.e. it is tessellated) and this can, at times, slow down a render significantly.

With Image Based Lighting (IBL), you can use the HDRI to simulate light from an infinitely distant environment. This is a much quicker and easier method for setting up HDRI, and is also faster to render and more effective for distant environments, such as sky. Virtual lights can be derived from the environment image which can cast shadows and contribute to Final Gather and Global Illumination simulations.

1 Open the scene file

- Open the scene file called *13-IBL_01.ma.*

This is the same scene as you used for the HDRI exercise, except that there is no sky dome, Final Gather is disabled and there is no light source.

2 Create the IBL sphere

- Open the mental ray Render Settings.

- Scroll down to the **Image Based Lighting** section and click the **Create** button.

A mental ray environment sphere will be created and placed at the origin.

Lesson 13

3 Map the image

- In the Attribute Editor for the *mentalraylblShape1* node, under **Image Based Lighting Attributes**, map *nappaValley.tif* file to **Image Name**.

- Render the scene.

Render using image based lighting

Tip: *Experiment with different values for* **Color Gain** *and* **Color Offset** *to achieve the effect that you desire.*

4 Adjusting illumination

You may find the scene is lacking shadows. The **Emit Light** option will further illuminate your scene.

- In the Attribute Editor for the *mentalraylblShape1* node, under the **Light Emission** section, set **Emit Light** to **On**.

This will allow us to emit light from the infinitely distant IBL environment.

- Set both **Quality U** and **Quality V** to **64**.

These values represent the resolution for a control texture for light emission. Every pixel in that texture corresponds to a virtual directional light. The higher these values, the longer it will take to render, so it's best to start with low values and gradually increase them.

5   Adjust samples

To sample all the directional lights in the control texture would be very expensive. The **Samples** attribute allows you to control the sampling of the strongest lights. The first parameter specifies the number of important lights that must be sampled. The second parameter quasi-randomly selects a certain number of remaining light. The higher the sample values, the longer the render.

- Set the first **Samples** parameter to a value of **10** and the second to a value of **4**.

- Render the scene.

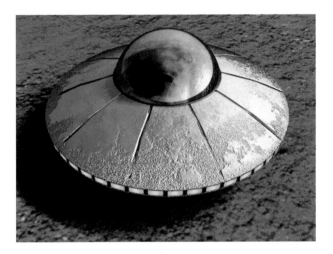

Image based lighting results with Emit Light option

Tip: *If you find that the **Emit Light** option is slowing down your render too much, you can add regular lights into the scene for illumination instead.*

6   Save your work

- Save the scene as *13-IBL_02.ma*.

Conclusion

Final Gather and HDRI both allow precise diffuse light contributions in your scene and can help to create photorealistic images.

In the next lesson, you will learn about some of the mental ray shaders.

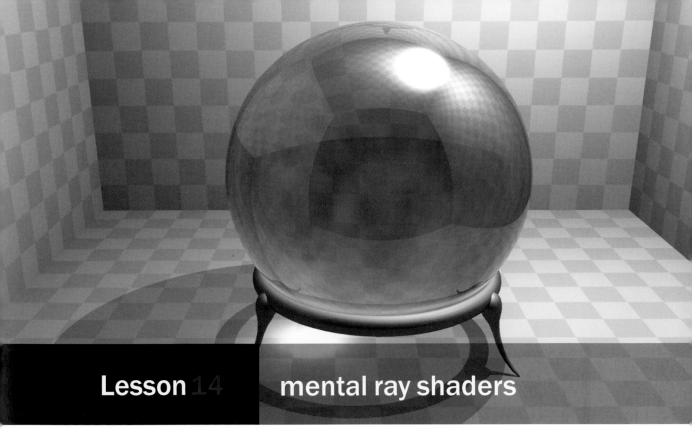

Lesson 14   mental ray shaders

mental ray supports all Maya shaders, textures and lights, but it is also possible to use custom mental ray shaders. This lesson will cover several examples of how to use custom mental ray shaders to create complex effects that may not be easily reproduced using another renderer.

In this lesson you will learn the following:

- mental ray's shader library;

- How to use mental ray material shaders, photon shaders, shadow shaders, volume shaders and light shaders;

- How to create a mental ray double-sided shader;

- How to use contour shaders;

- How to view the mental ray approximation node tessellation structure;

- How to build an Elliptical Filtering shading network;

- How to assemble a mental ray bump map;

- How to create a mental ray phenomenon.

Shader library

mental ray includes an extensive library of custom mental ray shaders. In addition to standard shaders, user defined shaders written in standard C or C++ can be precompiled and linked at runtime, or can be both compiled and linked at runtime.

You can create mental ray custom shaders the same way you create Maya shading nodes, which is either within the Hypershade **Create** bar, the Hypershade **Create** menu, or the **Create Render Node** window.

mental ray shader nodes are available by default in the Hypershade. If the Hypershade does not include the **mental ray** section in the **Create Render Node** window, the mental ray plug-in is probably not loaded. Use the **Window** → **Settings/Preferences** → **Plug-in Manager** to load the *Mayatomr.mll* plug-in.

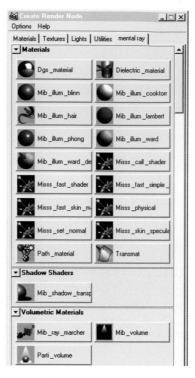

mental ray shader section of the Create Render Node window

Note: It is possible to selectively load and unload the mental ray libraries using the Shader Manager. This handy interface is located under **Window** → **Rendering Editors** → **mental ray** → **Shader Manager**.

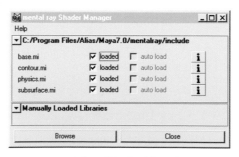

mental ray Shader Manager

Material shaders

The mental ray material shaders are similar to the Maya surface materials.

Two mental ray material shaders will be discussed here: *dgs_material* and *dielectric_material*. These two shaders implement different physically based models of reflection and refraction.

The *dgs* in *dgs_material* stands for *diffuse-glossy-specular*. The *dgs_material* shader can simulate mirrors, glossy paint or plastic, anisotropic glossy materials such as brushed metal, diffuse materials such as paper, translucent materials such as frosted glass and any combination of these.

The *dielectric_material* shader is a physically based material shader which can be used to simulate dielectric media such as glass, water and other liquids.

In this exercise, you will learn to use these mental ray material shaders.

1 Scene file

- Open the file called *14-crystalBall_01.ma*.

This scene has been set up for rendering with mental ray using Caustics. There is one point light in the scene and it has been set to emit photons. The objects in the scene use regular Maya shaders.

- Render the scene.

Crystal ball render with Caustics

2 Assign a mental ray material shader

You will use mental ray custom shaders to replace the regular phong shader on the crystal ball.

- Select the *crystal ball* surface.

- Open Hypershade and click the **Graph Materials on Selected Objects** button.

This will display the phong1 material and the phong1SG shading group.

- Select *phong1SG* and open the Attribute Editor.

- In the *phong1SG* tab, expand the **mental ray** → **Custom Shaders** attributes section.

Lesson 14

- Open the **Create mental ray Nodes** bar in Hypershade and expand the **Materials** section.

- **MMB-click+drag** a *dielectric_material* node to the *phong1SG's* **Material Shader** attribute.

> **Note:** *The dielectric material has built-in absorption fresnel reflection. It simulates dielectric media very well. Technically, a dielectric material is a poor conductor of electricity but is a good supporter of electrostatic fields. Dielectric materials are generally solid. Some examples include porcelain, ceramic, plastics and glass.*

3 Assign a mental ray photon shader

The regular Maya shaders such as phong, lambert and blinn, have photon attributes by default. This is not the case with mental ray material shaders; in order to use photonic effects such as Caustics with a mental ray material shader, a photon shader must be connected to the shading group.

- Select *phong1SG* and open its Attribute Editor.

- In the *phong1SG* tab, expand the **mental ray** → **Custom Shaders** attributes section.

- Open the **Create mental ray Nodes** bar in Hypershade and expand the **Photonic Materials** section.

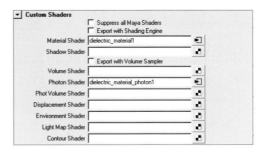

Custom material and photon shaders

- **MMB-click+drag** a *dielectric_material_photon* node to the *phong1SG's* **Photon Shader** attribute.

4 Change the settings for the custom shaders

The various settings for the custom mental ray shaders are at zero by default; they must be changed in order for the shaders to render properly. You can read more about the settings for these custom shaders in the mental ray shader reference section of the Maya documentation.

- Select *dielectric_material1* in the Hypershade and open its Attribute Editor.

- Set the **Col** attribute as follows:

  H to **198**;

  S to **0.13**;

  V to **1.0**.

- Set the **Index of Refraction (Ior)** attribute to **2.0**.

2.0 is the refractive index of crystal.

- Set the **Phong_coef** attribute to **140**.

This setting is used to compute normalized phong highlights. It is similar to the **Cosine Power** *attribute of a regular phong shader.*

Tip: *If* **Phong_coef** *is zero, only reflected rays will create highlight effects. Therefore,* **Phong_coef** *could be left at zero if Final Gather or a mental ray physical light was being used to light the scene. This is not the case in this scene, so the* **Phong_coef** *attribute must be set in order for there to be highlights on the material. If the* **Col_out** *color is different from the color for* **Col** *and the* **Ior_out** *value is different than zero, the reflected color will be a combination of the two colors (***Col_out** *and* **Col***).*

- Select the *dielectric_material_photon1* node and open its Attribute Editor.

- The settings for the *dielectric_material_photon1* shader should match the *dielectric_material1* shader:

  Col to **pale blue**;

  Ior to **2.00**;

  Phong_coef to **140**.

Note: *If the* **Col_out** *color is different from the color for* **Col** *and the* **Ior_out** *value is different than zero, the color of the Caustics will be taken from* **Col_out**.

---

5   Render the scene

You may notice that it renders faster than it did at the beginning of this exercise.

Lesson 14

Crystal ball with dielectric shader

6 Save your work

- Save your scene as *14-crystalBall_02.ma*.

Shadow shaders

It is possible to use mental ray shadow shaders to further customize the appearance of your object's shadows.

Note: *If photon effects such as Caustics or Global Illumination are used, using shadow shaders is generally not recommended because light effects are properly determined by the photons. Shadow shaders used with Caustics or Global Illumination will not produce physically correct results, but can be used to fake certain shadow effects.*

1 Scene file

- Continue with your own scene.

Or

- Open the scene called *14-crystalBall_02.ma*.

2 Assign a shadow shader

- Open the Hypershade and select the *phong1* material.

- Select **Graph** → **Output Connections**.

This will display the phong1SG shading group.

- Select *phong1SG* and open its Attribute Editor.

- Under the *phong1SG* tab, expand the **mental ray** section.

- Expand the **Shadow Shaders** section of the **Create mental ray Nodes** bar in the Hypershade.

- **MMB-click+drag** a *mib_shadow_transparency* node to the *phong1SG*'s **Shadow Shader** attribute.

3 Adjust the shadow shader

- In the Attribute Editor for the *mib_shadow_transparency1* node, set **Mode** to **3**.

Doing so will remove light dependency. You will not get any shadows if you leave this at 0.

- Set the **Color** attribute as follows:

  H to **198**;

  S to **0.3**;

  V to **0.8**.

Doing so will determine the shadow color.

Tip: *You can soften your shadows by enabling Area Light in your light's mental ray attributes in order to convert it to a mental ray area light. This may slow down rendering time.*

---

4 Render the scene

5 Save your work

- Save your scene as *14-crystalBall_03.ma*.

Transparent blue shadow shader

Lesson 14

Volume shaders

Volumetric materials scatter light to a certain degree, and can be used to realistically simulate effects such as fog, smoke, translucent glass, etc. **Volume shaders** can be assigned to particular objects by connecting them to their shading group.

In this exercise, you will apply a volume shader to the crystal ball from the previous exercises.

1 Scene file

- Continue with your own scene.

Or

- Open the scene called *14-crystalBall_03.ma*.

2 Assign a volume shader

- Open the Hypershade and select the *phong1* material.

- Select **Graph** → **Output Connections**.

This will display the phong1SG shading group.

- Select *phong1SG* and open its Attribute Editor.

- Under the *phong1SG* tab, expand the **mental ray** section.

- Expand the **Volumetric Materials** section of the **Create mental ray Nodes** bar in the Hypershade.

- **MMB-click+drag** a *parti_volume* node to the *phong1SG*'s mental ray **Volume Shader** attribute.

> **Note:** *Make sure you connect the volume shader to the shading group's Volume Shader attribute, found in the mental ray attribute section. Do not connect it to the Volume Material attribute found in the Shading Group attributes section.*

3 Assign a photon volume shader

In order for the Caustic effects in this scene to work, the volume shader needs an equivalent photon volume shader as well.

- Expand the **Photonic Materials** section of the **Create mental ray Nodes** bar in the Hypershade.

- **MMB-click+drag** a *parti_volume_photon* node to the *phong1SG*'s mental ray **Photon Volume Shader** attribute.

4   Adjust the volume shader

In order for the volume shaders to render properly, their settings must be adjusted. In this scene, the volume shader and the photon volume shader will use identical settings.

- In the Hypershade, select the *parti_volume1* node and open the Attribute Editor.

- Set the following settings:

  Set **Scatter** to be **aqua**.

  Scatter is the color of the scattering medium.

  Set **Extinction** to **0.3**.

  Extinction *determines how much light is absorbed or scattered in the medium. The higher the value, the denser the medium, and the more light is scattered. A value of* **0** *would indicate clean air or vacuum.*

  Min_step_len to **0.03**;

  Max_step_len to **0.1**.

  Min_step_len and **Max_step_len** *determine the step length for rays marching in a non-homogeneous medium. In other words, they regulate accuracy.*

- Select the *parti_volume_photon* node and give it the same settings.

Tip: *You can also try experimenting with different settings.*

5   Adjust the light energy

Adjust the photon energy to get a nice Caustic effect.

- In the Hypershade's **Lights** tab, select *pointLightShape1* and open its Attribute Editor.

- In the **mental ray** → **Caustics and Global Illumination** section, change the **Photon Intensity** values to between **400** and **1000**.

6 Increase Caustic photon radius

If you render the scene now, you will see dots scattered throughout your image - these are the photons. Increasing the photon radius is one way to correct this effect.

- Open the Render Settings.

- Click on the **mental ray** tab, then scroll to the **Caustics and Global Illumination** section.

- Set **Caustic Radius** to **2.000**.

7 Render the scene

Your crystal ball should now be uniformly translucent.

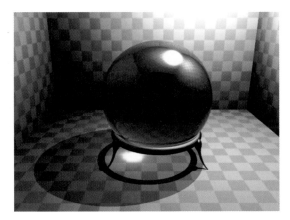

Volume Shader creates translucent glass effect

8 Save your work

- Save your scene as *14-crystalBall_04.ma*.

Volume noise

You will now use some Maya textures and utility nodes to further enhance the appearance of the volume shader.

1 Scene file

- Continue with your own scene.

Or

- Open the scene called *14-crystalBall_04.ma*.

2 Create a volume noise texture

A volume noise texture will be used to color the volume shader's scatter attribute.

- In the **Create Maya Node** bar of the Hypershade, scroll to the **3D Textures** section and create a **Volume Noise** texture.

- Adjust the texture's attributes as follows:

  Amplitude to **0.86**;

  Frequency Ratio to **1.37**;

  Frequency to **10.0**;

  Noise Type to **Wispy**;

  Color Gain to **dull yellow**;

  Color Offset to **dark blue-green**.

3 Connect the volume noise texture to the volume shaders

- Select the *parti_volume1* node in the Hypershade and open its Attribute Editor.

- **MMB-click+drag** the *volumeNoise1* texture to the *parti_volume1*'s **Scatter** attribute.

- Repeat the above steps with the *parti_volume_photon1* node.

4 Adjust the volume shaders

If you render the scene now, you should see a wispy color effect inside your crystal ball, but the smoke is still uniformly distributed. You can increase the **Non-uniform** attribute of the volume shaders to randomize the distribution of the volumetric material. The non-uniform attribute can be set to any number between 0 and 1.

- Select the *parti_volume1* node and increase the **Non-uniform** attribute to **0.95**.

- Repeat the above steps with the *parti_volume_photon1* node.

5 Restrict the height of the smoke

Currently, the volumetric material fills the entire sphere. You can use the volume shader's **Height** attribute to limit the height of the material. When the volume shader's **Mode** value is set to **0**, the volumetric material fills the entire volume. When **Mode** is **1**, there will be clear air or vacuum anywhere above the **Height** setting.

- Select the *parti_volume1* node and open its Attribute Editor.

- Set the **Mode** attribute to **1**.

- Set the **Height** attribute to **3**.

- Repeat the above steps with the *parti_volume_photon1* node.

> **Note:** *To more clearly see the effect of changing the height attribute, try setting the **Ior** attribute to **1** and the **Transp** attribute to **1**. The glass will now render making the volumetric effect much more evident.*

6 Randomize the smoke height

A noise texture will be used to make the height a little less even.

- In the **Create Maya Nodes** bar of the Hypershade, scroll to the **2D Textures** section and create a **Noise** texture.

- Adjust the *noise1* texture's as follows:

  Amplitude to **0.79**;

  Ratio to **0.32**;

  Frequency Ratio to **1.97**;

  Noise Type to **Wispy.**

- Open the **General Utilities** section of the Hypershade and create a **Set Range** node.

*The noise texture's output will return a value between 0 and 1, but the **Height** value for the smoke in the crystal ball should be higher than that. The Set Range utility will allow you to specify a new output range.*

- **MMB-click+drag** the *noise1* texture onto the *setRange1* node and choose **Other** from the pop-up menu.

- In the **Connection Editor**, connect *noise1*'s **Out Alpha** attribute to *setRange1*'s **Value X** attribute.

- Select *setRange1* and open its Attribute Editor.

- Set the following:

  Min X to **2.0**;

  Max X to **4.0**;

> **Old Min** to **0.0**;
>
> **Old Max** to **1.0**.

- **MMB-click+drag** the *setRange1* onto the *parti_volume1* node, then select **Other** from the pop-up menu.

- **Connect** *setRange1*'s **Out Value X** attribute to *parti_volume1*'s **Height** attribute.

- Repeat the previous steps to connect *setRange1*'s **Out Value X** attribute with the *parti_volume_photon1* node's **Height** attribute.

7 Render the scene

The smoke inside the crystal ball now has uneven distribution and height. The *crystalBall_smoke_finished.mb* file has the final results of this exercise.

Smoke effect

8 Save your work

- Save your scene as *14-crystalBall_05.ma*.

Double-sided shaders

The mental ray custom *mib_twosided* shader can be used to create a surface material with different properties for each side of the geometry to which it is assigned (e.g. specular, diffuse, bump). This is known as a double-sided material.

In order to achieve the **double-sided shader** effect with mental ray, you will have to use a different workflow than the one used with Maya.

1 Scene file

- Open the file called *14-doubleSided_01.ma*.

2 Create the required shaders and textures

- In the **Create All Nodes** bar of the Hypershade, create a blinn and a lambert shader.

- Change the *blinn* **Color** to **gold** and the *lambert* **Color** to **deep blue**.

- Scroll to the **2D Textures** section of the Hypershade.

- **MMB-click+drag** a **Bulge** texture on top of the *blinn* shader and choose **Bump Map** from the pop-up menu.

- Open the Attribute Editor for the **2D placement** of the *bulge* texture and set the following values:

  Coverage to **0.675, 1.0**;

  Translate Frame to **0.06, -0.065**;

  Repeat UV to **22.0, 22.0**.

- From the **Create 2D Textures** section of the Hypershade, **MMB-click+drag** a **Grid** texture on top of the *lambert* shader and choose **Bump Map** from the pop-up menu.

- Open the Attribute Editor for the *grid* texture and set the following values:

  U Width to **0.0**;

  V Width to **0.12**.

- Open the Attribute Editor for the *grid*'s 2D placement node and set the following values:

  Repeat UV to **0.0, 50.0**.

3 Create a mib_twosided

- Assign the *blinn* material to the goblet surface.

- With the *blinn* and *lambert* selected, select **Graph → Input and Output Connections** in the Hypershade.

This will display the shading group node used by the materials.

- Select *blinnSG* and open its Attribute Editor.

- Make sure the *blinnSG* tab is selected.

Project Four

- Open the **Create mental ray Nodes** bar in the Hypershade and expand the **Sample Compositing** section.

- **MMB-click+drag** a *mib_twosided* node onto the **Material Shader** port of *blinnSG*.

Doing so will break the existing connection to the blinn material, which is what you want.

4   Assign materials to mib_twosided

- Open the Attribute Editor for the *mib_twosided* node.

- **MMB-click+drag** the lambert material onto the **Front** attribute of *mib_twosided*.

- **MMB-click+drag** the blinn material onto the **Back** attribute of *mib_twosided*.

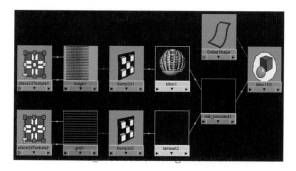

5   Render the scene

- In the Render Settings, set **Render Using** to **mental ray**.

- Render the scene.

mib_twosided used to create a double-sided shader effect

Lesson 14

Light shaders

The mental ray light shaders can be used to replace the regular Maya lights at render time. This workflow will be illustrated in this exercise.

1 Scene file

- Open the file called *14-lightShader_01.ma*.

2 Create a mental ray light shader

- In the **Create mental ray Nodes** bar in the Hypershade, expand the **mentalRay Lights** section and create a *mib_light_spot* node.

- Open the Attribute Editor for the *spotLight* in the scene and scroll to the mental ray → **Custom Shaders** section.

- **MMB-click+drag** the *mib_light_spot* node into the **Light Shader** port of the *spotLight*.

- In the Hypershade, select the *spotLight* node and display its **Input and Output Connections**.

- Open the Attribute Editor for the *coneShape* node and expand the **Render Stats** section.

- Set the following under the Render Stats section:

  Volume Samples Override to **On**;

  Depth Jitter to **On**;

  Volume Samples to **12**.

3 Adjust mib_light_spot node

- Set the **Color** attribute of the *mib_light_spot* to a pale yellow.

- Make sure **Shadow** is set to **On**.

This will result in volumetric shadows.

- Make sure **Attenuation** is set to **On**.

*If **Attenuation** is **On**, the light will start from the **Start** value and will fade at the **Stop** value.*

- Set the **Cone** value to **4**.

Note: *If **Factor** is different than **0**, you will not get a volumetric shadow.*

4   Render the scene

- Render the scene using mental ray.

Light shader with shadows

Tip: *Increase the* **Color** *of the mib_light_spot node to get brighter lighting.*

Contour shaders

In the following image, the Software Renderer was used to create a cartoon-like image of a vase with a ramp shader assigned. It is possible to use mental ray **Contour Shaders** for greater flexibility to achieve similar results.

Ramp shader

Lesson 14

Lesson 14

Contour shaders

Contour shaders, along with other custom mental ray shaders, are found in the Create mental ray Nodes bar of the Hypershade. They are further controlled using the Render Settings' **Contour Lines** section.

In this exercise, you will create a simple toon shader based on normal direction with respect to the camera point of view.

1 Scene file

- Open the file called *14-contour_01.ma*.

The file contains a vase on a table top that will be used to illustrate the general workflow associated with mental ray contour shaders.

2 Assign a new shader

- Apply a new **Blinn** shader to the *vase* geometry.

3 Enable contour rendering

- Click on the **Input and Output Connections** button in the Hypershade for the *blinn1* shader and select the *blinn2SG* node.

- In the *blinn2SG* node's Attribute Editor, expand the **mental ray** → **Contours** section and set **Enable Contour Rendering** to **On**.

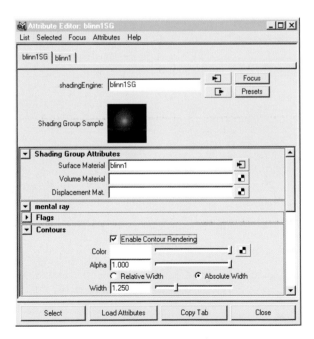

Contour Shading enabled for the blinn's Shading Group node

You will notice in the Contours section, there are a few attributes that allow you to control the width and color of the contour lines on a shader basis.

Color attribute

Allows you to control the color of the individual lines of the shader.

Width attribute

Controls the contour line width. If **Relative Width** is enabled, then contour width is specified as a percentage of the horizontal image resolution. This option in effect maintains the relative contour size if the image resolution changes. If the default **Absolute Width** is enabled, the contour width is specified as the fractional number of pixels.

4 Adjust the contour shader settings

- Set the following:

    Relative Width to **0.5**;

    Color to **Red**.

5 Render Settings

If you render at this point you will not see any contour lines. To see the contour lines you need to enable **Contour Rendering** in the mental ray Render Settings.

- Open the Render Settings and make sure to render using mental ray.

- Under the **mental ray** tab, set the **Quality Presets** to **Preview** quality.

- Expand the **Contours** section and set **Enable Contour Rendering** to **On**.

If you render now you will still not see any contour lines. There are two methods to render the scene at this point. You can draw contours on your model based on **Property Difference** *or* **Sample Contrast**.

- In the **Draw Contours** section, set **Between Different Materials** to **On**.

6 Render the scene

- Render the scene.

mental ray contour shader between different materials

Lesson 14

Tip: Set **Raytracing** to **Off** *in the* **General** *section to speed up render time.*

Following are some explanations about the different contour options.

Enable Contour Rendering

This is the global switch for contour rendering.

Hide Source

Hides the underlying image. Only contours are drawn.

Flood Color

The color for image clearing.

Over Sample

This is the number of super samples used for contour line rasterization.

Filter Type

This attribute defines the downsampling of contours to image resolution.

Filter Support

Defines the fractional number of pixels used for filtering.

Contours Around Coverage

Draws contours between samples that hit something and those that do not.

Between Different Primitives

Draws contours between samples that contact different primitives (draws the tessellation).

Between Different Instances

Draws contours between samples that contact different instances.

Between Different Materials

Draws contours between samples that contact primitives with different materials.

Between Different Labels

Draws contours between samples that contact instances with different labels.

Around Co-planar Faces

Draws contours between samples that have different geometric normals.

Front vs. Backface Contours

Draws contours if the value of the dot product of the normal vector and the view vector differs from one sample to the other.

Color Contrast

If the color difference of samples is larger than what is set here, a contour is drawn.

Depth Contrast

If the color difference of samples in camera space exceeds this contrast, a contour is drawn.

Distance Contrast

If the sample distance difference exceeds this contrast, a contour is draw.

Normal Contrast

If the normal difference measured in degrees of samples is larger than what is stipulated here, a contour is drawn.

UV Contours

A contour is drawn at every Uth and Vth isoline in the primary UV space.

Approximation node tessellation with contour render

By using the Between Different Primitives option in the mental ray Render Settings, it is possible to review NURBS surface tessellation topology.

1   Create an Approximation Node

- Open **Window** → **Rendering Editors** → **mental ray** → **Approximation Editor**.

- Click the **Create** button for the **Surface Approx. (NURBS)**.

- Select the vase geometry.

- Make sure the *mentalraySurfaceApprox1* is selected in the **Surface Approx. (NURBS)** field, then click the **Assign** button.

Doing so will assign the approximation node to the vase geometry.

> **Note:** *You can also create a default Approximation node as a Global Override.*

2 Adjust Render Settings

- Open the Render Settings and set **Between Different Primitives** to **On** under the **Contours** section of the **mental ray** tab.

3 Tweak the approximation node

- In the Approximation Editor, click the **Edit** button for *mentalraySurfaceApprox1*.

- Change the **Presets** to **Angle Tolerance Low Quality**.

- Render the scene.

You can now see the tessellation of the vase at render time. This workflow can be very useful to see how mental ray's surface approximation nodes tessellate NURBS geometry and to study areas that may not be tessellating as you might expect.

Surface Approximation Node used to view the tessellation

Elliptical filtering

mental ray has a high quality sampling technique called **Elliptical Filtering**. This can be very useful where high quality texture sampling is required on a shader by shader basis. It can be of particular use where an object in your scene recedes into the distance and requires very high sampling in order to remove, for example, moire patterns. For instance, this option would be useful when rendering a detailed carpet.

Notice in the following image how the detailing of pixels in the distance is fine, producing an image of greater quality.

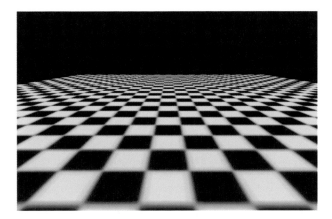

Checker texture with Elliptical Filtering

With conventional filtering techniques, the pixels that make up the pattern in the distance require very high point sampling to remove moire patterns. In order to fix the problem, you would need to turn anti-aliasing levels up, which comes at quite a price in terms of rendering performance.

In the following example, you will see how Elliptical Filtering works.

1   Scene file

- Open the file called *14-ellipticalFiltering_01.ma*.

  This file contains two NURBS planes with a checker texture assigned on them.

2   Create a lambert

- In the Hypershade, create a lambert material and assign it to the plane on the right.

3   Create mental ray shader nodes.

- In the Hypershade, select **Create mental ray Nodes** at the top of the Create bar.

- Create the following nodes:

      Textures → **mib_texture_vector**;

      Textures → **mib_texture_remap**;

      Textures → **mib_texture_filter_lookup**.

4 Connect the mental ray shader nodes.

- **MMB+drag** and **connect** the nodes as follows:

    mib_texture_vector.out value to *mib_texture_remap.input;*

    mib_texture_remap.out value to *mib_texture_filter_lookup.coord;*

    mib_texture_remap.message to *mib_texture_filter_lookup.remap;*

    mib_texture_filter_lookup.out value to *Lambert.color.*

Note: *You may need to go in the* **Left** *or* **Right Display** *menu and choose* **Show Hidden** *in the Connection Editor to see the attribute described here.*

5 Create a mental ray texture node

- Open the Attribute Editor for the *mib_texture_filter_lookup* node.

- In the **mental ray Texture** section, click on the **map** button.

Doing so will create a mental ray texture node.

- In the Attribute Editor for the new *mentalrayTexture1* node, click on the **browse** button, and select the file *checker.tif* from the *sourceimages* directory.

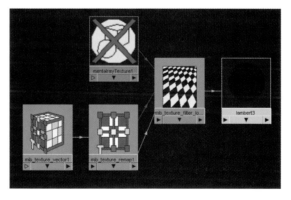

Elliptical Filtering shading network

- Render the scene.

Notice how the right plane's distant pixels are well rendered compared to the left plane.

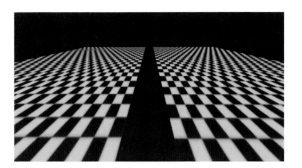

Elliptical Filtering render

Bump maps

mental ray bump maps work a little differently than the Maya bump maps. The
workflow is not initially intuitive. The following workflow is for a file texture based
bump map. If a procedural bump map is required, either convert the texture to a
file or use normal bump mapping.

The mental ray bump network makes use of the following mental ray custom
shader nodes:

dgs_material;

mib_color_mix;

mib_passthrough_bump_map;

mib_bump_basis;

mentalrayTexture;

mib_texture_remap;

mib_texture_vector.

1 Scene file

- Open the file called *14-bumpmap_01.ma*.

The file contains a NURBS sphere and directional light.

2 Create a dgs_material

- In the Hypershade, go to the **Materials** section of the **Create mental ray
Nodes** bar.

- Create a *dgs_material* and assign it to the sphere.

Lesson 14

- Set the following on the newly created node:

  Shiny to **20.0**;

  Diffuse to **white**;

  Glossy to **grey**.

3 Create a mib_color_mix node

- Go to the **Data Conversion** section of the **Create mental ray Nodes** bar.

- Create a *mib_color_mix* node and connect its **outValue** attribute to the **Specular** attribute of the *dgs_material*.

Note: *The mib_color_mix node is required to return problematic surface normals back to normal prior to color calculation.*

4 Create required mental ray textures

- Go to the **Textures** section of the **Create mental ray Nodes** bar.

- Create the following nodes:

  mib_passthrough_bump_map;

  mib_bump_basis;

  mib_texture_remap;

  mib_texture_vector.

5 Connect the bump network

- Make the following connections:

  mib_texture_vector1.outValue to *mib_texture_remap1.input;*

  mib_texture_remap1.outValue to *mib_passthrough_bump_map1.coord;*

  mib_passthrough_bump_map1.outValue to *mib_color_mix.colorBase;*

  mib_bump_basis.u and .v to *mib_passthrough_bump_map.u and .v.*

6 Create the mentalrayTexture node

- Select the *mib_passthrough_bump_map1* node and open its Attribute Editor.

- Click on the **mental ray Texture map** button.

A new node will be created that allows for the file texture information to be input.

- Select the *mentalrayTexture* node and open its Attribute Editor.

- Click the **Browse** button, then select *scratches.tif* as basis of the bump map.

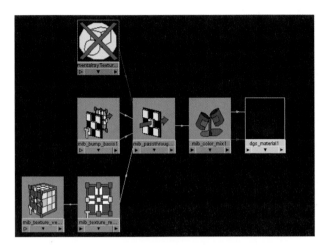

Bump map network

7 Test the bump

- Select the *mib_passthrough_bump_map1* node and open its Attribute Editor.

- Change the **factor** attribute to **-2.0**.

This defines the orientation of the bump along with its depth.

- Render the scene.

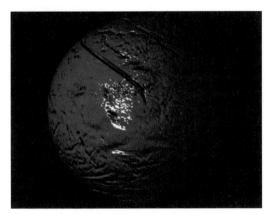

mental ray bump map

Lesson 14

Phenomenon

Essentially, a mental ray **Phenomenon** is a user customized and packaged set of nodes that are re-assembled as a single node entity at subsequent Maya startup. Attributes that a user would want to adjust in the shader graph are all accessed through one node. From a production standpoint, this is good news as complex shading graphs can be designed and then packed into a single user node that can be used over and over. Because mental ray's shader architecture makes use of many separate nodes to get the job done, having the ability to package these separate nodes into a single interface for users is very helpful.

After creating the mental ray custom shader network, the new phenomenon node is created and connected to the mental ray material shader graph. The phenomenon is then exported and subsequently declared in the *maya.rayrc* file. Upon restarting Maya, the phenomenon node will be created by mental ray's node factory. The newly created phenomenon will be placed into the appropriate folder of the Hypershade's Create mental ray Node section.

In order to create a phenomenon node, you can go in the **Hypershade** → **Create mental ray Nodes** → **Miscellaneous** section and create a **mentalrayPhenomenon** node. A phenomenon requires connections in two directions. The first connection is from the material to the phenomenon and the second is backwards from the phenomenon to the individual attributes that you want included in the phenomenon when created on subsequent startups.

```
#*****************************************************************************
# Copyright 1986-2003 by mental images GmbH & Co.KG, Fasanenstr. 81, D-10623
# Berlin, Germany. All rights reserved.
#*****************************************************************************
# Evaluated at startup time of the plug-in to fill the mental ray registry.
#*****************************************************************************/

registry "(MAYABASE)"    value   "C:/Program Files/Alias/Maya7.0/mentalray" end registry

registry "(SYSTEM)" value   "windows"        end registry
registry "(DSO)"    value   "dll"       end registry

$lookup "(MAYABASE)"
$lookup "(SYSTEM)"
$lookup "(DSO)"

registry "(MRMAYA_START)"
    link    "(MAYABASE)/lib/base.(DSO)"
    link    "(MAYABASE)/lib/physics.(DSO)"
    link    "(MAYABASE)/lib/mayabase.(DSO)"
    link    "(MAYABASE)/lib/contour.(DSO)"
    link    "(MAYABASE)/lib/subsurface.(DSO)"
    link    "(MAYABASE)/lib/mi_openexr.(DSO)"
    link    "(MAYABASE)/lib/mayahair.(DSO)"
    mi   "(MAYABASE)/include/dgs_reflective.mi"
    mi   "(MAYABASE)/include/mayabase.mi"
    mi   "(MAYABASE)/include/base.mi"
    mi   "(MAYABASE)/include/physics.mi"
    mi   "(MAYABASE)/include/contour.mi"
    mi   "(MAYABASE)/include/subsurface.mi"
    mi   "(MAYABASE)/include/mayahair.mi"
    echo    "mental ray for Maya - startup done"
end registry

$lookup "(MRMAYA_START)"
```

Edited maya.rayrc file

Once the customization of the node is achieved, you must export the phenomenon using **File → Export Selection → ❑** and setting the appropriate options. You must then edit the file *C:\Program Files\Alias\Mayav7.0\mentalray\maya.rayrc* using a text editor. Adding the line indicated below at the top of the listed .mi files section will create the phenomenon node called *dsg_reflective* upon the start of Maya.

Note: *It is important that the phenomenon declaration line be at the top of the list of .mi files as shown. mental ray evaluates the list from bottom to top and requires the information from reading these files to understand the phenomenon declaration.*

Upon restarting Maya, you will find the newly created custom phenomenon in the appropriate section under **Hypershade → Create mental ray Node.**

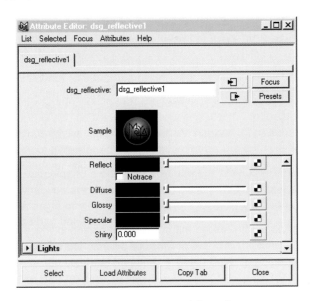

The new phenomenon node's attributes

Conclusion

Custom mental ray shaders can allow you to create complex shading and lighting effects. Custom shaders can be used with standard Maya texture and utility nodes, and their rendering is fully supported.

In the next project, you will start the dynamics section of the book, where you will learn about rigid bodies.

THE CHUBB CHUBBS GALLERY

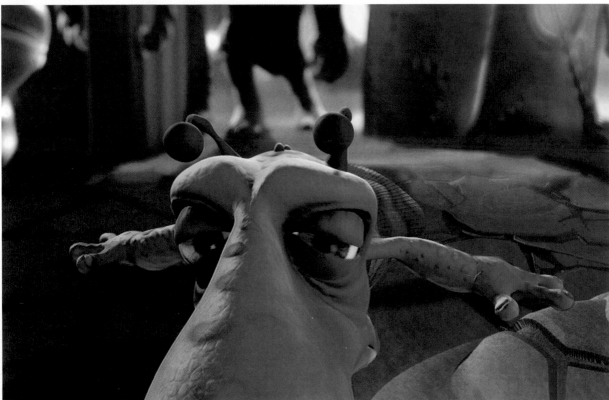

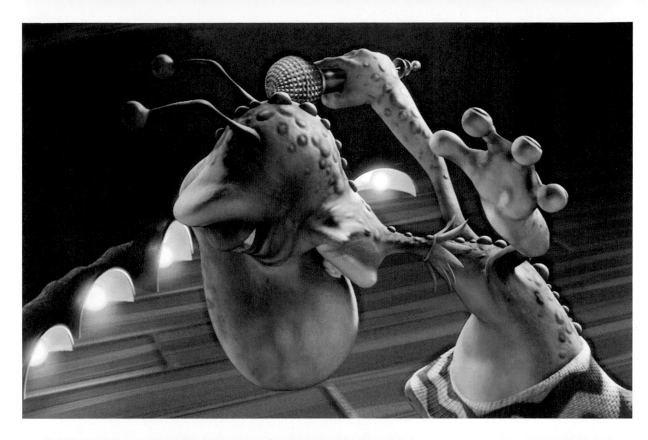

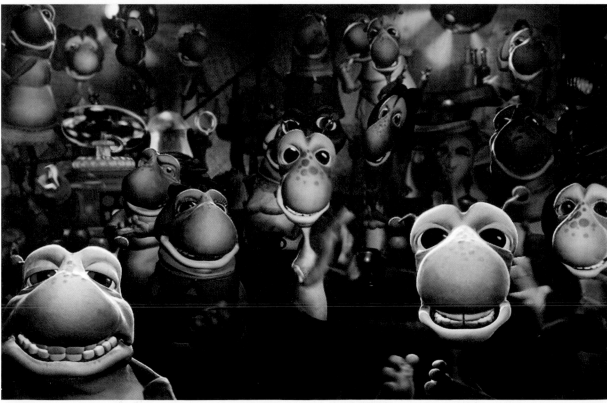

THE CHUBB CHUBBS GALLERY

Project

In Project Five, you will start the overview of the Maya dynamic systems by learning about rigid bodies. Rigid bodies are objects that can collide and interact with each other, resulting in dynamic animation. Such animation can add a good amount of realism to a scene, which could be extremely hard to recreate by hand.

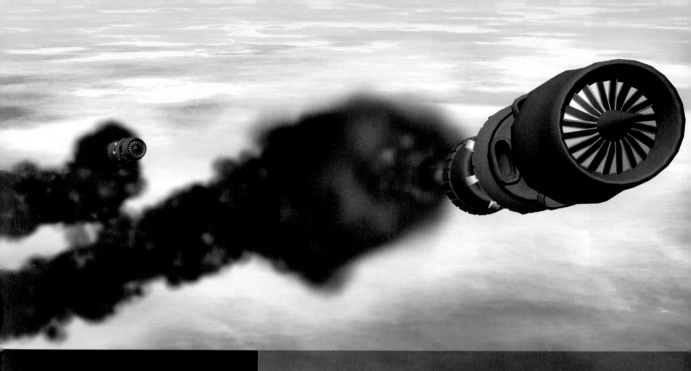

Lesson 15   Maya dynamics

Dynamics in Maya uses rules of physics to let you simulate natural forces in your animation. Effects with complex motion, such as smoke, rain, fire or colliding objects, lend themselves well to dynamically controlled animation. This animation is typically achieved by creating elements in a scene that react to the forces applied to them. By creating an environment of fields, expressions, goals, etc., the animator has artistic control over the affected objects, balancing the need for realism and animation requirements.

In this lesson you will learn the following:

- Different types of rigid bodies;

- Particle terms;

- Different clip effects available;

- Particle instancing terms;

- Particle goals;

- Soft bodies terms;

- Particle rendering.

Dynamics

Maya dynamics is the animation of rigid bodies, soft bodies, and particles, the use of dynamic constraints, and the rendering strategies for hardware and software particle types.

The following section provides a brief overview of some of the key topics discussed in the upcoming dynamics section of the book.

Rigid bodies

The rigid body system in Maya provides animation of geometric objects in a dynamically controlled, collision-based system.

Active and passive rigid bodies

Active and passive rigid bodies are created to collide and react with one another in a realistic manner. Active objects typically fall, move, spin and collide with passive objects.

Rigid body constraints

Rigid body constraints allow dynamic objects to be constrained or constrain each other. Spring, hinge, pin, etc. are some of the constraint types that will be explored.

Particles

Particles are objects that have no size or volume. They are reference points that are displayed, selected, animated and rendered differently than other objects in Maya.

Particle object and Array attributes

Like other nodes in Maya, particles can be thought of as objects with a collective transform. They also contain attributes that control the individual particles using Array attributes. Individual particle behavior can be controlled with ramps, scripts and expressions.

Fields

Fields such as gravity, turbulence, air and others are used to easily move particles around your scene without the use of MEL and expressions.

Particle expressions

Particle expressions are a powerful and almost limitless method of controlling particle parameters. Particle expressions share the MEL syntax and methodology. Functions such as *linstep()*, *sin()*, and *rand()* provide mathematical control over particle appearance and motion.

Particle collisions

Particle collision events provide a method for creating and killing particles when they collide with geometry. Particle collision event procedures can be used to trigger specific MEL-scripted commands at collision time.

Emit function

The emit function allows the user to create and position particles based on information directly derived from MEL and expressions. It requires an ample amount of MEL knowledge, as more complicated usage of the emit function can be MEL intensive.

Clip effects

Clip effects provide you with powerful and flexible tools for creating common dynamic effects. These are typically MEL scripts and expressions that automate the setup of the effect for the user. They also provide an excellent set of MEL and expression examples.

Fire

This clip effect will light an object on fire for both hardware and software rendering.

Smoke

The smoke clip effect makes use of hardware sprites and is a good example of how to setup hardware sprites.

Fireworks

The fireworks effect allows you to make fireworks that are set up for software rendering quickly and easily.

Lightning

The lightning clip effect lets you create an electrical arc between two or more objects.

Shatter

The shatter clip effect lets you break up objects into parts you can use for dynamic simulations.

Curve Flow

The curve flow clip effect allows you to select a curve as a motion path for particles.

Surface Flow

The surface flow clip effect allows you to use a surface as a path for particles.

Lesson 15

Particle instancing

With particle instancing, you can use particles to control the position and motion of instanced geometry.

Animated instance

Particle instancing is only part of the functionality. You can instance a keyframed object to particles in the scene.

Cycled instance

With the particle instancer, you can cycle through a sequence of snapshot objects to create the instanced motion.

Software sprites

The particle instancer also provides aim control of the instanced object. If this instanced object is a textured plane, it can be aimed at the camera, creating a software renderable sprite method.

Goals

Goals are a very powerful method of animating particles. A goal is a destination point that a particle wants to achieve. Particles can have multiple goal objects and per particle attributes designed specifically for goal-based interaction.

These can be animated to provide particle movement that would be otherwise difficult to create with fields or expressions.

Per Particle Goal attributes

Goal attributes such as **parentU** and **goalPP** provide individual particle control. With the use of the **parentId** attribute, these values can be transferred from one particle to another.

Soft bodies

Animating geometry for fluid-like motion or with dynamic response is accomplished with soft body particles.

Soft bodies

Soft bodies are geometry that have particles controlling the position and movement of the CVs or poly vertices of the objects.

Goals

Goals are a fundamental part of controlling soft bodies. The **Goal Weight** controls the deviation of the soft body from its goal object.

Springs

Although springs can be applied to any particle, even to dynamic geometry, they are especially suited to binding soft body components together. Spring parameters such as **Stiffness**, **Rest Length** and **Damping** can be controlled on a per object or per spring basis.

Particle rendering

What good is all this particle animation if you cannot render it out to contribute to the final shot?

Hardware rendering

Hardware rendering of particles provides a quick method of image creation. Typically, these images are taken to the compositor who sweetens and integrates them with the rest of the scene elements.

Software rendering

Software rendering allows for scene integration of particles and rendered objects. Volumetric particle rendering is also created with software rendered particle types. Shadowing, glows and other lighting effects are also combined.

Compositing

Without compositing, much of this process would not be possible. Dynamics should always be viewed as another contributor to the elements that will make up the final image.

Conclusion

Maya dynamics can be quite simple or very complex. The topics presented in the following projects are shown in a progressive manner, in order to take you through as many tools and techniques as possible. Lots of self-experimentation will be required in order to fully control the dynamic simulations and create astonishing results.

In the next lesson, you will learn about rigid bodies.

Lesson 16   Rigid body dynamics

This lesson introduces the fundamental tools and techniques required to achieve realistic solid collisions in Maya using rigid bodies.

In this lesson you will learn the following:

- The differences between active and passive rigid bodies;

- How to create rigid bodies;

- How to create and connect fields to rigid bodies;

- Stand-ins;

- How to work with the rigid body solver and its attributes;

- How to combine keyframing with rigid body dynamics.

Rigid body

A rigid body is defined as any object whose surface does not deform when a collision occurs. Common examples in nature would be billiard balls, floors and ceilings, or a bowling ball. Of course, in the real world these surfaces do actually deform to a very small extent when a collision occurs. This minimal deformation will be overlooked and the objects will be considered as either rigid or not rigid to simplify the process.

Any NURBS or polygonal surface can contain rigid body properties. Curves, particles and lattices, for example, cannot become rigid bodies since they contain no surface information. Surfaces, however, that are made from curves, particles or lattices, for example, can be rigid bodies.

Opposed to rigid bodies, soft bodies are NURBS or polygonal surfaces that have particle-like control of their respective vertices. Soft bodies will be explored in Lesson 27.

Active vs. passive rigid bodies

Rigid bodies are divided into two categories: *active* and *passive*. There are important distinctions between these two types of rigid bodies.

	ACTIVE	PASSIVE
Can be keyframed	No	Yes
Responds to collisions	Yes	No
Causes collisions	Yes	Yes
Affected by fields	Yes	No

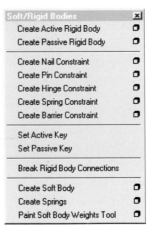

Soft/Rigid Bodies menu

A comparison of active vs. passive rigid bodies

The Soft/Rigid Bodies menu

The **Soft/Rigid Bodies** menu is used to create rigid and soft bodies, create dynamic constraints, and keyframe the active and passive state of objects.

> **Alias** *I love the Dynamics menu set. Because the Maya dynamics solvers are*
> **Tip:** *relatively easy to use and anyone, with little or no knowledge of physics and dynamics can produce some interesting and realistic simulations in a short amount of time.*
>
> *Julio Lopez | Sr. Multimedia Specialist*

Important rigid body nodes

The rigid body command you choose will create several new important nodes and attributes for each selected object. These nodes and their associated attributes can be viewed in the Channel Box, Hypergraph, Outliner or Attribute Editor. In the Channel Box, you will notice the following nodes are created for each selected object:

rigidBody

The *rigidBody* node is located under the **Shapes** section for each selected rigid body object in the Channel Box.

To view and select a *rigidBody* node from the Outliner, you may first need to show shapes by selecting **Outliner** → **Display** → **Shapes**. The *rigidBody* node will appear as a child of the object's transform node.

The attributes within this node contain information that determines the active or passive status of the rigid body and various controls relating to the properties of each specific rigid body object.

rigidSolver

The *rigidSolver* node provides control over the evaluation of the rigid body dynamics. This node is listed under both the **Inputs** and **Outputs** sections within the Channel Box for the selected item. By default, one *rigidSolver* node is used to control the evaluation of all rigid bodies in the scene.

time

The *time* node determines when the *rigidSolver*'s evaluations will take place. This is useful if you wish to have multiple simulations running within the same scene based on different time parameters.

Collapsing armor

This example incorporates the use of active and passive rigid bodies and is intended to familiarize you with the process of setting up a simple rigid body simulation.

1   Scene file

- Open the file named *16-armor_01.ma*.

This scene contains a ZyZak armor. You will use it to simulate the dynamics of the armor falling down on the ground as the ZyZak gets eaten by the ChubbChubbs.

A ZyZak armor and a ChubbChubb stand-in

2   Create the active rigid bodies

- From the Outliner, select all the armor surfaces.

- **Ctrl-click** *projectile* to add it to the selection.

- Select **Soft/Rigid Bodies** → **Create Active Rigid Body** → ❑ from the **Dynamics** menu set.

- In the **Rigid** Options, select **Edit** → **Reset Settings** to set the options to their default states.

- Press **Create**.

An active rigid body is created for every selected piece of geometry.

3   Create the passive rigid body

- Select the floor surface.

- Select **Soft/Rigid Bodies** → **Create Passive Rigid Body** → ❑.

- In the **Rigid** Options, select **Edit** → **Reset Settings** to set the options to their default states.

- Press **Create**.

A passive rigid body is created for the selected piece of geometry.

4   Set rigid body attributes for the projectile

- Select projectile.

- Locate the *rigidBody* node for this object in the **Shapes** section of the Channel Box.

- Set the following attribute values for the *rigidBody* node:

    InitialVelocityZ to **-50**;

    Mass to **100**;

    Apply Forces At to **verticesOrCVs**.

5 Set rigid body attributes for the armor

- Select all of the armor surfaces.

- Enter the following attribute values for the *rigidBody* nodes:

    Mass to **35**;

    Bounciness to **0.5**;

    Static Friction to **0.05**;

    Dynamic Friction to **0.05**;

    Apply Forces At to **verticesOrCVs**.

The specific definition of these attributes will be discussed in later lessons. For now, your goal is to have collisions occur at a decent playback speed.

> **Note:** *When multiple items are selected, changing an attribute value in the Channel Box will change the value for every selected item that contains that same attribute.*

6 Set rigid body attributes for the floor

- Select the floor.

- Enter the following attribute values for the *rigidBody* node:

    Bounciness to **0.5**;

    Static Friction to **0.5**;

    Dynamic Friction to **0.5**.

7 Enable dynamic labels

In some cases when dealing with complex scenes containing large numbers of rigid bodies, it is difficult to keep track of which rigid bodies are passive and active. When set to **On**, the **displayLabel** attribute will display a small label next to each rigid body in the viewport indicating if it is an active or passive rigid body.

Lesson 16

Note: *Other dynamic components, such as dynamic constraints, also have labels associated with them.*

- Select any *rigidBody* object in the scene.
- Click on the *rigidSolver* node near the bottom of the Channel Box.
- Set the **displayLabel** attribute to **On**.
- Rewind to display the dynamic labels.

The labels are placed at the object's center of mass, which is represented by a small **x** *on each object.*

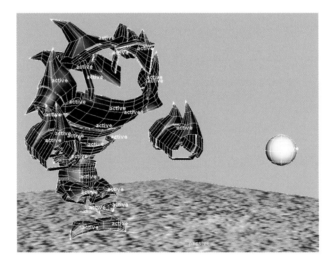

Displaying rigid body labels at the object's center of mass

8   Test the animation

- Make sure the **Playback Speed** in the preferences is set to **Play every frame**.

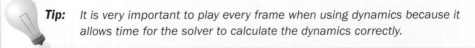

Tip: *It is very important to play every frame when using dynamics because it allows time for the solver to calculate the dynamics correctly.*

- Playback the animation to see how the armor reacts.

9 Create a gravity field

- Click in the viewport to deselect any currently selected objects.
- From the **Dynamics** menu, select **Fields → Gravity → □**.
- In the **Gravity** options, select **Edit → Reset Settings**.
- Press **Create**.

A new gravity field is created at the origin.

- Move the *gravityField* up above the scene so that it is easily selectable and visible.

10 Connect the objects to gravity

- Select all the armor pieces and the *projectile*.
- **Shift-select** the *gravityField* last.
- Select **Fields → Affect Selected Object(s)**.

Tip: *The same results could have been achieved by selecting the armor pieces and projectile, then creating the* **Fields → Gravity**. *This process would automatically connect the selected items to the chosen field. You could also use the Relationship Editor to connect fields and surfaces.*

11 Test the results

- Rewind and then playback the scene.

The simulated dynamics

*The ChubbChubb stand-in (projectile), is projected along the **Z-axis**. The projectile collides with the armor pieces and the armor pieces collide with each other and the floor surface. Notice that the floor remains stationary because it is a passive rigid body.*

Note: *When rigid bodies interpenetrate, they get selected by the rigidSolver to tell you that an interpenetration has occurred. This is normal and can be ignored at this stage.*

12 Save your work

- Save the scene as *16-armor_02.ma*.

Stand-Ins

All the rigid body nodes have a **Stand-In** attribute. This attribute allows you to speed up simple collisions by telling the rigid solver to calculate the piece of geometry as a simple primitive. By default, this attribute is set to **None**, which tells the solver to calculate the dynamics for each vertex of the geometry. Despite the fact that it will be much slower to calculate the simulation, the dynamic animation will be accurate.

The attribute can also be set to **Cube** or **Sphere** stand-ins delimited by the bounding box of the geometry. This can really speed up the dynamic simulation, but you might notice that the rigid bodies will not react exactly the same as if the full geometry was taken into account.

Another solution is to create a low resolution version of the models for dynamics and link their dynamic animation to the high resolution model. This will be discussed in Lesson 18.

Caching

Caching allows the dynamic solver to evaluate calculations once per frame and store the results of those calculations in memory (RAM) where they can be accessed during subsequent playback at much faster speeds. In addition to providing improved performance, caching allows you to scrub through the animation without problems.

When caching is enabled, the solver will continue to use the cached version of the data until the cache has been deleted. For this reason, any modifications made to the simulation after caching the data will not exist in the currently cached version of the playback, since those changes were not part of the original calculations that were computed during the cache run-up.

It is best to tweak values and then cache the scene. Once you have evaluated those changes and wish to make more, delete the cache, make the new changes, then re-cache the scene again.

Note: *The first playback cycle where the solver records the calculations into RAM is commonly referred to as a run-up.*

1 Scene file

- Continue with your own scene.

Or

- Open the scene file called *16-armor_02.ma*.

2 Cache the playback

- In the timeline, set the playback range to start at frame **1** and end at frame **100**.
- Select the projectile.
- Click on the *rigidSolver* node in the Channel Box and set **cacheData** to **1**.

*A value of **1** corresponds to **On**; a value of **0** corresponds to **Off**.*

Tip: *You can also enable or disable caching by selecting **Solvers** → **Memory Caching** → **Enable** or **Disable**.*

- Rewind and then playback the scene.

You should be able to scrub in the timeline after the simulation has completely played through once.

3 Delete the cache

- Select **Solvers** → **Memory Caching** → **Delete** to clear the previously cached data from memory.

4   Modify the attribute values

- Experiment with different values for InitialVelocityZ, InitialSpinX, Mass, and Bounciness to see how the simulation results differ.

- Re-cache the scene so you can see the result playback in real time.

- Repeat this process until you have achieved the desired motion.

5   Save your work

- Save the scene as *16-armor_03.ma*.

Combine keyframes with dynamics

In some cases, relying solely on the influence of fields, **InitialVelocity**, **InitialSpin**, and other dynamic attributes to animate objects may not provide the required level of control. In these cases, it is useful to combine keyframing techniques with dynamic techniques to tune the motion of the animation. You will learn how to ignore dynamics while an object is controlled by keyframes, and how to combine keyframes and dynamics.

1   Scene file

- Continue with your own scene.

Or

- Open the scene file called *16-armor_03.ma*.

2   Group the projectile

Creating a group on the projectile provides a second transform with which to apply hierarchical animation. In this case, you will use a motion path.

- Rewind to frame **1**.

- Select the projectile.

- Select **Edit → Group → ❐**.

- In the Group options, set **Group Pivot** to **Center**.

- Rename the new group to *projectileTranslate*.

- Rename the *projectile* to *projectileRotate*.

projectileTranslate will handle the translation of the ball along a motion path. projectileRotate is where you will keyframe rotation and use dynamics to control the motion of the ball after the motion path animation has been completed.

3 Disable the rigidSolver

You'll be setting up animation now and you do not want the dynamics to interfere with the keyframed animation. A quick way to do this is to disable the state of the *rigidSolver*.

- Select the projectile's *rigidSolver* node from the Channel Box.

- Set **State** to **Off**.

4 Draw a motion path

- Select **Create** → **EP Curve Tool**.

- From the side view, draw a curve as follows:

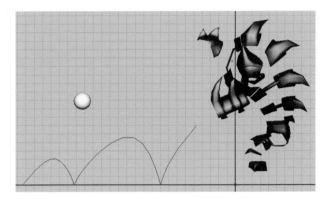

The motion path

5 Attach the projectile to the motion path

- Set the playback range from **1** to **40**.

- Set current frame to be **1**.

- Select *projectileTranslate,* then **Shift-select** the curve.

- From the **Animation** menu set, select **Animate** → **Motion Paths** → **Attach to Motion Path** → ❏.

Set the following options:

> **Time Range** to **Time Slider**;
>
> **Follow** to **Off**.

- Press **Attach** button.

The projectile should move at the beginning of the motion path.

Note: *If you drew the curve in the wrong direction, the projectile will go at the end of the motion path. To correct this, reverse the curve direction before attaching the motion path.*

6 Move the motion path

- Move the curve up so that the projectile doesn't interpenetrate with the floor surface.

7 Set playback range

- Set the playback frame range to start at frame **1** and end at frame **200**.

- Playback the scene.

The projectile should be animated correctly on the path, without dynamics.

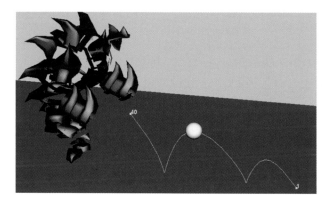

The projectile animated on the motion path

Keyframe the rotation

The ChubbChubb stand-in now moves along the curve, but it should also rotate a little as it bounces toward the ZyZak. You will need to put some secondary animation on the projectile by keyframing its rotation on the *projectileRotate* node.

1 Keyframe projectileRotate

- Go to frame **1**.

- Select *projectileRotate* node.

- Set a keyframe on the **Rotate X** channel of *projectileRotate* through the Channel Box.

Doing so will add a pairBlend on the node in order to be able to blend between the animation of the rigid body and the keyframes. Also note a new attribute called **Blend Rigid Body** *on the projectileRotate node.*

- Set the new **Blend Rigid Body** attribute to **1**.

Doing so specifies that you want to see and set keyframes on the projectile.

- Set other appropriate keyframes on the rotation until frame **40**.

- Set the **Blend Rigid Body** attribute to **0**.

2 Keyframe the active and passive state of the projectile

In order for the projectile to be either active or passive at different frames in the animation, you will keyframe its active state attribute using special menu items.

- Rewind to frame **1**.

- Select *projectileRotate* node.

- Highlight the *rigidBody* node for *projectileRotate* in the Channel Box.

- Select **Soft/Rigid Bodies** → **Set Passive Key** to key this as a passive body.

- Go to frame **40**.

- Select **Soft/Rigid Bodies** → **Set Active Key** to key this as an active body.

Note: *Keying the active/passive state using these menu items is the most reliable method for keyframing rigid bodies.*

Tip: *Sometimes setting the active/passive keyframe a frame or two before the motion path ends helps to prevent problems with order of evaluation.*

3 Enable the state of the rigidSolver

Now that you have completed the keyframe animation, you can enable dynamics again.

- With the *rigidBody* still selected, look under the **Inputs** section in the Channel Box and click on *rigidSolver*.

- Type **1** in the **State** attribute to set it back to **On**.

4   Keyframing the Ignore attribute

To speed up playback, since no substantial collisions occur in this animation until many frames into the simulation, the solver can ignore the computation of the armor until near the time of collision.

- Go to frame **1**.

- Select all the armor surfaces.

- In the Channel Box, go to the **Shapes** section and highlight the **Ignore** attribute of the *rigidBody* nodes.

- **RMB-click** and select **Key Selected** to set the following keyframes:

    Keyframe **Ignore** at frame **1** to **On**;

    Keyframe **Ignore** at frame **45** to **Off**.

5   Test the scene

- Playback the animation.

The ChubbChubb stand-in will translate and rotate along the motion path as a passive rigid body. It continues moving and rotating after the motion path animation has completed as an active rigid body. This continued motion is the combined result of the gravity field, motion inherited from the path animation and keyframed rotation.

Tip: *You can also playblast the scene in order to see a movie of the animation in real-time.*

6   Save your work

- Save the scene as *16-armor_04.ma*.

Tips and traps

The following are some additional tips to consider for this exercise and for rigid bodies in general:

- The **Ignore** attribute may cause some problems if it is keyframed **On** or **Off** at the same time some other important operation is done, such as a keyframed active state. To fix this, keyframe **Ignore** one frame before the other important action.

- Keyframing the **Ignore** flag while the simulation is cached or vice-versa may cause some unexpected behavior. Choose one or the other but avoid doing both simultaneously or the simulation may produce unexpected results. These results may include offsetting objects' positions or objects spinning off into space at the wrong time, etc.

- Avoid keyframing the **Active** attribute using the Channel Box on any objects containing hierarchies. Instead, use the **Set Active Key** or **Set Passive Key** menu items under the **Soft/Rigid Bodies** menu.

- If an object doesn't follow a motion path correctly, make sure the pivot point of the object is well placed. If an object appears to follow the basic shape of a path but is offset in space, this is likely the cause.

- If you playback the scene after the projectile is attached to the motion path, the projectile may offset itself from the motion path. To avoid this behavior, reopen the scene. After the **Ignore** attribute has been keyframed, select the *rigidSolver* node in the Channel Box and set the attribute **State** to **Off**. After the active and passive state of the ball has been keyframed, select the *rigidSolver* node and set the **State** attribute back to **On**.

- Verify that your **Undo Queue** in the **Preferences** is set to **Infinite** or to a high number. Realize that undo doesn't always work as reliably with dynamics due to the way dynamic simulations are being computed in the software. In general, when working with dynamics, you must work methodically and think about each step before progressing. Also, avoid scrubbing playback in the timeline if your scene is not cached.

- Changing the **Mass** attribute of an object will not affect how it falls under the force of gravity. However, it will affect how much force is exerted when a collision occurs. Also, changing the mass will affect how a non-gravity field (i.e. turbulence) will move the object around in the scene.

Lesson 16

- The file *16-friction.ma* has rigid body books that slide down a table. You can use this file to get a clear idea of how the **Static** and **Dynamic Friction** attributes work.

  *These attributes provide general changes and are not precision controls. Valid values normally range from **0** to **1** although you can use higher values. Static friction controls a threshold as to how high the angle will need to be before the object begins to slide. Dynamic friction controls the slipperiness (energy loss) of the object once it is in motion along the table surface. Values closer to **1** correspond to more energy lost or more stickiness in the collision.*

  It is important to remember that the friction values on the books and the table need to be taken into consideration since both contribute to the final simulation. Try adjusting the static and dynamic friction attributes for both objects and compare the different results.

  *The long arrows displayed from the rigidBodies in this file during playback show the direction of the velocity of the traveling rigidBody. This is a display feature called **displayVelocity** on the rigidSolver node that can be enabled or disabled.*

  *The **scaleVelocity** attribute also on the rigidSolver simply scales the length of this arrow and has no control of the motion of the objects on the solver.*

- Can a rigid body be deformed? By definition a rigidBody is rigid, which means non-deformable. You can apply a deformer to a rigid body, however, the collision calculations will be based on the shape of the original, non-deformed object also known as the intermediate object. This will not likely be the effect you are after. One exception to this rule is particle collisions. You can make particles collide with deforming geometry and deforming rigid bodies. Particle collisions are discussed in greater detail in later lessons.

Building a house of cards

Use what you have learned so far to build a house of cards on a table. Apply fields to the cards to make them collide with each other and the table.

Remember that the normal orientation of a surface is important in rigid body collisions. If you build the cards as a single-sided polygonal surface, you will find that some cards will not collide correctly. You can fix this quickly by selecting all the rigid body objects and selecting **Edit Polygons** → **Extrude Face**, then extruding a little to give the card some thickness. You can do this even after you have created the rigid bodies.

Conclusion

You now have a basic understanding of how rigid body dynamics work. Rigid bodies are objects that can cause and respond to collisions. Active rigid bodies cause and respond to collisions and fields and cannot be keyframed. Passive rigid bodies cause, but do not respond, to collisions, and do not respond to fields, but can be keyframed.

Rigid bodies are controlled by the *rigidSolver* and the *time* node. Important attributes of the *rigidBody* and the *rigidSolver* can be adjusted in the Channel Box. It is possible to keyframe the active and passive state of the *rigidBody* to combine keyframing and dynamic animation together.

In upcoming lessons, you will learn about the various rigid body attributes and solver attributes in greater detail.

In the next lesson, you will learn about rigid body constraints.

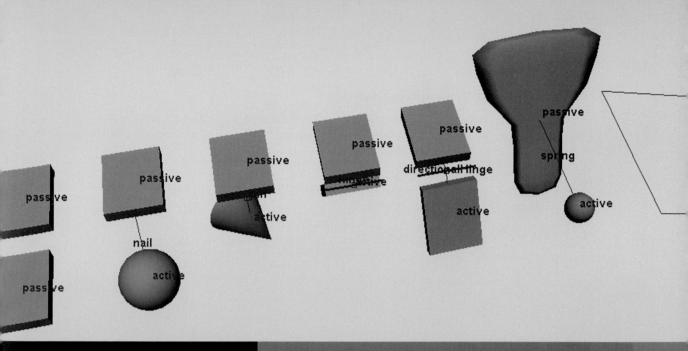

Lesson 17   Rigid body constraints

This lesson focuses on working with rigid body constraints. The three examples shown here are a hanging armor, a catapult and a pod engine setup.

In this lesson you will learn the following:

- Rigid body constraint types;

- How to parent constraints;

- How to animate constraint parameters;

- How to set the initial state;

- The different application for dynamic and non-dynamic constraints;

- Rigid body groups.

Dynamic constraint types

Rigid body constraints are created using **Soft/Rigid Bodies** → **Create Constraint**. There are six dynamic constraint types divided into two categories:

Dual body constraints

The dual body constraints allow for constraining of a rigid body to a point in space or to another rigid body.

- Pin
- Hinge
- DirectionalHinge
- Spring

Single body constraints

The single body constraints allow for the constraint of a rigid body to only a point in space or, in the case of the barrier, to a plane in space.

- Nail
- Barrier

Constraint descriptions

Pin

Constrains two active rigid bodies to each other, or an active and a passive rigid body to each other. It does not allow constraining to a point in space. The pinning point or pivot is adjustable and can be keyframed On and Off.

Hinge

Constrains an active rigid body to another active or passive rigid body with a user defined pivot orientation. This pivot constrains the motion to one axis. It can also constrain a rigid body to a point in space.

Directional hinge

Works just like a hinge constraint. The difference is that the orientation of the hinge axis will change depending on the motion of the object(s) that it is connected to. So, if you rotate an object that has a directionalHinge attached, the constraint will orient its axis to match. To use a Directional hinge, create a constraint, then set its constraint type to **directionalHinge** in the Attribute Editor.

Spring

Constrains an active or a passive rigid body to another active rigid body or to a point in space. The spring constraint contains attributes that control the elastic properties, **Stiffness, Restlength** and **Damping**.

Nail

Constrains an active rigid body to a point in space. This point can be grouped and translated under another object as a child.

Barrier

Creates a planar boundary that an active rigid body cannot pass through.

Auto Create Rigid Body

When you select an object to be dynamically constrained to a point or another object, Maya will automatically turn the necessary objects into rigid bodies if they are not already rigid bodies. This feature is controlled by the **Auto Create Rigid Body** flag in the **Dynamics** section of the **Window** → **Settings/Preferences** → **Preferences...**

Constraint examples

The scene file *17-constraints_01.ma* contains a sample application of each constraint type.

Constraint examples

Lesson 17

Hanging armor

In this exercise, you will use the armor scene from the last lesson, and hook it up into a free hanging kinetic armor using rigid body constraints.

1 Scene file

- Open the file called *17-hangingArmor_01.ma*.

In this scene, all the rigid bodies are already created and linked to a gravity field.

- Rewind and playback the simulation.

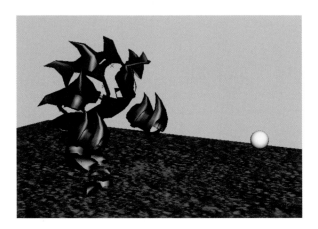

The armor geometry

2 Create a nail constraint to support the entire structure

You will now add rigid body constraints to hang the armor. A nail constraint will let you hang the structure from a point in space.

- Select the armor surface on the top of the upper back.

This will be the surface used to hang all the other pieces of the armor.

- Select **Soft/Rigid Bodies → Create Nail Constraint**.

- Translate the *rigidNailConstraint1* pivot up above the armor.

- Playback the animation.

Tip: *Moving the nail constraint's pivot in space will allow you to move the entire armor once it is hanging.*

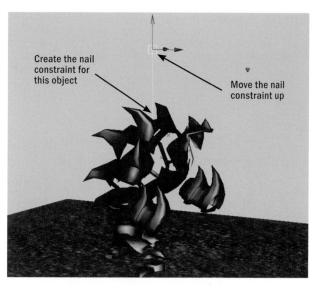

Create the nail
constraint for
this object

Move the nail
constraint up

Move the nail constraint point up above the armor

3   Create pin constraints for the hanging arms

Since each arm is hanging from the top armor surface, pin constraints will
be used. By using pins, the weight of each arm will influence the rotation of
the top armor object.

- Select the left upper
  arm armor piece, then
  Shift-select the top
  armor piece.

- Select **Soft/Rigid
  Bodies** → **Create
  Pin Constraint**.

*Notice that the pin
constraint is created
between the two object's
center of mass.*

- Translate
  rigidPinConstraint
  pivot so it is
  located at the
  shoulder location.

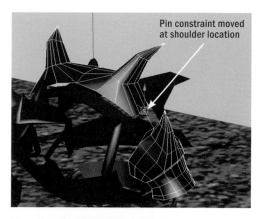

Pin constraint moved
at shoulder location

Move the pin constraint's pivot to the hanging point

4 Repeat for the forearm piece

- Repeat the last step to create a pin contraint between the left upper arm and the left forearm geometry.

- Move the pin's pivot to the elbow area.

- Playback the animation.

5 Repeat for the other arm

- **Repeat** the process to create the required pin constraints on the right arm pieces.

Tip: *You can use the **g** hotkey to repeat the last command, which will create a new pin constraint.*

6 Adjust the center of mass

Currently, each constraint hangs from the center of the surfaces. Ideally, the surfaces should hang from where the constraint is hooked to the piece above, as though a string was attached between the surfaces. You can easily move the **Center Of Mass** attributes on each rigid body to accomplish this. There is no manipulator for this, so you need to do it through the Channel Box.

- Select a forearm object.

- Highlight **Center Of Mass Z** attribute in the Channel Box for the rigid body.

- **MMB-click+drag** in the viewport to change the value.

*You will see the length of the nail constraint change and the small **x** representing the center of mass moving.*

- Move the center of mass to the back of the surface.

Tip: *Pressing **Ctrl** while you **MMB-click+drag** in the viewport changes the Channel Box attribute values in smaller increments.*

- Repeat for the other forearm.

Center of mass moved toward the back of the surface

7 Playback the simulation

- Playback the simulation to see how the arms react.

The arms will hang from the top armor surfaces while all the other unconstrained pieces fall to the ground.

The arms are now hanging from the top piece of the armor

8 Save your work

- Save the scene as *17-hangingArmor_02.ma*.

Rest of hanging armor

You will now continue to create pin constraints for the rest of the armor pieces.

1 Scene file

- Continue with your own scene file.

Or

- Open the scene called *17-hangingArmor_02.ma*.

2 Create a pin constraint for the back of the armor

- Create pin constraints between each of the armor's back surfaces.

- Move the constraints' pivots appropriately between the objects.

The pin constraints of the back armor pieces

3 Constrain the front of the armor

- Create a pin constraint between the top surface of the armor and the neck piece.

- Create four pin constraints between each of the armor's front surfaces and move their pivots as follows:

Creating these four pin constraints will ensure that the front plate and straps stay linked together.

- Test the simulation if needed.

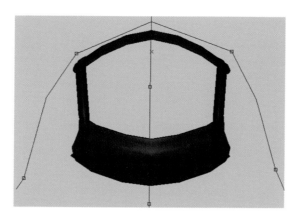

The pin constraints to be created on the front of the armor

4   Continue pinning the armor

Continue to create pin constraints in order to link up all the armor geometry together.

Tip: *The fewer constraints you use, the faster playback you will get out of the dynamic simulation.*

5   Playback

- Playback the simulation.

Tip: *If a simulation takes too long to calculate, you can press* **Escape** *to stop the simulation.*

6   Save your work

- Save the scene as *17-hangingArmor_03.ma*.

Initial state

You will now adjust the mass of the armor pieces and then play the simulation until the armor stabilizes. Once that is done, you will be able to set this pose as being the initial state of the armor.

1 Scene file

- Continue with your own scene file.

Or

- Open the scene called *17-hangingArmor_03.ma*.

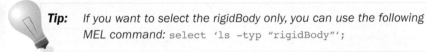

Note: *There might be warnings in the Script Editor upon the opening of this file. This is normal and can be ignored.*

2 Adjust the armor pieces' mass

Keep in mind that the mass of all rigid body pieces directly affects the motion of the simulation. The **Attribute Spread Sheet** is a great way to compare values of many objects and quickly make changes.

- Select the rigid body objects by selecting **Edit** → **Select All by Type** → **Rigid Bodies**.

- Select **Window** → **General Editors** → **Attribute Spread Sheet…**

- Click the **Shape Keyable** tab in the spreadsheet to locate the *rigidBody* nodes. You may have to scroll down to see the *rigidBody* nodes and their attributes.

Tip: *If you want to select the rigidBody only, you can use the following MEL command:* `select 'ls -typ "rigidBody"';`

This command will select all nodes that are the rigidBody type.

- Locate the **Mass** attributes of the selected objects and adjust them as desired.

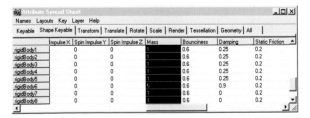

Attribute Spread Sheet

> **Tip:** You can **click+drag** to select multiple cells in single or multiple columns to make simultaneous value changes. You can use **Ctrl** or **Shift** select cells. Entire rows or columns can be selected by clicking on the row or column header.

3 Initial state

- Play the animation until the armor stabilizes and then stop the playback.

- Select **Solvers** → **Initial State** → **Set for All Dynamics**.

Doing so will save the current pose of the rigid bodies as the initial state.

- Rewind the animation to frame **1**.

Notice the pose of the armor at frame 1 is now the one you have just saved.

The stabilized armor and initial state

> **Tip:** If you feel that a stable initial state is not perfectly reached, you can play the simulation again and save the initial state a second time.

4 Add initial velocity on the projectile

Experiment with **Impulse**, **Spin Impulse** and **InitialVelocity** on the projectile. These attributes exist on passive and active rigid bodies but only have an effect with active rigid bodies.

Lesson 17

Impulse

A force that gets applied to a rigid body on every frame of the simulation. These can be useful if you always want to keep something moving in a given direction and you want that force to be reapplied continuously. Impulses are rarely used but can come in handy.

Spin Impulse

Adds a force to each frame that will cause the object to spin around the specified axis.

Initial Spin

Adds a force at the first frame of the simulation to cause spinning around the defined X,Y or Z-axis of the active rigid body.

- Get the *projectile* to smash into the hanging armor and watch how it reacts.

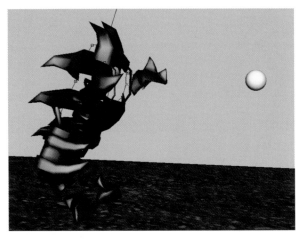

The projectile hits the armor, causing it to dangle

4   Save your work

- Save your scene as *17-hangingArmor_04.ma*.

Related exercises

- Try to animate the translation of the top nail constraint to see how it affects the armor's rigid bodies.

- There are extra example files in the *17-mobile* folder that require more effort in balancing and understanding mass and center of mass.

- The *mobile.mpg* movie shows you a sample render of this scene file.

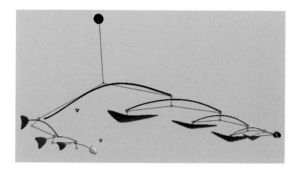

A balanced mobile

Catapult

In this exercise, you will construct a catapult using the hinge and spring constraints. You will also use two orient constraints that are non-dynamic. There are many ways this example could be set up; this is just one example that is used to show you some different ideas.

1   Open scene file

- Open the file *17-catapult_01.ma*.

This file contains the catapult geometry with the following inventory of objects:

overhead - static anchor for spring constraint;

lever - armature anchor for spring constraint;

frame - geometry of catapult frame;

wheels - geometry of catapult wheels;

boom - armature arm;

boomWheel - armature fulcrum.

Catapult geometry

2 Spring constrain the lever to the overhead

Use the spring constraint to pull the armature towards the overhead anchor, which will remain stationary.

- Select lever, then **Shift-select** the overhead objects.

- Select **Soft/Rigid Bodies** → **Create Spring Constraint**.

This converts lever and overhead to active rigid bodies and builds a spring constraint between them.

3 Change the overhead object to a passive rigid body

- Select the overhead object.

- In the Channel Box, set the **Active** attribute to **Off**.

- In the Channel Box, make sure the **cacheData** attribute for the *rigidSolver* node is set to **Off**.

If caching is accidentally on, there can be some strange object offsetting or rewind problems that will occur later. To help avoid these problems in this example, avoid scrubbing and excessive undoing.

4 Orient constrain the boomWheel to the lever

The lever object will rotate the boomWheel object so you must orient constrain the boomWheel to the lever.

- Select the lever first, then **Shift-select** the boomWheel object.

- In the **Animation** menu set, select **Constrain** → **Orient** → ❏.

- In the option window, make sure the **Maintain Offset** is set to **On**.

- Click the **Add** button.

This will create a boomWheel_orientConstraint under the boomWheel object.

Note: *Do not confuse the animation constraints with the dynamic rigid body constraints.*

5 Hinge constrain the lever object

To get the *lever* to only rotate about the same axis as the *boomWheel*, you will use a hinge constraint on the lever and then move the hinge to the center of the *boomWheel*.

- Select the lever object.

- Select **Soft/Rigid Bodies** → **Create Hinge Constraint.**

6   Reposition the hinge

- Select the hinge constraint object and rotate it so that it is parallel with the **X-axis** of the *boomWheel.*

Hinge constraint rotated

- Translate the hinge to the center of the *boomWheel.*

Note: *Use an Orthographic view to align this accurately.*

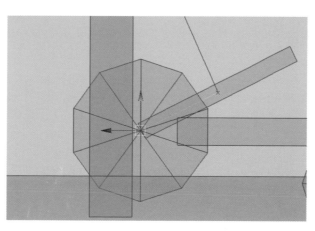

Hinge constraint positioned

Lesson 17

7   Test the setup at this point

- Select the *rigidSpring_Constraint*.

- In the Channel Box, set the **SpringRestLength** attribute to about half of its current value.

This will force the spring to try to assume this new length, thus pulling the lever towards the overhead object.

Note: *A quick way to change a value to half its original value is to type /=2 in the Channel Box.*

- Playback the animation.

- When you are done, make sure to rewind the scene.

8   Attach the boom to the boomWheel

You should have the boomWheel rotating correctly. You want the boom and its launcher to follow this rotation. To do this you will apply another orient constraint between the boomWheel and the boom.

- Select the boomWheel first, then **Shift-select** the boom object.

- Select **Constrain** → **Orient**.

The boom is now orient constrained to the boomWheel.

The boom also contains, as children, the geometry that will hold the projectile. It is named launcherPad.

9   Make the launcherPad into a passive rigid body group

- Select the *launcherPad* group, which contains the *stop* and *pad* geometry.

- Make this group a passive rigid body group by selecting **Soft/Rigid Bodies** → **Create Passive Rigid Body**.

Note: *You can make a hierarchy of objects into a single rigid body group by selecting the group and performing the create rigid body command. This works as long as there are no existing rigid bodies in this hierarchy.*

10 Create a bomb

- Create a primitive cylinder.

- Place the cylinder on the *launcherPad*, making sure to leave a little gap between it and the launch pad.

- Set this object to be an active rigid body.

- Apply a gravity field to the cylinder.

- Playback the scene.

The catapult in action

11 Tune the throw

- Tune the throw by setting the spring constraint attributes as follows:

    Spring Stiffness to **200**;

    Spring Damping to **5**;

    Spring Rest Length to **1**.

*For the springRestLength you have already tried a value that is one half its initial value. Other values will change the action but it is generally a good idea to keep this value constant and use the other values of **SpringStiffness** and **Damping** to control the catapult strength and recoil.*

***Damping** and **Friction** settings on the launcherPad and the bomb will also play a part in the simulation. Try to set **Friction** to **3** and **Damping** to **1** on both the bomb and launcherPad.*

Friction controls how much resistance occurs between surfaces. Damping can be thought of as air density.

Note: *A good solution for limiting the range of the catapult arm is to place a hidden passive rigid body object just behind the boomWheel so the lever collides with it, thus stopping it before the boom hits the overhead. If the rigidBody is placed up higher, interpenetrations are more likely to occur since the tip of the arm is traveling faster than the base of the arm. The solver might not be checking frequently enough to be able to catch interpenetrations that occur at such a fast pace.*

12 Save your work

- Save your scene as *17-catapult_02.ma.*

Pod engines

In this more complex example, you will learn how to control high resolution geometry via lower resolution rigid bodies. You will set up a network of constraints between control objects that will in turn drive higher resolution geometry.

In the second section of this example, you will learn how to attach the complex rigid body setup to a motion path for animation.

1 Open scene file

- Open the file *17-pods_01.ma.*

This file contains two pod engines. The engine on the right is already set up and will be used as reference for you to set up the engine on the left.

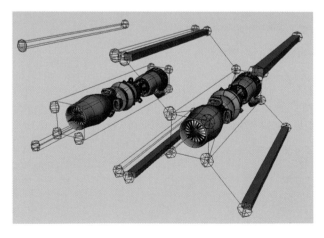

The pod setups

*Also note the display layers in the scene. You can use these to help organize
the scene. Several items are set as references so they are visible in shaded
mode but not selectable.*

2   Create passive rigid bodies

- Use the display layers to hide *engine1*, *engine2* and *controls2*.

- Individually, select the eight spheres at the ends of the *controlArmsGroup*.

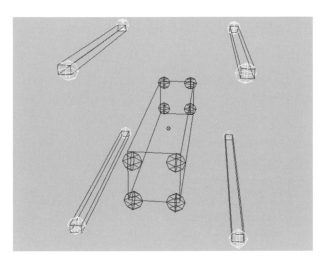

Geometry for anchoring the constraints

- Select **Soft/Rigid Bodies** → **Create Passive Rigid Body.**

- With the newly created passive rigid bodies still selected, set the
  following attributes in the Channel Box.

  Mass to **1**;

  Bounciness to **0.4**;

  Damping to **0.8**;

  Static Friction and **Dynamic Friction** to **0.6**;

  Stand In to **None**;

  Active to **Off**;

  Collisions to **Off** (very important);

  Apply Forces At to **boundingBox.**

Lesson 17

3   Create active rigid bodies

- Individually **Shift-select** the eight spheres surrounding the central box and also select the box.

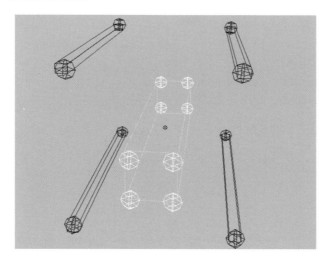

Spheres and surrounding box selected

- Select **Soft/Rigid Bodies** → **Create Active Rigid Body**.
- With these newly created active rigid bodies still selected, set the following attributes in the Channel Box:

  Mass to **1**;

  Bounciness to **0.4**;

  Damping to **0.8**;

  Static Friction and **Dynamic Friction** to **0.6**;

  StandIn to **None**;

  Active to **On**;

  Collisions to **Off** (very important);

  Apply Forces At to **boundingBox**.

4   Create spring constraints

- Make the *controls2* display layer visible, but keep it set to reference (**R**).

  Use the objects in control2 as a guide so you can see how to configure the constraints for control1.

- Select the upper left front sphere on the control arm and the upper left front sphere of the main box as shown below:

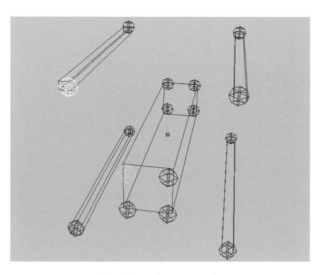

Rig with spring constraint

- Select **Soft/Rigid Bodies** → **Create Spring Constraint**.

- Set the following in the Channel Box:

    Stiffness to **200**;

    Damping to **10**;

    Spring Rest Length to **3.0**.

5 Repeat springs for remaining pairs of spheres

Create the same spring
constraint for the remaining
pairs of spheres, then
select all the constraints
and set their attributes
appropriately through the
Channel Box.

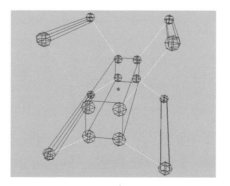

All spring constraints created

Lesson 17

Note: *You can press* **g** *to redo the last action, which is the constraint creation.*

6   Create pin constraints

Now you will create pin constraints between the central box object and each sphere at the corner of the box. This is done to keep the box from rotating out of control.

- Select the upper left box ball, and **Shift-select** the box as in the following image:

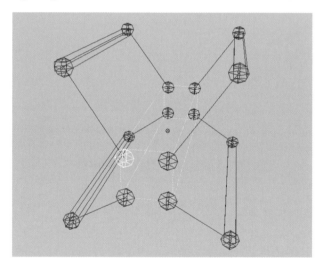

Objects for first pin constraint

- Select **Soft/Rigid Bodies** → **Create Pin Constraint**.

Leave the pin's pivot where it was created for now.

- Repeat the process for the remaining seven spheres around the box.

Pin constraints prior to positioning

7 Move the pins into place

Now you will move each pin to the center of each sphere.

Tip: *Set your selection mask so you can select only rigid constraints if needed.*

- Select one of the pin constraints.
- Use snap to point along with the front and side views to align the constraints' pivot so they are positioned at the centers of each sphere as shown below:

Tip: *Use the controls2 display layer for reference if you need.*

Pin constraints in position

8 Connect fields

- Select all seventeen rigid bodies you created; two sets of eight spheres and the main box.
- In the Outliner, **Ctrl-select** the *gravityField1* and *turbulenceField1* objects under the *engineOne* hierarchy.
- Select **Fields** → **Affect Selected Object(s)**.

9 Add the constraints to the controls1 layer

- Select all the new rigid constraints created so far.
- Press **Ctrl+g** to group them and rename the group to *constraints*.

- Parent the *constraints* group to the *engineOne* group.

- With the *constraints* group still selected, **RMB-click** on the *controls1* layer, then select **Add Selected Objects**.

10 Test the results

- Display the *engine1* layer and hide the *controls1* layer.

- Playback the animation.

The pod engine now appears to be moving because of its thrust.

- Rewind the animation.

11 Save your work

- Save the scene as *17-pods_02.ma*.

Animating along a path

1 Scene file

- Continue with your own file.

Or

- Open the scene called *17-pods_02.ma*.

2 Create a path

- Select **Create → EP Curve Tool**.

- From the top view, draw a curve to be used as a path.

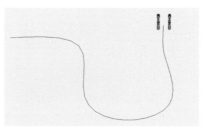

Curve to be used as a path

3 Attach a locator to the path

- Select **Create → Locator** and rename it to *pathLoc*.

- Select *pathLoc*, then **Shift-select** the path curve.

- Select **Animate → Motion Paths → Attach to Motion Path → ❒**.

- Set the following:

    Time Range to **Start/End**;

    Start Time to **30**;

    End Time to **230**;

Follow to **On**;

Front Axis to **X**;

Up Axis to **Y**;

World Up Type to **Scene Up**;

Bank to **On**;

Bank Scale to **5**;

Bank Limit to **90**.

- Click the **Attach** button.

When you playback the animation, the locator follows along the path.

Note: *Don't change the shape of the path unless you are at frame **1**. This can cause problems that are difficult to recover from.*

4 Parent the controlArms

- Make the *controls2* and *controls1* display layers visible.
- Parent both *controlArms* to the *pathLoc* locator.

5 Playback

- Playback the animation.

There is a lot going on here, including several layers of hierarchy, point and orient constraints, passive and active rigid bodies with fields, motion path control, etc., all affecting the motion of these objects and all being evaluated simultaneously.

6 Save your work

- Save the scene as *17-pods_03.ma*.

Note: *The scene file called 17-pods_04.ma contains a finalized version of the pod engines with particles.*

Hardware display of sprite smoke

Note: *This smoke only renders using the Hardware Render Buffer and would need to be composited into a final rendered image. Hardware rendering is covered in greater detail later in the book.*

Tips and traps

Some of the following issues may arise as you go through the examples of this lesson:

- Cycle warning messages are often displayed when you use dynamics. These messages can usually be ignored. Type `cycleCheck -e off` in the Command Line to disable this warning.

- Sometimes objects will not move back to their original position correctly upon rewinding the scene. If you notice that problem, check first if caching is enabled for the *rigidBody* solver since that might be the problem. This can also be caused if you are scrubbing in the timeline or using undos. This can be partially caused by the fact that there are dynamic and non-dynamic constraints working together. The undo queue may not be able to record all complex interdependent functions. In some cases, simply zeroing out the transforms on the offset geometry can serve as a temporary fix. A rule of thumb when doing dynamics is to save under incremented versions often. If you don't do so, you may have to restart and do your setup again. Try to keep scrubbing and undoing to a minimum.

- Notice that when geometry pieces are in the same hierarchy, you cannot make a parent surface a rigid body if one or more children are rigid bodies. You can only have one rigid body controlling a given hierarchy. The next optimization lesson will discuss some alternatives to this limitation.

- It is recommended to make the most of your dynamic changes while at frame 1. Not doing so might create unexpected results.

- Take advantage of the fact that you can keyframe a rigid body constraint On and Off in the Channel Box. For example, you can have a leaf dangling from a tree using a pin constraint, then disable the constraint to allow the leaf to fall to the ground at a specific time.

- If a lot of collisions are happening in your scene, try setting half the rigid bodies on one collision layer and the other half on another. Despite the fact that some interpenetration could happen, it could be much faster for the solver to calculate the scene.

Conclusion

Rigid body constraints are an important part of working with dynamically animated geometry. Understanding the various advantages of using a specific constraint for a specific application can greatly affect how you approach a shot. Alternative methods outlined here for building and controlling hierarchies of objects through parenting and constraints are important to consider as you build more complicated scenes or scenes that require more control.

In the next lesson, you will learn about rigid body optimization.

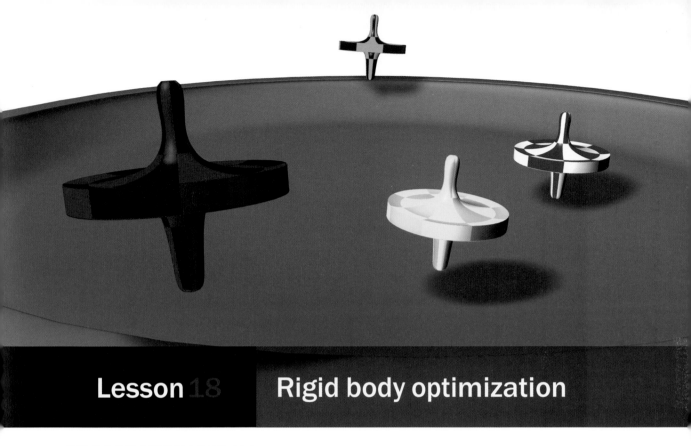

Lesson 18 Rigid body optimization

This lesson covers some fundamental tools and techniques for ensuring your rigid body simulations are as efficient as possible.

In this lesson you will learn the following:

- The importance of stand-in geometry;

- Rigid body and solver optimization settings;

- Collision and interpenetration troubleshooting;

- Baking simulations.

Optimization

There are several cases, if not all cases, when you should think about optimizing your scene's dynamics. The following guidelines can help you determine if you should think about optimizing your scene:

- When the scene runs excessively slow;

- When the dynamic simulation fails due to interpenetration errors;

- When the dynamics behave erratically and unpredictably.

You generally expect performance problems when running simulations in dense environments and expect lighter scenes to present less of a challenge to the interaction and playback.

The first objective is to ensure that a scene progresses through the simulation, only stopping or slowing down during an intensive calculation.

The second objective is to achieve playback as close to real-time as possible without having to render or playblast the scene. This is a good goal, but in many cases cannot be attained due to hardware and software performance limitations.

To achieve these objectives, you will look at some typical problem areas and the necessary steps to ensure that the solver is not driven into an unsolvable situation.

The rigid solver

The rigid solver calculates the transformation attributes for rigid bodies using the attributes on the *rigidBody* nodes and the global attributes set on the *rigid solver* node as input. The attributes on the *rigid solver* node control the accuracy of the solution. The following material will help you find the right balance of accuracy versus speed.

Unpredictable or wild results

This is typically caused by values being fed into the solver that are wildly changing or exceeding the proper expected range. The proper expected range encompasses values that make sense for the solver on a given attribute or dynamic state. If the solver encounters a value that is much larger or smaller than it was expecting, it may tell an object to travel much faster or farther than the other objects around it are prepared to do.

The solver must make assumptions to increase its performance. When you intentionally or unintentionally stress the simulation, you may exploit an assumption that the solver is making. This can result in errors. Remember, the simulation is only an approximation.

The goal is to set the approximation to an appropriate trade-off between accuracy and interaction.

Solver grinding or failing

When a scene is grinding or no longer making forward progress, it is time to take a look at what is going on more closely. The Script Editor is the first place to look for errors and information that may be produced by the solver. Even seemingly unimportant warnings can provide a clue as to why a solver is failing farther on. Your first step should be to investigate all warnings and errors.

You should learn to associate warnings and errors with symptoms and conditions that lead to solver problems.

Slow playback

In order to speed up playback, the load on the solver must be reduced. The solver attempts to determine where every rigid body vertex is at any given frame.

The first step is usually reducing the amount of vertices that the solver must keep track of. Using Stand Ins will accomplish this, as will tuning rigid body tessellation to more coarse values. A stand-in is a less complex shape that is used to represent a more complex shape, essentially an object with less data for the solver to monitor.

Reducing the overhead of other scene components and display functions can go a long way to improving playback. Think about displaying in wireframe, or hiding other unused objects, for instance.

Caching the animation is necessary for optimizing rigid bodies that have an unavoidable geometry density. Caching can use a lot of memory in scenes with dense geometric objects. Caching will not make it easier for the solver to calculate a solution, but it will help speed up your work because it reduces the time you have to wait for the solver.

Interpenetration errors

An interpenetration error occurs when the solver can no longer guarantee the accuracy of the simulation due to one object's geometry having passed through another object's geometry. Typically, the solver stops or slows down the simulation if this error occurs.

The solver slows down and tells you about the problem because this error is important in order for the dynamics to be properly simulated. This type of feedback is very important. You can use it to your advantage to help adjust simulation properties so that the solver does not enter into a corrupt or inaccurate situation.

Lesson 18

Imagine if a sharp piece of geometry spiked into another object creating an interpenetration. The only way for the object to continue on would be to reverse its direction, back itself out and continue in a less penetrating fashion. This would be a very laborious and computationally intensive moment and one that you want to avoid completely, if possible.

Avoid interpenetration errors by:

- Anticipating objects that are at risk;

- Using stand-in geometry;

- Adjusting tessellations;

- Adjusting *rigidSolver* **Step Size** and **Collision Tolerance** attributes in the Attribute Editor;

- Increasing **Damping** to avoid wild velocities;

- Using closed geometry surfaces;

- Checking the surface normal orientations;

- Positioning objects to have a little gap between them before the simulation starts.

Scene optimization example

This exercise steps you through some common scene problems that lead to optimization and troubleshooting. It is a very simple scene that has been constructed to demonstrate some of the more common things you can check for when optimizing a more complex scene.

1   Scene file

- Open the file called *18-battleTops_01.ma*.

This scene contains an arena with four battle tops.

2   Playback the scene

The scene is set up to a point where it is in need of some optimization. It also has some warnings that are creating problems. You can often learn about the problem by opening the Script Editor. Then you should ask yourself:

- What do you notice about performance?

- What do you notice in the Script Editor?
- What do you notice about the base object?
- What do you notice about the tops?

3   Display the normals of the objects

- Select the base area and the four *tops*.

Tip: *Make sure that you are in shaded mode to see the normals.*

- Select **Display** → **NURBS Components** → **Normals**.

The base and the tops' normals are pointing inward. This is a common problem that should be checked for with both NURBS and polygonal surfaces.

Tip: *It may be difficult to see that the normals are facing inward. It helps to dolly your camera inside one of the tops' geometry to clearly see the surface normal direction.*

Note: *When you first open the file, error messages are shown in the Script Editor, telling you that some objects' surfaces might be reversed.*

4   Reverse the surfaces

- Select the *base* area and the four *tops*.
- In the Modeling menu set, select **Edit NURBS** → **Reverse Surface Direction** → ❑.
- Reset the options.
- Click the **Reverse** button.

Although this may improve performance and alleviate interpenetration problems, for this particular scene it hasn't solved our slow performance problem yet. Sometimes, it is just one or two things that affect the entire situation. Nonetheless, having the normals facing outward is important.

Lesson 18

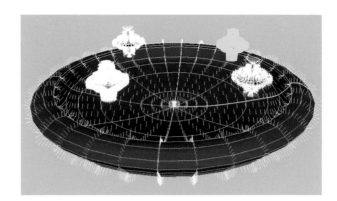

Normals with correct orientation

- Select **Display** → **NURBS Components** → **Normals** again to hide the normals on the selected objects.

5   Rebuild the geometry

Another reason for hampered playback can be geometry that is needlessly overbuilt, therefore, you will rebuild the tops' geometry to see if that will fix the slow playback.

- Select the four tops.

- Select **Edit NURBS** → **Rebuild Surfaces** → ❐.

- Set the following:

  > **Rebuild Type** to **Reduce**;
  >
  > **Parameter Range** to **0 to 1**;
  >
  > **Direction** to **U and V**;
  >
  > **Keep Originals** to **Off**;
  >
  > **Use Tolerance** to **Local**;
  >
  > **Positional Tolerance** to **1.0**;
  >
  > **Output Geometry** to **NURBS**.

- Click the **Rebuild** button.

- Playback to check for improvements.

Once again, doing so will not make a huge performance increase, but this step is still recommended to help prevent other problems that could be introduced.

Tessellation factor for NURBS rigid bodies

As you may know, when you render a NURBS object, the renderer tessellates the NURBS geometry into polygons prior to rendering. A similar process occurs when the dynamics engine encounters a NURBS rigid body object. The solver assigns a tessellation factor to the NURBS object that determines the polygonal approximation of the shape. You can adjust the accuracy of this approximation by adjusting the **Tessellation Factor** attribute under **Performance Attributes** for each rigid body object. This attribute has no effect on polygonal rigid body objects.

By default, the **Tessellation Factor** is **200**.

If you have a highly detailed NURBS object, 200 polygons may not be enough for the solver to accurately represent that shape when calculating collisions. Although lower tessellation factors will mean less computation work for the solver, you will also have less accurate representation of your NURBS geometry. Being aware of this attribute can help you tune your simulations to add more or less accuracy where necessary.

By rebuilding the tops objects, you have reduced the geometric load on the solver. Another way is to adjust the Tessellation Factor attribute. The main drawback is that you do not have control over where the tessellation is most needed. In this example, you want more tessellation at the tips to avoid a sharp interpenetrating point and also at the sides to avoid interpenetration when tops collide.

Another strategy might be to convert your rigid bodies to polygons during the rebuilding process, thus creating a stand-in object for collisions and simulation.

Stand Ins

One of the best ways to clean up the performance of rigid bodies is to use stand-in objects. This is very useful when you have dense or irregular objects that you want to attach rigid body dynamics to. The *rigidBody* node provides a choice of cube and sphere Stand Ins that you can select from. Alternatively, you may wish to create your own stand-in geometry, then make it a rigid body and simply parent your higher resolution object to that stand-in and hide the stand-in.

1   Substitute the base with the lower resolution object

One needlessly complex object in the scene is the base object; it has geometry not involved in collisions.

- Select base object.

- Select **Edit** → **Delete by Type** → **Rigid Body**.

- Select *lowRezBase* from the Outliner and make it visible by showing selection.

This object was created by duplicating the base object, then detaching the surface at the appropriate place and deleting the unnecessary geometry.

- Select **Soft/Rigid Bodies** → **Create Passive Rigid Body**.

Now the collisions will be computed only for the area of the base that is important for this particular simulation.

- Hide the *lowRezBase*.

- Playback the scene.

There should still be no major improvements.

Optimizing a dynamics scene is often like optimizing for rendering. You can try several different options until you find what works. During this process, you have cleaned up a lot of things and will continue to do so.

2   Set tessellation for the tops' rigid bodies

The rigid body dynamics are determined by an approximation of the rigid body object's shape. This approximation is controlled by the tessellation of the rigid body unless a stand-in object is specified.

- Select the *top1*.

- Open the Attribute Editor and locate the **Performance Attributes** section under the *rigidBody* tab.

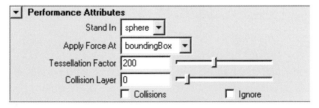

Performance Attributes section

- Following are explanations about the attributes found in this section:

   Stand In

   Selects a stand-in object, such as **sphere** or **cube**.

   Apply Force At

   Dynamic forces applied at **Center of Mass**, **Bounding Box** or **VerticesOrCVs**. **VerticiesOrCVs** is the most accurate, but the slowest.

   Tessellation Factor

   Adjusts geometric approximation of rigid body object.

Collision Layer

Selects the collision layer participation. Objects on the same collision layer number will collide with each other. Objects on different collision layer numbers will not collide with each other. An object on collision layer **-1** will collide with objects on any collision layer.

- Set the **Stand In** attribute to **none**.

- Set the **Apply Force At** attribute to **VerticiesOrCVs**.

- Set the **Tessellation Factor** attribute to **100**.

Below are the equivalent tessellations for the top1 object set to **100**, **150**, **200** *and* **500**.

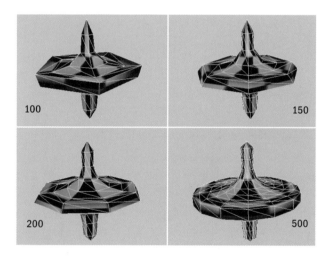

Tessellation values

Note: *At low tessellation values, the point of the top is much sharper. This affects how the top spins and also increases the likelihood of an interpenetration. At low tessellation values, the interaction of the edge of the top with other tops is less predictable.*

- Set the **Collisions** attribute to **On**.

- Repeat the above steps for the remaining tops.

3   Use the Attribute Spread Sheet

You have tried all of these things but nothing has solved the problem yet. When this happens, it is a good idea to have a look at the *rigidBody* nodes themselves and compare them against each other. You want to look for differences between the rigid bodies or values that stand out as excessively large or small.

- Select all the tops' *rigidBody* nodes.

Tip: *A quick way to select the rigid bodies is to select the surfaces, then pressing the* **down arrow** *followed by the* **right arrow** *on your keyboard.*

- Select **Window** → **General Editors** → **Attribute Spread Sheet...**

- Make sure the **Shape Keyable** tab is selected.

- Compare the attribute values.

The **InitialSpin** *settings are very high, with some at 30000 units per frame. This is potentially the root of the problem for this scene.*

- Lower the **InitialSpin** values around **2000** units.

With practice, you will learn valid ranges for the different attributes and also learn how many attributes rely on each other. In other words, if you change mass, you may have to change frictions to compensate for the new motion.

- In order to make the tops more aggressive, set the **Bounciness** value to **0.9**, and the **Damping** value to **0**.

- Playback the simulation again.

You should notice much faster performance in the playback.

Playback is now real-time

4 Save your work

- Save the scene as *18-battleTops_02.ma*.

Working through this process usually isn't too much fun but knowing what to check and being methodical about checking things will help you track down and solve problems. It will also help you design things correctly when starting from scratch to avoid potential problems.

Obviously, the scene file shown here is very simple by design. Chances are that your production scenes will not be this simple. Design your work smartly from the ground up and also know what you can reasonably expect as good performance from the solver. Always look for ways to keep the number of rigid body calculations to a minimum.

Bake animation

Maya is much faster at evaluating animation curves than at evaluating dynamic motions. The primary reason an evaluation of animation curve data is faster is because it knows where the object is going to be at any given point in time. This is not true for a rigid body simulation. The position and orientation of all rigid bodies are calculated using rules inside each frame to produce the final result.

In the following example, you will learn some additional optimization techniques. You will learn how to produce animation curve data from objects that are dynamically controlled. This process is called *baking*.

> **Tip:** *Baking animation is not limited to dynamics animation. For instance, you can also bake objects driven by constraints.*

This scene returns to the example of the ZyZak armor being destroyed by the ChubbChubb stand-in.

Another challenge here will be getting these interdependent objects reacting to each other without stalling the solution due to interpenetration. Hopefully, you can use what you learned in the previous section of this chapter to overcome any such interpenetration problems encountered.

1 Scene file

- Open the file called *18-armorOptimized_01.ma*.

This scene consists of the armor constrained together with rigid constraints and the ChubbChubb stand-in bouncing at it.

2   Playback the scene

As the armor is falling on its back, notice that some interpenetrations occurs and that the simulation slows down as it plays.

Performance Attributes section

3   Solver attributes

The solver attributes of **Step Size** and **Collision Tolerance** will need to be slightly lowered.

- Set the following for the current *rigidSolver* within the Attribute Editor:

    Step Size to **0.02**;

    Collision Tolerance to **0.03**;

    Rigid Solver Method to **Runge Kutta Adaptive**.

The solver settings are very important and are a good place to look at early in the process of reaching a good solution. If your scene generates persistent interpenetration problems, then the solver settings of Step Size and Collision Tolerance should be lowered slightly.

The solver method also influences performance. The **Runge Kutta Adaptive** *method is the default calculation method and is generally the most accurate setting. Experiment with these methods so that you are comfortable with their respective strengths and weaknesses.*

As you will learn, one small change in your scene can change all the interdependent and subsequent elements of the simulation. Having patience and being methodical are important. Also, making slight adjustments in the initial starting position of your simulation can have profound effects.

Controlling interpenetrations and collisions

Sometimes when creating a dynamic system, you might want to allow some rigid bodies to interpenetrate. Doing so can greatly speed up playback, at a minimal cost.

The following shows you how you can control the collisions between some of the rigid bodies on the ZyZak armor.

1 Allow interpenetration

- Select the following two surfaces:

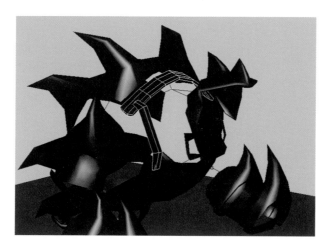

Select the objects that are allowed to interpenetrate

- Select **Solvers → Set Rigid Body Interpenetration**.

Those two objects are now allowed to interpenetrate.

2 Repeat

- Repeat the previous steps to allow interpenetration between the same strap and torso plate.

- Repeat the previous steps for all the other straps.

3 Playback the animation

You should notice a slight difference in the animation and in the playback since there are less collisions to be handled by the solver.

Lesson 18

4 Enable collisions

If you wish to enable the collisions again, do the following:

- Select the objects for which you would like to enable collisions.

- Select **Solvers** → **Set Rigid Body Collision**.

5 Save your work

- Save the scene as *18-armorOptimized_02.ma*.

Bake the armor

Once you have a decent simulation for all the rigid bodies, you can simplify things by baking the simulation. Baking converts the dynamics induced animation to animation curves. These curves can then be tweaked and manipulated like any other animation curve.

The baking process also provides other performance benefits and functionality. You will bake the dynamic motion of the armor and delete the *rigidBody* nodes.

1 Scene file

- Continue with your own scene file.

Or

- Open the file called *18-armorOptimized_02.ma*.

Tip: It is recommended to keep a version of the dynamic scene before baking the animation. Doing so will allow you to go back in the dynamic scene if needed.

2 Bake the armor and projectile falling down

- Select all of the armor and projectile objects.

- In the Channel Box, highlight the **Translate** and **Rotate** attributes.

Tip: **Click+drag** *across these attributes in the Channel Box to highlight them black.*

- Select **Edit** → **Keys** → **Bake Simulation** → ❑.

- Reset the options in the dialog box and then set them as follows:

  Hierarchy to **Selected**;

  You only want to bake the selected object, not the entire hierarchy.

  Channels to **From Channel Box**;

  You will highlight the appropriate transform attributes in the Channel Box.

  Time Range to **Time Slider**;

  You should only need to bake about **200** frames.

  Sample by to **1.0**.

  The resulting animation will have **1** key per frame.

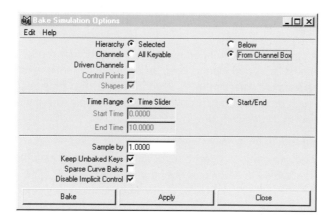

Bake Simulation Options

- Press the **Bake** button.

The animation will be played through, and keyframes will be set for each frame of the simulation for all selected objects. This will result in animation curves.

3 Delete the dynamics

Since the rigid bodies and rigid body constraints are no longer required, you will now delete them.

- Select **Edit** → **Delete All by Type** → **Rigid Bodies**.

- Select **Edit** → **Delete All by Type** → **Rigid Constraints**.

- Delete the *gravity* field.

Lesson 18

4 Delete static channels

Baking animation often creates static animation channels, which slows down the playback.

- Select **Edit** → **Delete All by Type** → **Static Channels**.

5 Playback

Confirm that the bake is accurate. Problems with baking can arise when either you are sampling by too coarse of a **Sample Rate** or you are trying to bake too many channels from **Control Points** or **Shape** nodes animation. Treat these other nodes and channels as separate passes.

Also, notice that if you select any animated objects, the timeline shows a series of red tick marks. These are the keyframes that now control the motion of the objects. You can also view and edit these keys using the Graph Editor.

Baking is strongly recommended as the last step before rendering any rigid body scene. It is a good idea to keep an unbaked dynamic version of your scene and a baked version that is used for rendering. Time-based rendering options, such as motion blur, work much more reliably with baked animation data than with dynamically driven animation.

Baking with the control points option enabled is a good method for baking out soft body animations prior to rendering them with motion blur. Soft bodies are covered in detail in a later lesson.

6 Save your work

- Save the scene as *18-armorOptimized_03.ma*.

Creating multiple rigid solvers

Using multiple rigid solvers gives you the ability to adjust solver settings independently. If you have groups of colliding objects that will not collide with each other (perhaps they are not in close proximity), then putting them on different solvers helps optimize the scene and hasten the playback.

To select the current solver:

- Select **Solvers** → **Current Rigid Solver** → **rigidSolver**.

To create a new solver:

- Select **Solvers** → **Create Rigid Body Solver**.

To move rigid bodies to another solver, simply select the objects and type the following command in the Command Line:

```
rigidBody -edit -solver rigidSolver1;
```

New solvers can have separate settings while maintaining the settings already in place for the existing simulations. Any new rigid bodies you create in the scene will be assigned to the selected current rigid solver and will only collide with other rigid bodies that are part of that solver. In a way, this is like using collision layers. The difference is that you can control each solvers' accuracy level independently.

Optimization reminder list

Tuning and troubleshooting rigid bodies can usually be approached by keeping the following in mind:

- **Adapt the tessellation** of NURBS and polygons so that the solver can minimize the amount of calculation to be done.

- **Double check the normals of your surfaces**, which can solve many problems.

- Use **stand Ins** for both NURBS and polygonal objects to help the solver work with this geometry.

- **Bake the simulation** to increase playback speed and add control to complex scenes.

- **Use collision layers** to separate objects for which the solver should not calculate collisions.

- Use **multiple solvers** to help localize control over a specific simulation, collision or interaction.

- The `rigidBody` and `rigidSolver` MEL commands can be used for creation and modification of *rigidBodies* and *rigidSolver* nodes in MEL scripts. Refer to the online MEL command reference for a list of all available flags for these commands.

- Use caching when possible to speed things up.

Lesson 18

Solver accuracy

It is important to remember that the solver is an approximation of real world physics. The solver doesn't evaluate detailed information about subtle surface properties. Doing this detailed level of calculation (such as some systems specifically designed for engineering purposes), would be slower than existing methods. The solver is not intended to give you accuracy down to the millionth decimal point. However, there is a decent level of accuracy control there if you need it. Use rigid bodies to get some dynamic motion happening, bake and modify where necessary, and be glad you don't have to keyframe it all by hand!

Units

You should always keep in mind your scene scale and units when working with dynamics and fields. In physics, gravity is measured in meters per second squared. In Maya, the same is true, however, usually people work in centimeters, not meters. Therefore, the effect of gravity seems to be off by a factor of 100. You will often see rigid body objects floating through the scene seemingly in slow motion because of this. Things may appear okay in your hardware playback, but when you view it in real time, you notice this floating motion.

For example, if you are trying to match live action motion, you will most likely need to crank your gravity much higher than a magnitude of **9.8**, for instance, **980**. In practice, it is best to keep the scene units at centimeters; you will find that you will have fewer problems. Using reference footage is very important.

The movie *dropBall.mpg* included with the *support_files* is reference footage that was shot to compare real world gravity with the Maya gravity in centimeters. Importing this movie footage into Maya via an image plane and mimicking the motion with rigid bodies is a good way to get an idea of how dynamics relate to real world physics.

Bake before render

Baking is highly recommend before you render rigid bodies or soft bodies, especially if you are rendering with motion blur. This is especially true when using a render farm, where each machine has different frames to render and where slight differences in the dynamic simulation can make the object flicker and ruin a render.

> **Note:** When baking animation, you should be aware of gimbal lock, where an object can do a 360 degree rotation in-between two frames. This behavior might cause motion blur to create a flicker as it thinks the object is moving at an incredible speed.

Conclusion

You are now experienced with dynamic optimization. Knowing about the different topics discussed here can greatly improve your animation, playback and renders.

In the next project, you will learn about particles and their uses.

Project Six

Lessons

In Project Six, you will learn about particles and their different uses. Particles are the heart of special effects such as fire, snow, rain and smoke. They can also be dynamic and collide with geometry and even affect rigid bodies. In this project, you will also learn about writing MEL expressions that can ease the creation and animation of your particle effects.

By the end of this project, you should feel comfortable creating, emitting and controlling particles' animation and look.

Lesson 19　Introduction to particles

This lesson focuses on the basic concepts required to understand and work efficiently with particles. It should be considered an essential framework to build upon for more advanced concepts that are discussed throughout the upcoming lessons.

In this lesson you will learn the following:

- The particle shape node;

- The basic particle attributes;

- Fields;

- Emitters.

Particle structure

Particles differ from geometry in the following ways:

- Particles are points in space. They require special handling at render time because they do not contain surface information.

- Particles can be rendered using hardware or software rendering methods. The particle's **Render Type** attribute controls which of these two methods is used.

- Individual particles belong to a common collection referred to as the *particleShape* object, just as vertices of a geometric object belong to their shape node. Individual particles can be thought of as components to the *particleShape* node.

- Particle attributes are commonly categorized into two types: **Per Particle** (array) and **Per Object**.

- Particles do not have volume, which means that you will not be able to stack particles on each other. For instance, if you poor water particles in a glass, the glass will not fill up.

Applications of particles

Particles are commonly used to simulate complex natural phenomena. Common examples include smoke, rain, sparks, gases, dust, snow, fire and other motions that consist of complex or random movement of many individual components.

Particles can be keyframed or controlled dynamically as a group.

Creating a particle galaxy

There are several methods for creating particle objects. In this first example, the focus will be on using the **Particle Tool**.

The **Par**ticle Tool is a quick and easy way of creating individual particles, particle grids and random collections of particles. This can be useful for generating some particles to begin working with. The tool also provides you with the ability to interactively place particles exactly where you want them.

1   Sketch some particles

- Select **Particles** → **Particle Tool** → ❑.

- Set the following:

  Particle Name to *galaxy*;

  Number of Particles to **20**;

  Maximum Radius to **3**;

  Sketch Particles to **On**;

  Sketch Interval to **5**.

- **Click+drag** to sketch a cross-like shape in the *top* view, then press **Enter**.

A cross of particles

- Open the Outliner to see the newly created particle object called *galaxy*.

You will need to show shapes in the Outliner to see the galaxyShape node.

- In the Outliner, enable the option **Display → Shapes**.

2   Vortex field

To make the particles spin like a galaxy, you will apply a vortex field.

- Select the *galaxy* particle object.

- Select **Fields → Vortex**.

- Playback to watch the particles spin.

Tip: *Increase the playback range as needed.*

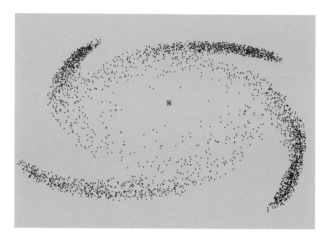

The vortex field effect on the particles

3 Set Initial State

Every time you rewind, the galaxy returns to the cross shape. To prevent this, you can set the **Initial State** of the particles.

- Playback until the particles are in a galaxy like shape.

- With the particles selected, select **Solvers** → **Initial State** → **Set For Selected**.

Now when you rewind, the galaxy is in the shape it was in when you set the initial state.

4 Adjust Conserve on the particles

To prevent the particles from immediately spinning out of control, you can lower the conserve attribute on the particle object.

- Select the *galaxy* particle object.

- Under the galaxyShape node in the Channel Box, set **Conserve** to **0.8**.

- Set the *vortex*'s **Magnitude** attribute to **200**.

- Rewind and playback the animation.

Conserve *is a very important particle attribute. Conserve is short for conservation of momentum. By default it is set to* **1**, *which means the particles will never lose any of their motion as they move through space. This is a very sensitive attribute so lowering it in very small increments is usually best. Normally, lowering conserve just a little, such as* **0.99**, *will give your particle's motion a more realistic looking appearance.*

5 Keyframe the particles

Traditionally, particles have been animated exclusively through fields and dynamic expressions. You also have the option to animate the particle object's transform like any non-dynamic object. Translate, scale and rotation can be keyframed to provide many common effects.

- Select the *galaxy* particle object.

- Set **Rotate Z** to about **-25** degrees so the galaxy is tilted at an angle.

- Playback the animation.

Things look fine at the first frame of the simulation but as you playback, you may notice that the particles are not orbiting around relative to the new rotation you introduced. Instead, they are revolving around the world axis defined by the vortex field's axis attributes axis attributes – **0**, **1**, **0** *(Y-axis).*

Note: *The axis of the vortex is specified to be* **0, 1, 0** *because of its attributes* **Axis X**, **Axis Y** *and* **Axis Z**. *These attributes define the direction of the force, in this case the Y-axis.*

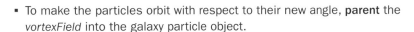

- To make the particles orbit with respect to their new angle, **parent** the *vortexField* into the galaxy particle object.

- Set **Forces In World** to **Off** in the Channel Box for the *galaxyShape* object.

Now, the vortex's axis is being calculated in local space to the particle object instead of the world space. Also, the field is conveniently parented into this effect so you can keyframe the entire galaxy's translation, rotation and scale as you wish.

6 Save your work

- Save your work as *19-galaxy_01.ma*.

Lesson 19

Note: *It is also possible to create an empty particle object by setting the number of particles to* **0** *in the Particle Tool options, or by typing* `particle;` *in the Script Editor or Command Line. Empty particle objects are commonly needed when working with particle emitters, which are discussed in the next section.*

Emitters

An emitter is like a cannon that projects particles into space. Below is a list of the different kinds of emitters available to you:

> **Directional**;
>
> **Omni**;
>
> **Volume**;
>
> **Curve**;
>
> **Surface**;
>
> **Per-Point**;
>
> **Texture**.

Open the file *19-emitterTypes_01.ma* to see an example of each of these types.

Tip: *Shaded mode display is recommended to see the colored particles. You may also want to use the display layers provided in the scene to keep the viewport from getting overly cluttered.*

Water fountain example

1 Scene file

A fountain is a very simple effect that you will create to learn how to work with the particle system.

- Open the file *19-fountain_01.ma*.

This file contains geometry of a simple fountain with no dynamics. You will add a directional emitter and modify some of its attributes.

2   Create a directional emitter

A directional emitter allows you to specify exactly what direction in world space to emit the particles.

- Select **Particles** → **Create Emitter** → ❒.

- Set the following:

    Emitter Type to **Directional**.

- Press **Create**.

This creates two new objects. Emitter1 is the directional emitter that emits particles, and the particle object particle1.

3   Position and name the emitter

- Select *emitter1* in the Outliner and position it slightly below the tip of the fountain's *spout*.

- **Rename** *emitter1* to *spray.*

- **Rename** *particle1* to *mist.*

4   Playback the animation

- Set the playback range to start at frame **1** and end at frame **500**.

- Playback the animation.

By default, the particle emitter direction occurs along the **X-axis***.*

5   Modify the emitter's attributes using manipulators

- With the *spray* emitter selected, press the **t** key to switch to the **Show Manipulator Tool.**

Tip: *You may need to hide the NURBS surfaces to see the emitter.*

The small circular icon below the emitter is a toggle switch that cycles the manipulator through different attributes on the emitter, so that each attribute can be quickly edited graphically. This manipulator functions similarly to manipulators on spot lights, which you may already be familiar with. The value manip will change based on the attribute manip selection. It can be **click+dragged** *to change the attribute value.*

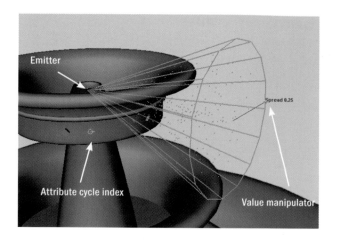

Show Manipulator Tool on emitter

- Use the manipulators or Channel Box to adjust the **Direction, Speed, Rate** and **Spread** of the emitter.

- The following values work well for the *spray* emitter:

  Direction to **0, 1, 0**;

  Rate to **1000**;

  Spread to **0.17**.

Emitter spraying on Y direction

Note: *A* **Spread** *value of* **1** *corresponds to a 180 degree emission cone.* **Rate** *is a measurement of the number of particles per time unit that are emitted. The default time unit is seconds.* **Speed** *determines how fast the particles leave the emitter.*

6 Change the particle render type

- Select the *mist* object.

- Open the Attribute Editor, and select the *mistShape* tab.

- Under the **Render Attributes** section, set the following:

    Particle Render Type to **MultiStreak**;

    Depth Sort to **On**.

- Press the **Current Render Type** button and set the following:

    Color Accum to **On**;

    Use Lighting to **On**.

These options determine the draw, shading and lighting properties of this particle object. These settings make the particles appear somewhat more like water droplets in motion. The specific details of these options will be discussed more in the upcoming lesson.

7 Add gravity and turbulence to the droplets

Adding fields will help better define the particles' motion.

- With *mist* still selected, select **Fields** → **Gravity**.

- Select *mist* again, then select **Fields** → **Turbulence**.

- Playback the scene to test the gravity and turbulence fields.

Note: *When a field is chosen from the Fields menu, all selected objects will be connected to that field automatically. If nothing is selected, the field is created in the scene and objects can be connected to it using the Dynamic Relationship Editor. Another method is selecting the object(s), then the fields, then selecting* **Fields** → **Affect Selected Object(s)**. *If you want the field to automatically be parented to the selected object, use* **Field** → **Use Selected as Source of Field**.

8 Increase spray's Speed attribute

Using a higher speed value causes the particles to leave the emitter faster which, in turn, allows them to travel higher before being overcome by gravity.

- Select *spray*.

- Set **Speed** to **10** in the Channel Box.

- Playback the scene.

The effect of the fields on the droplets

9 Save your work

- Save the scene as *19-fountain_02.ma*.

Add a second particle object

To give the impression of water droplets in the water, you will now add a second particle object for the emitter to emit into. The attributes of this particle object can be controlled independently from the *mist* particles.

1 Scene file

- Continue with the previous scene file.

2 Create an empty particle object

An empty particle object will be created to have an empty storage place for the emitter to later emit into. The particles will be created by the emitter, using the attributes set on the *particleShape* node.

- In the Command Line, type the following:

  ```
  particle -name droplets;
  ```

- Press **Enter**.

- Check the Outliner to make sure the *droplets* particle object was created.

3 Establish emission for droplets

Currently, there is no relationship between *droplets* and *spray*. You will now establish a connection between the two.

- Select *droplets* in the Outliner.

- **Ctrl+select** to select *spray*.

- Select **Particles** → **Use Selected Emitter**.

- **Rewind** and **playback**.

The spray emitter now emits into both mist and droplets.

4 Set display attributes for droplets

Just as you defined descriptive attributes for *mist*, you can do the same for *droplets*.

- In the Attribute Editor, set the following attribute values for *droplets*:

    Particle Render Type to **MultiPoint**;

    Depth Sort to **On**;

    Color Accum to **Off**;

    Use Lighting to **On**.

Turning **Color Accum** *Off for droplets creates contrast against the mist particles whose* **Color Accum** *setting was turned On. Depth sorting simply draws the particles on the screen from back to front.*

Tip: When **Color Accum** *is On, overlapping particles within the same particle object get their RGB values added together. This creates a more washed-out or additive appearance. You will only notice the Color Accum effect later, once the particles have an opacity attribute.*

---

5 Connect droplets to the existing gravity

- Select *droplets* in the Outliner.

- **Ctrl-select** *gravity1*.

- Select **Fields** → **Affect Selected Object(s)**.

> **Note:** *You can also use the Dynamic Relationship Editor to connect fields, emitters and particles together.*

- **Playback** the scene.

The droplets particles should fall along with the mist.

The spray emitter emitting droplets and mist particles

6 Save your work

- Save the scene as *19-fountain_03.ma*.

Understanding particle attributes

The next step is to add more specific controls to *droplets* and *mist*. This requires a clear understanding of some important concepts that will be discussed here briefly before continuing with the fountain:

- The most commonly used particle attributes exist on the *particleShape* node. The transform node contains the traditional transform attributes such as translate, scale and rotate.

- All particle objects use position, velocity, acceleration and mass attributes. Therefore, these attributes are part of the *particleShape* node.

- There are many other attributes, such as lifespan, radius, color and incandescence that can be added to particles if needed. This allows you to customize each particle shape to your specific needs and also keeps things more efficient.

- Some attributes are intended to be used for only specific particle render types. For example, *spriteNum* is only intended to be used with sprite particles.

Per particle vs. per object attributes

It is important to understand the difference between the *per particle* and *per object* attributes.

- **Per Particle Attribute** allows each particle to store its own value for a given attribute.

- **Per Object Attribute** assigns one attribute value to the entire particle object.

    It is a common convention to name per particle attributes with a PP at the end. For instance: radiusPP, rgbPP, etc. However, it is not an absolute requirement.

Tip: *For more information regarding various particle attributes, visit Maya's online documentation.*

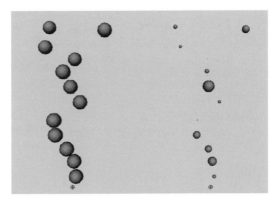

Per Object Radius vs. Per Particle Radius

In the picture above, the particles emitted from the left emitter were given a per object radius attribute (**radius**). The particles emitted from the emitter on the right are in the same relative position as those emitted from the emitter on the left. However, each particle has its own radius value (**radiusPP**).

Color, lifespan and opacity attributes

You will now add per object attributes and per particle attributes.

1 Scene file

- Continue with the previous scene file.

2 Per object attributes for the droplet particles

The lifespan attribute gives you control over how long the particles stay in the scene before they disappear. For now, you will assign the same lifespan value to all the particles to keep things simple.

- Select *droplets* and open the Attribute Editor.

- In the **Lifespan Attributes** section, in **Lifespan Mode**, select **Constant**.

- Set **Lifespan** to **2.5**.

This is the number of seconds that the particles will live. This number means the particles will die just before they touch the base of the fountain.

- In the **Add Dynamic Attributes** section, press **Color** and select **Add Per Object Attribute**.

- Press **Add Attribute**.

Fields for editing **RGB** *are added in the* **Render Attributes** *section and in the Channel Box for this particle object as shown below.*

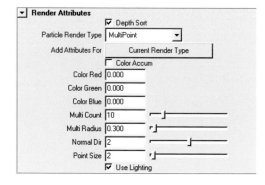

Color per object attribute

- Set the following attributes for **Color**:

    Color Red to **0.5**;

    Color Green to **0.5**;

    Color Blue to **1.0**.

3 Mist particles life span

The lifespan attribute of the mist particles should be the same as the droplet particles.

- Select *mist* and open the Attribute Editor.

- In the **Lifespan Attributes** section, in **Lifespan Mode**, select **Constant**.

- Set **Lifespan** to **2.5**.

4 Per particle attributes for the mist particles

You will now add a per particle opacity attribute, which will control the fading out of each particle as it falls down in the fountain.

- In the **Add Dynamic Attributes** section, press **Opacity** and select **Add Per Particle Attribute**.

- Press **Add Attribute**.

This adds a **opacityPP** *field in the* **Per Particle (Array) Attributes** *section of the Attribute Editor.*

- **RMB-click** in the **opacityPP** field, then select **Create Ramp**.

A ramp texture now controls the opacity of each particle.

- **Rewind** and **playback** the scene.

Notice that the mist particles are opaque at the top of the fountain and fully transparent just before dying at the bottom of the fountain.

- **RMB-click** in the **opacityPP** field, then select **arrayMapper1.outValuePP** →
  Edit Ramp.

The Attribute Editor will display the ramp that controls the particles' opacity.

- Reverse the ramp color so that it is white at the top and black at
  the bottom.

Doing so will make the mist less apparent at the top of the fountain and more apparent toward the bottom of the fountain.

The vertical axis of the ramp represents the particle's normalized age, thus going from 0 to 1. The bottom of the ramp corresponds to the particle's birth and the top of the ramp corresponds to its death.

Tip: *It is usually recommended to set up the ramp as you want it, then add color handles to make the particle fully transparent at birth and just before death. Doing so will prevent the particles from popping when they appear and die.*

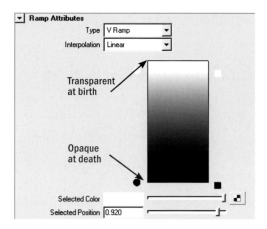

Opacity during life of mist particles

5 Test the animation

- Rewind and playback the animation.

- If necessary, adjust the lifespan so the particles die near the time they are at the bottom pool of the fountain.

> **Note:** *The unit for lifespan is seconds, so it is important to be aware of your frames per second settings and the different results that can occur if the same file is used on two different machines with different time settings. This can happen when you use import instead of open. When you use* **File →** **Open Scene,** *the time setting will be read from the scene file. To check the time setting, open* **Window → Settings/Preferences → Settings...**

- Make sure the *lighting* and *backgroundGeo* layer is visible.

- Press **7** on the keyboard to display the scene with hardware lighting.

- Playback the animation.

Now the particles are displayed with color and lighting.

6 Increase the resolution

For better results when rendering this fountain, increase the *spray's* **Rate** to **2000** and also add an **opacityPP** attribute to the *droplets*.

You may notice that the particles do not collide with the fountain in this example. Particle collisions will be discussed in a later lesson.

The refined fountain particles

7 Save your work

- Save the scene as *19-fountain_04.ma*.

Omni emitters

An omni emitter causes particle emission to occur equally in all directions. Adding omni emitters to NURBS surfaces, polygons and curves will cause particle emission to occur from the vertices of the object it is added to.

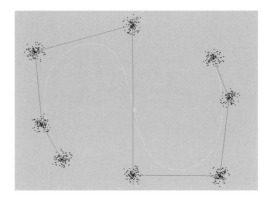

An omni emitter emitting from a curve's CVs

Curve emitters

Although it is possible to add a directional or omni emitter to a curve, doing so will cause emission to occur only from the CVs of that curve, not from the portions of the curve between the CVs or from points on the curve.

A curve emitter is designed to allow omni emission to occur along the entire curve, instead of only from the CVs.

1 Create a simple curve emitter

- Create your own curve using the **EP Curve Tool**.

- Select the curve and add a curve emitter by selecting **Particles** → **Emit from Object** → ☐.

- Set the **Emitter Type** to **Curve**.

2 Test the animation

- Playback the animation to view the curve emission.

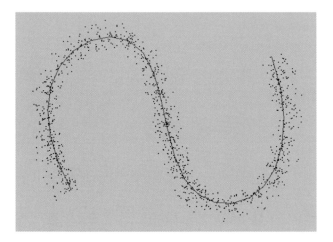

Curve emission

Tip: It is possible to change the emitter type after the emitter has been created by editing the **emitterType** attribute in the Channel Box or the selected emitter's Attribute Editor.

Curve emitter example

The following illustrates a quick example of using curve emitters and also introduces you to more per particle attributes.

1 Open the scene file

- Open the scene file called *19-curveEmit_01.ma*.

This simple scene contains a microphone and a wire, which you will set on fire.

- Playback the animation.

The microphone is animated and the curve used to create the wire is deformed by a cluster deformer.

2 Add a curve emitter to the wire

- Rewind to frame **1**.

- Select the *wire* curve from the Outliner.

This is the curve that was used to create the wire geometry.

Note: *If the curve is not available, you could also select an isoparm and then use* **Edit Curves** → **Duplicate Surface Curves***.*

- Add a curve emitter to it by selecting **Particles** → **Emit from Object** → ❐.

- Set the **Emitter Type** to **Curve**, then click the **Create** button.

- Rename the resulting particle object *fire* and the resulting emitter *fireEmitter*.

Tip: *You can also add curve emitters to a curve on surface. You can create a curve on surface by using tools like* **Intersection** *or* **Project Curve***, or by making the surface live using* **Modify** → **Make Live***, then drawing a curve directly on the geometry.*

3 Adjust lifespan attribute

- Select the *fireShape* particles and change the **Particle Render Type** to **Cloud (s/w)** in the Channel Box or Attribute Editor.

- In **Lifespan Attributes**, change **Lifespan Mode** to **Constant**.

The default setting of **1.0** *is fine for now.*

Lesson 19

4   Add a radiusPP attribute

Adding a **radiusPP** attribute will provide control over the radius of each cloud particle emitted.

- Press the **General** button in the **Add Dynamic Attributes** section of the Attribute Editor.

- Click on the **Particle** tab and select **radiusPP** from the list of particle attributes.

- Press **OK**.

A **radiusPP** *attribute field is added to the* **Per Particle (Array) Attributes** *section of the Attribute Editor.*

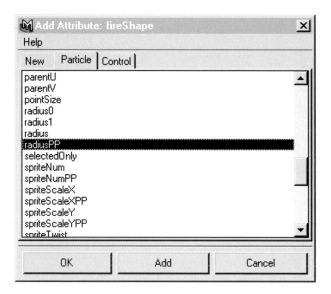

Adding a radiusPP from the Add Attributes window

5   Add a ramp to control each particle's radius

- **RMB-click** on the **radiusPP** field in the **Per Particle (Array) Attributes** section.

- Select **Create Ramp** from the pop-up menu.

- **RMB-click** on the same **radiusPP** field and select **arrayMapper1. outValue1PP** → **Edit Ramp**.

The ramp is displayed in the Attribute Editor.

6 Edit the ramp color

- Edit the ramp so there is a white handle at the bottom of the ramp and a black handle at the top as shown below:

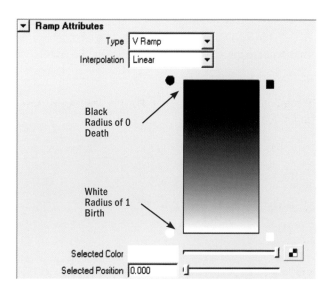

The ramp of radiusPP over age

*Black corresponds to a radius value of **0**, white to a value of **1**. Therefore, with the current ramp configuration, the radius will be **1** when the particle is born and decrease to **0** when the particle dies by the end of its lifespan. The age of a particle is normalized, so you are sure that each particle will go from the bottom of the ramp all the way to the top of the ramp.*

Note: *Normalized age is the relationship between a particle's age and its lifespan (**age / lifespan**).*

Tip: *In order to assign values greater than 1 for float attributes such as **radiusPP** with a ramp, open the Color Chooser window and switch to **HSV** mode. Then simply enter the desired value in the **V** field.*

7   Test the animation

- Rewind and playback the animation.

The radius decreases smoothly over the particle's age.

- Using what you have seen so far, try to make the particles emit with a radius of 0.0, then quickly increase to **1.2**, stay at **1.2** until halfway through their life, then decrease to a radius of **0.1** when they die.

Tip: *You may want to decrease the emission rate of the emitter while you adjust the effect and boost it back up when you have satisfying settings.*

Note: *Adjusting* **Noise** *and* **Noise Frequency** *in the ramp is an interesting way to achieve randomness. This works better with some attributes than others.*

8   Adjust the Inherit Factor of the particles

The **Inherit Factor** attribute controls how much of the emitting object's velocity is transferred to the particles during emission.

- Select the emitted particles and set **Inherit Factor** in the Channel Box to **1.0**.
- Rewind and playback the animation.

When **Inherit Factor** *is* **0**, *the particle velocity is not affected by the wire's motion. A setting of* **1** *causes the particles to emit with the same velocity as their emitting point.*

9   Add reverse gravity

In order to have the particles flying up, like real fire would do, you will create a gravity field and inverse its magnitude.

- Select the *fire* particles.
- Select **Field** → **Gravity.**
- Change the new *gravity*'s **Magnitude** to **-9.8.**

10 Tweak the fire particles

You will now tweak the particles so they look more like fire.

- Open the Hypershade.

- In the Create bar, create a **Particle Cloud** shader from the **Volumetric** section.

- Select the *fire* particles.

- **RMB-click** on the new *particleCloud* shader and select **Assign Material to Selection.**

- Open the Attribute Editor for the *particleCloud* shader.

- Set the following:

    Color to **yellow;**

    Incandescense to **white;**

    Glow Intensity to **0.2;**

    Density to **0.2.**

- Click on the **Map** button for the **Blob Map** attribute.

- Create a **3D Crater** texture.

- Set the following:

    Shaker to **1.0;**

    Channel1 to **white;**

    Channel2 to **black;**

    Channel3 to **black;**

    Melt to **0.2.**

11 Test render the scene

- Increase the amount of emitted particles.

- Play the animation until there are some particles visible.

- Render the scene using the Software Renderer.

Note: *Curve emission is also useful for simulating effects, like shockwaves or energy pulses, by adding an emitter to a curve and scaling the curve over time. This could be a stand alone effect or a grayscale rendering used as a displacement effect in compositing.*

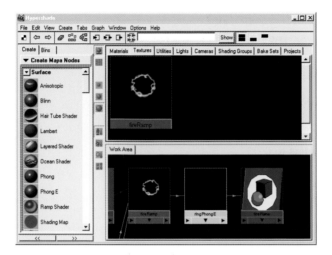

The fire emitted from the wire curve

12 Save your work

- Save the scene as *19-curveEmit_02.ma*.

Surface emitters

Surface emitters can be applied to NURBS and polygonal surfaces and cause emission to come from the entire surface rather than just from the vertices.

1 Scene file

- Open the file *19-glass_01.ma*.

This scene contains a drinking glass with ice cubes.

- Press **4** to go in wireframe mode.

2 Add a surface emitter

- Use the Outliner to select *glassBase*.

- Choose **Particles** → **Emit from Object** → ❑ and set **Emitter Type** to **Surface**.

- Click the **Create** button.

- Rename the emitter *bubbleEmitter* and the particles *bubbles*.

3   Change the render type

- Select *bubbles* and open the Attribute Editor.

- In the **Render Attributes** section of the Attribute Editor, set **Particle Render Type** to **Spheres**;

- Press the **Current Render Type** button.

This displays the attributes specific to that type of particle.

- Set **Radius** to **0.06**.

4   Test the animation

- Set the playback range to go from **1** to **500**.

- Playback the animation.

The particles emit from the base towards the top of the glass, but remain in the scene indefinitely.

Note: *The particles are emitting up because the normals of the surface point in that direction.*

5   Add a turbulence field

Turbulence will add some fluctuation to the movement of the particles to add realism.

- Select *bubbles*.

- Select **Fields → Turbulence**.

- Position the field near *glassBase*.

- In the Channel Box, set the following:

     Magnitude to **2**;

     Attenuation to **2**;

     Frequency to **2**.

Attenuation *controls an exponential relationship between the strength of the field and the distance between the affected objects and that field. For instance, imagine a curtain being blown by the air from a fan. In reality, as the distance between the fan and the curtain increases, the effect of the air from the fan*

Lesson 19

on the curtain diminishes. It is this relationship between distance and field strength that attenuation controls. An attenuation of **0** *causes a constant force, regardless of the distance between the field and the affected object.*

6   Set the Per Object Lifespan attribute

▪ Set the **Lifespan** attribute to **Constant** for the *bubbles*.

Choose a lifespan value that causes the particles to die before they reach the top of the glass.

7   Add color to the particles

▪ Use the Attribute Editor to add an **rgbPP** attribute to *bubbles*.

Note: *If an* **rgbPP** *attribute is added without a specified lifespan,* **Lifespan** *will automatically be set.*

▪ Add a default *ramp* to the **rgbPP** attribute.

▪ Make the *outerGlass* layer template.

▪ Press **5** to switch to shaded mode.

8   Test the animation

▪ Rewind and playback the animation.

As a particle's age approaches its lifespan, its color corresponds to a color higher along the vertical axis of the ramp.

The bubbles going up

- Edit the ramp so the color smoothly interpolates from white to a slightly light blue tint.

9 Save your work

- Save the scene as *19-glass_02.ma*.

Tangent speed and normal speed

Two attributes that are noteworthy when working with surface emission are **Tangent Speed** and **Normal Speed**.

These are closely related to the speed attribute that was previously discussed. Normal Speed controls the particle's speed along the vector that is normal to the point of emission. Tangent Speed controls the particle's speed along a randomly selected vector that is tangent to the surface of emission.

A good way to see what normal speed and tangent speed do, is to create a NURBS sphere and add a surface emitter to it. Increase the rate to around **300** and playback. If you view the sphere from the top view, you'll see a radial emission pattern.

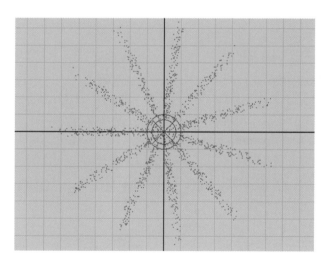

Radial emission pattern

The pattern emerges because the particles are emitted from tessellated geometry. The default **Tangent Speed** is **0**, causing the particles to move perpendicularly to the faces of the tessellated geometry from which they were emitted. Adding a bit of tangent speed eliminates this problem. Select the emitter and increase the tangent speed and the particles will now be given some velocity along the surface tangent from which they originate. This causes them to shoot off the surface at angles and gets rid of the radial emission pattern.

> **Tip:** When setting both the **Normal Speed** and **Tangent Speed** to **0**, the emitted particles will have no speed.

1   Scene file

- Continue with your own scene.

Or

- Open the scene called *19-glass_02.ma*.

2   Add water droplets to the glass surface

- Untemplate the *outerGlass* layer.

- Add a surface emitter to the *drinkingGlass*.

- Rename the new emitter *glassEmitter*.

- Rename the corresponding particle object *droplets*.

- Set the following attributes for the *glassEmitter*:

  Tangent Speed to **0**;

  Normal Speed to **0**.

3   Change the droplets render type

- Select *droplets* and open the Attribute Editor.

- In the **Render Attributes** section of the Attribute Editor, set **Particle Render Type** to **Spheres**;

- Press the **Current Render Type** button.

This displays the attributes specific to that type of particle.

- Set **Radius** to **0.08**.

4   Test the animation

- Rewind and playback the animation.

The emitted particles are emitted without any speed, and thus appear to stick to the glass.

5   Adjust the Max Count attribute

At this time, there are too many particles being emitted on the glass. Adjusting the emitter rate and particle lifespan to get the precise number of particles can be difficult. Fortunately, the **Max Count** attribute can control the number of particles directly to limit the emission.

- Open the Attribute Editor for the *droplets*.

- Set **Max Count** to **50** near the top of the Attribute Editor.

6   Test the animation

- Rewind and play the animation.

The **Max Count** *attribute limits the total number of particles the selected particle object is allowed to hold.*

Note: *When a particle object is created,* **Max Count** *is set to* **-1** *by default. This means no limits on the number of particles it can hold.*

7   Use a ramp to control acceleration

Currently, the *droplets* remain stationary during playback. It is possible to control their acceleration using a ramp. This is an alternative to attaching a gravity field.

- Open the Attribute Editor for *droplets*.

- In the **Per Particle (Array) Attribute** section, **RMB** in the **rampAcceleration** field and select **Create Ramp** from the pop-up menu.

- Adjust the ramp so there is only a single color handle at the bottom of the ramp.

- Open the Color Chooser for that handle's color.

- Set the **RGB** values for the color entry to **0, -0.5, 0**, respectively.

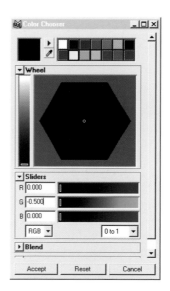

Setting a vector quantity (acceleration) using RGB

Lesson 19

> **Note:** *When using the Ramp Editor to control* **vector** *quantities such as position, acceleration and velocity, RGB corresponds to the particle's X, Y, Z respectively.*

8 Use a ramp to control acceleration

Currently, the *droplets* remain stationary during playback. It is possible to control their acceleration using a ramp. This is an alternative to attaching a gravity field.

- Open the Attribute Editor for *droplets*.

- Experiment with different **RGB** values to see how the acceleration of the particles is affected.

Controlling particle motion with ramps is not really all that common. This example is very simple as it's intended to show you the purpose of this feature and also help give you some ideas of other ways to move particles around. You could potentially use textures that are mapped to the ramp handles to push particles around your scene. This would require some additional set up, but is a technique that some studios are currently using to help modify existing motion of particles without changing too much in the simulation.

9 Map radiusPP

- Use what you have learned so far to map a ramp to the droplets **radiusPP**.

- Have the particles grow in size as they move down the glass and then vanish.

10 Save your work

- Save the scene as *19-glass_03.ma*.

Texture emission

With surface emitters, it is possible to control emission rate and location based on characteristics of a texture file or any 2D procedural texture. Texture emission works with textures only, not materials.

1 Scene file

- Open the file *19-paperBurn_01.ma*.

2 Add a surface emitter

- Select the *paper* surface, then choose **Particles** → **Emit from Object** → ❐.

- **Rename** the emitter *textureEmitter* and the particle object *textureParticles*.

3 Set tangent and normal speed

- Select *textureEmitter*.

- Set the **Tangent Speed** to **0.5** and **Normal Speed** to **1.0**.

This prevents the particles from emitting directly at the normal of the surface, providing a more randomized emission appearance.

4 Add a rgbPP attribute to textureParticles

An **rgbPP** attribute is required for the **Inherit Color** option of texture emission to work. This is a common oversight when setting up texture emission.

- In the Attribute Editor for *textureParticles*, add an **rgbPP** attribute.

5 Set the rate of textureEmitter

- Select *textureEmitter*.

- Set the **Rate** to **200** particles per second in the Channel Box.

- Set **scaleRateByObject Size** to **On**.

If this attribute is enabled, the size of the object emitting the particles affects the rate of the particles emitted per frame. The larger the object, the greater the rate of emission.

6 Specify a texture for coloring the particles

Now you will connect a pre-made animated procedural texture to the emitter, which will determine the color of the particles emitted.

- Open the Attribute Editor for *textureEmitter*.

- Select **Window** → **Rendering Editors** → **Hypershade...** and position it next to the Attribute Editor.

- In the Hypershade, select the **Textures** tab.

This displays all of the textures currently in the scene file. An animated fireRamp texture has already been prepared for this example and should be visible in the Hypershade window.

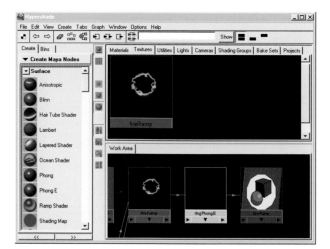

Displaying the fireRamp texture in the Hypershade window

- With the *textureEmitter* still selected, locate the **Texture Emission Attributes** section of the Attribute Editor.

- **MMB-click+drag** and **drop** the *fireRamp* texture icon from the Hypershade window onto **Particle Color** in the Attribute Editor for *textureEmitter*.

- Turn **Inherit Color** to **On** for the emitter.

- Press **6** to switch to hardware texture mode.

7 Test the animation

- Rewind and play the animation.

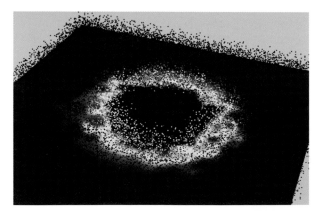

Using an animated ramp texture to color the emitted particles

Notice the emitted particles have inherited the RGB values from the texture at the location where they were emitted. Notice that black particles are emitting from the outer edge of the texture where the color is not present. You will be fixing this shortly.

Note: *To use a 3D texture for texture emission, you'll first need to convert it to a 2D UV mapped image using* **Convert To File Texture** *in the Hypershade.*

8 Change Lifespan attribute

- Set the **Lifespan Mode** to **Constant**.

9 Add opacity so the particles fade out

Now you will add opacity and a ramp to control it based on the age of the particles.

- Create a **Per Particle Attribute** for **Opacity**.

- Add a ramp to **opacityPP**.

- Edit the ramp handle position so it has the following properties:

    Color entry 1: **Selected Position** to **0**; **RGB** to **0.9, 0, 0**;

    Color entry 2: **Selected Position** to **1.0**; **RGB** to **0, 0, 0**.

10 Save your work

- Save the scene as *19-paperBurn_02.ma*.

Scaling emission rate with a texture

Similar to how you mapped a color image to control the color of emitted particles, you can also use the values of a grayscale image as multipliers on the emission rate of the emitter. This provides control over which portions of the surface will emit more than others. In this example, you want to shut off emission from the black areas of the ramp texture and leave emission on for the areas where there is color in the burning ring.

1 Scene file

- Continue with your own scene.

Or

- Open the scene called *19-paperBurn_02.ma*.

Lesson 19

2 Connect a ramp to the rate

Since the areas of emission that you are interested in controlling correspond exactly to the color ramp that is being animated, the same ramp can be mapped to **Texture Rate**.

- Use the same method used in Step 6 above to **MMB-click+drag** the *fireRamp* from the Hypershade onto the Texture Rate slider of the *textureEmitter*'s Attribute Editor.

- Set **Enable Texture Rate** to **On**.

3 Test the results

- Rewind and playback.

Although fireRamp is a color image, when mapped to Texture Rate, the luminance values are extracted from the texture and those values are used as multipliers against the emission rate at the corresponding location of the surface.

Areas of the color map with a luminance of 0 (black), use a 0 emission rate. Areas of the color map with luminance of 1 use 100% of the emitter's rate.

Once rendered, this fire ring could be rendered with a matte channel and combined with other textured surfaces using compositing software. These techniques will be discussed later.

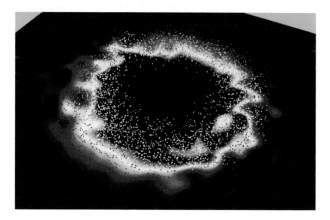

Texture mapped to texture rate

4 Save your work

- Save the scene as *19-paperBurn_03.ma*.

Per point emission

When working with particles, you may want to have some points on a curve or a surface emit at a different rate than other points. This can be achieved to some extent using texture emission controls. Another option that offers some additional control is **Per Point Emission**.

1 Scene file

- Open the scene called *19-perPoint_01.ma*.

This scene is the same scene you worked with when using curve emission, except that the curve emitter was deleted, leaving the fire particles in the scene to be reused.

2 Create an emitter

- Set the *microphoneLayer* to be templated.

- Select the *wire* curve.

- Press **F8** to go in **Component mode**.

- Set the selection mask to have only the **Edit Points** available for selection.

- **Click+drag** over the entire *wire* curve to select all of its edit points.

- Select **Particles → Emit from Object → ❐**.

- Change the **Emitter Type** to **Omni**, then click the **Create** button.

- Rename the new emitter to *perPointEmitter*.

3 Test the animation

- Rewind and playback the animation.

An even emission rate occurs from the edit points, as illustrated in the following image:

An even omni emission from the curve's edit points

Lesson 19

Note: *You may need to hide the fire particles to see the per point emissions.*

4   Per point emission control

You can easily vary the emission rate for each edit point using per-point emission:

- Select the *perPointEmitter*.

- Select **Particles** → **Per Point Emission Rates**.

The **Use Rate PP** *attribute of perPointEmitter gets automatically unlocked and set to* **On** *in the Channel Box.*

- Select the *wire* curve and change the **RatePP** for each edit point in the Channel Box as follows:

wireShape
Per Point Emitter Rate PP[0] 100
Per Point Emitter Rate PP[1] 500
Per Point Emitter Rate PP[2] 0
Per Point Emitter Rate PP[3] 0
Per Point Emitter Rate PP[4] 0
Per Point Emitter Rate PP[5] 0

Per Point emission rates in the Channel Box

5   Reconnect the fire particles

In order to reuse the fire particles created earlier, you must use the Relationship Editor.

- Select the *fire* particles.

- Select **Window** → **Relationship Editors** → **Dynamic Relationships**.

- In the Relationship Editor, change the selection mode to **Emitters**.

- Click on the *perPointEmitter* to highlight it.

Doing so will allow the emitter to release the fire particles.

- Delete the *particle1* object since it is no longer required.

6   Test the animation

- Rewind and playback the animation.

The emission rates of each edit point correspond to the changes made in the Channel Box. This style of emission can be combined with the curve emitter to add some variation to the overall effect.

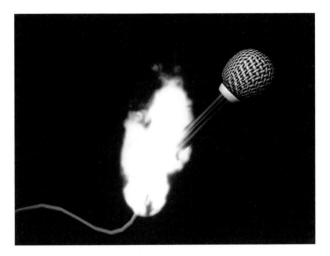

Per-point emission rates

7   Save your work

- Save the scene as *19-perPoint_02.ma*.

There are more practical examples of when you might use per-point emission, but these often require the use of particle expressions, which you will cover in a later lesson.

For example, perhaps you have a car crashing into a wall. Points that collide with the wall at a higher velocity could be made to emit more particles at the collision point.

Tips and traps

The following tips and traps will give you some additional information relating to these lessons, and also some possible explanations for things you may run into while working with the provided examples:

- People often ask about the **currentTime** attribute found on particles. By default, a particle system is plugged into the default scene time. As you advance the timeline, the particles evaluate. It is possible to break the connection from the main scene time and create your own custom time curve for the particles to evaluate from.

Lesson 19

The file 19-reverseTime.ma demonstrates a simple example of this. For example, perhaps you want to have particles shoot out into a scene and freeze in space while other animation continues.

- To set up a reverse time, do the following:

  Create an emitter.

  Set timeline to end at frame **100** and advance to frame **100**.

  Select the associated particle object and cache it using **Solvers** → **Memory Caching** → **Enable**, then rewind and playback, the scene.

  Select the particle object and **RMB** → **Break Connection** on the **Current Time** attribute in the Channel Box

  Set a key at frame **1** on *currentTime* to **1**.

  Set a key at frame **50** on *currentTime* to **25**.

  Set a key at frame **100** on *currentTime* to **50**.

  Playback and see that particles play at half speed.

  Now select the particle object and edit its time curve in the Graph Editor. Since the data is cached, you can actually make the time curve cause the particles to get sucked back into the emitter by pulling the time keyframes down near values of **1** at frame **100**. You can also add keyframes in the Graph Editor and adjust the curve however you want.

- To connect the particle object back to the default time, break its connection from time again, then select **Particles** → **Connect to Time**.

- The *geoConnector* node on the surface associated with the emitter has a **Tessellation Factor** control. This is very similar to the tessellation factor used with rigid bodies. However, this controls the level of detail of the surface that the emitter uses to emit particles from. Increasing this attribute will slow things down but provide more even/accurate emission from the surface. If you have a highly detailed surface that you need very accurate emission from, increasing this number will likely be necessary.

- Patchy or sputtering emission can also be caused by the **Real-time** playback setting in your general preferences. Set the playback to **Play Every Frame** in the animation preferences to correct the problem.

Conclusion

You have now been introduced to some different ways of creating and working with particles. At this stage, you have experimented with the basics of particles, such as learning where everything is, and the basic particle and dynamic terminology. You also worked on controlling simple motion and characteristics of particles using per object attributes and per particle attributes. There are many more attributes specific to particles that can be used. Several will be discussed in greater detail throughout the rest of this book. Keep in mind that they are all created, accessed and manipulated in the same way.

In the next lesson, you will learn how to combine particles with rigid bodies.

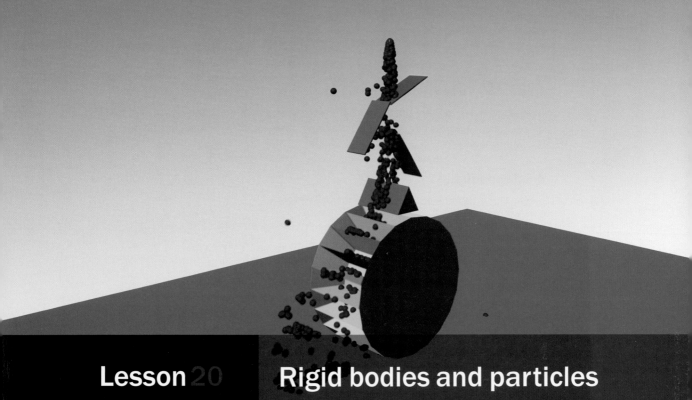

Lesson 20   Rigid bodies and particles

Now that you have been introduced to particles and rigid bodies, you will combine the two into one exercise to learn some ways they can work together. It is common for particles to collide and interact with rigid bodies. Getting the two to work together can help create realistic movement that otherwise would require intensive keyframing.

In this lesson you will learn the following:

- How to add particle and rigid body collisions;

- How to set particle mass in a creation expression;

- How to change geoConnector's attributes;

- How to set collision layers.

Particle driven mechanism

In this example, you are going to create a particle driven mechanism. You will be incorporating some of the tools that you have been working with up to this point, as well as some new techniques.

1 Scene file

- Open the scene called *20-particleRigidBodies_01.ma*.

This scene consists of some simple geometry already placed to create a simple mechanism.

2 Active rigid bodies

In order for the mechanism to move, some pieces need to be made into active rigid bodies.

- Select the three flat pieces of geometry and the big cylinder.

- Select **Soft/Rigid Bodies → Create Active Rigid Body**.

3 Hinge constraints

- For each active rigid body, create a **Hinge** constraint.

4 Passive rigid bodies

- Select the prism and the plane surfaces.

- Select **Soft/Rigid Bodies → Create Passive Rigid Body**.

5 Emitter

- Select **Particles → Create Emitter → ❑**.

- Make sure **Emitter Type** is set to **Omni**, then click the **Create** button.

- Move the new *emitter* on the Y-axis, above all the geometry.

The emitter position

6 Gravity field

- Select the particle object.

- Select **Fields → Gravity → ❑** and reset the options.

- Playback the animation.

At this time, the particles are falling down, straight through the geometry.

7 Make the particles collide

- Select the *particle* object, then **Shift-select** the first flat surface at the top of the mechanism.

- Select **Particles** → **Make Collide**.

- Playback the animation.

The particles now collide with the first rigid body.

- Repeat the previous steps in order to make the particles collide with all the other rigid bodies in the scene.

8 Enable the rigid bodies' particle collision

- Select all of the rigid bodies.

- In the Channel Box, scroll down and set **Particle Collision** to **On**.

- Playback the animation.

The particles now collide with all the rigid bodies, which in turn react to the collisions. You will notice that the particles fly unexpectedly and that the collisions are much too pronounced. You will now fix this.

9 Change the particles' settings

- Select the *particle* object.

- From the Attribute Editor, change the **Particle Render Type** to **Spheres**.

- Set the **Lifespan Mode** to **Constant**.

- Set the **Lifespan** to **7**.

- Set the **Conserve** attribute to **0.99**.

10 Change the particles' mass

- Still in the Attribute Editor, scroll down to the **Per Particle (Array) Attributes**.

- **RMB-click** in the **Mass** field and select **Creation Expression**.

The Expression Editor will appear.

- Type the following in the **Expression** field:

```
particleShape1.mass = 5;
```

- Click on the **Create** button, then click on the **Close** button to close the editor.

*Each particle will now have a weight of **5** assigned when it is born. But if you playback the scene, the dynamics are still chaotic.*

11 Change the mass of the rigid bodies

- Select the top three rigid bodies.

- In the Channel Box, set their **Mass** to **200**.

- Select the big cylinder rigid body.

- In the Channel Box, set its **Mass** to **1000**.

12 Change the geoConnector settings

- Select the *particle* object.

- In the **Inputs** section of the Channel Box, locate the *geoConnector* nodes.

*There is one geoConnector node per surface, which the particles collide into. This node defines some dynamic attributes, such as **Resilience** and **Friction**. The following are some explanations about these attributes:*

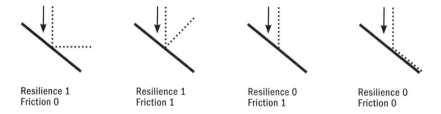

Resilience 1 Friction 0	Resilience 1 Friction 1	Resilience 0 Friction 1	Resilience 0 Friction 0

Resilience and Friction attributes

- For each geoConnector node, set the following:

    Resilience to **0.2**;

    Friction to **0.2**.

13 Playback the results

- Playback the results.

You should see the particles going through the first three flaps, then being distributed in the big cylinder's grooves. When there is enough weight at the top of the cylinder, it starts rotating.

Spend some time adjusting the various rigid body and field attributes to change the motion to your liking. You can also try incorporating some of what you learned in previous lessons to add more interesting characteristics to the particles, such as color or opacity.

The simple mechanism is now working

Tips and traps

- **Resilience** controls how much rebound occurs in the particle collision. You can even use negative numbers with Resilience, however it is rare that you would need this.

- If rigid bodies keep colliding together and you don't want them to, you can change their **Collision Layer** attribute to be different values. Doing so will prevent them from colliding and could increase the solver's calculation speed, especially in scenes with heavy dynamics.

- You can also use the Set Rigid Body Interpenetration and Set Rigid Body Collision menu options under the Solvers menu to produce the same basic result of setting different objects on different collision layers. Set Rigid Body Interpenetration has the same effect as putting all selected objects on different collision layers. Set Rigid Body Collision has the effect of all selected objects being on the same collision layer. This is just another way of doing the same thing, but makes it faster since you don't have to manually change all the numbers. However, it can be tricky to keep track of which things are set to collide and which things are not. The advantage of collision layers is that you can very clearly see which objects will be colliding just by looking in the Attribute Spread Sheet.

Conclusion

You should now have a good idea how to set up and work with particle collisions, as well as understand methods for integrating particles with rigid bodies. You also learned how to produce a creation expression to control the mass of each particle.

In the next lesson, you will take this a step further to work with particle collision events, which cause a user defined action to occur when a particle collision occurs.

Lesson 21 — Particle collisions

In this lesson you will learn how to create and tune particle collisions. Such a task can involve creating particle collision events and defining a collision procedure. The straightforward examples in this lesson will teach you how to use this approach to create refined dynamic simulations.

In this lesson you will learn the following:

- How to create particle surface collisions;

- How to create and edit particle collision events;

- How to use the Particle Collision Event Editor;

- How to implement particle collision event procedures;

- Different particle collision applications.

Particle to surface collisions

As you have seen in the previous lesson, you are able to implement particle collisions onto rigid bodies, but you are not limited to rigid bodies. To enable a particle to collide and interact with any geometric object (including soft bodies, trimmed objects and deforming geometry), you can use the **Particles** → **Make Collide** command.

Note: *Particles can collide with geometry but cannot collide with each other.*

Particle collision events

With the particle collision event, you can trigger the following events when a particle collides with a collision object:

- Emit new particles from the colliding point;

- Execute a MEL script procedure;

- Kill the colliding particles.

Note: *The collision can be caused by either moving particles or by moving or deforming geometry.*

Raindrops

This exercise will introduce you to the Collision Event Editor.

1 Scene file

- Open the scene file called *21-rainDrops_01.ma*.

This scene file contains three pieces of geometry:

rainCloud - polygonal plane;

rainSurface - NURBS surface obtained from trim;

mounds - NURBS surface.

2 Add a surface emitter

- Select the rainCloud plane.

- Select **Particles** → **Emit from Object** → ❑.

- Set **Emitter Type** to **Surface**.

- Press the **Create** button.

- Set the new emitter's **Rate** to **2** and **Speed** to **10**.

Tip: *The rain particles will move down because the surface's normals are pointing down.*

3 Set attributes for the particles

- Set the following attributes for *particleShape1*:

    Particle Render Type to **Streak**;

    Line Width to **1**;

    Normal Dir to **2**;

    Tail Fade to **0.5**;

    Tail Size to **0.5**;

    Use Lighing to **On**.

4 Make rainSurface a collidable object

- Clear the selection.

- Select the rainSurface.

- Select **Particles** → **Make Collide**.

This will create and connect a geoConnector node to the rainSurface object. The rainSurface geometry will now appear as an option for connecting the particle object as a collision through the Dynamics Relationship Editor.

5 Connect rainSurface to particle1

- Open the Dynamic Relationships Editor by selecting **Window** → **Relationship Editors** → **Dynamic Relationships...**

- Select the *particle1* object.

- Select **Collisions** under **Selection Modes**.

- Highlight *rainSurfaceShape1*.

The connection is made between the rainSurfaceShape1 and the particleShape1 nodes via the geoConnector node. Now, the particles will collide with that surface.

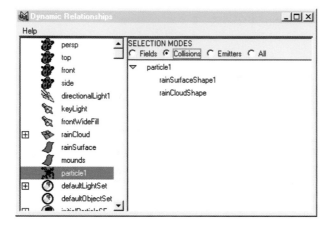

Connecting collisions to rainSurfaceShape1

Tip: *You can also do this collision and connection in one step by first selecting the particle, then the surface it is to collide with, then select **Particles →
Make Collide.***

6 Test the scene

- Playback the scene.

You should see the particles now colliding with rainSurface.

- Adjust the **Resilience** and **Friction** attributes as desired on the *rainSurface1's geoConnector.*

7 Create an empty particle object

You will soon make the colliding particles split into new particles. Creating an empty particle object now will allow you to emit those new particles.

- Type `particle` in the Command Line, then hit **Enter**.

An empty particle object is created.

8 Set the new particle object to collide

You can set up collision and connection in one step without using the Dynamic Relationship Editor.

- Select *particle2*, then **Shift- select** the rainSurface object.

- Select **Particles** → **Make Collide**.

Using the Particle Collision Event Editor

This Particle Collision Event Editor is the graphical interface to the event MEL command. From this editor, you can choose actions to occur when a particle collides with its collision objects.

The top two panes provide selection of valid objects to create and edit events for the selected particle object. The next section provides fields that give information about the selected event and allow for editing the event name.

You can create multiple events for each particle object selected in the left list. You can also update the list of particle objects by pressing the **Update Object List** button.

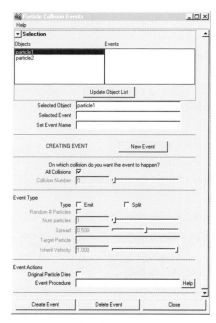

Particle collision events

Below that section is a section that displays whether you are in edit or creation mode and a button to add a new event to the particle object you are working with.

The next section lets you define the collision event to occur when any of the particle objects collide.

Emit vs. Split

Emit is when the particle emits new particles, while **Split** is when the particle emits new particles and dies. If a new target particle is not specified for Split, it uses the same particle object as the colliding particle. Also, when Emit is used, the age of the new particles start at 0. When Split is used, the age of the new particles is inherited from the colliding particle.

Lesson 21

Random # Particles

Checking this option will create a random amount of emitted particles with a min range of **0** and a max range of the **Num Particles** attribute.

Num Particles

Sets the amount of particles emitted at collision time, or the max range of particles if **Random # Particles** is enabled.

Spread

Controls the spread of emitted particles. Valid values are from **0** to **1**.

Target Particles

The **Target Particles** field is where you can choose the *particleShape* that you want to emit upon the collision event. If you do not select a particle, the colliding one is used.

Inherit Velocity

This value controls the percentage of parent particle velocity that will be transferred by the new particles.

Original Particle Dies

This option specifics whether or not the original particle dies upon collision.

Event Procedure

The event procedure is where you can call a MEL script procedure at the time of collision. You will use this option later in this lesson.

1 Open Collision Event Editor

- Select **Particles** → **Particle Collision Events…**

2 Set event options

- Highlight *particle1* in the **Objects** section.

- Set the following options as directed:

    All Collisions to **On**;

    Type to **Split**;

    Num particles to **20**;

    Spread to **1**;

Target Particle to *particleShape2*;

Inherit Velocity to **0.8**.

3 Create Event

- Press the **Create Event** button.

4 Play the animation

- Select *particle2*, then select **Fields** → **Gravity**.

- Playback the simulation.

5 Add two events to the particle2

- Select **Particles** → **Particle Collision Events...**

- Select *particle2* in the object list.

- Press the **Create Event** button.

- Rename this event from *event0* to *firstEvent* in the **Set Event Name** field.

- Press **New Event**.

You are now in create mode.

- Press **Create Event** at the bottom of the window.

You have now created another new event for particle2 called event1.

- Rename this event *secondEvent*.

6 Event options for firstEvent

- Highlight the *firstEvent*.

- Set the following options:

    All Collisions to **Off**;

    Collision Number to **1**;

    Type to **Split**;

    Num Particles to **2**;

    Spread to **0.5**;

    Target Particle to **particleShape2**;

    Inherit Velocity to **0.5**.

7   Event options for secondEvent

- Highlight the *secondEvent*.
- Set the following options:

     All Collisions to **Off**;

     Collision Number to **2**;

     Type to **Split**;

     Num Particles to **1**;

     Spread to **0.5**;

     Target Particle to **particleShape2**;

     Inherit Velocity to **0.5**.

- Close the editor.

8   Test the scene and tune

- Playback the scene.
- Adjust the lifespan and render attributes for *particle1* and *particle2* to help refine the simulation.

The particle splashes as they collide

9   Save your work

- Save the scene as *21-rainDrops_02.ma*.

Dust raising while walking

The following example scene contains Meeper walking through a floor of particles. You will make Meeper kick up a cloud of particles as he walks through the scene.

1 Scene file

- Open the scene file called *21-footDust_01.ma*.

- Playback the animation.

You will see Meeper walk through the particles.

2 Create a radial field

- Select *particle1*.

- Select **Fields** → **Radial** → ❑.

- Set the following:

> **Magnitude** to **1**;
>
> **Attenuation** to **1**;
>
> **Use Max Distance** to **On**;
>
> **Max Distance** to **5**;
>
> **Volume shape** to **none**.

- Click on the **Create** button.

3 Point constrain the field

- Select the *LeftToeBase* joint and **Shift-select** the radial field.

- Select **Constrain** → **Point** → ❑.

- Make sure **Maintain Offset** is set to **Off**.

- Click on the **Add** button.

4 Radial field on the other foot

- Repeat the last two steps to create and point constraint another radial field to the other foot.

5 Test the animation

- Playback the scene to ensure that the fields and particles are interacting.

Lesson 21

6 Set the floor particles to collide with the floor object

- Select the *particle1* object, then **Shift-select** the *stage* object.

- Select **Particles** → **Make Collide**.

7 Create a collision event for the floor particles

- Select **Particles** → **Particle Collision Event...**

- Highlight *particle1* in the **Objects** section.

- Press **Create Event**.

- Highlight *event1* in the **Events** list for *particle1*.

- Set the following options:

> **All Collisions** to **On**;
>
> **Type** to **Emit**;
>
> **Random # Particles** to **On**;
>
> **Num Particles** to **10**;
>
> **Spread** to **1**;
>
> **Target Particle** to *particleShape2*;
>
> **Inherit Velocity** to **1**;
>
> **Original Particle Dies** to **On**.

- Click the **Close** button.

8 Tweak the secondary particles

- Select the *particle2* object.

- Select **Fields** → **Gravity**.

- Set the new *gravity*'s **Magnitude** to **-9.8**.

- Change the *particle2*'s **Render Type** to **Cloud**.

- Set the *particle2*'s **Lifespan** to **1.0**.

9 Playback the scene

There are various places to fine-tune this example. Particle **Lifespan** and **Max Count** on *particle2* control how many particles are in the scene. Adjusting the field attributes such as **Magnitude** and **Max Distance**, will also make a big difference.

The particle splashes as they collide

10 Save your work

- Save the scene as *21-footDust_02.ma*.

Particle collision event procedure

You have learned how to create and edit collision events. Now, you will take things further and explore the options for triggering a more complex animation at the time of collision.

The particle collision event also has a section called **Event Actions**. From this section you can enter an **Event Procedure**. An event procedure is typically a MEL script that is called when a collision occurs and the event is triggered. There are a multitude of applications that can utilize this functionality. For example, perhaps you want to move an object to the location of a particle collision, or perhaps you want to query the UV coordinates and determine or modify the shading information at a collision point. In many production environments, there may be other proprietary rendering systems or software applications that require you to pass information on to them. Having access to this level of information and being able to modify that information is what makes this a powerful feature.

One requirement for the script that is called by the particle collision event is that it must have the following format and argument list:

```
global proc myEventProc

        (string $particleName, int $particleId,
    string $objectName)
```

Where `myEventProc` is the name of the MEL procedure and also the name of the script file (*myEventProc.mel*), `$particleName` is the name of the particle object that owns the event, `$particleId` is the particle number of the particle that has collided, and `$objectName` is the name of the object that the particle has collided with.

These arguments, which are also variables, are the place holders for holding the information that is passed to the script from the particle collision event.

1   Scene file

- Open the scene called *21-collisionScript_01.ma*.

This scene contains a raining backdrop and it will be set up to execute a specific particle collision event procedure.

2   MEL commands

Enter the following commands in the Script Editor to create a special node and establish the connection to the *ground* surface:

```
createNode closestPointOnSurface;

connectAttr —f

            ground.worldSpace[0]
closestPointOnSurface1.inputSurface;
```

Note: *The closestPointOnSurface node is a very useful node for querying the world and UV position of a point on a surface.*

3   Set particle1 to collide with ground

- Select *particle1*, then **Shift-select** the *ground* surface.
- Select **Particles** → **Make Collide**.

4   Add a script procedure to the particle collision event

- Select **Particles** → **Particle Collision Event...**
- Press the **Create Event** button.
- Set **Original Particle Dies** to **On**.

Note: Do not select **Emit** or **Split** as the **Event Type**.

- Enter *partCollisionPrnt* into the **Event Procedure** field under the **Event Actions** section.

This is the name of a script that is included as part of the dynamics support files.

- In order to make sure that Maya knows about the script, **click+drag** the *partCollisionPrnt.mel* file into the viewport.

Doing so will automatically source the script.

Note: Another way to source a script is to open the Script Editor and choose **File → Source Script**.

Tip: You can also copy the script file *partCollisionPrnt.mel* from the support directory to your current Maya script folder, such as the \My Documents\ maya\scripts\ directory. The next time you launch Maya, the script will be foundautomatically found.

5 Create a point light in the scene

The script that will be executed at collision time will do two things: first, it will print out the collision information, then it will take a point light and move it to the X,Y, Z location of collision. You will thus need to create a point light for the script to execute without error.

- Select **Create → Lights → Point Light** .

- Make sure the name of the light is *pointLight1*.

- Press **7** on your keyboard to switch to hardware lighting mode.

6 Test the scene

- Open the Script Editor.

- Playback the scene.

The partCollisionPrnt script is executed each time a particle collides with the surface. The script then prints the position on the surface where the collision occurred. The script also moves the point light you created to these world coordinates.

Sample output from the Script Editor:

```
partCollisionPrnt("particleShape1", 0, " ground");

CPOS XYZ          10.51686562 2.943025257e-15 -10.38921561

CPOS UV           0.9370036721 0.9316994754

POS Position      10.51686562 2.943025257e-15 -10.38921561

POS UV Position 0.9370036721 0.9316994754
```

7 Save your work

- Save the scene as *21-collisionScript_02.ma*.

8 Open the partCollisionPrnt.mel script

If you want, you can use a Text Editor or the Script Editor to read through the *partCollisionPrnt.mel* script. Unless you know MEL, this script may not make a lot of sense to you. But, you will be able to see the basic framework of the collision event procedure and get an idea of how this type of effect is set up.

The procedure *partCollisionPrnt* does a few things. First, it takes the arguments given to it from the particle collision event and puts these values into global variables:

```
$particlePositions

$particleVelocitys

$hitTimes

$particleHitCount

$currentHitTime
```

These variables can then be accessed from other procedures or expressions. Use this upper portion of the script as a template for your own particle collision event script.

The second portion uses two types of point-on-surface nodes to get and maintain collision information as it pertains to the surface.

closestPointOnSurface returns information about a point on the surface in relation to the world space position information that the `$particlePositions` variable is getting from the particle collision event each time a particle collides with the surface.

pointOnSurface is an operation that can create a *pointOnSurfaceInfo* node. This node will maintain information about a point on a surface even if the surface is animating and deforming.

The script then moves the point light into position.

Lastly, some clean up is made in order to delete nodes no longer required by the scene. This last step is optional, but will optimize this specific example.

Note: *Several lines in the partCollisionPrnt.mel script are only for human readable feedback and are not neccessarily useful to the script's task.*

Tips and traps

- People often ask about the difference between Emit vs. Split. The two functions determine what happens to the particle that originally collided. Emit keeps it in the scene, while Split will kill the particle. This also affects what happens to the age of th -e new particle. Emit resets the age of the new particle to 0 and Split starts the age of the new particle at whatever value the old particle's age was when the collision occurred.

  The file 21-emitVsSplit.ma is a very basic demonstration of this.

- As Meeper walks through the grid of particles, everything may appear to work fine for the first part of the walk, but then particles can stop emitting later in the cycle. This is because there is a **Max Count** set for *particle2*. This is just to keep the number of particles in the scene to a reasonable level. If you want, you can set the value to **-1** and use the **Level Of Detail** attribute on *particle2*, instead of Max Count.

- When entering the name of a script to be executed by the collision event procedure, do not type the *.mel* portion of the script name into the Particle Collision Event Editor.

- If errors occur, check to make sure the script is in your scripts directory. If you make any changes to the *partCollisionPrnt.mel* script yourself, make sure to source the script by dragging the script file in the viewport. Always check the output to the Script Editor to help track down problems.

- A great way to find out where Maya is looking for your scripts is to type the following line in the Script Editor:

```
internalVar -userScriptDir;
```

- If using IRIX, a fun example is to play a sound when a collision occurs. To do this, use a system command and the `sfplay` command along with any **.aiff* or sound file. Store the following commands as *soundPlay.mel* in the Maya *scripts* directory:

```
global proc soundPlay

            (string $particleName, int $particleId,
string $objectName)

{

      system ("sfplay mySound.aiff");

}
```

  There is a completed version of this script in the support files. There are also some example sound files included in the sound directory of the current project. `sfplay` *is an IRIX command, so this will not work on Windows systems.*

- The file *21-dieOnFrustumExit.ma* shows how to make particles die when they leave the camera frustum. This is a very simple file where a polygon has been fit to the camera frustum and a collision event is used to kill the particles. This can be useful when dealing with very large numbers of particles for memory management.

- The event MEL command can be used in MEL scripts and expressions to customize the behavior of particle collision events beyond what is in the Particle Collision Event Editor. Additionally, particles have **Event** attributes that keep track of how many collisions each particle has had. For more information on this and many other particle attributes, refer to the *particle node* entry in the Maya online documentation.

Conclusion

Particle collision event is a very powerful method of controlling particles and their behavior. It provides a logical method of emission or death, based on collision. The ability to execute a procedure at collision also opens up a large range of possibilities for creating geometry or manipulating virtually any other part of the scene, or even your system, at times of collision.

In the next lesson, you will learn about particle expressions.

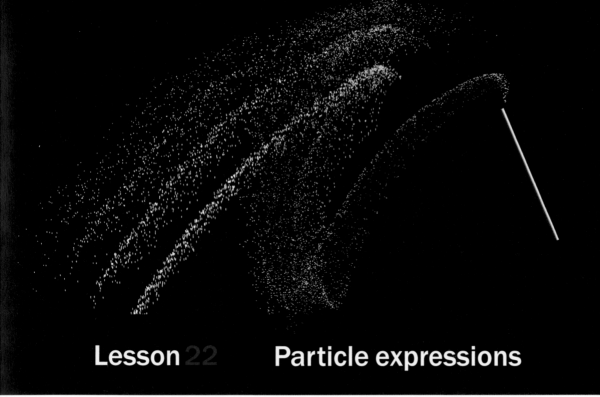

Lesson 22   Particle expressions

This lesson focuses on different techniques for controlling particle motion with special attention placed on particle expressions.

In this lesson you will learn the following:

- Fundamental physics concepts;

- The Maya particle evaluation process;

- Initial State;

- The difference between creation and runtime expressions;

- The linstep and smoothstep functions;

- How to use the particleId attribute;

- Absolute value;

- The sine and cosine functions.

Fundamental physics concepts

There are some basic rules that govern the motion of objects in the universe that are directly applicable to a discussion of particles. Newton's first law states the following:

```
Force = Mass x Acceleration
```

Note: *This is more commonly written as* `F = ma`.

Force and **mass** are known quantities when dealing with particles. Acceleration is calculated by the dynamic system based on these values. The resulting values are used to control the particle's motion.

Force

A generated quantity that can come from things like fields, springs and expressions.

Mass

An attribute that exists by default on particle objects. Therefore, since two items in the equation are known, the third item, the acceleration, can be determined through the following simple division:

```
a = F/m
```

This rule forms the basis of the underlying architecture Maya uses to calculate particle attributes such as position, velocity and acceleration. Understanding this relationship is not always necessary, but can be useful when deciding how to set something up, or when troubleshooting.

Some useful definitions

There are some common terms and definitions that come up frequently regarding particle attributes and quantities related to particles.

Scalar

A numerical quantity with only one specific component. Time and mass are examples of scalar values represented by values like 20 or -3.5.

Vector

A quantity with magnitude and direction. This is represented as three distinct numerical components grouped together in brackets, i.e. <<1,2,3>> or <<5,-2,1>>.

Float

A decimal numerical value, i.e. 2.3, 0.001, 3.14, etc.

Integer

A non-decimal whole number, i.e. -1, 0, 57, etc.

String

A collection of alphanumeric characters, i.e. *"hello123"*

Boolean

A value that is either true or false, on or off, 1 or 0.

Variable

A location in memory used to store information that is one of the above data types, i.e. `float $hello` defines `$hello` as a storage space for decimal numerical information that can be accessed in expressions and scripts.

Position (vector)

A particle's location in the world is its **position**.

Velocity (vector)

A particle's change in position over time. This is a measurement of both **rate** and **direction**. To visualize velocity, imagine an arrow pointing in the direction of the object's motion with the arrow's length proportional to the speed of the object.

Speed (scalar)

A particle's measurement of rate only without respect to direction.

Acceleration (vector)

A particle's measurement of the change in velocity over time.

Propagation: the evaluation process

Propagation is the method Maya uses to determine a particle's attribute values by basing the calculations for the current frame on the result that was determined from the previous frame.

Propagation is like a *piggy-back* effect. For example, frame 2 gets information from frame 1, it does some calculations, then positions the particles.

Lesson 22

Next, frame 3 gets the result from frame 2, does its calculations, positions the particles, and moves to frame 4. The cycle continues throughout the playback of the animation.

So what happens at frame 1?

Frame 1 in the above example is the **Initial State** of the system. Initial state refers to the values that exist in any dynamic object's attributes at the initial frame of a dynamic simulation. It is from this initial state that propagation occurs.

Note: *The* **Initial State** *of a simulation is not necessarily the first frame in the playback frame range but, instead, is determined by the* **Start Frame** *attribute on each particle object.*

Creation vs. Runtime Expressions

It is important to understand the difference between creation and runtime expressions.

Note: *Particle expressions are also commonly referred to as rules.*

Creation Expression
Evaluated only once for each particle in the particle object when the particle is born.

Runtime Expression
Evaluated at least once per particle per frame, but not at particle birth.

Two types of runtime expressions are available, **Runtime before Dynamics** and **Runtime after Dynamics**.

Each particle object stores all of its expressions in one of two places: the **Creation Expression** or the **Runtime Expression**.

The Expression Editor can toggle between displaying the runtime and creation expressions for the selected *particleShape* node. The expressions are evaluated in the order they appear in the Expression Editor.

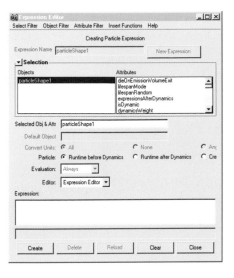

The Expression Editor

All Creation Expressions are stored in the creation portion of the Expression Editor for that particle object.

Likewise, all Runtime Expressions on a given particle object reside in the runtime segment of that particle object.

Tip: *Runtime and creation will be greyed out unless the particleShape node is the selected item. If you select the particle object, you can press the down arrow on the keyboard to navigate to the particleShape node.*

Expression examples

The following exercise will take you through the process of creating both types of particle expressions.

1 Scene file

- Open the file called *22-expressions_01.ma*.

This file contains two *pre-made* directional emitters.

2 Creation expression

Now you will write a simple particle expression.

Tip: *Remember that typing the expression is good practice and is recommended if this is new territory for you.*

- Playback the scene.

The emitters both have an **rgbPP** *attribute already added to both particleShape nodes. Right now, the rgbPP value is* <<0,0,0>>, *so the emitted particles are black.*

- Open the Attribute Editor for *particleShape1*.

- **RMB-click** on the **rgbPP** attribute and select **Creation Expression**.

- Enter the following expression in the Expression Editor:

```
rgbPP = <<rand(1),0,0>>;
```

In the above syntax, the double brackets indicate a vector quantity. There are three entries in a vector quantity, called X, Y and Z components. The components are separated by commas. In this case, the first X component corresponds to a red color, the second Y component to a green color and the third Z component corresponds to blue.

Note: *It is common to see many different attributes assigned values on the same line in the Expression Editor. Each should be separated by semicolons as follows:* rgbPP = <<1,0,1>>; lifespanPP = rand(4,6);

- Click the **Create** button.

3   Runtime expression

- Select *particleShape2*.

- **RMB** on the **rgbPP** attribute and select **Runtime Expression Before Dynamics**.

- Enter the following expression in the Expression Editor:

```
rgbPP = <<0,0,rand(1)>>;
```

- Click the **Create** button.

4 Test the results

- Press **5** to switch to shaded mode.

- Rewind and then playback the scene.

The particle shape with the creation expression gets a random red color assigned to it only once during the animation. The particle shape with the runtime expression reassigns a new random blue value on each frame of the animation.

The resulting particle color

> **Note:** The syntax `rand(1)` picks a random value between **0** and **1**. The result is always greater than **0** and less than **1**. You can also define a more specific range by using two numbers. For example, `rand(20, 30)` picks a random value greater than **20** and less than **30**. This example uses a range from **0** to **1**, since RGB values range from **0** to **1**.

- Use the same techniques to create additional creation and runtime expressions to control other attributes such as **radiusPP** or **opacityPP**.

5 Save your work

- Save the scene as *22-expressions_02.ma*.

Applied particle expressions

You should now have a better understanding of the difference between runtime and creation expressions. The next step is to use these concepts in conjunction with normalized age to establish a relationship between time and the attribute values.

Lesson 22

The following template can be used when writing a particle expression to animate from **quantity A** to **quantity B** over the particle's age:

```
A+((B-A)*(age/lifespan))
```

1 Scene file

- Open the file called *22-fountainExpression_01.ma*.

This file contains the fountain done in a previous lesson.

2 Mimic a ramp behavior with a particle expression

So far, you have learned to change the color of a particle over its age based on a ramp. This exercise teaches you how to do the same thing using an expression. This is handy if you need some specific control that you can't get from a ramp.

- Open the Attribute Editor for *mist*.

- Add an **rgbPP** attribute to *mist*.

- **RMB-click** in the **rgbPP** field and choose **Runtime Expression Before Dynamics...**

- Following the template shown above, substitute values for white(A), light blue(B), and normalized age into the Expression Editor as shown below:

```
$normAge = age/lifespan;

vector $startColor = <<1,1,1>>;

vector $endColor = <<0,0,0.8>>;

rgbPP = $startColor + (($endColor - $startColor) *
$normAge);
```

- Highlight the text you have just entered, then **MMB-click+drag** the contents of this expression to the shelf.

Doing so will save the expression to your shelf so that you can later reuse this expression.

- Press **Create** and **Close** the Expression Editor.

- Press **5** to switch to shaded mode.

- Rewind and play the animation.

The expression causes the particles to slowly transition from white to blue over the particles' age in the same way ramps controlled their related attribute. You can adjust the start and end colors in the expression to your liking once you see the effect the expression is having.

The resulting particle color

3 Save your work

- Save the scene as *22-fountainExpression_02.ma*.

linstep and smoothstep

linstep and smoothstep are MEL commands that return a value between **0** and **1** over a specified range for a given unit (frames, fps, lifespan, age, etc).

linstep produces a linear curve, while smoothstep produces a linear curve with an ease-in and ease-out appearance at the tangents.

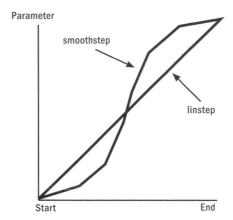

Resulting value curves

The syntax template for a `linstep` or `smoothstep` statement is as follows:

```
linstep (start, end, unitParameter);

smoothstep (start, end, unitParameter);
```

One advantage of using `linstep` and `smoothstep` is that the range of the effect can occur over any defined interval instead of being limited to the particle's age.

It is also possible to make the range of the values for `linstep` or `smoothstep` extend beyond the range of **0** to **1**. For example, to make a particle's radius increase from **0** to **5** over the course of frames **8** to **20**, the following runtime expression could be used:

```
radiusPP = 5 * linstep(8, 20, frame);
```

To make a `linstep` curve decrease instead of increase, subtract the `linstep` statement from **1**. Below is a common linstep function that will cause opacity to fade out linearly over the particle's age if placed in the runtime expression.

```
opacityPP = 1 - (smoothstep(0, lifespanPP, age));
```

Taking it a step beyond ramps

So far, what you have done could be done using ramps. The idea has been to get you familiar with how to enter expressions and how their evaluation works. Now, you will control a particle attribute such as **radiusPP** using a dynamic attribute like velocity. This is more difficult to accomplish with ramps and lends itself well to an expression.

1   Scene file

- Continue from the previous fountain example file.

2   Sphere render type

- Change the *mist* particle **Render Type** to **Spheres**.

Although you may not want to render the final shot in sphere mode, for this example you will use the sphere render type, since the effects of the expression are easiest to see with that render type.

3   Add a radiusPP attribute and enter a runtime expression

- Add a **radiusPP** attribute to the *mist* particles by clicking the **General** button and going to the **Particle** tab.

- Add to the existing runtime expression as follows:

```
float $startRadius = 0.1;

float $endRadius = 0.5;

vector $vel = velocity;

float $y = $vel.y;

radiusPP = $y / 10 * ($startRadius + ($endRadius -
$startRadius) * $normAge);
```

Tip: *You may want to enter a few carriage returns below the existing rgbPP expression to make things more readable.*

The above expression changes the radius of the spheres based on a factor of their velocity in the Y direction and also based on their normalized age. Notice that the radius decreases when the particle drops slow down and increases as they speed back up.

Problem with the particle color

4 Problem with the rgbPP values

While in shaded mode, you will notice that the spheres begin white, but turn black at some point instead of being colored. The numeric render type is useful for determining what values a specific particle attribute holds.

- Select the *mist* particles.

- Set **Particle Render Type** to **Numeric**.

- Press the **Current Render Type** button and enter *radiusPP* in the **Attribute Name** field.

This displays the numeric radius value held for each particle. As you playback, the values start positive, then become negative. Since the expression used is returning negative radius values, the spheres get turned inside out. This is why you see black instead of color.

5 Correct the expression

- Open the Expression Editor for the expression written in the previous step.

- Edit the last line of the expression so it appears as follows:

```
mistShape.radiusPP = abs($y / 10 * ($startRadius +
($endRadius -

$startRadius) * $normAge));
```

The only difference is that you enclosed what you previously had within abs(). abs *is a function that takes the absolute value of the value within parentheses. This tells the expression to check the value and always make it positive.*

- Press **Edit** and **Close**.

6 Test the results

- Playback in numeric mode again to verify that the numbers stay positive throughout.

- Switch **Render Type** back to **Sphere** and playback to see that the RGB values now display correctly.

The corrected particle color

7 Save your work

- Save the scene as *22-fountainExpression_03.ma*.

Particle motion examples

The file *22-expressionExamples.ma* contains several particle objects in different display layers. Each particle object has its own creation and runtime expression illustrating a common or interesting technique used with particle expressions.

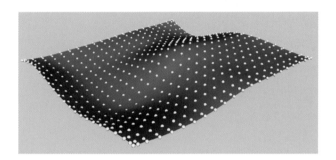

A wave example

Magic wand

This is an application for controlling particle color over time to create the common pixie dust effect.

1 Scene file

- Open the file *22-magicWand_01.ma*.

This scene consists of an animated cylinder object called wand and some standard lighting.

2 Create an emitter and parent it to the wand geometry

- Create a directional emitter with default values.

- Rename emitter *dustEmitter*.

- In the Outliner, **MMB-click+drag** *dustEmitter* onto *wand*.

- Select *dustEmitter* and translate it to the end of the *wand* geometry.

3 Set the emitter to emit dust particles

- Rename *particle1* to *dust*.

Lesson 22

- Select *dust*.

- Select **Particles** → **Emit from Object**.

This creates an emitter that will emit particles from the dust particles. It also creates another particle object.

- Rename the added emitter to *trailEmitter*.

- Rename the new particle object *dustTrail*.

4   Emitter attributes

- For the *dustEmitter* set the following:

  Emitter Type to **Directional**;

  Rate to **800**;

  Direction X, Y, Z to **0, 1, 0**;

  Spread to **0.5**;

  Speed to **2**.

- For the *trailEmitter* set the following:

  Emitter Type to **Directional**;

  Rate to **1**;

  Direction X, Y, Z to **0, 1, 0**;

  Spread to **0.2**;

  Speed to **0**.

5   Create fields for the pixie dust

- Add **Gravity** to *dust* and decrease **Magnitude** to **1**.

- Add a separate **Gravity** field to *dustTrail* with **Magnitude** to **1**.

- Add **Turbulence** to *dust* and set **Magnitude** to **2**.

6   Adjust dust particle shape attributes

- For the *dust,* set the following:

  Particle Render Type to **Points**;

  Normal Dir to **2**;

  Point Size to **2**.

7 Adjust dustTrail particle shape attributes

- For the *dustTrail* set the following:

  Particle Render Type to Streak;

  Line Width to 1;

  Normal Dir to 2;

  Tail Fade to 1;

  Tail Size to 0.05.

8 Per particle attributes to the dust particle

- Select *dust* particle shape.

- Add an **rgbPP** attribute.

9 Per particle attributes to the dustTrail particle

- Select *dustTrail* particle shape.

- Add an **rgbPP** attribute.

- Add an **opacityPP** attribute.

10 Creation expression for the lifespanPP of the dust particle

- Select *dust* particle shape.

- Set **Lifespan Mode** to **LifespanPP Only**.

- Use the following creation expression to control the dust particle lifespan on a per particle basis:

```
lifespanPP = rand(1,3);
```

This expression assigns a random lifespan value greater than 1 second and less than 3 seconds to each particle.

- Click the **Create** button.

11 Runtime expression for the rgbPP of the dust particle

- Switch the Expression Editor to its **Runtime Before Dynamics** mode.

- Enter the following twinkle expression to control the color of the particles on a per particle basis:

```
rgbPP = <<1,1,1>> * (sin(0.5 * id + time * 20));
```

The following is a breakdown of what it is doing:

<<1,1,1>> : *This is the rgb vector value of white. The expression multiplies a number against this value to change its overall value by <<0,0,0>> (black) and <<1,1,1>> (white).*

sin(0.5 * id + time * 20) : `sin` *is a function that can create an oscillating value between* **1** *and* **-1**.

By multiplying sin by variables like `particleId` *and* `time`, *we can get values that are unique and changing rhythmically. This is a very important function of expressions, especially particle expressions.*

0.5 * id : *When working with per particle expressions, it is useful to work with the* `particleShape.particleId` *attribute. This attribute, as you have seen, gives us a unique value for each particle that the runtime expression is applied to.*

0.5 * id + time * 20 : *Again, time is a great incrementer. Multiplying by 20 in this case dictates the frequency or how fast this sin functions repetitively.*

- Click the **Create** button.

Alternate expression #1:

Here is an alternate expression that does not use negative values against the rgb vector:

```
rgbPP = <<1,1,1>> * ((sin(0.5 * id + time * 20) *
0.5) + 0.5);
```

This example offsets the sin function to provide values that fall between 0 and 1. To do this, the sin is multiplied by 0.5 to cut the amplitude in half. An offset has also been added to keep its values above 0.

Alternate expression #2:

How about even a simpler method? Just like tossing a coin, we can make some of the particles dark gray and some white to cause a blinking effect:

```
if (rand(1)> 0.5)
    rgbPP = <<1,1,1>>;
else
    rgbPP = <<0.3,0.3,0.3>>;
```

There are always many different ways to do similar things. Be careful about making things overly complicated when you don't really need to. But, at the same time, you should allow enough control in your expressions to be able to achieve the effects you want.

12 Creation expression for the lifespanPP

- Select *dustTrail* particle shape.

- Enter the following creation expression:

```
lifespanPP = rand(2,5);
```

This will cause these particles to live a little longer.

- Press the **Edit** button.

13 Runtime expressions for the rgbPP and opacityPP of the dustTrail particle shape

You will create the same type of expression for the **rgbPP** and **opacityPP** to control not only the **Color**, but also the **Transparency** of the particles.

- Select *dustTrail* particle shape.

- Update the runtime expression for the following:

```
rgbPP = <<1,1,1>> * ((sin(0.5 * id + time * 20) * 0.5) + 0.5);

opacityPP=(1 - ((linstep(0, lifespanPP, age))) * 0.0005);
```

1-linstep(0,lifespanPP,age) : *The linstep function is used here to provide a linear change of value between 0 and 1 over time.* **1-linstep** *gives us the reverse, returning values from 1 to 0 over the particle's age. This value is different for each particle based on the lifespanPP creation expression you already made.*

- Press the **Edit** button.

14 Playback

Experiment with field attributes, render types or multiplier values in the expressions to tune the results.

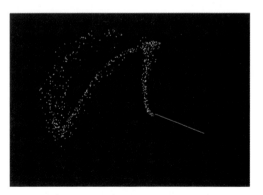

Pixie dust

15 Save your work

- Save the scene as *22-magicWand_02.ma*.

Tips and traps

- In the fountain exercise of this lesson, the fountain may emit black particles on the first frame. To fix this, add a creation expression that sets the color to white. The runtime expression doesn't evaluate when the particle's age is equal to **0** (birth).

- `mag` is a function that finds the magnitude of a vector, also known as the length. This is useful for representing a 3 component vector with a single value. `mag` does the following math automatically for the user:

      distance^2 = (x2-x1)^2 + (y2-y1)^2 + (z2-z1)^2

  `mag` is often useful to help determine the distance one point in space is from another point in space. For an example of this, look at the 22-waveDistCam.ma file. The `mag` function is used to determine the distance from each wave particle to the camera. When moving the camera closer to the surface, the waves diminish in intensity and vice versa.

- People often look through some of the expression examples and see things like `position0` and `velocity0` and wonder what they are.

  *When you save **Intial State** on a particle object, that information needs to be stored somewhere. Most static particle attributes (i.e. position, velocity, acceleration, mass, etc.), have an **Initial State** attribute that is designated by the 0 as in `position0`. Also, when you add a new array attribute to a particle object via **Modify → Add Attribute...**, there is an option to **Add Inital State Attribute**. When you check this **On**, it adds a 0 attribute for the custom attribute.*

- Expressions are evaluated in the order they are typed in the Expression Editor from top to bottom. For more specific information about the order of evaluation of dynamics, refer to Lesson 24 .

- Lesson 24 provides a more in-depth explanation of each expression type and shows more specific expression syntax.

Conclusion

You now have a foundation for creating some of your own particle expressions. Keep in mind that particle expression applications are limitless, and are comprehensive topics on their own. In this lesson, you have seen how to get started with some basic examples. Particle expressions should be considered as an entire tool within the Maya dynamic system. Not all situations lend themselves well to using expressions. However, they give you access to a lower level of information that, in some cases, is not accessible through graphical methods such as ramps or the Attribute Editor. Expressions can also provide a solution for getting results that would be difficult or impossible to keyframe and can give your simulations the ability to have decision-making built into them.

In the next lesson, you will learn about the particle emit function.

Lesson 23

The emit function

In this lesson, you will learn about additional control provided for particle placement and emission using the MEL command called `emit`.

In this lesson you will learn the following:

- Common uses for the emit function;

- Common emit syntax and options;

- How to use simple conditional statements;

- How to add and work with custom attributes;

- How to construct MEL commands with strings;

- How to use the `eval` MEL command;

- Emitting particles when rigid body collisions occur.

Emitting particles

Up to this point, the examples have relied on the Particle Tool and predefined emitters such as surface, directional and omni to place particles in the scene. For most applications, these provide an adequate starting point.

There are cases where some additional control may be required that is difficult or not possible using the default emitters.

For example, if you create a cloud of particles with the Particle Tool and realize you need to add a few more particles to change its shape, one common practice is to use the `emit` command.

Emit function with position flag

1 Create a particle object

- Type `particle` in the Command Line, then press **Enter**.

- Rename the particles *addParticles*.

- Set the **Particle Render Type** to **Sphere**.

- Click the **Current Render Type** button and set the **Radius** to **0.3**.

2 Add three particles to the existing particle object using emit

- Select **Window** → **General Editors** → **Script Editor**.

- Enter the following lines in the lower window of the Script Editor:

```
emit -object addParticles -position 1 1 1;

emit -object addParticles -position 2 2 2;

emit -object addParticles -position 3 3 3;
```

- Press the Enter key on the numeric keypad or select **Script** → **Execute**.

Each line above adds one particle to the existing addParticles particle object. The `position` *flag is followed by the world space coordinate where the particle gets placed into the scene.*

Tip: *Individual particles cannot be removed from a particle object. However, you can set an individual particle's* **opacityPP** *to* **0** *or its* **lifespanPP** *to* **0** *using its* **particleId** *in an expression, or by setting the value in the Component Editor.*

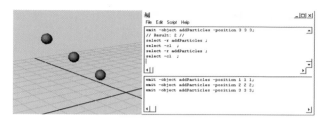

Emitting individual particles

Define particle placement with a locator

You can make this process more interactive by setting it up so the `emit` command places the particle at the coordinates of a locator.

- Select **Create** → **Locator**.

- Type the following in the Script Editor:

```
float $locX = `getAttr locator1.tx`;

float $locY = `getAttr locator1.ty`;

float $locZ = `getAttr locator1.tz`;

string $partObject[] = `ls -type "particle"`;

emit -object $partObject[0] -position $locX $locY $locZ;
```

- Highlight and **MMB-click+drag** the script to the shelf.

- Move the locator to a location in space where you want to add a new particle.

- Click the shelf button.

This will automatically add a new particle into the particle object at the locator position.

- Repeat the process as desired.

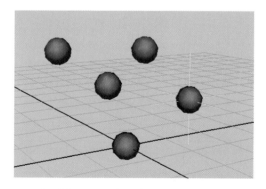

Particles created at the locator position

Emitting based on other particles

The `emit` function can set any attribute for a particle, not just its position. In the following example, `emit` is used to set position and velocity on newly spawned particles to make it appear as though the dying particles are emitting new particles.

1 Create a directional emitter

- In a new scene, select **Particles** → **Create Emitter** → ❑.

- Set the **Emitter Type** to **Directional**.

- Rename the emitter *primaryEmitter*.

- Rename the particles *primaryParticles*.

- Set the following attributes for *primaryEmitter*:

> **Rate** to **100**;
>
> **Direction** to **0, 1, 0**;
>
> **Spread** to **0.25**;
>
> **Speed** to **10**.

- Set the following attributes for *primaryParticles:*

> **Particle Render Type** to **Spheres**;
>
> **Radius** to **0.2**;
>
> **Lifespan Mode** to **lifespanPP only**.

2 Create an empty particle object

- In the Command Line, type the following, then press Enter:

```
particle -n secondaryParticles;
```

This will create an empty particle object named secondaryParticles.

3 Render type for secondaryParticles

- Select *secondaryParticles*.

- Set the following:

> **Particle Render Type** to **Multi-Streak**;
>
> **Lifespan Mode** to **lifespanPP only**.

4 Connect gravity to primaryParticles

- Select *primaryParticles*.

- Select **Fields** → **Gravity**.

5 Runtime expression to lifespanPP for primaryParticles

- Add the following to *primaryParticles'* runtime expression:

```
$pos = position;

$vel = velocity;

if ($vel.y<0)

{

        lifespanPP = 0;

        emit -object secondaryParticles

                -position ($pos.x) ($pos.y) ($pos.z)

                -at velocity -vectorValue ($vel.x) ($vel.y)
($vel.z);

}
```

- Click the **Create** button.

6 Test the expression

- Set the playback range to go from **1** to **500**.

- Rewind and playback.

Just as primaryParticles begin to fall, the emit function is invoked and new secondaryParticles replace them with the same velocity and position.

New particles emitted from runtime expression

Lesson 23

> **Tip:** *A full description of the flags used by the* emit *function are listed in the online MEL documentation in the scene commands section.*

7 Edit the expression to add color to secondaryParticles

- Add an **rgbPP** to *secondaryParticles*.

- Edit the runtime expression on *primaryParticles* as shown:

```
$pos = position;

$vel = velocity;

$col = sphrand(1);

if ($vel.y<0)

{
        lifespanPP = 0;

        emit -object secondaryParticles

                -position ($pos.x) ($pos.y) ($pos.z)

                -at velocity -vectorValue ($vel.x) ($vel.y)
($vel.z)

                -at rgbPP -vectorValue ($col.x) ($col.y) ($col.
z);

}
```

- Click the **Edit** button.

8 Test the results

- Press **5** for shaded mode.

- Rewind and playback.

A random color is assigned to each particle in secondaryParticles.

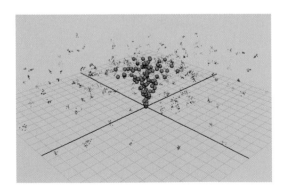

Colored particles

Fireworks

In the last lesson, you created the framework for a fireworks effect. You can take the `emit` function a step further by repeatedly invoking the command in a looping structure to create a fireworks effect. Here you will create a fireworks effect and will also learn how to add custom attributes to the particle object and emitter. This will allow you to customize the launching and explosion characteristics.

1 Emitting cannon

- Open a new scene.

- Create a **Directional** emitter with the following settings:

  Rate to **5**;

  Direction X to **0**;

  Direction Y to **1**;

  Direction Z to **0**;

  Spread to **0.25**;

  Speed to **10**.

- Rename the emitter *launcher* and the particle object *fireworks1*.

2 Add custom attributes to launcher

Custom attributes are attributes that the user can tailor to his or her specific needs. Below you will add several custom attributes to the emitter that will later be used in particle expressions to modify the motion of the particles and the amount of emission that occurs.

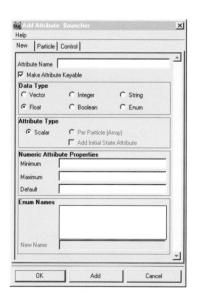

To add custom attributes to the emitter, follow these steps:

- Select *launcher* and choose **Modify** → **Add Attribute...**

- Add the following custom attributes to *launcher*:

The Add Attributes window

Lesson 23

Note: *All the custom attribute should be* **Interger, Scalar** *and* **Keyable.**

antiGrav with a **Default Value** of **5**;

showerUpper with a **Default Value** of **30**;

showerLower with a **Default Value** of **30**;

streamUpper with a **Default Value** of **1**;

streamLower with a **Default Value** of **1**;

3 Add and adjust attributes for fireworks1

- Add a per object **Color** attribute to *fireworks1*.

- Set the attribute values for *fireworks1* as follows:

    Max Count to **3**;

    Particle Render Type to **Streak**;

    Red to **0.8**;

    Green to **0**;

    Blue to **0**;

    Line Width to **1**;

    Tail Fade to **0.1**;

    Tail Size to **3.6**;

    Lifespan Mode to **lifespanPP** only.

4 Connect fireworks1 to gravity

- Select *fireworks1*.

- Select **Fields** → **Gravity**.

5 Save your work

- Save your scene as *23-fireworks_01.ma*.

Make the secondary particle object

The secondary particle object represents the small projectiles that leave the initial projectile when its velocity reaches 0. These will be created using the `emit` function.

These secondary particles will act as leading particles for the long streaks of sparks that will be added later. Wherever the leading particles go, the streaks of sparks will follow. The secondary particles are the glowing tips of the streaks.

1   Scene file

- Continue working with the scene from the last exercise.

2   Create the "leading" particle object

- Type the following in the Script Editor:

```
particle -n fireworks2;
```

This will create an empty particle object named fireworks2.

3   Add and modify attributes for fireworks2

- Select the *fireworks2* particles.

- Change the **Particle Render Type** to **Spheres**.

- Set a **Radius** value of **0.05**.

- Set **Lifespan Mode** to **lifespanPP only**.

4   Create and connect gravity

- Select *fireworks2*.

- Select **Fields** → **Gravity**.

Create the final particle object and emitter

Now you will create the stream of sparks that follow behind the leading particles.

1   Add a directional emitter to fireworks2

- Select *fireworks2*.

- Select **Particles** → **Emit from Object**.

- Make sure the new emitter is **Directional**.

- Rename the emitter *sparkEmitter* and the new particle object *fireworks3*.

2 Adjust attributes for sparkEmit

- Select *sparkEmitter* and set the following attributes:

    Rate to **40**;

    Direction to **0, 1, 0**.

    Spread to **0.25**;

    Speed to **1**;

3 Set the attributes for fireworks3

- Select *fireworks3* and set the following attributes:

    Depth Sort to **On**;

    Particle Render Type to **MultiPoint**;

    Color Accum to **On**;

    Multi Count to **15**;

    Multi Radius to **0.2**.

- Set **Lifespan Mode** to **lifespanPP only**.

Add expressions to the particle objects

Now that the particle objects have been built and the appropriate fields connected, you can add expressions to the various particle objects.

1 Use emit to spawn the leading particles

- Select **Window** → **Animation Editors** → **Expression Editor**.

- Select *fireworks1Shape*.

- In the Expression Editor, make sure to select the **Runtime Before Dynamics** option.

- Add the following runtime expression to *fireworks1*:

```
vector $pos = fireworks1Shape.position;

vector $vel = fireworks1Shape.velocity;

float $antiGrav = launcher.antiGrav;

int $upperCount = launcher.showerUpper;

int $lowerCount = launcher.showerLower;

int $upperLife = launcher.streamUpper;
```

```
int $lowerLife = launcher.streamLower;

if ($vel.y < 0)

{

    fireworks1Shape.lifespanPP = 0;

    int $numPars = rand ($lowerCount, $upperCount);

    string $emitCmd = "emit -o fireworks2Shape ";

    for ($i=1; $i<=$numPars; $i++)

    {

        $emitCmd += "-pos " + $pos + " ";

        vector $vrand = sphrand(10);

        $vrand = <<$vrand.x, $vrand.y + $antiGrav,
$vrand.z>>;

        $emitCmd += "-at velocity ";

        $emitCmd += "-vv " + $vrand + " ";

        float $lsrand = rand ($lowerLife, $upperLife);

        $emitCmd += "-at lifespanPP ";

        $emitCmd += "-fv " + $lsrand + " ";

    }

    eval ($emitCmd);

}
```

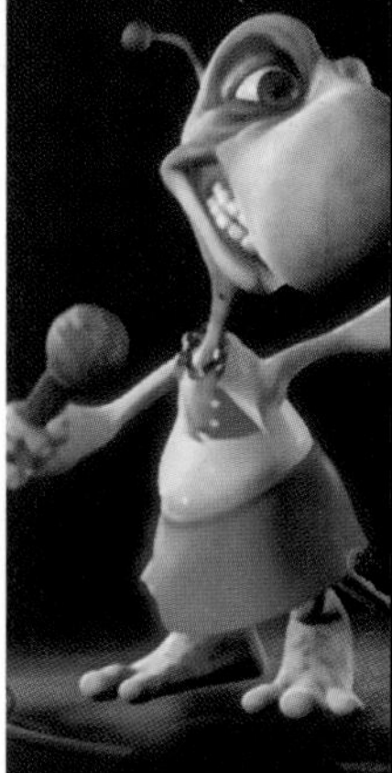

Note: *If you get the following execution error it means that the names mismatch between the expression and your scene:*

```
//Error: An execution error occurred in the runtime expression
for fireworks1Shape.
//Error: line 1: fireworksShape2: Object not found for -object
flag.//
```

In the error shown above, the name fireworksShape2 is not found and should be changed to fireworks2Shape within the expression.

This expression creates the flares at the tips of the fireworks trails.

- Click the **Create** button.

Lesson 23

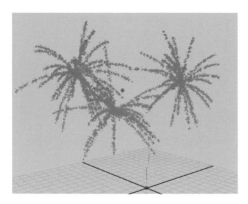

The rough fireworks expression

2   Create a non-dynamic expression to control launcher's rate

A non-dynamic expression is an expression that is not contained within a runtime or creation expression. Non-dynamic expressions are evaluated once per frame.

- Select *launcher* and add the following in the Expression Editor:

```
launcher.speed = rand (12,18);

if (frame%20==0)

launcher.speed = 22;
```

This expression varies the speed at which a particle leaves the cannon so the fireworks explode at different heights. Every 20th frame, a particle gets launched much higher.

- Click the **Create** button.

Note: *The* **Creation** *and* **Runtime** *options are greyed out in the Expression Editor since the expression is being added to* launcher, *which is not a particle shape object.*

---

3   Assign a random lifespan to the spark trails

- To control how long the spark trail burns, add the following to the creation expression of *fireworksShape3*:

```
fireworksShape3.lifespanPP = rand (0.3, 0.7);
```

This causes each particle in the spark trails of the fireworks to die before they are one second old.

- Click the **Create** button.

4 Playback

- Playback the animation.

Now that you are comfortable with how this process works, try setting different values for lifespanPP *and other particle and attribute values, including the custom attributes you added to the emitter.*

5 Save your work

- Save your scene as *23-fireworks_02.ma*.

The files *23-fireworks_03.ma* and *23-fireworks_04.ma* are finished versions of this example.

Final fireworks effect

Emission on contact

In the following exercise, you will learn how to emit particles at the location where rigid bodies collide. To test this functionality, you will drop a rigid body object on the ground and you will emit particles at the contact points.

1 Open File

- Open *23-bucket_01.ma*.

This file contains a bucket set up to fall and collide with the ground. The rigid bodies and field are already set up.

2   Create an empty particle object

- Type `particle` in the Command Line and press Enter.

This empty particle object will be used later to hold the particles that are emitted when a collision occurs.

- Set the following attributes:

    Conserve to **0.9**;

    Max Count to **600**;

    Particle Render Type to **MultiStreak**;

    Color Accum to **On**;

    Line Width to **2.0**;

    MultiCount to **7**;

    MultiRadius to **0.3**;

    Lifespan Mode to **lifespanPP only**.

- Add an **rgbPP** attribute.

- Add an **opacityPP** attribute and add the default ramp to it.

3   Enable contact data attribute on the rigidSolver

The rigidSolver has an attribute called *contactData*. If this attribute is **On**, you can use MEL to find out information about when and where rigid body collisions occur. This attribute is **Off** by default since it requires extra work for the solver to manage this data.

- Select the *bucket*.

- Locate the *rigidSolver* node in the Channel Box and set the **contactData** attribute to **On**.

4   Add a non-dynamic expression

An expression applied to the bucket will be used to check the velocity of the rigid body, find out when and where a contact has occurred and emit particles into *particle1* at that location.

- Select *bucket* and open the Expression Editor.

- Enter the following expression:

```
float $vel[] = `rigidBody -q -vel bucket`;

float $speed = mag(<<$vel[0],$vel[1],$vel[2]>>);

int $num = $speed * 3;

int $contact = `rigidBody -q -cc bucket`;

string $cPos[];

string $each;

if(($contact > 0) && ($num > 0))

{

        $cPos = `rigidBody -q -cp bucket`;

        for ($each in $cPos)

        {

                string $emit = ("emit -o particle1 -pos "
+$each);

                for ($x = 1; $x < $num; $x++)

                {

                        $emit += (" -pos " + $each);

                }

                $emit += (" -attribute velocity");

                for ($x= 1; $x <= $num; $x++)

                {

                        vector $rand = (sphrand(1) + <<0,4,0>>);

                        $emit += (" -vectorValue " +

                                $rand.x + " " +

                                $rand.y + " " +

                                $rand.z);

                }

                eval($emit);

        }

}
```

- Click the **Create** button.

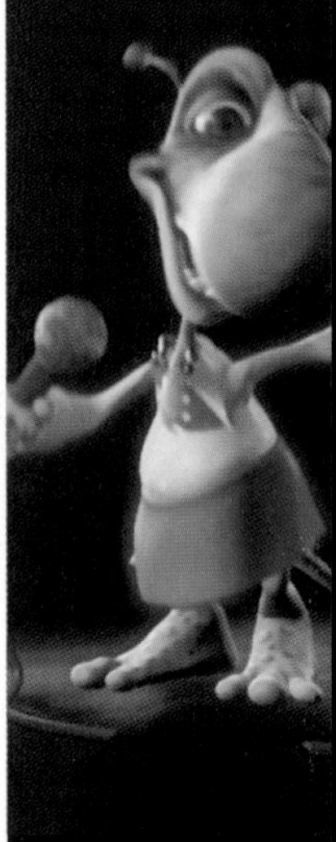

Lesson 23

5   Connect particles to gravity

- Connect the *gravity* already in the scene to the particles.

6   Make particles collide with ground

- Select *particle1*, then **Shift-select** *ground*.
- Select **Particles** → **Make Collide**.

7   Add creation expression to particles

- Enter the following creation expression for the particles:

```
mass = 50;

lifespanPP = rand(0.8,1);

rgbPP = <<0.8,0.4,0.3>>;
```

- Click the **Create** button.

8   Playback the scene

Particles are getting emitted wherever the bucket rigid body collides.

Collision emit

9   Save your work

- Save the scene as *23-bucket_02.ma*.

Conclusion

In this lesson, you learned about several key concepts such as using the `emit` command to add and place new particles, building complex MEL expressions using loops and `eval` commands, and emitting particles from other particles and at rigid body collision points. Now that you have had some exposure to the `emit` command, you have another tool available to achieve the effects you are working on.

You will likely come across cases where the methods discussed here are applicable to a situation you are trying to simulate. Be careful about getting sidetracked by the more technical approach of using `emit` if the same effect is easily accomplished using the particle tools already available.

In the next lesson, you will go even more in-depth with particle expressions.

Lesson 24   Advanced particle expressions

This lesson provides a more in-depth discussion of the expressions and steps used to build some examples contained in the file 22-expressionExamples.ma. You will now learn how they were built and obtain a description of how some expressions work. This section also discusses the order of evaluation for the various elements in the dynamics system. Lastly, you acquire more detailed descriptions of the expressions using the emit command in the fireworks example.

In this lesson you will learn the following:

- How to move particles with expressions;

- How to create random motion;

- How to change the color of particles based on their motion;

- How to vary the emission rate with expressions;

- How to use particleId;

- The order of evaluation.

Moving particles with expressions

You have been dealing primarily with expressions to control rendering attributes such as color or opacity. Here, you will apply similar methods on position, velocity and acceleration attributes to dynamically control the motion of the particles.

> **Note:** *If you don't feel comfortable with expressions and algorithms, this lesson can help you understand some fundamental concepts.*

Position control expression

1 Create a particle in the scene

- Use the **Particle Tool** to create a single particle near the origin.
- Set **Particle Render Type** to **Spheres**.

2 Add a runtime expression

- Enter the following runtime expression for **position**:

```
position = <<0, time, 0 >>;
```

- Click the **Create** button.

3 Test the results

- Set the frame range to go from **1** to **300**.
- Rewind and playback.

The particle moves up on the **Y-axis** *as* time *increases. As the animation plays back,* time *is a constantly changing value determined using the following relationship:*

```
Time = Current Frame Number / Frames Per Second
```

Random motion expression

- Create a cloud of **100** particles.
- Try each of the following on their own in the runtime expression to see the interesting effects they produce:

```
velocity = dnoise (position);

acceleration = dnoise (position);

velocity = sphrand(10);

acceleration = sphrand(10);

position = position + dnoise(position);
```

sphrand *returns a random vector value that exists within a spherical or ellipsoidal region of your choice.* dnoise *returns a vector with each component containing a random number from -1 to 1.*

Acceleration using variables and magnitude

1   Create a new scene file with a cloud of particles in it

- Select **File** → **New Scene**.

- Create an **Omni** emitter.

- Set **Rate** to **10**.

- Set **Particle Render Type** to **Spheres**.

- Set **Radius** to **0.3**.

2   Runtime expression for acceleration

- Enter the following in the runtime expression for **acceleration**:

```
int $frequency = 65;

float $distance = mag (position);

int $limit = 3;

if ($distance > $limit)

    acceleration = acceleration - (position * $frequency);
```

- Click **Create** in the Expression Editor.

3   Playback the animation

The particles move in a swarming pattern. Watch one particle to see what it is doing. It is swinging between a range in 3D space defined by $limit. When the *magnitude* of the position is greater than the limit, the expression begins subtracting acceleration from the particle, which increases its acceleration in the opposite direction.

Lesson 24

Swarming particles

If this is unclear to you, try the same expression on a single particle instead of an emitter. Also, try changing the values used for frequency and limit.

Noise position expression and custom attribute

1 Grid of particles

- Select **File** → **New Scene**.

- Select **Particles** → **Particle Tool** → ☐.

- Set the following in the options:

    Create Particle Grid to On;

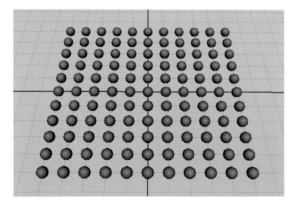

A grid of particles

Particle Spacing to **1.0**;

Placement to **With Text Fields**;

Minimum Corner to **5, 0, 5**;

Maximum Corner to **-5, 0, -5**.

- Press **Enter** in the viewport to create the grid.

- Set **Particle Render Type** to **Spheres**.

- Set **Radius** to **0.3**.

2 Custom vector attribute

Adding a custom vector attribute will give us a place to store the original position of each particle.

- Select *particleShape1* and open its Attribute Editor.

- In the **Add Dynamics Attributes** section, click the **General** button.

- Set the following:

  Attribute Name to *origPos*;

  Data Type to **Vector**;

  Attribute Type to **Per Particle (Array)**;

  Add Initial State Attribute to **On**.

- Press the **OK** button.

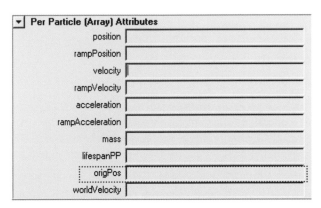

Your custom per particle attribute

An origPos field is added to the **Per Particle (Array) Attributes** *section of the Attribute Editor. Since the* **Attribute Type** *was set to* **Array**, *you just made your own custom per particle attribute.*

3 Creation expression for origPos

- Add the following creation expression to **origPos** to store the position of each particle at the initial frame:

```
origPos = position;
```

Note: *Since it is a creation expression, the original position will be saved only on the first frame of the simulation.*

- Click the **Create** button.

- Make sure to **rewind** the scene in order to execute the creation expression.

4 Runtime expression to position

- Click the **Runtime Before Dynamics** radio button in the Expression Editor.

- Enter the following Runtime Expression to control position:

```
position = origPos +

            << 0, (0.8 * noise (origPos *
3+time*<<0,1,2>>)), 0>>;
```

- Click the **Create** button.

5 Test the results

- Rewind and playback.

Each particle moves in a wave-like fashion up and down along only the **Y-axis**. *The above expression is just adding a vector to* **origPos**. *The Y component of that vector is a statement that generates a random stream.* **0.8** *controls the amplitude of that stream,* **3** *controls the frequency and* **<<0,1,2>>** *controls the direction of the phase.*

The noise *function produces a smoother random number stream than the previously discussed* rand *function.*

Notice how you are setting a value for **origPos** in the creation, then modifying that value again in the runtime expression. This is a very common technique for working with particle expressions.

The noise expression effect

Change color based on position

- In a new scene, create an **Omni** emitter.

- Add an **rgbPP** attribute.

- Add the following runtime expression to **position**:

```
vector $pos = position;

if ($pos.y >=0)

    rgbPP = <<1,0,0>>;

else

    rgbPP = <<0,0,1>>;
```

- Switch to shaded mode.

- Rewind and playback.

This expression stores the position for each particle in a vector variable called $pos. *The* if *statement checks the Y component of that vector to see if it is above or below the Y-axis. If the particle is above, it is red, otherwise it is blue.*

You can try the same idea with acceleration or velocity instead of position.

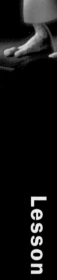

Lesson 24

Tip: *The individual elements of a vector (i.e. <<x, y, z>>) are called components.*

Emitter examples

Although emitters are closely related to particles, they do not use creation and runtime expressions. The following example is good for obtaining a randomized emission rate that can be used to simulate an eruption, geyser, or puffing smoke effect. This example shows you a concept on which you can build upon when working with emitters.

1   Start with an empty scene file

- Select **File** → **New Scene**.

2   Create a directional emitter

- Create a **Directional** emitter.

- Set the following for the emitter:

  Direction to **0, 1, 0**;

  Spread to **0.25**;

  Speed to **10**.

- Set the following for the particles:

  Particle Render Type to **Clouds (s/w)**;

  Radius to **0.2**;

  Lifespan to **Constant**.

3   Add gravity to the particles

- Select the particles, then select **Fields** → **Gravity**.

4   Add an expression to control rate

- Select *emitter1*.

- Open the Expression Editor and enter the following expression:

```
emitter1.rate = 200*noise (time*1000);
```

- Click the **Create** button.

This expression uses noise *as opposed to* dnoise, *since rate is a scalar quantity. You would only use* dnoise *if you were working with a vector quantity such as position or color. You then multiply* noise *and* time *by* **1000** *to increase the amplitude and frequency of the noise values, since they are far too small without these multipliers.*

Particle ID

Just as each building on a street has its own address number, each particle in a particle object has its own unique numerical identity called the **particleId**. ParticleId is an integer value ranging from **0** to **n-1**. The **particleId** attribute makes it easier to control attributes of specific particles independently of other particles within the same particle object. This is especially useful for adding variation to attributes of a particle object.

The following example will control color based on particleId.

1 Create a new scene file

- Select **File** → **New Scene**.

2 Create an Omni emitter

- Select **Particles** → **Create Emitter**.
- Set **Emitter Type** to **Omni**.

3 Add an rgbPP attribute to particleShape1

4 Add a runtime expression to rgbPP

- Add the following to the runtime expression for *particleShape1:*

```
if (particleId == 10)

    rgbPP = <<0,1,0>>;
```

- Press the **Create** button.
- Make sure you are in shaded mode.
- Rewind and play the animation.

The first particle in a particle object is always particleId **0**. *Therefore, the 11th particle emitted into particleShape2 is particleId* **10** *and is colored green due to the conditional statement of the expression.*

▪ Below is another particleId example you can add as a runtime or creation expression for **rgbPP** to produce some interesting results.

```
if (particleId % 10 == 0)

      rgbPP = sphrand(1);
```

The % *symbol stands for the modulus operation, which is the remainder produced when two numbers are divided. The above expression divides the particleId by 10. If the remainder of that division is* **0**, *then the* sphrand *function picks a random vector value between <<0,0,0>> and <<1,1,1>>. In other words, every 10th particle will get a random color assigned.*

Order of evaluation

The following is a breakdown of the order in which the dynamics system evaluates the elements of a simulation.

▪ First, the **acceleration** is cleared at the beginning of each frame or evaluation.

▪ Particle **Runtime Expressions before Dynamics** are then evaluated. The expressions can be set or added to the current values of the particle's attributes.

▪ Next, the **forces** are computed. Forces include **fields**, **springs** and **goals**. These forces are added to whatever is currently in the acceleration, which includes whatever a particle expression may have put there.

▪ The **velocity** is computed from the **acceleration**. This also just adds to whatever value is currently in the velocity, which may have previously been set in an expression.

▪ The **positions** are computed from the velocity. Just as with acceleration and velocity, position is added to whatever is currently stored in position from expressions or forces already computed.

▪ Finally, the **Runtime Expressions after Dynamics** are evaluated.

The expressions do not override the dynamics. The dynamics happen after the expressions are evaluated, and their results are added together. It is possible to have expressions calculated before dynamics on a per object basis by disabling the **Expressions After Dynamics** checkbox of the *particleShape* object.

Emit expression

Below is the runtime expression used for the *fireworks1* particles in the scene called *23-fireworks_03*. The short command flags have been replaced with the long flag names for additional clarity. A detailed description is provided after the expression.

```
vector $pos = fireworksShape1.position;

vector $vel = fireworksShape1.velocity;

float $antiGrav = launcher.antiGrav;

int $upperCount = launcher.showerUpper;

int $lowerCount = launcher.showerLower;

int $upperLife = 0.8 ;   //launcher.streamUpper;

int $lowerLife = 2 ;   //launcher.streamLower;


string $emitCmd = "emit -object fireworks2 ";

if ($vel.y < 0)

{//opening bracket for the if statement

    // kill this particle

    fireworksShape1.lifespanPP = 0;


    // emit a shower of new particles in this particle's place

    int $numPars = rand($lowerCount, $upperCount);


    for ($i = 1; $i <= $numPars; $i++)

    {//opening bracket for the for loop

        $emitCmd += "-position " + $pos + " ";

        vector $vrand = sphrand(60);

        $vrand = <<$vrand.x, $vrand.y + $antiGrav, $vrand.z>>;

        $emitCmd += "-attribute velocity ";

        $emitCmd += "-vectorValue " + $vrand + " ";

        float $lsrand = rand($lowerLife, $upperLife);
```

```
        $emitCmd += «-attribute lifespanPP «;

        $emitCmd += «-floatValue « + $lsrand + « «;

    }//closing bracket for the for loop


    eval($emitCmd);

}//closing bracket for the if statement
```

Step-by-step explanation

```
vector $pos = fireworksShape1.position;

vector $vel = fireworksShape1.velocity;
```

- Stores the values for the position and velocity of a particle to be used later in the expression.

```
float $antiGrav = launcher.antiGrav;
```

- Stores the value for `antiGrav` into a float (decimal) variable called `$antiGrav`. This variable is one of the custom attributes added to the *launcher* object.

The `$antiGrav` variable will be used later in this expression to add or remove velocity in the Y-axis as particles fall. This provides a way to add to or counteract the effect of gravity.

```
int $upperCount = launcher.showerUpper;

int $lowerCount = launcher.showerLower;
```

- `showerLower` and `showerUpper` are two custom attributes previously added to *launcher*.

These attributes define a range (lower and upper bound) out of which a random number will be picked later in the expression. That random number will then be used to control the number of fireworks2 particles emitted.

```
int $upperLife = launcher.streamUpper;

int $lowerLife = launcher.streamLower;
```

- `streamUpper` and `streamLower` are two more of the custom attributes previously added to *launcher*.

*These attributes define a range (lower and upper bound) out of which a random number will be chosen later in the expression. That random number will then be used to control the **Lifespan** of fireworks2 particles emitted.*

```
string $emitCmd = "emit -object fireworks2 ";
```

- The expression is designed to piece together the `emit` command and execute it once it has been fully assembled.

- Each particle created in *fireworks2* will be the result of using the same basic syntax framework for the `emit` command. The only difference will be substituting in different attribute values (position, velocity, etc.) for each particle.

- `$emitCmd` stores the emit command while it is being constructed in the expression. The text between quotes is the first piece of the `emit` command. The remaining elements will be appended in the looping structure.

```
if ($vel.y < 0)
```

- This is a conditional statement that needs the velocity on the Y-axis of the particle to become negative in order to return true and execute the portion of the expression between its brackets.

```
fireworksShape1.lifespanPP = 0;
```

- This line will kill the particle from which the explosion is happening on the next frame by setting its lifespan to **0**.

```
int $numPars = rand($lowerCount, $upperCount);
```

- Choose a random integer number from within the range of values defined by `$lowerCount` and `$upperCount` and assign that random value to `$numPars`.

- `$numPars` will be used in the next line to control the number of times the commands within a loop will be executed.

```
for ($i=1; $i<=$numPars; $i++)
```

- This is a looping structure that will execute the commands enclosed between its brackets.

- The random value assigned to `$numParts` controls the number of times those commands are executed.

- The basic syntax of a `for` loop is:

```
for (startValue; endValue; increment)
{
    statements;
}
```

- In the expression's loop, $i is the *startValue* and represents how many times it has cycled through the loop to this point.

The first time through the loop, $i has the startValue of **1**.

Then, $i is incremented by **1**, *by the $i++ in the increment portion of the loop.*

Therefore, the second time through the loop $i = 2.

As long as the condition $i <= $numParts, *which defines the endValue, is* **true**, *$i will be incremented and the loop will continue.*

When the endValue condition is **false**, *the loop is exited and the next line in the expression is evaluated.*

```
$emitCmd += "-position " + $pos + " ";

vector $vrand = sphrand(60);

$vrand = <<$vrand.x, $vrand.y + $antiGrav, $vrand.z>>;

$emitCmd += "-attribute velocity ";

$emitCmd += "-vectorValue " + $vrand + " ";

float $lsrand = rand($lowerLife, $upperLife);

$emitCmd += "-attribute lifespanPP ";

$emitCmd += "-floatValue " + $lsrand + " ";
```

- The syntax += will take what is currently stored in $emitCmd and append what is on the right side of the symbol to the end of $emitCmd.

- $vrand uses the sphrand function to select a random vector value between **<<0,0,0>>** and **<<60,60,60>>**. This provides a random value to use for velocity.

- The expression constantly appends to $emitCmd. Each line is setting a different attribute for the emit command.

```
eval($emitCmd);
```

- So far in the expression, you have entered and constructed the emit command in the $emitCmd variable. After the loop is finished, the emit command is complete and ready to be executed.

- eval is a command that is much like the = button on a calculator. It will execute the content of the $emitCmd variable. This will actually place particles in the correct locations and assign them the correct attribute values.

Conclusion

In this lesson, you have taken a deeper look into ways of using advanced expressions to control particles and emitters. You learned about several new MEL commands and also how to add custom per particle attributes. You also experimented with using particleId to add an extra level of control to your particles.

In the next project, you will learn about several dynamic features that will help you create astonishing particle effects.

Project Seven

Lessons

In Project Seven, you will learn about dynamic features that will contribute to the creation of advanced particle effects. You will start by experimenting with particle flow, which controls particles over a path. You will then learn about particle goals, soft bodies and springs, which, when used together, can achieve great dynamic object deformations. Lastly, you will create a particle instance, which allows you to replace particles with pieces of geometry.

By the end of this project, you should have a basic understanding of some advanced dynamic features.

Lesson 25   Flow

This lesson focuses on flow, which is a preset clip effect that allows you to quickly and easily make particles follow the shape of a specified curve. The main example of this lesson will have you create a simplified version of a tornado, such as the one following the ZyZaks in The ChubbChubbs! movie.

In this lesson you will learn the following:

- How to make particles flow along a NURBS curve;

- How to combine deformers and animation with dynamics;

- How to use objects as the source of fields;

- How to adjust important flow parameters.

Using flow

There are many ways to create a tornado effect. In the following example, you'll give your brain a rest from particle expressions to demonstrate the simple and easy to use flow effect.

1   New Scene

- Open a new scene.
- Select **Create → EP Curve Tool**.
- In the front view, create a curve as follows:

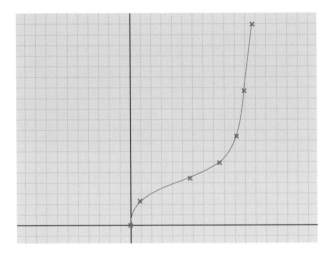

Tornado profile curve

- Rename the curve to *tornadoCurve*.

2   Apply a lattice deformer

- Select *tornadoCurve*.
- Select **Deform → Create Lattice → ❑**.
- Set the following:

    Divisions to **5, 9, 2**;

    Autoparent to Selection to **On**.

- Press the **Create** button.

3 Add relative clusters

- Select the *ffd1Lattice* node, then press **RMB-click** on it and select **Lattice Point**.

- Select the top three rows of lattice points.

- Choose **Deform** → **Create Cluster** → ❑.

- Make sure **Relative Mode** is **On**.

*Making a cluster **Relative** forces the cluster to receive its transform information from the transform node directly above it in the hierarchy. This prevents the double transformations that normally occur when clusters are parented to geometry. It is possible to toggle the relative mode **On** and **Off** in the Attribute Editor on a cluster that has already been created.*

- Press the **Create** button.

- Repeat the previous steps in order to create two additional clusters for the three middle and three bottom rows.

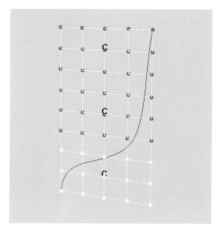

Adding clusters to the lattice points

4 Group the clusters under the tornadoCurve

- Select the three clusters, then **Shift-select** the *tornadoCurve*.

- Press **p** to parent the clusters to the curve.

Note: *Groups will be created between the clusters and the curve. This is normal and will maintain the clusters' position.*

Lesson 25

5 Animate the curve

- Select *tornadoCurve*.

- Rewind to frame **1**.

- Move *tornadoCurve* to **-12**, **0**, **12**.

- Press **Shift+w** to keyframe the translation channels.

- Advance to frame **110** and set another keyframe using **Shift+w**.

- Advance to frame **160**.

- Move the *tornadoCurve* to **0**, **0**, **0** and set another keyframe.

- Advance to frame **300**.

- Move the *tornadoCurve* to **-12**, **0**, **-12** and set another keyframe.

Note: *You can also add keyframes to the cluster handles if you wish to animate the shape of the funnel, instead of only the position. It is best to get the motion of the curve the way you want it before animating the clusters.*

6 Add flow to the curve

- Select *tornadoCurveShape*.

Note: *Make sure to pick the shape node. A quick way to do this is by selecting the curve and then pressing the **down arrow** on your keyboard.*

- Select **Effects** → **Create Curve Flow** → ❐ from the **Dynamics** menu set.
- Set the following:

    Flow Group Name to *tornadoFlow*;

    Num Control Segments to **6**;

    Particle Lifespan to **3**;

    Goal Weight to **0.5**.

- Press the **Create** button.

A new node called tornadoFlow is created. This hierarchy contains all the flow components and attributes needed to control the flow of particles along the curve. If you receive an error stating that the `command failed to execute`, make sure you have selected the tornadoCurveShape node before creating the flow.

> **Note:** Deformers can be added to a flow path curve after flow has already been applied. Flow does not interrupt the curve history.

7 Test the results

• Rewind and playback the animation.

The particles follow the shape of the curve as they are emitted. They reach the end of the curve in three seconds (90 frames) since **Lifespan** is set to **3**.

The particles don't flow exactly along the curve's path. This is due to a low **Goal Weight** setting. **Goal Weight** values closer to **1** cause the particles to adhere more closely to the curve's shape.

If you want to animate either the **Lifespan** or the **Goal Weight**, these attributes can be found on the tornadoCurveFlow group in the Outliner.

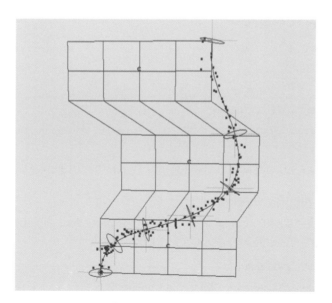

The basic particle flow

8 Adjust flow parameters

- Select the *control_Circle_6* located at the upper end of *tornadoCurve*.

- Scale the control circle up.

- Scale the other circles along the curve in a similar fashion so they increase in scale from the bottom of the curve to the top as shown:

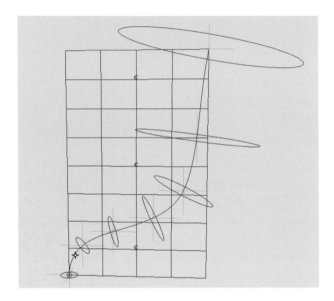

Flow circles from small to large

Tip: *To adjust the control segments along the length of the curve, pick the tornadoFlow group, then edit the attributes called Locator_xx_pos in the Channel Box.*

9 Enable display thickness

You can get a better sense of the volume the particles will fill by enabling the display thickness attribute for refining your circles.

- Select *tornadoFlow*.

- Set **Display Thickness** to **On** in the Channel Box.

*There are additional display attributes, such as **Display Subcircles** and **Display All Sections**. These values are used for advanced refinement of the curve and to help smooth out sharp bends in the flow path, if necessary.*

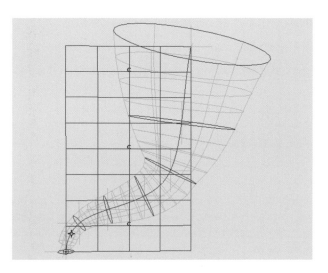

Display Thickness enabled

- Once satisfied with the shape, set all display attributes back to **Off**.

10 Vortex field

- Select the *tornadoFlow_particles*, then choose **Fields** → **Vortex** → ❒.
- Set the following:

  Magnitude to **10**;

  Attenuation to **0**.

- Click the **Create** button.
- Parent the vortex field to *tornadoCurve*.
- Select the *tornadoCurveShape*, then **Shift-select** the new vortex field.
- Select **Fields** → **Use Selected as Source of Field**.

This makes the curve the source of the field.

- Select vortex field, then set **Apply Per Vertex** to **On**.

This makes every point on the curve emit field force.

11 Add a ramp to control radius over age

- Switch the **Particle Render Type** to **Cloud (s/w)**.
- Add a **radiusPP** attribute.

Lesson 25

- **RMB-click** and select **Create Ramp** for **radiusPP**.

- **RMB-click** again and select **arrayMapper** → **Edit Ramp**.

- Adjust the values of the ramp so the **Radius** starts at **0.1** and dies at **0.9**.

> **Tip:** *The radius could also be increased over age using the following runtime expression:* `radiusPP = 0.1+((0.9-0.1) * smoothstep(0,lifespan,age));`

Since the **Goal Weight** *is fairly low, the vortex field adds to the acceleration of the particles and allows them to spin as they flow. As the* **Goal Weight** *value is increased, the effect from the vortex is less, but the particles adhere more closely to the curve.*

When combining fields with flow effects, the curve usually acts as a general guide for the particles, not an absolute pathway for them. This allows the field to influence the particle.

12 Playback and test render

- Playback the scene.

- Test render the scene to see the look of the tornado.

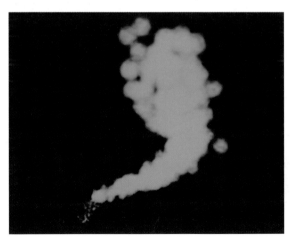

Render of the tornado

- Tweak the results if wanted.

13 Save your work

- Save the scene as *25-tornado_01.ma*.

- The movie *tornadoMovie.mpg* from the support files shows a final rendered effect.

Surface flow

You can also guide particles along a NURBS *surface* using a different but closely related clip effect called *Surface Flow*. To see how this works, do the following:

- Create a simple NURBS plane.

- Deform it so it looks like a slide.

- Select the plane and choose **Effects** → **Create Surface Flow**.

- Adjust the resulting attributes for the surface flow in the Channel Box.

When used with blobby surface particles, you can easily achieve effects like slime, water, lava, etc.

- Open the scene file called *25-slime_01.ma* for a surface flow example.

Slime effect

Tips and traps

- If double transformations occur when moving the lattice, turn **On** relative mode on the cluster.

- You can change the location of flow control objects along the length of the curve or surface by changing the different attributes in the Channel Box on the flow group. The proximity of the control objects to each other controls the amount of time it takes the particles to jump between each section.

- By default, there is not an easy way to make each particle travel along a path with an individual lifespan, (i.e. some particles take five seconds to reach the end whereas others take three seconds). This could be done with expressions but it's not part of the built-in functionality of the flow effect.

- Sometimes, there are some particles that can seem to be getting away or shooting out from the flow object. This can be fixed by setting the opacity on these particles to **0** or by killing it using a creation expression based on its ID. In order to kill the particle, the **Lifespan Mode** will need to be **lifespanPP only**. Here is the expression used to kill a single particle:

```
if (id == 0)

    lifespanPP = 0;
```

- Both flow clip effects are MEL scripts that simply set up a variety of settings for the user. If you would like to view the contents of the flow MEL script, you can type `whatIs flowAlongCurves` in the Script Editor and then view the resulting script with a Text Editor.

Tip: *Looking at pre-existing MEL scripts is a great way to learn MEL.*

- The flow clip effect adds many expressions into your scene. This is good reference information for you to learn more about expressions and expression syntax. Look at the different expressions in the Expression Editor; you may be able to pick up some tips. These expressions primarily focus on goalU, goalV, and goalOffset. These are covered in greater detail later in the next lesson.

Conclusion

The flow clip effect is a handy method for getting particles to go where you want them to go. In some cases, it can provide as much control as complicated expressions, without having to write them yourself. You can use flow for things like water, energy streams, flocking, smoke, or any other cases where you need to guide particles and fields alone do not provide enough control.

In the next lesson, you will learn about goals, which allow you to specify target points for particles.

Lesson 26   Goals

This lesson focuses on working with particle goal functionality. A goal is an object that particles follow or move towards. You can use goals to give trailing particles a flowing motion that's hard to generate with other animation techniques. The trailing particles move as if connected to the goal by invisible springs.

In this lesson you will learn the following:

- How to create goal objects;

- The different goal parameters;

- How to animate goal attributes;

- Per particle goal attributes and their functionality.

Particle goals

One of the most powerful methods that you have at your disposal for controlling particle position and motion is the use of goals. A *goal* is a location in space that a particle will move towards. You can create goals out of curves, lattices, polygons, NURBS surfaces, particles or transform nodes. A particle can also have multiple goal objects.

When a goal is created, new attributes are added to the *particleShape*. In the Attribute Editor, under the **Goal Weights and Objects** section, you will see an attribute with the name of the goal. This is the **Goal Weight**. In the **Per Particle (Array) Attributes** section, you will see a **goalPP** attribute. Together with the **Goal Smoothness** attribute, these attributes control how each particle moves towards the goal.

Particle goals are a big part of soft body dynamics. You will be looking at goals for soft bodies in the soft body section as well. The concepts covered in this lesson will also be utilized in the soft body lessons.

Creating particle and non-particle goals

Creating a particle goal object involves selecting the particles, selecting the object or objects that will be used as the goal objects and then selecting the menu item **Particles → Goal**. You have the option of using particles or geometry objects as the goal objects. In the Goal options, you can specify if you want to use the transform of the object as the goal. By default, this option is Off, and the components of the goal object will be used as the goal. When more than one object is an active goal for a particle, the resulting goal will be a combination of the goal objects' positions and the Goal Weights that have been set for each goal on the *particleShape*.

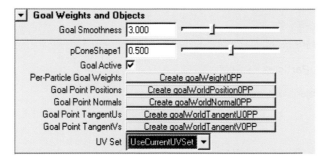

A goal object in the Attribute Editor

Goal Weights and goalPP

Goal weights can be set for all particles at the same time or on a per particle basis. The per particle goal weight is controlled by the goalPP attribute. This is a dynamically added attribute. It is automatically added when a goal is created for a particle object. The goalPP weight is then multiplied by the **Goal Weight** of the particle object for a total particle goal weight. A **Goal Weight** of **1** means the particle will stick to its goal immediately. A **Goal Weight** of **0** means it will not move towards the goal at all.

Goal Smoothness

Goal Smoothness controls how particles accelerate toward a goal object. A low Goal Smoothness value will make the particle take large steps towards the goals, a higher value will cause the particle to take smaller steps. The ratio between Goal Smoothness and Goal Weight controls how far the particle will travel towards the goal in each step.

Simple example

In this example, you will learn the basics of creating goal weights.

1 New scene

- Open a new scene.
- Create an **Omni** emitter with default attributes.
- Select **Create** → **Polygon Primitives** → **Sphere**.
- Move the *sphere* by **5** on the **Z-axis**.

2 Add a goal object

- Select the *particles*, then **Shift-select** the *sphere*.
- Select **Particles** → **Goal**.

A goal object was added to the particles.

3 Playback

- Set the playback range to go from **1** to **1000**.
- Playback the scene.

You will notice that as the particles are being emitted, they get attracted by the component on the sphere with the same identification number.

Lesson 26

For instance, the particleId 0 moves toward its goal, which is the vertex 0 of the sphere.

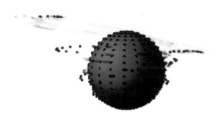

Particles with a sphere goal object

> **Note:** *Once the amount of particles as the goal object's vertices are emitted, the particles start over at the first vertex of the goal object. If a particle dies before a certain goal point, a new one will be emitted.*

4 Goal attributes

- Select the particles.

- In the Channel Box, locate the **Goal Smoothness** attribute.

- Experiment with different values for the **Goal Smoothness**, **Goal Weight[0]** and **Goal Active[0]** attributes.

> **Note:** *These attributes have the [0] suffix because they represent the first goal object. Particles can have multiple goal objects.*

5 Add another goal object

- Select **Create** → **Polygon Primitives** → **Torus**.

- Move the *torus* beside the *sphere*.

- Select the *particles*, then **Shift-select** the *torus*.

- Select **Particles** → **Goal**.

6   Change the goal weight

- Set both **Goal Weight[0]** and **Goal Weight[1]** to **0.5**.

- Playback the scene.

Since the particles are influenced by both goal objects equally, they will be exactly between the two goal objects.

- Experiment with different values for the **Goal Weight** attributes.

7   Per particle goal

A goalPP attribute is automatically added to the particles when a goal is created. This attribute allows you to set Goal Weights on a per particle basis. The total Goal Weight per particle is the object Goal Weight multiplied by the goalPP value. The default value of **goalPP** is **1**.

- Select the particle object and open its Attribute Editor.

- Under the **Per Particle (Array) Attributes**, **RMB-click** in the **goalPP** field and select **Create Ramp**.

Note: *Doing so automatically changes the* **Lifespan** *of the particles to* **Constant**.

- **RMB-click** in the **goalPP** field again and select **arrayMapper** → **Edit Ramp**.

- Set the bottom (birth) of the ramp to white and the top of the ramp (death) to black.

- Playback the scene.

The particles will first be attracted to their goal because of the white section of the ramp. They will then fly off because of the black section of the ramp.

GoalPP used with a ramp

- Set the bottom (birth) of the ramp to black and the top of the ramp (death) to white.

- Playback the scene.

The particles will first be emitted normally, and they will then get attracted to their goal object.

Ray gun

In this example, you will control particle movement with goal objects to create a ray gun effect. You will notice that using goals instead of expressions and fields has many advantages.

1 Scene file

- Open the file *26-goal_01.ma*.

This scene file consists of a ray gun and a target object. The rayGun_group has several objects underneath as children:

> *Gun* - This is the group that holds the *rayGun* geometry.
>
> *targetFocus* - This is the goal for the particles.
>
> *circleEmitter* - This is the particle emitter curve.
>
> *coneControl* - This is another object that is used for particle control.

2 Curve emitter

- Select the *circleEmitter* object.

- Select **Particles** → **Emit from Object** → □.

- Set **Emitter type** to **Curve**.

- Press the **Create** button.

This emitter will serve as the particle source.

3 Add targetFocus as a goal object

- Select the particle object, then **Shift-select** the *targetFocus* object.

- Select **Particles** → **Goal**.

The targetFocus object will be the main destination for the emitted particles.

Note: *Notice that the targetFocus object is animated to rotate on itself to give an added effect.*

Project Seven

4 Playback to see the results

- Open the **Goal Weights and Objects** section in the Attribute Editor for the particle object.

- Experiment with these values to see their effect on the particles.

- Also experiment with the attributes that affect particle motion in general, such as:

    Dynamics Weight;

    Conserve;

    Inherit Factor.

Dynamics Weight *may not have much of an effect, but notice that if it is* **0**, *the simulation will not compute. This is a global control for the particle object, scaling how much the various dynamic contributors, such as fields, affect this particle object. If you want to scale the effect of all fields by a little, it is much easier to lower this value than to try and adjust all field magnitudes, especially if they are all keyframed.*

Conserve *is a very important attribute for controlling the acceleration of particles. If you find that particles are overshooting their goal object, you may be able to dampen their movement with this attribute.*

Inherit Factor *controls the amount of velocity inherited from the emitting object. This only comes into play here if the position of the gun is animated.*

The main attributes to use in the case of the ray gun are **Conserve, Goal Weight** *and* **Goal Smoothness**.

Ray of particles

Note: *You can hide the goal objects using the pre-made display layers.*

Lesson 26

5   Add coneControl as another goal object

- Add *the coneControl* object as another goal object for the particles.

- Experiment with the particle **Goal Weight[0]** and **Goal Weight[1]**.

A different ray look

Tip: *To remove a goal object's influence, set the object's* **Goal Active** *to* **Off** *for the particle object.*

6   Experiment with different animation, scale and position settings on the goal objects

- Note that if you set the **goalWeight** to **0.5** for the coneControl object and **0** for the targetFocus object, the particles line up on the CVs of the coneControl. Conversely, if you set the **goalWeight** to **0.5** for targetFocus and **0** for coneControl, the particles gather on the CVs of the *targetFocus* object.

- You can animate the goal objects around the scene if you want. Notice in this case the *targetShape* object is already animated.

- Mixing the Goal Weights between the two objects produces some very interesting results.

Tip: *Don't forget to also lower* **Conserve** *and adjust* **goalSmoothness** *values.*

Project Seven

7 Animate the rayGun_group

- Animate the *rayGun_group* as if it was trying to disintegrate a moving target.

8 Parent the particle object

When you animate the *rayGun_group* transform, all of the child objects, including the goal objects, will translate and rotate together. The particles will move towards their respective goals but will react in world space.

- **Parent** the *particle* object into the *rayGun_group*.

> **Note:** *If you get strange offsetting of the particles after you parent them, toggle the* **Emission In World** *attribute for the particle object.*

9 Save your work

- Save your work as *26-goal_02.ma*.

Goal U and goal V

In this example, you will make particles travel along a NURBS surface as though they are water droplets. You will keep track of where the particle is emitted on the surface and move it along the surface by incrementing the goal values for each particle on each frame of the animation.

In the last example, the particles traveled directly to the CVs of the goal objects. Now, you will learn how to move them on the surface using the **Goal U** and **Goal V** attributes in a runtime expression.

1 Scene file

- Open *26-faucet_01.ma*.

2 Surface emitter

- Select the *faucetSpout* surface.

- Create a **Surface** emitter with a **Rate** of **15**.

3 Adjust attributes

- Select the *emitter* and set **Need Parent UV** to **On**.

- Select the *particles* and set **Lifespan Mode** to use **lifespanPP only**.

4 Goal object

- Select the *particles*, then **Shift-select** the *faucetSpout*.

- Select **Particles → Goal**.

- Set the new **Goal Weight** attribute to **0.9**.

- Playback to watch the particles build up on the surface of the faucet.

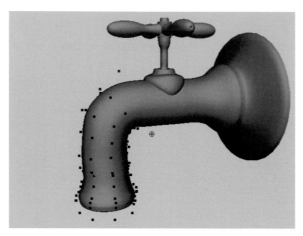

Particles building up on the faucet

5 Add per particle attributes

- Select the particles and press the **General** button in the **Add Dynamics Attributes** section of the Attribute Editor.

- Select the **Particles** tab and add **goalU**, **goalV**, **parentU** and **parentV** attributes.

6 Add expressions

The **parentUV** attributes establish the UV coordinates where a particle is emitted from the surface. At birth, the goal and the parent should be the same, so the particle has a goal on the surface instead of at the CV of the surface.

- **RMB-click** in one of the new attributes' fields and select **Creation Expression**.

- Enter the following creation expression:

```
goalU = parentU;

goalV = parentV;
```

- Press the **Create** button.

To get the particles to move along the U direction of the surface, you will change the **goalU** attribute on each frame.

- Select the **Runtime Before Dynamics** option in the Expression Editor.

- Enter the following runtime expression:

```
goalU = goalU - 0.1;
```

- Press the **Create** button.

7 Test the scene

- Playback the simulation to see the effect of the expressions.

The particles get emitted on the surface and move toward the tip of the faucet.

8 Refine region of emission and make particles drip off

The expressions below have some new lines added to them, allowing particles to exist only on a specific part of the faucet. The runtime expression has been modified to have the Goal Weight for each particle shut off when the particle reaches a certain U location on the surface.

- Modify the existing creation expression with the following:

```
goalU = parentU;

goalV = parentV;

if ((parentU > 10) || (parentU < 2))

        lifespanPP = 0;

else

        lifespanPP = 5;
```

Note: *The double pipe* || *stands for the* **Or** *operator. In this case, if the particle was emitted between U values of* **10** *and* **2***, which is the lower part of the faucet, it will stay alive for* **5** *second. Otherwise, it will be killed.*

- Press the **Edit** button.

- Modify the existing runtime expression so that it looks as follows:

```
goalU = goalU - 0.1;

if (goalU <= 2)

        goalPP = 0;

else

        goalPP = 1;
```

- Press the **Edit** button.

9 Add gravity to the particles

Adding gravity gives the particles downward motion after the **Goal Weight** has been set to **0**.

- Select the particles.
- Select **Fields** → **Gravity**.

10 Playback

- Playback the animation.
- Tweak the look of the particles as wanted.

Sphere particles with increasing radiusPP with a ramp

11 Save your work

- Save the scene as *27-faucet_02.ma*.

Tips and traps

- Errors might occur if **Dynamic Weight** is set to **0**, so set it above 0 when using goals.

*Dynamics weight allows you to scale the effects of dynamics (fields, collisions, springs, goals). A value of **0** causes fields, collisions, springs and goals connected to the particle object to have no effect. A value of **1** provides the full effect. A value less than **1** sets a proportional effect. For example, **0.6** scales the effect to 60% of full strength.*

Note: *Expressions are unaffected by* **Dynamics Weight.**

- The **Min Max Range U** and **Min Max Range V** attributes in the Attribute Editor of a NURBS surface make it easy for you to determine the UV range of a surface. This is useful when working with **goalUV** expressions. Also, the feedback line will show you this information to select isoparms on the surface.

- In the faucet example, the runtime expression is what moves each particle along the surface. Incrementing the goal on each frame of the simulation is what moves it along the U or V direction. This expression also determines when the goalPP value will be set to **0**. This is what causes the particle to drip off the end of the faucet. You may want to add a collision object beneath the faucet that makes the particles die on contact rather than setting their lifespan.

- If setting a value using goalPP, it is good practice to set the Goal Weight slider to **1** when creating the goal. This is important because the goalPP attribute always gets multiplied by that number. Therefore, if the goal is created with a value of **0** and **goalPP** is set to **0.5**, the resulting **goalPP** value will be **0**, not **0.5** as would normally be expected.

- By default, the first particle will go to the first CV or vertex of a goal object. This mapping cannot be changed.

- People commonly ask if there is an easy way to apply a black and white ramp to the surface and have the grayscale of the ramp control the particle Goal Weight. Currently, this involves quite a convoluted work around to accomplish, so the short answer is no. Applying a ramp to goalPP will change the goalPP weight of all particles in that particle object with respect to the particle's lifespan, not the surface UV coordinates. This doesn't mean that it isn't doable; it just isn't a quick and simple solution.

Normalize goalPP

The file *26-goalNormalized.ma* is a simple example of a more advanced usage of goal weights. It first shows how to write using particles. Secondly, it shows how to use an expression to check to see if a given particle has reached its goal. The particles are colored using the values of a ramp. The particle's color is at the bottom of the RGB ramp at birth and at the top of the ramp once it reaches the goal.

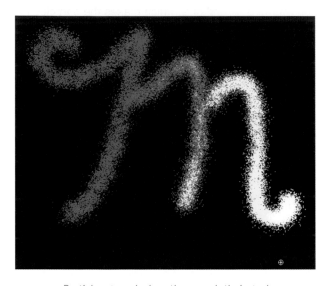

Particles go red when they reach their goal

Tip: Make sure to display this example scene in shaded mode.

Goal from point A to point B

The file called *26-goalAtoB.ma* shows an interesting application of goalPP, particle expressions and blobby surface rendering. Here is how the effect was achieved:

- First, two polygonal letters were created with the **Text Tool**.

- A surface emitter was added to each letter.

- The scene was played until the A surface filled up with particles.

- The **Max Count** of the B particles was set to the **Count** of the A particles.

- B particles were made to be a goal for A particles.

- A locator was animated in the scene to check the distance between the B particles and the moving locator. This distance check was done using a runtime expression. As the locator moves further from the B particles, the goalPP value of the A particles gets set to **1**. The goalPP value gets multiplied by the number that the original goal was created at. The goalPP is set to **0** until the locator gets closer to the A particles, then they transition over to a setting of **1**, which makes the particles jump to stick to B particles.

- The particles were set to be blobby surfaces and an expression was added to control the radius size.

Particles moving from point A to point B

Conclusion

Goals are an intuitive, fun and powerful method of particle manipulation. They can be used to solve particle movement problems, a feat shared only by complex expressions. Mixing goals with fields and other animation is often the best way to achieve good control over your particles.

In the next lesson, you will learn about soft bodies and springs, which usually use particle goals.

Lesson 27 Soft bodies and springs

In this lesson, you will learn how to create dynamic motion on surfaces using soft bodies and springs, along with collisions and rigid bodies.

In this lesson you will learn the following:

- How to create soft bodies;

- How to change soft body parameters;

- How to create particle springs;

- How to delete particle springs;

- How to use goal weights on soft bodies;

- How to use soft bodies as influence objects;

- How to have an object follow a particle with an expression.

Soft bodies

When you make geometry or a lattice a soft body, a corresponding particle object is created. The particle object is placed in relation to the surface, based on options that you select when you create the soft body. A duplicate surface can be created and used as a goal object to help control the soft body and maintain its shape.

NURBS and polygonal surfaces can be made into soft bodies. The particles are created and placed at the corresponding CVs or vertices. If the particles move, the corresponding vertices follow, thus changing the shape of the geometry. Soft bodies are great for achieving flowing-like motion of a geometry object, such as a flag in the wind or a candle flame.

Dynamic springs can also be applied to the particles to control the tension that exists between the particles and thus, the vertices.

Creating soft bodies

Creating a soft body object involves selecting the geometry to be made a soft body and then selecting **Soft/Rigid Bodies** → **Create Soft Body** from the Dynamics menu set.

The soft body creation options allow you to make the selected object a soft body in the following manner:

Make Soft

This option directly makes the selected object a soft body.

Duplicate, Make Copy Soft

This option duplicates the object and makes this duplicate the soft body. This is useful for keeping the original object. The original object can then be used as a goal object.

Duplicate, Make Original Soft

This option duplicates the object in question but makes the original selected object the soft body. This option enables the creation of a duplicate for use as a goal object.

If you are duplicating, you can choose to **Duplicate Input Graph** of the selected object as well as automatically **Hiding** or making the **Non-Soft Object** a **Goal**. It is often necessary to Duplicate Input Graph if the object you are making soft contains deformers or animation.

Water bucket

In this example, you will make the water in the bucket a soft body. You will then add particles dropping from the faucet to deform the soft body. The water surface will use a goal to return to its original rest position. You will also see how to make particles as fields.

1   Scene file

- Open the file *27-waterbucket_01.ma*.

This scene file consists of a faucet and Meeper's water bucket.

The water bucket

2   Make the water into a soft body

- Select the *water* object.

- Select **Soft/Rigid Bodies** → **Create Soft Body** → ❑.

- Set **Creation Option** to **Make Soft**.

- Press the **Create** button.

This will turn the water object into a soft body. Notice that a particle object was created and parented under the water object.

3 Make a goal object

- Duplicate the *water* object.

- Rename the new *water1* object to *waterGoal*.

- Delete the particles that are children of *waterGoal* as they are not required.

- Select the *waterParticle* object, then **Shift-select** the *waterGoal* object.

- Select **Particles** → **Goal** → ❐.

- Make sure **Goal Weight** to **0.5**.

- Press the **Create** button.

Note: *This entire process could have been automated by using the* **Duplicate,** **Make Original Soft** *option and enabling* **Make Non-soft a Goal** *in the* **Create** **Soft Body** *options.*

4 Set up for animation

In order to be able to animate the water bucket, you will need to parent the goal object to the bucket.

- **Parent** the *waterGoal* surface to the bucket object.

- **Hide** the *waterGoal* surface.

5 Create an emitter

- Select **Particles** → **Create Emitter** → ❐.

- Set the following:

    Emitter Type to **Omni**;

    Rate to **5**;

    Speed to **0.3**.

- Press the **Create** button.

- Rename this emitter *dripEmitter*.

- Rename the new particle object to *dripParticles*.

- Move the *dripEmitter* to the nozzle of the faucet.

6 Gravity field

- Select the *dripParticles*.

- Select **Fields** → **Gravity**.

7 Tweak the particles

- Select the *dripParticles*.

- Set the following:

    Lifespan Mode to **Constant**;

    Lifespan to **2.0**;

    Render Type to **Spheres**;

    Radius to **0.05**;

- Add an **RGB** attribute and set the particle color to be **0.8**, **0.8**, **1.0**.

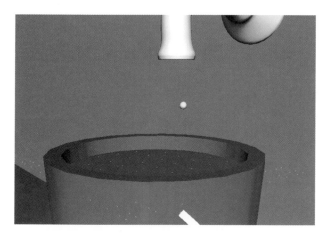

The dripping particles

8 Make a field out of the particles

- Make sure nothing is selected, then select **Fields** → **Radial**.

- With the radial field selected, **Shift-select** the *dripParticles*.

- Select **Fields** → **Use Selected as Source of Field**.

Each particle is now a radial field. You must now link the radial field to affect the soft body water.

Lesson 27

- With the radial field selected, **Shift-select** the *waterParticles*.
- Select **Fields** → **Affect Selected Objects**.

9 Tweak the radial field

- Select the **radial** field.
- Set the following in the Channel Box:

    Magnitude to **20.0**;

    Attenuation to **5.0**;

    Use Max Distance to **On**;

    Max Distance to **2.0**;

    Apply Per Vertex to **On**;

10 Make the soft body particles colide with the bucket

- Select the *waterParticles*, then **Shift-select** the *bucket* geometry.
- Select **Particles** → **Make Collide**.

11 Adjust the goal weight

- Select the *waterParticles*.
- Set the **Goal Weight[0]** to **0.2**.

12 Playback the result

- Set the playback range to go from **1** to **500**.

The disturbed water

- Playback the scene.

You will notice that each dripParticle disturbs the water surface. Also, since the soft body collides with the bucket, they do not interpenetrate with the bucket geometry.

Note: *Since the radial force is emitted uniformly around each drip particle, the water will start moving before the drip touches the water. This issue will be overlooked for simplicity reasons.*

Springs

Springs and soft bodies are often used together. You will sometimes find that a goal object is not always appropriate for controlling a soft body that is deforming or colliding with another object. This is where springs come in.

- Springs are useful for controlling particles that will respond to forces with cohesion.

- Springs can be established between particles.

- Springs can be established between particles and surface CVs or polygonal vertices.

- Springs can be established between surface CVs or polygonal vertices.

Springs often require **Stiffness** settings above **100**. They may gain little benefit from higher **Damping** values, though. Experimentation is required for each application, but if you find that a higher Damping value results in poorer spring response, your object may require more springs, or you may need to increase the **Oversampling** of the simulation.

Overlapping springs and springs connected in multiple directions will have profound results on the simulation. Generally, you want to build a framework of springs on your object. In the following exercises, you will use springs, but experimentation is required in all cases.

Adding springs

The scene file *27-springCompare_01.ma* contains three examples of soft body spring approaches. They are all under a gravity field and will collide with the floor.

- The first sphere is a soft body with no springs.

- The second example is a sphere with a wrap deformer, which is a soft body with springs.

- The third example is a sphere with a lattice deformer that has been made into a soft body with springs applied.

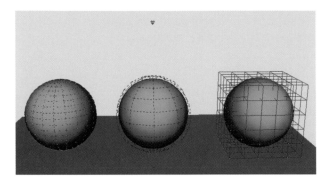

Spring examples

When you play this scene, you will notice some strange behavior. Only the lattice sphere is resisting the force of the floor when it collides. This is because only the lattice example has springs in place positioned to oppose this force. The other two spheres either explode or simply collapse. These objects need to have springs added in specific places and also need to have their spring attributes adjusted.

There are several methods to create or add springs to a spring object. You will learn each of these methods on a very basic example so you can clearly see how the process works.

Wire Walk Length

Adds springs along the wireframe segment as determined by the **Wire Walk Length**.

All

Adds springs between all the components that are selected.

Min/Max

Adds springs between the selected components that fall between the **Min** and **Max** criteria.

Set Exclusive

Used to make the spring creation take place between objects and not between the components on the object.

1   Scene file

- Create a new scene.

2   Set up

- Create a floor surface, then add a polygonal sphere above the floor.
- Select the *sphere*, then select **Soft/Rigid Bodies** → **Create Soft Body** → ❑.
- Make sure the **Creation Options** is set to **Make Soft**.
- Press the **Create** button.
- Select the *sphere*'s particles, then **Shift-select** the *floor*.
- Select **Particles** → **Make Collide**.
- With the *sphere*'s particles still selected, select **Field** → **Gravity**.
- Set the attributes on the *floor*'s *geoConnector* as follows:

    Resilience to **0.2**;

    Friction to **0.5**;

3   Playback the scene

You will notice that the soft body simply goes flat on the floor. You will now learn different ways to add springs to the particle object.

4   Add springs using Wire Walk Length

- Select the *sphere*'s particle object from the Outliner.
- Select **Soft/Rigid Bodies** → **Create Springs** → ❑.
- Set the following:

    Add to Existing Spring to **Off**;

    Don't Duplicate Springs to **Off**;

    Creation Method to **WireFrame**;

    Wire Walk Length to **2**.

- Press the **Create** button.

A **Wire Walk Length** *of* **2** *means that each component will have springs created for all of its neighbors, up to two components away in the wireframe.*

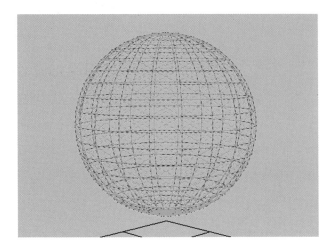

Sphere with springs with a walk length of 2

5 Playback the animation

Note the sphere still collapses. There are still no springs directly opposing the particles journey to the floor.

6 Add springs using selected particles

- Select the *sphere*'s particle object, then press **F8** to go in Component mode.

- Select a couple of rows of particle components that lie on the bottom of the sphere and the top of the sphere from the *side* view.

- **Ctrl-select** the *spring* object in the Outliner.

- Select **Soft/Rigid Bodies** → **Create Springs** → ❒.

- Set the following:

    Add to Existing Spring to **On**;

    Don't Duplicate Springs to **On**;

    Creation Method to **All**.

- Press the **Create** button.

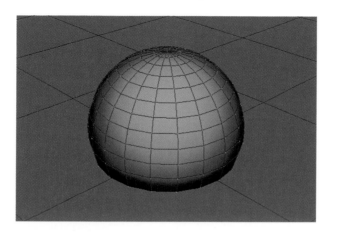

More springs on the sphere

7 Playback the animation

Note the sphere still collapses, but this time with more resistence between the top and bottom particles.

8 Add springs using MinMax

When you find that selecting all the components and manually building springs is too tedious, you may find that you can use the **Min** and **Max** options to distribute the springs in the right quantity.

- Select the *sphere's* particle object, then **Ctrl-select** the *spring* object in the Outliner.

- Select **Soft/Rigid Bodies** → **Create Springs** → ❐.

- Set the following:

  Add to Existing Spring to **On**;

  Don't Duplicate Springs to **On**;

  Creation Method to **MinMax**;

  Min Distance to **1.8**;

  Max Distance to **2.0**.

- Press the **Create** button.

Lesson 27

> **Note:** You may find that trial and error is the best method for determining what **Min** and **Max** will work best. Another method is to use the **Modify** → **Measure** → **Distance Tool**.

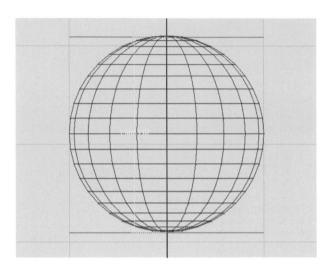

Using the Distance Tool

9   Playback the animation

Despite the fact that you have added lots of springs, when you play the animation, it seems like the resistance of the springs cannot overcome the force of the gravity. In order to fix this you will add more springs and you will tweak the springs' attributes.

10 Add more springs

- Select the *sphere's* particle object, then **Ctrl-select** the *spring* object in the Outliner.

- Select **Soft/Rigid Bodies** → **Create Springs** → ❐.

- Set the following:

  > **Add to Existing Spring** to **On**;

  > **Don't Duplicate Springs** to **On**;

  > **Creation Method** to **All**;

- Press the **Create** button.

If you playback the scene, you will notice that the sphere now explodes.

Tip: *Hide the spring object for a faster playback.*

11 Adjust the springs

- Select the *spring* object.
- In the Channel Box, set the following:

    Stiffness to **0.4**;

    Damping to **0.1**.

- Playback the scene.

The sphere should now conserve most of its shape as it collides with the floor.

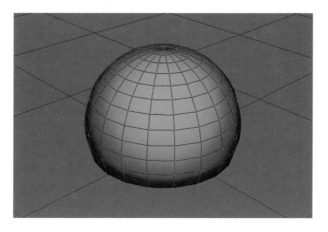

The sphere colliding with the floor correctly

Per spring attributes

On the spring object, you can see three attributes called **StiffnessPS**, **DampingPS** and **RestLengthPS**. These are per spring attributes that can have values set for individual springs through the Component Editor.

In the following example, you will learn how to set per spring attributes.

Lesson 27

1 Scene file

- Open the scene file called *27-springCube_01.ma*.

*The scene contains a polygonal cube that is about **3.8** units in width, height and length. This cube also has springs applied to it with a **Wire Walk Length** of **1**.*

Soft body cube with springs at each corner

Note: *The spring object's **Rest Length** is set to **4.0**.*

- Playback the scene.

*Because the spring's **Rest Length** is set to **4.0**, when you play the scene, the cube will move to accommodate this length.*

2 Enable the restLengthPS on one of the springs

- Set the **RestLengthPS** to **On** in the Channel Box for the *spring* object.

- **RMB-click** on the *spring* object, then select **Spring** from the contextual menu.

- Select a single spring.

Note: *You may need to hide the cube to select an individual spring. It is sometimes hard to see if a spring is selected. When in doubt, look in the Channel Box to see the name of the selection.*

- Select **Window → General Editor → Component Editor**.
- Select the **Springs** tab.

If spring components are selected, they will be listed under this tab.

- Enter a value of **2.0** for the **restLengthPS** attribute.

Note: *The default value of the* **restLengthPS** *attribute is the original length of the spring when it was created.*

- Playback the scene.

Notice how the per spring attribute modification affects only the selected spring.

Spring restLengthPS set to 2.0

Lesson 27

3 Change the value of the spring object's End1 Weight

- Select the spring object in the Outliner and enter 0 for the **End1 Weight** attribute.

This will eliminate the force acting on the start of the spring. All of the force of the added **restLength** *will be applied to the end of the spring.*

End1 Weight *and* **End2 Weight** *control at what percentage forces will act on either end of the spring.*

1 (default) = 100%

0 = 0%

- Playback the scene to see the effect of the new weight.

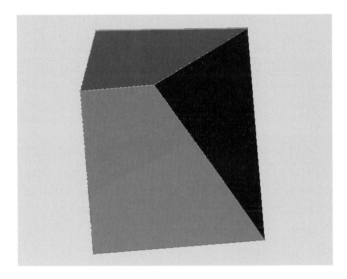

Spring End1 Weight set to 0

4 Experiment with StiffnessPS and DampingPS

- Add gravity and make the cube collide with the floor.
- Try to alter the springs' **StiffnessPS** and **DampingPS** to see their effects.

Springs between objects

Springs are not limited to being part of the same object; they can also be created between different soft body objects or even between soft bodies and geometry. The following example shows how to create springs between objects to create a basic clothesline.

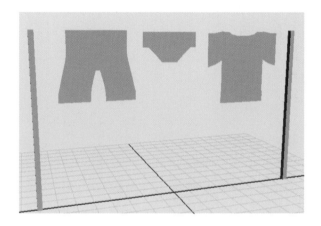

A simple clothesline

1   Scene file

- Open the scene file called *27-clothesline_01.ma*.

This file contains a simple clothesline to be used with springs.

2   Make soft bodies

- Select all three pieces of clothing.

- Select **Soft/Rigid Bodies** → **Create Soft Body** → ❑.

- Make sure the **Creation Options** is set to **Make Soft**.

- Press the **Create** button.

3   Add springs

- Select one of the newly created particle objects from the Outliner.

- Select **Soft/Rigid Bodies** → **Create Springs** → ❑.

- Set the following:

    Add to Existing Spring to **Off**;

Lesson 27

Don't Duplicate Springs to **On**;

Creation Method to **WireFrame**;

Wire Walk Length to **2**.

- Press the **Create** button.

- Repeat the last action by selecting another particle object and pressing the **g** hotkey.

4 Add gravity

- Select all three particle objects.

- Select **Fields** → **Gravity**.

5 Add specific springs

- Select all three particle objects, then press **F8** to go in Component mode.

- Select individual particles on the clothes as follows:

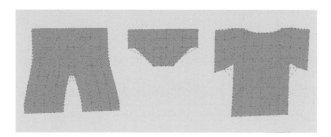

A simple clothesline

- **RMB-click** on the *poles*, then select **Vertex**.

- **Shift-select** the top vertices of the poles.

- Select **Soft/Rigid Bodies** → **Create Springs** → ❐.

- Set the following:

Add to Existing Spring to **Off**;

Don't Duplicate Springs to **On**;

Creation Method to **MinMax**;

Min Distance to **0.5**;

Max Distance to **5.0**.

- Press the **Create** button.

Soft bodies and springs
Springs between objects
583

A new spring object will connect the selected components together. ·

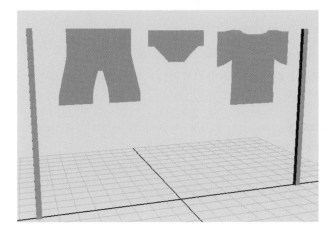

Springs now connect the clothes and poles together

6   Playback the scene

- Set the playback range to go from **1** to **500**.

- Playback the animation.

The spring simulation will require more stiffness, but doing so will also require the dynamic solver's oversampling to be increased. You will see how to do this in the following step.

7   Fine-tune the scene

In order for the simulation to run correctly without jittering, you will need to increase the dynamics oversampling.

- Set the three particle object's **Conserve** to **0.95**.

Doing so will help settle down the relax position of the clothesline.

- Add more springs to the top particles of each clothing piece in order to reinforce their strength.

- Select **Solvers** → **Edit Oversampling or Cache Settings**.

Doing so will display the Attribute Editor for the dynamic solver.

- Set **Over Samples** to **2**.

A dialog box will appear telling you that you will need to modify the playback speed in order for the playback to match the final simulation at render time.

- Click the **OK** button, then close the Attribute Editor.

- Select **Window** → **Settings/Preferences** → **Preferences**.

- Highlight the **Timeline** section, then set the following:

   Playback Speed to **Play every frame**;

   Playback by to **0.5**.

- Click the **Save** button.

The playback speed will now be slower, but the simulation will be more accurate.

- Select the three spring objects for the clothes.

- Set the following in the Channel Box:

   Stiffness to **150**;

   Damping to **0.05**.

- Select the spring object for the clothesline.

- Set the following in the Channel Box:

   Stiffness to **1000**;

   Damping to **0.1**.

- Playback the animation.

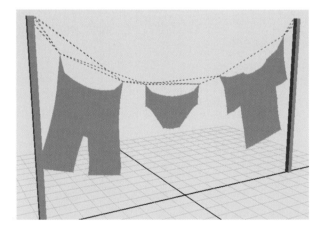

The clothesline simulation with higher oversampling

8 Save your work

- Save the scene as *27-clothesline_02.ma*.

Delete individual springs

It is possible to delete individual springs. You might want to do this when springs are created between unwanted components.

1 Scene file

- Continue with the scene file from the last exercise.

2 Delete a spring

- Playback the scene until the clothesline settles, then stop the playback.

At this point, you should clearly see the different springs forming the clothesline.

- Select the clothesline spring object.

- Go in to **Component mode**, then enable the **Springs** selection mask.

You can now select individual springs.

- Select some springs, then press the **Delete** button on your keyboard.

Doing so will delete the selected springs.

- Continue to playback the scene to see the results.

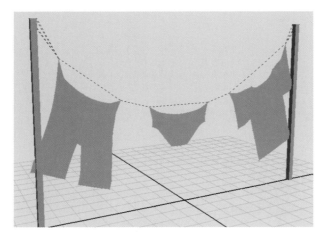

Extra springs deleted

3 Save your work

- Save the scene as *27-clothesline_03.ma*.

Drapes

In this example, you will simulate drapes dynamics. To do so, you will be using soft bodies with springs and a goal, a rigid body and fields.

1 Open File

You will now open the example scene and also reset the playback speed to its original value.

- Open *27-drape_01.ma*.

This file contains a NURBS drape hanging from a frame and a collision object.

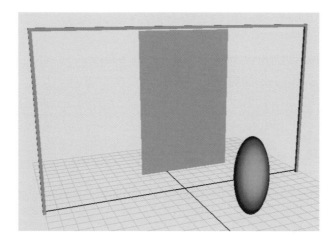

The drapes scene

- Select **Window** → **Settings/Preferences** → **Preferences**.
- Highlight the **Timeline** section, then set the following:

  Playback Speed to **Play every frame**;

  Playback by to **1**.

- Click the **Save** button.

2 Soft body

- Select the *drape* object, then select **Soft/Rigid Bodies** → **Create Soft Body** → ❐.
- Set the following:

Creation Options to Duplicate, Make Original Soft;

Hide Non-Soft Object to On;

Make Non-Soft a Goal to On;

Weight to 0.5.

- Click the **Create** button.

3 Collision

- Select the new particle object, then **Shift-select** the *sphere* object.

- Select **Particles** → **Make Collide**.

- Select the *sphere* object, then locate the *geoConnector1* node in the Channel Box.

- Set **Resilience** to **0.2** and **Friction** to **0.5**.

4 Fields

- Select the new particle object, then select **Fields** → **Gravity**.

- Adjust the field or add more fields as wanted.

5 Playback the scene

Since there are no springs in the scene at this time, when you play the simulation, the colliding sphere goes straight through the drape.

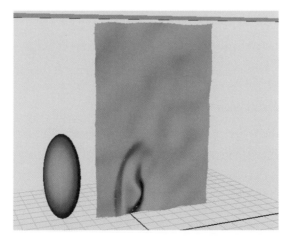

The collision object goes straight through the soft body

Lesson 27

6 Per particle goal weight

You will now change the goal weight on the drape's particles in order to have it freely moving.

- Select the *drape*'s particle object.

- Set the **Goal Weight[0]** to **1.0**.

This will make all the particles stick to the goal object.

- With the particle object still selected, go in to Component mode.

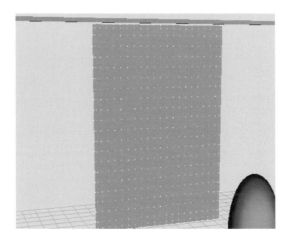

Select all the particles except the first two rows

- Select all the particles except the first two top rows of the drape.

- Select **Window** → **General Editor** → **Component Editor**.

- Under the **Particles** tab, highlight the entire **goalPP** column by clicking on its header.

- Enter **0.2**, then press **Enter**.

*Doing so will change all the selected particles' **goalPP** to be **0.2**, thus letting the lower portion of the drape move almost freely.*

Tip: *You can also paint the **goalPP** attributes rather than manually entering values. To do so, **RMB-click** on the soft body object and select **Paint** → **particles** → **goalPP**. This will enter the **Paint Attribute Tool**, allowing you to paint the **goalPP** attributes.*

7   Add springs to the soft body

To further refine the motion of the particles, you can add springs.

- Select the *drape*'s particle object.

- Select **Soft/Rigid Bodies** → **Create Springs** → ❑.

- Set the following spring options:

    Add to Existing Spring to **Off**;

    Don't Duplicate Springs to **On**;

    Creation Method to **Wireframe**;

    Wire Walk Length to **1**;

    Use Per-Spring RestLength to **On**;

    Stiffness to **20**;

    Damping to **0.05**.

- Press the **Create** button.

- Hide the spring object for faster playback.

8   Adjust attributes to tune the simulation

As you play the simulation, you might have the feeling that the springs are not stiff enough. The sphere might also go through the drape. To fix this, do the following:

- Select the *spring* object.

- Set the following:

    Stiffness to **300**;

    Damping to **0.1**.

- Select the *sphere*'s *geoConnector*.

- Set **Friction** to **1.0**.

> **Tip:**   To prevent stretching of the drape caused by particles intersecting with the colliding object, you may need to increase the oversampling slightly. However, changing the oversampling will slow the playback down and may require you to adjust other attributes to compensate for the new motion.

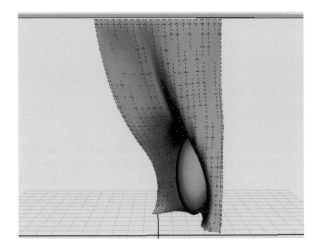

The collision object moves the drape correctly

9 Save your work

- Save the scene as *27-drape_02.ma*.

Diva dress

In this exercise, you will use soft bodies to create dynamic influence objects to control Diva's dress. Influence objects are used with smooth skinning to create movements cause by secondary objects such as geometry. By making a NURBS surface underneath the dress an influence object and making it dynamic, the dress will react to gravity and collisions, and will inherit the forces imparted from the character's movement.

1 Scene file

- Open the scene file called *27-dress_01.ma*.

This scene file contains Diva, who was animated to follow a simple beat. If you playback the scene, you will notice that the dress is interpenetrating quite a lot with the legs. That will be corrected using a dynamic influence object.

Diva dancing

2 Bind pose

To add an influence object to a smooth skinned model, you need to first make sure the skeleton is in its bind pose.

- Make sure you are at frame **1**.

*In order to simplify things, a bind pose keyframe was set at frame **1**.*

Tip: *If your character is not at bind pose, you may have to disable the IK solvers temporarily and have the skeleton go to its bind pose. To do so, disable* **Modify** → **Evaluate Nodes** → **IK Solvers,** *then select* **Skin** → **Go To Bind Pose.**

3 Make an influence object

You will now create an influence object starting from the skirt already modeled.

- Select *Diva*'s geometry.
- Press **Ctrl+d** to duplicate it.
- Press **Shift+p** to unparent it from its group.
- Rename the new geometry to *influenceObject*.
- Hide both the *divaLayer* and *rigLayer*.
- With the *influenceObject* selected, press **F11** to enable the face components display.
- Delete all the faces other than the skirt faces.

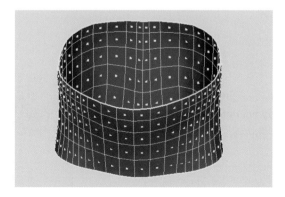

The dress faces

- Go back in Object mode.

Lesson 27

592

Project Seven

4   Have the dress influence object smaller than the actual dress

In order to have the influence object colliding with the legs and not the actual dress, you need the influence object to be slightly smaller to make room for small collision interpenetration.

- Select the *influenceObject*.

- Select **Edit Polygons** → **Sculpt Geometry Tool** → □.

- In the options, set the following:

  Operation to **Push**;

  Reference Vector to **Normal**;

  Max Displacement to **1.0**.

- Click the **Flood** button.

Doing so will push the entire geometry inwards, between the real dress and Diva's legs.

Note: *You might want to click the* **Flood** *button several times in order to push the geometry a bit more. Make sure the surface does not interpenetrate with Diva's legs.*

5   Add the influence object to Diva's skin

- Select the *influenceObject*, then **Shift-select** the *Diva* geometry.

- Select **Skin** → **Edit Smooth Skin** → **Add Influence** → □.

- Set the options as follows:

  Use Geometry to **On**;

  Dropoff to **4.0**;

  Lock Weights to **On**;

  Default Weight to **0.0**.

Setting **Geometry** *to* **Use Geometry** *will take the influence object's shape into consideration, including deformations that occur on the influence object.*

Setting the **Weight Locking On** *with a* **Default Weight** *of* **0.0** *will ensure that the new influence object does not disrupt the existing weighting of the smooth skinned surface.*

- Click the **Add** button to add the influence object to the selected skin.

> **Note:** *Creating an influence object will duplicate the geometry so that a reference object can compare the deformation to be applied on the skin.*

6 Update Diva's skin

Since the vertices of the influence object will deform the dress' skin, you must enable an option on the skin cluster to specify that you want the skin to be influenced by the components of the *influenceObject*.

- Select the *Diva* geometry.

- In the Channel Box, highlight the *skinCluster* node from the **Inputs** section.

- Set **Use Components** to **On**.

7 Paint skin weights

- Select the *Diva* geometry.

- Open the **Skin** → **Edit Smooth Skin** → **Paint Skin Weights Tool** → ◻.

- Scroll all the way to the bottom of the **Influence** list, then highlight the *influenceObject (Hold)* item.

- Click the **Toggle Hold Weights On Selected** button to enable the weight painting for that influence.

- Set the following options:

   Profile to the fully opaque brush preset;

   Paint Operation to **Replace**;

   Value to **1.0**;

> **Tip:** *Hold down* **b**, *then* **MMB-click+drag** *to change the size of the brush in the viewport.*

- **Paint** the dress' weights as follows:

The dress influence's weights

- Press **q** to exit the Paint Skin Weights Tool.

8 Create a soft body out of the influence object

The influence object will have flexibility and react dynamically to Diva's movement and gravity. As a soft body with springs, the influence object will use particles to dynamically control its shape and position.

- Select the *influenceObject* object.

- Select **Soft/Rigid Bodies** → **Create Soft Body** → ⏹.

- Set the following options:

    Creation Options to **Duplicate, Make Original Soft**;

    Hide Non-Soft Object to **On**;

    Make Non-Soft a Goal to **On**;

    Weight to **1.0**;

- Click the **Create** button.

Note: *These settings will create a duplicate copy of the surface to be a goal object. The goal surface will be prefixed with copyOf.*

Note: *You will paint the **goalPP** later in the exercise. For now, leave it at **1.0**.*

9   Collisions and springs

The influence objects need to collide against the legs and also maintain their shape with springs. That will allow the object to bounce and move with consistency.

- Select the *influenceObject*'s particles, then **Shift-select** the *collisionObject* geometry.

The collision object represents a simplified version of Diva's hips and legs. Using such a piece of geometry for collision rather than the entire Diva skin will speed up the playback time.

- Select **Particles** → **Make Collide**.

- Set the following on the *collisionObject*'s *geoConnector*:

    Resilience to **0.2**;

    Friction to **0.2**.

- Select the *influenceObject*'s particles.

- Select **Soft/Rigid Bodies** → **Create Springs** → ❐.

- Reset the options and set the following:

    Add to Existing Spring to **Off**;

    Creation Method to **Wireframe**;

    Wire Walk Length to **2**;

    Stiffness to **180.0**;

    Damping to **0.5**.

- Click the **Create** button.

10 Binding the goal object

At this point, the influence object is working, but you will notice that the dress doesn't move with the character. This is because the goal object must be bound to Diva's skeleton.

- Hide the *influenceObject* and *spring* objects.

- Hide the *collisionLayer*.

- Show the *copyOfinfluenceObject*.

This is the goal object for the soft body's particles.

- Select the *copyOfinfluenceObject,* then **Shift-select** all six *dressJoint's* and *HipsOverride* joints.

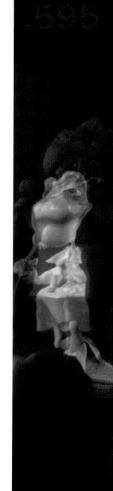

- Select **Skin** → **Bind Skin** → **Smooth Bind** → ☐.

- Make sure **Bind to** is set to **Selected Joints**, then click the **Bind Skin** button.

- Select the *copyOfinfluenceObject*.

- Open the **Skin** → **Edit Smooth Skin** → **Paint Skin Weights Tool** → ☐.

- Set the operation to **Smooth**, then click the **Flood** button for all the influences and smooth their weighting.

- Hide the *copyOfinfluenceObject* object.

11 Playback the scene

At this time, if you playback the scene while watching Diva, you will see that the collision prevents the interpenetration of the dress with Diva's legs.

12 Paint the goalPP

You will now paint the goalPP attribute of the particles with lower values in order to have the dress sway on its own.

- **RMB-click** on the *influenceObject* and select **Paint** → **particles** → **goalPP**.

*This will enter the **Paint Attribute Tool**, allowing you to paint the* **goalPP** *attributes.*

- **Double-click** on the tool in the tool box to bring up the Paint Attribute Tool settings.

At this time, the entire surface is white because all the **goalPP** *attributes are set to* **1.0**.

- **Paint** and **smooth** the **goalPP** of the dress as follows:

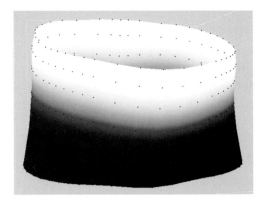

The soft body dress' goalPP

13 Fine-tune

- Select the *influenceObject*'s particles, then select **Fields** → **Gravity**.

- Set the particle object's **Conserve** to **0.95**.

14 Playblast the scene

Since the playback of the simulation with Diva displayed can be quite slow, it is recommended to playblast the scene.

Final dress simulation

15 Save your work

- Save the scene as *27-dress_02.ma*.

Microphone cord

In this exercise, you will have Meeper drop his microphone and hold it with a cord that will dangle from his hand. You will use a soft body curve to create the cord. The microphone will be made into a rigid body and connected to the soft body cord with a dynamic constraint.

1 Scene file

- Open the scene file called *27-microphoneCord_01.ma*.

This scene contains a simple animation along with a curve to be used as a soft body with springs.

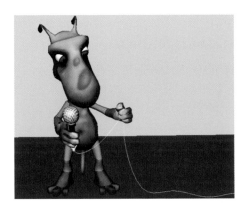

Start pose of Meeper and the microphone

2 Rebuild the curve

The curve should have refined definition. You will now display the CVs and then rebuild the curve to have more spans.

- Select the *cord* curve.

- Enable CV display by selecting **Display** → **NURBS Components** → **CVs**.

- Select **Edit Curves** → **Rebuild Curves** → ❑.

- Set the following:

> **Rebuild Type** to **Uniform**;
>
> **Parameter Range** to **0 to 1**;
>
> **Keep CVs** to **Off**;
>
> **Keep Ends** to **On**;
>
> **Number of Spans** to **28**;
>
> **Degree** to **3**.

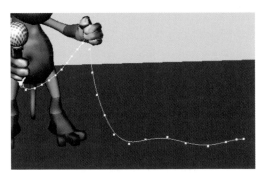

Rebuilt curves

- Click the **Rebuild** button.

- Disable **Display** → **NURBS Components** → **CVs** for both curves.

3 Create a soft body

- Select the *cord* curve.
- Select **Soft/Rigid Bodies** → **Create Soft Body** → □.
- Set the **Creation Options** to **Make Soft**.
- Click on **Create**.

> **Note:** *You will tweak the goalPP later.*

4 Numeric Display for the particles

- Select the new particle object from the Outliner.
- In the Channel Box, set **Particle Render Type** to **Numeric**.

Doing so will automatically display the particle IDs.

> **Note:** *By not clicking the Current Render Type button in the Attribute Editor, the particle IDs are displayed as integers rather than floats, making the numbers easier to read.*

5 Add springs

- With the *cord* curve selected, select **Soft/Rigid Bodies** → **Create Springs** → □.
- Select **Edit** → **Reset Settings**.
- Set the following:

    Creation Method to **Wireframe**;

    Wire Walk Length to **1**;

    Use Per-Spring RestLength to **On**.

- Click on the **Create** button.
- Select the second curve and press **g** to repeat the spring creation.

6 Add a goal

The cord now needs to be anchored in Meeper's left hand. To do so, you will use a locator and make it a goal for the particle object, but only the one particle in Meeper's left hand will have a **goalPP** of **1**. That particle will then drag along the other particles, since they are connected by springs.

- Select **Create** → **Locator**.

- Rename the *locator* to *leftHandLocator*.

- Holding down **c** to snap to curve, move the locator on the *cord* curve in Meeper's left hand.

- **Parent** the *leftHandLocator* to Meeper's *LeftHand*.

- Select the particle object, then **Shift-select** the *leftHandLocator*.

- Select **Particles** → **Goal** → ❑.

- Set the **Goal Weight** to **1.0**, and set **Use Transform as Goal** to **On**.

- Click the **Create** button.

A goal has been added to the dynamic curve.

7 GoalPP

You must now set the appropriate goal weights for the curve CVs.

- Select the particle object.

- Go in Component mode, and select all the particle components for the *cord* curve.

- Select **Window** → **General Editors** → **Component Editor**.

- Select the **Particles** tab, then set **pt[8]** to have a **goalPP** of **1.0**.

Tip: *Look at the displayed particle IDs in order to know which particle is in Meeper's left hand.*

- Make sure all the other particles have a **goalPP** of **0.0**.

Tip: *You can hold down **Ctrl** and **click+drag** to select multiple cells to change at the same time.*

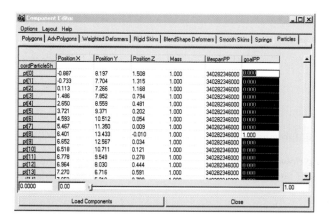

The Component Editor

8 Gravity

- Select the particle object.

- Select **Fields** → **Gravity**.

9 Collisions

- Select the two particle objects, then **Shift-select** the *floor* surface.

- Select **Particles** → **Make Collide**.

- Set the following for the *floor*'s *geoConnector*:

    Resilience *to* **0.2**;

    Friction *to* **0.2**.

10 Playback the animation

- Set the playback range to go from **1** to **500**.

- Playback the simulation.

Confirm that one particle stays in Meeper's left hand.

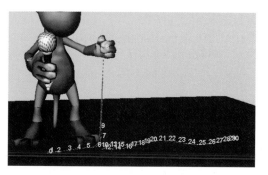

Particle sticking to Meeper's left hand

Lesson 27

11 Adjust the springs

Notice that the cord now drops much too far.

- Select the particle object and set **Conserve** to **0.95** in the Channel Box:

- Select the spring object and set the following in the Channel Box:

    Stiffness to **500**;

    Damping to **1**.

- Playback the scene.

The cord should now be hanging from Meeper's hand like this:

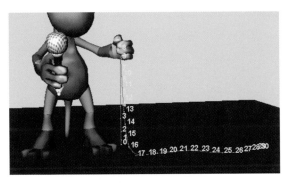

The cord hanging correctly

12 Place an object at the end of the cord

The microphone should not be connected to the cord directly. A simple object can be used to connect the microphone to the cord, for which an expression will place it at the world space position of the particle at the tip of the cord.

- Create a primitive cube.

- Rename the cube to *anchor*.

- With the cube still selected, highlight on the translate attribute in the Channel Box, then **RMB-click** and select **Expressions**.

- Type the following expression to get the position of *cordParticle.pt[0]*:

```
float $cordPosition[] =

    `getParticleAttr -at worldPosition cordParticle.pt[0]`;

anchor.translateX = $cordPosition[0];

anchor.translateY = $cordPosition[1];

anchor.translateZ = $cordPosition[2];
```

- Click the **Create** button.

- Playback the scene.

Notice how anchor remains attached to the end of the curve.

> **Note:** *It is not possible to attach the microphone to the cord directly, since the microphone will end up being a rigid body. Expressions cannot control the position of a rigid body object.*

13 Rigid bodies

- Make sure that you are at frame **1**.

- Select *anchor* and *floor*.

- Select **Soft/Rigid Bodies** → **Create Passive Rigid Body**.

- Set the **Collision Layer** of *anchor* to **1**.

- Hide *anchor*.

- Select *microphoneGeometry*.

- Select **Soft/Rigid Bodies** → **Create Active Rigid Body**.

14 Pin constraint

In order to have the microphone and pin constraint react correctly while colliding with the floor, you will need to offset the microphone's center of mass.

- Select the *microphoneGeometry*.

- In the Channel Box, change the **Center Of Mass Y** so that the center of mass is in the middle of the ball of the microphone.

- Select *microphoneGeometry*, then **Shift-select** *anchor*.

- Select **Soft/Rigid Bodies** → **Create Pin Constraint**.

- Move the pin constraint so that it is at the exact same position as the *anchor* center of mass.

> **Tip:** *Use snap to curve to move the pin constraint at the anchor's position.*

15 Connect the microphone to the gravity

- Select *microphoneGeometry*, then **Shift-select** *gravity1*.

- Select **Fields** → **Affect Selected Object(s)**.

- Hide the particles, springs and gravity objects.

16 Playback the scene

17 Final adjustments

Following are some extra refinement ideas that you can add to the scene.

- Create a NURBS circle and use it to extrude geometry along the cord.

- Animate Meeper's left arm in order to drag the microphone on the ground.

- Have Meeper drop the cord by animating the goal weight of the soft body.

Final simulation

18 Save your work

- Save the scene as *27-microphoneCord_02.ma*.

Conclusion

Soft bodies provide a direct manipulation of surface geometry with dynamic forces. They can also indirectly affect skinned surfaces through the use of dynamic influence objects.

There are several other applications for soft bodies including modeling, collision modeling and fluid-like effects. The main limitation to using soft bodies is that the particles do not collide with each other or obey interpenetration checking of the surface. This is where the Maya Unlimited Cloth feature takes over for dynamically simulating fabrics and materials that must react to themselves.

In the next lesson, you will learn about particle instancing.

This lesson focuses on particle instancing, a tool for placing geometry at the location of individual particles.

In this lesson you will learn the following:

- How to make geometry match particle movement;

- How to add animated geometry to particles;

- How to use cycles to instance a sequence of geometry;

- How particle instancing uses custom attributes;

- How to add randomness to particle instanced geometry;

- Important qualities of hardware sprites;

- How to create software sprites using particle instancing;

- How to use the velocity as an aim vector.

Instancing

An **instance** is similar to a duplicated object. The primary difference is that an instance contains no actual surface information, but is just a redrawn version of an original object. That original object acts like a master to all of its instances. The instance takes on all shading and surface characteristics of the original and will update as the original is updated. Since instances contain less information than duplicates, they can be handled and redrawn faster.

Particle instancing

Particle instancing is the process of using the position and behavior of particles to control the position and behavior of instanced geometry. For example, you could model a honey bee, animate it flapping its wings, then use particle instancing to apply that flapping bee to a number of particles. By replacing each particle with a piece of instanced geometry, you can easily create a scene with swarming bees at a decent playback rate.

Although some complex results can be obtained using particle instancing, it is important not to interpret it as a full-featured behavioral animation system or flocking system. For example, you could build a fish swimming, then instance that swimming fish onto particles to simulate a school of fish. However, each fish just follows its own particle; there are no behavioral relationships established between the individual instanced elements.

The instancer node

The *instancer* node can be considered the **engine** to perform particle instancing. Although use of the instancer node is not limited to particles, the most common inputs it receives are from particles and from the geometry that will be instanced to those particles.

Inputs to the instancer node in the dependency graph

Instancing example

1 Scene file

- Open the scene file called *28-dragonFly_01.ma*.

2 Animate the wings flapping

- Select *lWing*, then **Shift-select** *rWing*.

- Use **Shift+e** to keyframe the rotation attributes of both wings as follows:

    Frame **1**, wings down;

    Frame **2**, wings straight;

    Frame **3**, wings up;

    Frame **4**, wings straight;

    Frame **5**, wings down.

Tip: You can **MMB-click+drag** *in the timeline to advance frames without scrubbing through the animation. This makes it easier to set up one position at two different frame numbers for cycling. You can also use the* **RMB** *menu in the timeline to* **Cut**, **Copy** *and* **Paste** *keyframes.*

The dragonfly with animated wings

- With both wings selected, open the Graph Editor and set the **Pre-Infinity** and **Post-Infinity** to **Cycle**.

Doing so will make the dragonfly flap its wings repeatedly.

3 Create a grid of particles

- Select **Particle** → **Particle Tool** → ❑.

- Set the following:

   Particle Name to *flyParticles*;

   Conserve to **1**;

   Create Particle Grid to **On**;

   Particle Spacing to **12**;

   Placement to **With Text Fields**;

   Minimum Corner to **-25, 0, -25**;

   Maximum Corner to **25, 0, 25**.

- Click anywhere in the viewport, then press **Enter**.

Setting particle spacing to **12** *allows enough space in-between each particle so that the instanced dragonflies don't intersect.*

4 Randomly offset the particles

- Add the following creation expression to the position attribute of **flyParticles**:

```
float $randY = rand (-3,3);

float $randXZ = rand (-1,1);

vector $offset = <<$randXZ, $randY, $randXZ>>;

position = position + $offset;
```

- Press **Create**.

- Press the **Rewind** button to offset the particles.

 Tip: *You can repeatedly execute the creation expression and offset the particles by pressing the rewind button several times.*

- With the *flyParticles* selected, select **Solvers** → **Initial State** → **Set for Selected**.

- Delete the creation expression created earlier, then close the Expression Editor.

Offset particle initial state

5 Instance the dragonfly to the particles

- In the Outliner, select *dragonFly* group.

- Select **Particles** → **Instancer (Replacement)** → ❏.

- Set **Particle Instancer Name** to *flyInstanced*.

- Make sure that *dragonFly* is the only listed object in the **Instanced Objects** list.

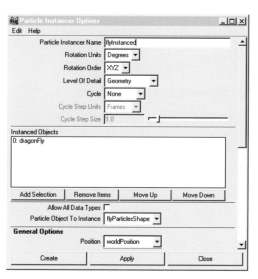

Particle instancer options

- Press the **Create** button.

This creates an instancer node in the scene and creates an instanced version of the dragonfly for each particle.

The instanced dragonflies

6   Hide the original dragonfly

Since the original object is still in the scene and there is one instance per particle, you will need to hide the original dragonfly.

- Select the *dragonFly* group.

- Press **Ctrl+h** to hide it.

7   Add a vector attribute to the particles

Now, you will add some variation to the size of each of the instanced dragonflies. Since the radiusPP of the particles does not affect the size of the instanced geometry, you will need a custom attribute.

- Open the Attribute Editor for *flyParticlesShape*.

- Press the **General** button in the **Add Dynamic Attributes** section.

- Set the following under the **New** tab:

    Attribute Name to *flyScaler*;

    Data Type to **Vector**;

    Attribute Type to **Per Particle (Array)**;

    Add Initial State Attribute to **On**.

- Press the **OK** button.

8 Assign values to the attribute with a creation expression

- **RMB-click** in the new **flyScaler** field in the Attribute Editor, then select **Creation Expression**.

- Add the following to the Expression Editor:

```
$rand = rand (0.4, 1.5);

flyScaler = <<$rand, $rand, $rand>>;
```

This expression picks a random number greater than **0.4** *and less than* **1.5** *for each particle and assigns that value to the* **flyScaler** *attribute.*

- Press **Create** and close the Expression Editor.

9 Set the instancer to use flyScaler

- Select *flyParticlesShape*, then expand the **Instancer (Geometry Replacement)** tab in the Attribute Editor.

- Under **General Options**, set **Scale** to **flyScaler**.

Any attribute added to the particle object can be fed into the various control attributes of the instancer node. In this case, you are computing a value with an expression, storing that value in the flyScaler attribute, then assigning flyScaler to the scale option in the instancer node. The ability to use any attribute value for any of the connections to the instancer is what gives the instancer its flexible control, since you are able to control the contents of those attributes with your own expressions.

Instanced dragonflies with random positioning and scaling

Lesson 28

10 Comment out the expression and set the initial state

Since *flyScaler* changes in a creation expression, the scale of the bugs will change every time the Rewind button is pressed. Once you are satisfied with the scale of the bugs, you can delete or comment out the expression and set the initial state of the particles. Use two forward slashes (//) at the beginning of each line to comment out the expression.

If the bugs disappear upon rewind, that means that the *flyScaler* attribute resets to **0** and that you probably forgot to set the initial state for the particles.

Tip: It is a good idea to save your file before setting the initial state.

- Select the particle shape and open the Expression Editor.
- **Comment** out the creation expression by placing // in front of the expression lines.

Or

- Delete the expression.
- Select **Solvers** → **Initial State** → **Set for Selected**.

11 Apply a uniform field to the particles

- Select the particle object, then select **Fields** → **Uniform**.
- Use the following settings for the uniform field:

    Direction X, **Y**, **Z** to **1**, **0**, **0**, respectively;

    Magnitude to **15**;

    Attenuation to **0**.

- Playback the animation.

The flies are now moving forward and flapping their wings according to the original dragonfly. Since the instances are animated like the original object, they flap their wings altogether. This issue will be discussed in the next exercise.

Tip: If you want each particle to move differently, you could apply an acceleration runtime expression to the particles instead of using a uniform field.

Instance cycling

One way of having different animation cycles for all the instances is creating duplicates of the different poses of the original object, and then telling the instances to use different sequences for the animation cycle.

In this example, you will see how to randomly animate a flock of butterflies.

1   Scene file

- Open the scene file called *28-butterfly_01.ma*.

This scene contains one butterfly with no animation. You will create an animated cycle using the instancer and several duplicates of the butterfly.

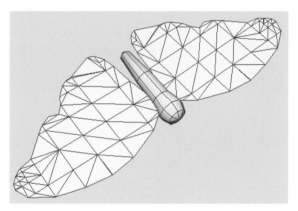

A simple butterfly

Note: *Since there could possibly be lots of butterfly instances in the scene, the butterfly used here is quite low resolution.*

2   Set up a cycle using duplicated butterflies

- Select the *butterfly* group from the Outliner.

- Duplicate the *butterfly* eight times.

- Move each butterfly on the **Y-axis**.

Note: *Do not select the butterfly geometry when translating. You must move the butterfly's top group. If you move the geometry, it causes the items to be offset from the base object's coordinate system and will cause offsetting from the particles during instancing.*

Lesson 28
Instance cycling

- Hide the original *butterfly*.

- Rotate the wings of each duplicate as shown here:

> **Tip:** You can rotate both wings simultaneously. They have been set up to have *inverse rotations.*

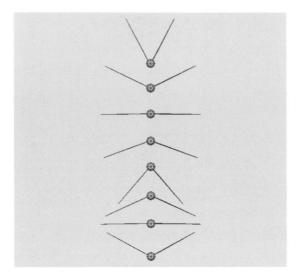

Eight butterflies producing a complete flap cycle

- Make sure the duplicated butterfly's groups are named from *butterfly1* through *butterfly8.*

> **Tip:** It is important to have the groups correctly named in sequence. That will make it easier to place the different positions in order.

3 Create particles in the scene

- Use the **Particle Tool** to create a cloud of **20** particles within a radius of **40**.

- Rename the particles *butterflyParticles*.

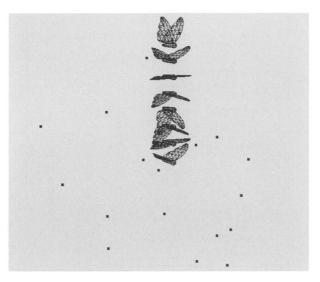

Cloud of twenty particles to be used for butterfly instancing

4 Set basic instancer options

- Use the Outliner to select *butterfly1* through *butterfly8* in order.

The order they are selected will determine the cycling order used by the instancer.

- Select **Particles** → **Instancer (Replacement)** → ❑.

- Set the following options:

  Particle Instancer Name to *butterflyInstancer*;

  Cycle to **Sequential**;

  Cycle Step Size to **1**.

- Press the **Create** button.

The list of objects the instancer will use is shown in the **Instanced Objects** *list. The number beside the object is called the* **Object Index**. *The first object in the list is always index* **0**. *The instancer uses this index value to determine which object in the sequence of butterflies to display at a given point in time.*

A cycle setting of **Sequential** *causes the instancer to cycle through the object indices in sequence rather than not using any cycling at all. A* **Cycle Step Size** *of* **1** *causes the instancer to display each object index for* **1** *frame before changing to the next item in the list.*

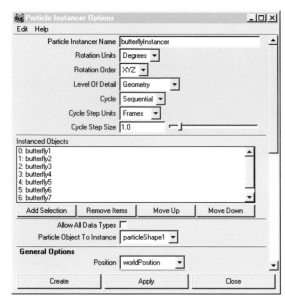

List of instanced objects and their object indices in the instancer options

5 Make a test run

- Hide *position1* through *position8*.

- Playback the scene to view the instanced objects cycling.

All butterflies cycle through the eight positions in exactly the same fashion.

Instanced butterflies all with the same initial object index

Project Seven

6   Add a custom attribute to control cycling on a per particle basis

It was previously stated that the Cycle Step Size determines how long the instancer will display each object index before switching to the next item in the list. Since the particleId is unique for each particle, it can be used to control this duration on a per particle basis. This is accomplished by multiplying the particleId by the age and storing the result in a custom attribute which, in turn, gets fed into the **Age** control of the instancer's cycling options as explained below.

- Select *butterflyParticles* and open the Attribute Editor.

- Press the **General** button in the **Add Dynamic Attribute** section.

- Set the following options:

  Attribute Name to *customAge*;

  Data Type to **Float**;

  Attribute Type to **Per Particle (Array)**;

  Add Initial State Attribute to **On**.

- Press the **OK** button.

7   Assign values to customAge with a runtime expression

Now that you have added the custom age attribute, you need to assign values to it for each particle. Since age changes over time, you will use a runtime expression instead of a creation expression.

- **RMB-click** on the *customAge* field and select **Runtime Expression Before Dynamics**.

- Enter the following runtime expression:

```
if (particleId == 0)

    customAge = age;

else if (particleId == 1)

    customAge = age * 0.5;

else if ((particleId % 2 == 0) && (particleId % 3 == 0))

    customAge = age * 0.25 * particleId / 4;

else if (particleId % 2 == 0)

    customAge = age * 0.4 * particleId / 4;
```

```
        else if (particleId % 3 == 0)

                customAge = age * 0.35 *particleId / 4;

        else

                customAge = age * 0.2 * (particleId) / 4;
```

This expression assigns a different value to customAge based on multiplication of the particleId. Since these particles are not being emitted, they have the same age. To get around this, age is multiplied by a decimal value which was arbitrarily selected to provide variation in age for each particle. This value is then multiplied by the particleId which is, again, another unique value. The particleId is divided by 4 to keep the values small. If this division wasn't done, the values in customAge would grow rapidly and cause the cycle to occur too quickly.

8 Set particle render type to numeric

To get a better idea of which portion of the expression is controlling which particles, you can use the **Numeric Render Type**.

- Select *butterflyParticles*.

- Set **Particle Render Type** to **Numeric.**

By default, the Numeric Render Type displays the particleId attribute for each particle. This makes it easier for you to see which particle will be affected by which portion of the expression. For example, particleId 12 is evenly divisible by both 3 and 2, so it will therefore be set by the following portion of the expression:

```
        else if ((particleId % 2 == 0) && (particleId % 3 == 0))

                customAge = age * 0.25 * particleId / 4;
```

Tip: *You can change the attribute displayed by the **Numeric Render Type** by pressing the **Current Render Type** button in the Attribute Editor, then typing in the name of the attribute to display in the field provided. Attributes such as **rgbPP** and **Mass** are other useful attributes to view in numeric mode.*

9 Set the cycle options

- In the **Instancer (Geometry Replacement)** section of *butterflyParticles'* Attribute Editor, choose **customAge** from the **Age** pull-down menu in the **Cycle Options** sub-section.

LEARNING MAYA | THE SPECIAL EFFECTS HANDBOOK

If you playback the simulation, you should see the butterflies update with various cycle speed.

10 Add a float array attribute to control the starting object index

Currently, all butterflies begin their sequence from object index 0 (position1). They all cycle through the instanced object list starting from *position1* and ending at *position8*, then repeating.

You can change the object index the sequence starts on by setting the **CycleStartObject** attribute in the instancer. In this case, you will create another custom attribute called *startPick* to control CycleStartObject on a per particle basis, similar to the way you set up *customAge*.

- Using what you have learned so far, add a custom particle **Float Array** attribute with initial state to *butterflyParticles* and name it *startPick*.

- Add the following creation expression to *startPick*:

```
if (particleId == 0)

        startPick = 0;

else if (particleId == 1)

        startPick = 1;

else if ((particleId % 2 == 0) && (particleId % 3 == 0))

        startPick = 2;

else if (particleId % 2 == 0)

        startPick = 3;

else if (particleId % 3 == 0)

        startPick = 4;

else

        startPick = 5;
```

Note: *The value chosen for startPick in this expression will determine which butterfly the instancer chooses to begin the cycle on.*

Lesson 28

11 Set the cycle options

- In the **Instancer** (**Geometry Replacement**) section of *butterflyParticles'* Attribute Editor, choose **startPick** from the **cycleStartObject** pull-down menu in the **Cycle Options** sub-section.

The butterflies' intial frame is now more random.

Tip: *The above method shows you a customized approach to selecting a starting object. A similar result can be achieved simply by setting* **cycleStartObject** *to* **particleId**.

12 Add uniform and radial fields to move the particles

- Add fields or expressions to control the motion of the individual particles as desired.

13 Playback

- Hide the particle object.

- Playback the simulation.

Butterflies animated with different cycle start and speed

Planning, optimizing and rendering considerations

Now you have used the instancer with an animated object and a cycled sequence of snapshots. There are advantages and disadvantages to both methods. Using an animated object allows you to use 2D and 3D motion blur when rendering. Motion blur is not available when cycling through a sequence of instanced objects. Therefore, it is best to consider rendering requirements when setting up shots requiring instancing.

It is also important to keep your geometry as simple as possible. Making your surfaces single-sided and keeping NURBS patches low or poly count low will make a big difference.

One advantage to using a sequence of snapshots is that you have control over the duration of each snapshot and also the starting point of the cycle.

Tip: *You can also instance Paint Effects strokes to particles.*

Hardware sprites

The **Sprite** render type is used for displaying 2D file texture images on particles.

The scene file *28_snowHW.ma* illustrates a simple application of hardware sprites. Open this file and playback the animation to see its effect.

The scene contains a *phongE* shading group with a file texture of a snowflake that has an alpha channel assigned to the particles. If you tumble the camera, the sprite images will always aim at the camera. This is a built-in feature of hardware sprites. You cannot make the hardware sprite type aim at some other object or direction.

Hardware sprites

Software sprites using the instancer

The hardware **Sprite** render type is only available for rendering using the Hardware Renderer or the Hardware Render Buffer. Therefore, you cannot render 3D motion blur, reflections, refractions, or shadows like you can when using software rendering. The following exercise outlines a method for creating software renderable particle sprites using the instancer. This will allow you to take advantage of these important software rendering features while maintaining the core functionality that the hardware sprite render type provides.

Sprite/camera set up (optional)

Sprites should always face directly at the camera. Hence, you will need to set up your camera so there is some information available to tell the sprites where to point. You will eventually use a polygon plane, particles and the instancer node to make the software sprite objects.

1 Scene file

- Select **File** → **New Scene**.

2 Create a camera at the origin

- Select **Create** → **Cameras** → **Camera**.

For this example, you will use a single node camera with the default options.

- Rename the new camera to *spriteCam*.

3 Create a locator at the origin and make it a child of spriteCam

- Select **Create** → **Locator**.

- Rename this locator to *camLocal*.

- **Parent** the locator under *SpriteCam*.

camLocal represents the local coordinate system of spriteCam at the back of the lens of the camera.

4 Duplicate the locator

- Duplicate the *camLocal* locator.

- Rename the new locator to *camUpLocal*.

- Move it up by **2** units on its **Y-axis** so that it is directly above *camLocal*.

The locator camUpLocal will be used to find out which direction is up for spriteCam within its own local coordinate system.

5 Create another locator at the origin

- Create a new locator at the origin.

- Rename this locator *camWorld*.

This locator should not be placed within the spriteCam hierarchy. camWorld will be used to find out what world space coordinate marks the center of the camera lens.

6   Duplicate the camWorld locator

- Duplicate the *camWorld* locator.

- Rename this locator *camUpWorld*.

camUpWorld will be used to find out what world space coordinate is considered up for the camera.

7   Point constrain camWorld to camLocal

Point constraining *camWorld* to *camLocal* will cause *camWorld* to always follow the position but not the rotational orientation of *camLocal*.

- Select *camLocal*, then **Shift-select** the *camWorld*.

- Select **Constrain → Point → ☐**.

- Make sure the **Maintain Offset** checkbox is turned **Off**, then click the **Add** button.

8   Point constrain camUpWorld to camUpLocal

Point constraining *camUpWorld* to *camUpLocal* will cause *camUpWorld* to always follow the position but not the rotational orientation of *camUpLocal*.

- Select *camUpLocal*, then **Shift-select** the *camUpWorld*.

- Select **Constrain → Point**.

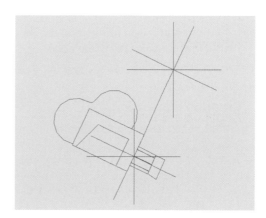

Side view of spriteCam with locators for world and local axes

Instancing set up

Now, you will add custom attributes to a particle object. These custom attributes will later be selected as options in the pop-up menus of the instancer.

1   Create a polygon plane

- Select **Create → Polygon Primitives → Plane**.

- Rename the plane to *spritePlane*.

- Set the plane's construction history to have only **1** subdivision for width and height.

2 Create particles

- Use the **Particle Tool** to make a cloud of particles.

3 Add vector array attributes to the particles

- Open the Attribute Editor for the particles.

- Press the **General** button under **Add Dynamic Attributes**.

- Add four **Vector Array** attributes with initial state, named as follows:

    spriteWorldUp;

    spriteAimPos;

    spriteAimAxis;

    spriteAimUpAxis.

Tip: *Click the **Add** button rather than the **OK** button to continue adding attributes without closing the editor.*

4 Creation expression

- **RMB** select **Creation Expression** in the *spriteWorldUp* attribute field.

- Enter the following expression:

```
spriteAimAxis = << 0, 1, 0 >>;

spriteAimUpAxis = << 0, 0, 1 >>;

vector $camPos = <<camWorld.tx,camWorld.ty,camWorld.tz>>;

vector $camUp = <<camUpWorld.tx,camUpWorld.ty,camUpWorld.tz>>;

vector $upDir = $camUp - $camPos;

spriteWorldUp= $upDir;
```

- Click the **Create** button.

5 Runtime expression

- Select the Runtime Before Dynamics radio button in the Expression Editor.

- Enter the following expression:

```
spriteAimPos = <<spriteCam.tx, spriteCam.ty, spriteCam.tz >>;

vector $camPos = <<camWorld.tx,camWorld.ty,camWorld.tz>>;

vector $camUp = <<camUpWorld.tx,camUpWorld.ty,camUpWorld.
tz>>;

vector $upDir = $camUp - $camPos;

spriteWorldUp = $upDir;
```

- Click the **Create** button.

6 Particle instancer for the plane object

- Select the *spritePlane* object.

- Select **Particles** → **Instancer (Replacement)** → ❒.

- Select **Edit** → **Reset Settings**.

- Click the **Create** button.

An instanced plane should now be at each particle position.

7 Instancer options

You have put all the pieces in place. You will now hook the particle attributes up to the instancer.

- In the *particleShape1* Attribute Editor, open the **Instancer** section.

- Set the following in the **Rotation Options** section:

  AimPosition to **spriteAimPos**;

  AimAxis to **spriteAimAxis**;

  AimUpAxis to **spriteAimUpAxis**;

  AimWorldUp to **spriteWorldUp**.

Note: *If **None** is selected for **AimDirection**, a default value of **<<1,0,0>>** will be used. If **None** is selected for **AimPosition**, **<<0,0,0>>** is used. If **None** is selected for **AimAxis**, **<<1,0,0>>** is used. If **None** is selected for **AimUpAxis**, **<<0,1,0>>** is used.*

Lesson 28

8 Test the particle instancing

- Rewind the scene to evaluate the various expressions entered earlier.

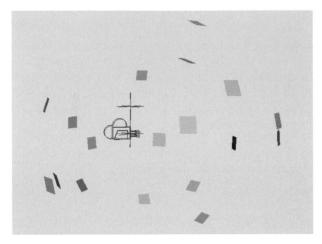

View of sprite particles from the Perspective view

- Select **Panels** → **Perspective** → **spriteCamShape**.

- Move the *spriteCam* view around to see the effect on the particles' orientation.

Tip: *A good test is to set the* **Particle Render Type** *to* **Sprites**. *You should see that the instanced plane and sprites match perfectly.*

How do these expressions work?

Determining the `spriteWorldUp` vector:

```
vector $camPos = <<camWorld.tx,camWorld.ty,camWorld.tz>>;

vector $camUp = <<camUpWorld.tx,camUpWorld.ty,camUpWorld.tz>>;
```

- `$camPos` is a vector determined by the current camera position in world space. The expression gets this value from the point constrained locator `camWorld`.

- `$camUp` is another vector determined by the current position of the `camUpWorld` locator that is offset from the `camWorld` locator.

```
vector $upDir = $camUp - $camPos;

spriteWorldUp = $upDir;
```

- $upDir is a vector determined by the difference between *camWorld* and *ºcamUpWorld*.

- spriteWorldUp is given this difference.

As the camera moves and rotates in world space, spriteWorldUp is reduced to a single vector that is used to compute each instanced object's current reference point for what is straight up. Since the camera may have rotated, what is straight up to the camera is not the same as what is straight up to the rest of the world. Without this information, the instancer would just assume that world up is the same as the Y-up presented by the world up setting, and the sprites would orient themselves to the wrong up reference point.

9 Assign a snowflake texture

- Assign a **lambert** shader to the original plane, then **map** the **Color** with a **File** texture.

- Browse for *snowflake_wAlpha.rgb* found in the *sourceImages* directory as the file texture.

- Hide the particle and original *spritePlane* objects.

10 Ready for rendering

Now that you have established control of the software sprites, they are ready for software rendering. You can render with shadows, raytracing, motion blur, etc.

spriteCam render

Tip: *Raytracing will be needed in order to cast shadows through the snowflakes.*

11 Save your work

- Save the scene as *28-snowSW.ma*.

swSprite.mel

The *swSprite.mel* script found in the support files will automatically set up the above steps for you. Create a new scene, create a cloud of particles, select them, then type `swSprites` in the Script Editor to test it out.

Tips and traps

- Dragonflies may disappear when the scene is rewound. This happens if the initial state isn't set after the expression has evaluated once, or if you have not set the scale pop-up menu to *flyScaler* in the instancer section of the *particleShape* node.

  Make sure the initial state is set immediately after the creation expression is evaluated once. If you cannot get your dragonflies to come back, delete the creation expression and try entering a runtime expression like this:

      bugScaler0=<<1,1,1>>;

  Playback to see if the dragonflies reappear but don't rewind. If they do appear, set the initial state and delete the runtime expression. Now you are back where you started before the problem arose and you can add the creation expression back in. Press **Edit** and **Delete** for the creation expression and set the initial state one final time.

> **Tip:** Restarting the example from scratch may be easier.

- If nothing happens after expressions are entered, it's usually because you forgot to hook up the custom attribute from within the instancing section's pop-up menus in the Attribute Editor.

- If the custom attribute you created doesn't show up in the pop-up menus, you likely created the custom attribute as a different data type than what that pop-up menu expects. Enabling **Allow All Data Types** refreshes the menus and allows the attribute to show up. The better solution is to recreate the attribute as the correct data type: float for object index numbers and vector for nearly all other instancer attributes.

- A very quick way to make each particle start on a different cycle index is to set *CycleStartObject* to *particleId*. This is faster than typing in an expression and gets the same basic results. It is still good, however, to understand the expression used in the butterfly example.

- The file *28-arrows.ma* is good for illustrating how to make an object aim in the direction of its velocity.

  To do so, you simply need to set the **AimDirection** *of the instancer to* **Velocity** *on the particle object.*

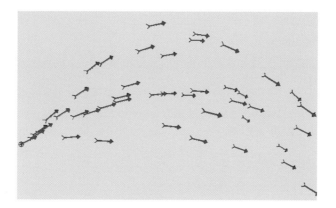

Arrows aiming at velocity

- If the snowflake texture does not appear with the example files, reassign the file *snowflake_wAlpha.rgb* found in the *sourceImages* directory to the **Color** attribute of the phongE material shader.

- The *swSprites.mel* script does the camera set up, instancing and shader set up automatically. It is normal for you to have to rewind and playback to get the sprites to align properly. It is also normal for the sprites to not align on the first frame until the expressions are evaluated.

- To play different sequences of images on software sprites, you need to animate the file texture for the plane. In addition, each poly plane needs to be a duplicate rather than an instance, so the current set up would not suffice.

- People often ask if there is a way to fade the instanced objects out based on the **opacityPP** of the particle it is instanced to. This is a limitation of particle instancing, since there is currently no direct connection between shading attributes of the particles and the objects that are instanced to them.

- The different aim attributes on the particle instancer can be confusing. Here's a quick breakdown:

  AimPosition

  Where the polygon plane will point.

  AimAxis

  Determines which axis of the polygon plane will point at the AimPosition

  AimUpAxis

  Determines which axis of the polygon plane is considered the up axis.

  AimWorldUp

  Determines which axis of the polygon plane is considered up in world space.

- **Particles** → **Sprite Wizard** is a script that automatically sets up animation of file textures on sprite particles.

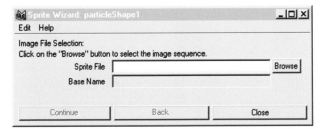

Sprite Wizard

- One trick for keeping particles away from each other is to use each particle as an individual radial field. To do so, do the following:

  With nothing selected, create a radial field with **Attenuation** *of 0 and* **Volume Shape** *set to* **none***.*

  Select the particles, then the field, and choose **Fields** → **Use Selected as Source of Field.**

  Connect the radial field up to the particles by selecting **Fields** → **Affect Selected Object(s)***.*

  Select the radial field and enable **Apply per vertex** *in the Attribute Editor under the* **Special Effects** *section.*

Now each particle is a small repelling field. You don't have control over the individual field magnitudes for each particle, but this is at least a start in keeping all the particles pushing away from each other. You can experiment with different **Max Distance**, **Attenuation** *and* **Magnitude** *settings for better results.*

Conclusion

Particle instancing is a built-in way to move geometry around using particles. Although the geometry will not detect the other instanced geometry, you can still come up with some pretty good effects using particle instancing. The fact that each parameter of the instancer is open to MEL scripting is a big benefit for customizing the parameters you use for your instanced animations.

In the next project, you will learn about rendering and compositing particles.

Project Eight

Lessons

Lesson 29 *Rendering particles*

Lesson 30 *Compositing*

In Project Eight, you will learn about the various particle rendering types, particle caching and useful particle rendering attributes. You will also get a glimpse of how to render a complex scene with layers on a composite workflow.

By the end of this project, you should feel comfortable rendering both software and hardware particles and compositing rendered layers together.

Lesson 29 Rendering particles

This lesson covers rendering types and techniques used for particles.

In this lesson you will learn the following:

- Hardware particle rendering types;

- Software particle rendering types;

- Particle caching in memory and on disk;

- Particle Sampler Info utility node;

- Particle cloud rendering.

Particle render types

Maya provides two types of rendering for particles: hardware and software.

Hardware rendering uses the graphics buffer and graphics memory of your computer to draw the image to the display and then take a snapshot of this image. This snapshot is then written to a file as a rendered image. This technique of using the hardware rendering capabilities of your computer has the advantage of being very fast, but also the limitation of few rendering advantages such as shadows, reflections and post-process effects like glow. Often particles are rendered only for the positional and matte or alpha information using the Hardware Renderer. The actual look of the particle effect is obtained by adding color, shadows, reflections, or environment lighting in the compositing stage of production. Again, speed and flexibility for aesthetic change of mind is behind this pipeline of image creation.

The hardware render types are:

Numeric;   **Points;**   **Spheres;**

Sprites;   **Streak.**

As a subset of these types, there are also two versions of point and streak that utilize multi-pass rendering. These are the **MultiPoint** and **MultiStreak** particle render types. It is probably safe to say that these two are the most commonly used hardware render types for most of the particular type of effects you create. Sprite comes in at a close second. As seen in the lesson on particle instancing, the sprite render type is used for displaying 2D images on particles. The sphere and point render type are more commonly used just to visualize where the particles are in space, while the numeric type is used especially to debug particle values. The point render type is the simplest and one that the display draws the quickest.

The **software render** types are:

Blobby Surface;

Cloud;

Tube.

These render types allow for various combinations of surface and volumetric shading techniques, which will be discussed in an upcoming section of this lesson. Their shaders are constructed from the similar shading nodes that are applied to geometry and lights.

When you software render, any hardware render type particles are skipped. When you hardware render, software render type particles are rendered as their respective hardware display appearance and filled circles.

Hardware rendering

Maya has two hardware renderers: the **Hardware Render Buffer** and the **Hardware Renderer.**

The Hardware Render Buffer

The Hardware Render Buffer can be found under **Window** → **Rendering Editors** → **Hardware Render Buffer...** This window will assume the size of the selected resolution format. It is recommended to ensure there are no windows beneath or in front of this window when you are rendering to it. It is also suggested to use an absolute black desktop background if you are going to be doing a lot of hardware rendering. Also, shut off your screen saver. The Hardware Render Buffer simply snapshots what is on the screen therefore, you should avoid moving the window around during rendering.

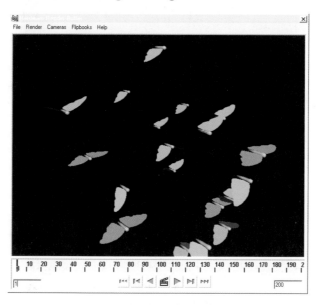

Hardware Render Buffer

Hardware rendering can also be used as a quick animation test. Geometry can be hardware rendered with lighting and textures, but without shadows or advanced lighting effects. There are also many options that allow geometry matting to be generated to aid in the compositing process.

The Hardware Renderer

The Hardware Renderer is one of the renderers listed in the Render Settings under **Render Using**. While it doesn't provide all the same options as the Hardware Render Buffer, it has significant advantages. Most importantly, it can render depth mapped shadows for hardware particle types. The exception is the sprite render type, because sprites cannot cast shadows. A workaround for rendering sprites that cast shadows is to use instanced geometry.

Hardware Renderer

Starting and stopping the Hardware Render Buffer

You invoke a render in the Hardware Render Buffer using **Render** → **Render Sequence** or by pressing the test button in the bottom center of the window to test a single frame. You can cancel a render by pressing and holding the **Esc** key, or by clicking the mouse inside the Hardware Render Buffer window.

Multipass hardware rendering

Multipass hardware rendering creates a softer rendered look for your particles. It can also anti-alias the geometry that is being hardware rendered. Multipass rendering requires you to use multipass render type as your particle render type. As mentioned earlier in this lesson, you have the choice of MultiPoint or MultiStreak.

For each of these render types, you will have several particle attributes that control the multi-pass effect:

Multi Count

Controls the number of added and offset pseudo-particles to distribute around the original particle.

Multi Radius

Controls how far away from the actual particle the additional pseudo-particles are drawn.

Hardware render attributes:

Render Passes

Controls the number of times a render is averaged.

Edge Smoothing

Controls anti-aliasing of geometry.

Motion Blur

Controls samples of time taken to blur particles and geometry. Values and approach differ from Maya software motion blur.

Motion blur and caching

Motion blur allows you to average the look of particles over time. To use motion blur, it is strongly recommended that you cache your particle motion. Otherwise, you will often get strange and unpredictable results.

Note: *It is possible that you encounter problems using hardware multi-pass motion blur.*

Cigarette smoke

In this example, you will create and render particles for cigarette smoke using hardware rendering techniques. The file contains props and dynamic elements ready for particle rendering. The animation of this setup is interesting as well. The main trick to the particle movement is two turbulence fields that have their phase animated with a simple `sin` expression. The only difference between the two fields is that the second turbulence field has a slightly slower frequency. These two fields work to reinforce each other while moving the particles. Rotation is obtained with a vortex field.

1   Scene file

- Open the scene file called *29-cig_01.ma*.

This scene file consists of a cigarette, an ashtray and several fields. There are two emitters parented under the cigarette group. You will use these emitters as your source for the particle smoke.

- Playback the scene to get an idea of how the particles are moving.

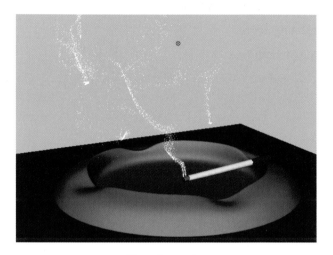

Cigarette smoke

2   Open the hardware render window

- Select **Window** → **Rendering Editors** → **Hardware Render Buffer...**

This will open the Hardware Render Buffer.

Note: *This window cannot be minimized or sized.*

3   Set hardware render attributes

- In the Hardware Render Buffer window, select **Render** → **Attributes...**
- Set the following in the **Image Output Files** section:

  Filename to *cigSmokeTest*;

  Extension to **name.0001.ext**;

  Start Frame to **1**;

End Frame to **100**;

By Frame to **1**;

Alpha Source to **Luminance**.

- Set the following in the **Render Modes** section:

    Lighting Mode to **All Lights**;

    Draw Style to **Smooth Shaded**;

    Texturing to **On**;

    Line Smoothing to **On**.

The **Line Smoothing** *option helps smooth out the particle tails when rendering streak or multiStreak particles.*

Note: *Hardware rendering has a maximum limit of eight lights.*

- Set the following in the **Multi-Pass Render Options** section:

    Multi Pass Rendering to **On**;

    Render Passes to **9**;

    Anti-alias Polygons to **On**;

    Edge Smoothing to **1.0**;

    Motion Blur to **4.0**.

- Following are descriptions of additional options:

    Full Image Resolution

    Turn this On if you are rendering at a resolution larger than screen resolution. An example would be rendering large images for film. The render will split the image into tiles, render each tile, then sew the tiles together into one image.

    Geometry Mask

    If turned On, you will only get particles in the final rendered image; no geometry is included. This can be useful when rendering a particle pass that will be composited over a separately rendered geometry pass.

    When this is on, the geometry will not be rendered into the hardware rendered image. However, the geometry will mask the appropriate particles so that layering occurs correctly during the compositing stage.

You should be aware that geometry masking is not perfect. For example, if you are layering your particles over a software rendered geometry pass and that geometry pass has software motion blur, it is unlikely that the hardware particle pass' geometry masking will match the motion blurred alpha channel from the software render. This is because the Software Renderer is much more accurate than the Hardware Renderer. Changing your object's tessellation will not necessarily increase the quality of the geometry masking. Also, geometry masking is not anti-aliased. Often you will need to use matte creation or modification tools in your compositing software to adjust how the particles will layer over the geometry.

Display Shadows

Some graphics cards support hardware shadowing. If your graphics card supports this feature, enabling this option will allow you to render shadows into your hardware rendered images.

4   Test render

- Playback the simulation until you are happy with the particle position.

- In the Hardware Render Buffer, select **Render** → **Test Render**.

This will render a single frame of the particles at the current time slider position.

Tip: *While rendering in the Hardware Render Buffer, if the rendered image doesn't stay in the view, make sure to clear the selection before rendering.*

5   Set Particle Render Type to MultiStreak

This render type will provide streaking and multiple jittered pseudo-particles.

- Select the *particleShape*.

- Change the **Particle Render Type** to **MultiStreak**.

- In the Attribute Editor, click the **Add Attributes For Current Render Type** button.

- Set the following:

  Depth Sort to **On**;

  Color Accum to **On**;

  Line Width to **1**;

Multi Count to **5**;

Multi Radius to **0.1**;

Normal Dir to **2**;

Tail Fade to **-0.5**;

Tail Size to **0.75**;

Use Lighting to **On**.

- Render the scene in the Hardware Render Buffer to see the difference.

MultiStreak cigarette smoke

6 Fine-tune lighting of particles

For hardware rendering, you will find that lighting values are often different than what is appropriate for software rendering.

Note: *You may want to use separate light sets for hardware and software rendering. You can then use light linking to limit the number of lights affecting the objects in the scene.*

- Toggle **Color Accum** to see its effect on the particle rendering.

When transparent particles are in front of one another they can either render the nearest particle or add the overlapping particle's colors. By using color accumulation, you can more closely simulate transparent particle effects.

Color accumulation also works to hide orphaned particles that are not contributing to the overall smoke trail. This adds to the smooth look of the smoke.

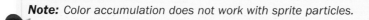

Note: *Color accumulation does not work with sprite particles.*

- Toggle **Normal Dir** to see its effect on the particle rendering.

The **Normal Dir** *attribute on the particles is an attribute available on many of the hardware render types. Normal Dir affects how particles are lit. Usually you won't need to adjust this unless your particles are moving in and out of lighting.*

- To maximize particle illumination, set Normal Dir as follows:

Set to **1** if most or all particles are moving towards the light. Example: smoke rising toward a light.

Set to **2** if most or all particles are stationary or passing in front of the light. Examples: rain passing in front of headlights, or stationary particles creating a glow around a point light.

Set to **3** if most or all particles are moving away from the light. Example: rain falling down past a street light.

7   Save your work

- Save the scene as *29-cig_02.ma.*

Caching particles

In order to apply hardware motion blur to a sequence of rendered images, you will need to cache the simulation. Motion blur requires knowing where the particle is and was, in order to determine the correct motion of the particle and determine the correct tail shape. Because future particle position is evaluated as the dynamic simulation calculates each frame, the renderer will not be able to predetermine the motion blur future frames unless the calculations have already been performed and stored in memory or on disk. Caching also makes it easier to evaluate timing since you can scrub in the timeline once the particles have been cached.

Memory caching vs. Disk caching

You have two choices for caching particles: **Memory caching** and **Disk caching**. Memory caching for particles works very much like memory caching of rigid bodies. You select the particle objects you want to cache and enable caching via a menu. The particle information is stored in RAM the first time.

Subsequent playbacks are read from the RAM making evaluation much faster, but the cache is only usable by the current Maya session. Disk caching is similar to memory chaching, except that it writes the cache on your computer's hard drive. Doing so thus makes the cache accessible between Maya sessions and between computers.

Memory caching workflow

Memory caching is good to use when you have a short simulation that doesn't have a huge number of particles. It is also useful when you know you will not be using distributed rendering across multiple computers. Currently, hardware rendering cannot be distributed in this manner but software rendering can. Memory caching provides a quick way of caching your particles without having to keep track of cache data files on your hard disk. However, memory caching can quickly eat up your computer's available RAM, so be aware of that before using it.

Following is a typical memory caching workflow:

- Select the particle object(s).

- Select **Solvers** → **Memory Caching** → **Enable**.

The particleShape will now show **Cache Data** *attribute as* **Enabled**.

To disable caching for a particular particle, you can deselect this attribute.

Note: *Each time you make a change to your scene, either to field values or particleShape attributes, you will need to delete the cache. To delete the cache, select each affected particle and* **Solvers** → **Memory Caching** → **Delete**.

Disk caching workflow

Disk caching creates particle disk cache files (*.pdc*) on your hard drive containing all the particle attribute information in your scene. One *.pdc* file is written for each particle object on each frame of playback. These files can be read very quickly so near real time scrubbing is still possible. You are only limited by available disk space, rather than available RAM. The *.pdc* files can be transferred to other machines if necessary, or accessed remotely, such as when using distributed rendering.

Following is a typical disk cache workflow:

- Save your scene.

- Select **Solvers** → **Create Particle Disk Cache** → ☐.

- Read the dialog description, and set the appropriate options.

- Press the **Create** button.

Maya will not draw the particles on the screen but will record all their attribute information to disk.

- Save the file again.

You are doing this so Maya knows this file has a disk cache going with it.

Following is how to disable or delete a particle disk cache:

- To temporarily disable the cache, select **Solvers** → **Edit Oversampling or Cache Settings**, then disable the **Use Particle Disk Cache** option.

- To permanently remove the disk caching, you need to locate the *particles* directory in your current project using your operating system. The directories inside the particles contain all the *.pdc* files for the various particle objects you have cached.

Tip: *For more specific control of which particle attributes will be written to disk cache, refer to the* dynExport *command in the MEL documentation.*

1 Scene file

- Continue with your own cigarette smoke scene.

Or

- Open the scene file called *29-cig_02.ma*.

2 Cache the particles

- Set the **playback range** to go from **1** to **200**.

- **Cache** the particles to disk using the workflow stated previously.

3 Adjust the motion blur

Now that you have cached the particles, experiment with different values of hardware motion blur.

- Open the Hardware Render Buffer attributes.

- In the **Multi-Pass Render Options** section, set **Motion Blur** to a value to **6**.

> **Note:** *Some older hardware graphics configurations do not support hardware motion blur.*

4   Adjust opacity over lifespan

The opacity of the particles should thin out as they get older.

- Add the **opacityPP** attribute and add a ramp to control the particle opacity.

5   Save your work

- Save the scene as *29-cig_03.ma*.

Graininess

Graininess is to be expected in your final smoke renders. This should be smoothed and blurred during the compositing stage, so you should not work too hard to get rid of it. Anticipate that the small particles that are orphaned or not contributing greatly to the effect will get removed during blurring and softening that takes place in the compositing stage.

Using low opacity values with a lot of particles can really help your hardware renders have a computer generated look and appear less flat. Also, you can simulate self-shadowing in hardware rendered smoke by using expressions to randomly assign gray values to the particles at creation time.

Glow and incandescence

People often ask if you can make hardware particles glow or produce self-illumination. **Color Accumulation** is currently the closest possible effect. This task is much better suited for compositing effects that let you make this adjustment very quickly. Even the most basic compositing packages generally have some nice tools for adding in incandescence and glowing effects. For hardware rendering, focus more on the motion and shadowing qualities inside of Maya. Sweetening effects like blurs, halos, glows, etc., are traditionally easier to add during compositing.

Final composited render

Software rendering

Software rendering of particles will allow you to do post-process effects such as glow and incandescence, as well as interactive effects of reflection, object occlusion and shadows. These particles are really nice to work with, but they are expensive in terms of rendering time.

There are three types of software particle render types. They each serve a separate purpose but can be combined as well.

Blobby particles

Blobby particles depend on each other to form blobs or connected shapes based on their radius and proximity to each other. There are two attributes related to the blobby particle object that control this behavior:

Radius

Sets the diameter of the blob particle.

Threshold

Sets the amount of flow between adjacent particles. The resultant blobbiness is a function of the particle radius, threshold and distance between particles. A setting of **0** generally means no blending. Values closer to **1** will normally produce more blending, assuming that there are particles close to each other. All of these factors are interdependent, so experimentation is almost always necessary.

Project Eight

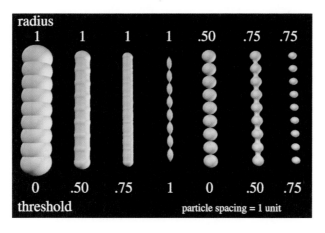

Blobby particle comparison of Radius vs. Threshold

To see a comparison of **Radius** vs. **Threshold**, open the scene file *29-blobCompare.ma*.

> **Note:** A high **Threshold** with big gaps between particles or a Threshold value that is larger than the particle's **Radius** may result in invisible particles.

Blobby particles are also the only render type to which you can assign shading groups and render in the same way you would assign shading groups to geometry.

It is generally recommended that you avoid depending on 2D mapping on blobby particles as blobbies use an averaging of UV space to calculate their respective mapping coordinates. This can result in artifacts or incorrect mapping of the resulting blobby surface. 3D mapping works the same as you would expect for any surface. It is often best to keyframe your 3D texture placement nodes to approximate the motion of your particles, as this helps to reduce the appearance of texture swimming during rendering. However, it can be difficult to totally eliminate the appearance of swimming when rendering blobbies using 3D textures, since particles may be moving at different speeds.

Bump mapping can be used with blobby surfaces, but displacement mapping might not work as you would expect.

Motion blur is not supported by any software render types.

Cloud particles

The cloud particle render type, as its name implies, is designed to create volumetric rendering effects. It has an additional attribute called **Surface Shading**, which controls how much blob the cloud will have. There are three attributes related to the cloud particle render type that control this behavior:

Radius

Sets the diameter of the cloud particles.

Threshold

Works like the blobby surface.

Surface Shading

Adjusts the degree of surface shading applied to the *particleCloud* shader via the **Surface Material** input on the shading group.

Tube particles

Tube particles are the software counterpart to the hardware streak particle render type. The tube particle has attributes to control the size of either end of the particle as well as tube length. The tube particle type does not have the surface shading capability that the cloud and blobby type have. The tube particle is velocity dependent like the hardware streak types. The **Tail Length** and **Direction** are dependent on the velocity and direction of the particle.

Radius0

Controls the tail size.

Radius1

Controls the head size.

Tail Size

Controls the tail length, but is also proportional to the particle velocity.

> **Note:** Radius0 *and* **Radius1** *are per object attributes only.*

Shading group organization

The software rendering engine accepts three basic types of shader information: **Surface Material**, **Volume Material** and **Displacement Material**. These three types are passed to the rendering partition through the shading group node. The shading group node acts as a place holder that tells the rendering partition what will be rendered and which shaders are to be used on which objects. The light linking partition also looks to the shading group to determine which lights will work with which shaders or objects.

Software particle rendering makes use of the Surface and Volume inputs to the shading group node. You can connect surface shaders and volume shaders to the three different types of particle render types via the particleCloud shading group (particleCloudSG). Surface shading is plugged into the Surface Material input of the shading group and volumetric shading is plugged into the Volume Material input.

Blobby particles make use of the standard surface material shaders, such as anisotropic, phong, lambert, blinn, etc.

Cloud particles make use of the surface materials and the volumetric particleCloud shader by plugging the particleCloud in both the Surface Material input and the Volume material input.

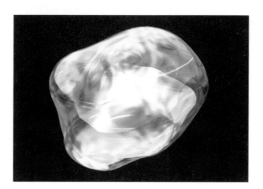

Blobby particles with phong shader and reflection map

Tube particles make use of the volumetric shader particleCloud only. ParticleCloud shader is plugged into the Volume Material input of the shading group.

Water bucket

In this exercise, you will create a very simple blobby water rendering. This will give you a chance to experiment with the blobby attributes and shading parameters.

1   Open scene file

- Open the file *29-waterBlob_01.ma*.

This scene consists of Meeper's bucket falling on the ground. The bucket contains water deformed with an animated wave deformer. You will have water to splash around using blobby surfaces.

Lesson 29

- Playback the scene to see the animation.

Note: *The bucket starts falling on the ground only at frame 20 because that will give you enough time to fill the bucket with particles.*

The dynamic bucket

2 Emit from surface

- Select the hidden *waterEmitter* surface from the Outliner.

- Select **Particles** → **Emit from Object**.

- Set the emitter attributes from the Channel Box as follows:

    Emitter Type to **Surface**;

    Rate to **1000**;

    Spread to **0.5**;

    Speed to **0**;

    Direction to **0, 1, 0**.

- Set the particle attributes as follows:

    Conserve to **0.95**;

    Inherit Factor to **3**;

    Particle Render Type to **Blobby Surface**.

- **Add Attributes** for the **Current Render Type** in the Attribute Editor.

- Set the following:

   Radius to **0.2**;

   Threshold to **0.75**.

3 Keyframe the emission

- Keyframe the **Rate** of the emitter as follows:

   Frame **15** to **1000**;

   Frame **16** to **0**.

4 Collisions and gravity

- Select the particle object, then **Shift-select** the gravity field.

- Select **Fields** → **Affect Selected Object(s)**.

- Select the particle object, then **Shift-select** the *bucket*.

- Select **Particles** → **Make Collide**.

- Repeat so the particles also collide with the *background* and the *water* surface.

- Select the *water* surface and set its *geoConnector* as follows:

   Resilience to **1**;

   Friction to **0.8**.

5 Apply phong shader to the blobby particles

You will use a phong material as the basis for the blobby particle shader. From this material, you will add other rendering nodes to control color, reflection and specularity.

- In the Hypershade window, create a **Phong** material.

- Select the particles, then **RMB-click** on the new phong material and select **Assign Material To Selection**.

6 Create the color and specular map

Because you want the blob to mimic clear water-like material, it will get most of its color from its environment. But, you will still want some method to control the color and specularity. The 3D texture, marble, makes a good sky texture.

Lesson 29

- Open the Attribute Editor for the phong.

- Press the **Map** button for the **Color** attribute.

- In the **Create Render Node** window, press **Marble** under the 3D Textures section.

- Adjust the values as follows:

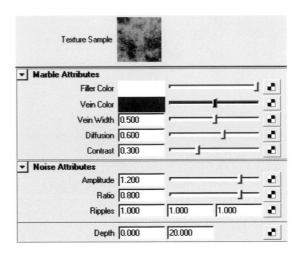

Marble settings

- Rename the marble node to *skyMarble*.

- **MMB-click+drag** *skyMarble* and drop it on to the **Specular Color** of the phong.

7 Environment map reflection

An environment map is a quick method for mimicking raytraced reflections and refraction.

- Set the following values for the phong material node:

- **Map** the **Reflected Color** attribute with an **Env Chrome** texture.

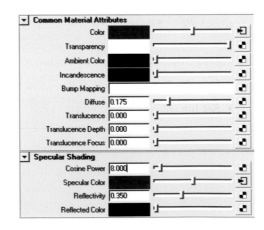

Phong settings

- Set the following values for the *chromeEnv* node:

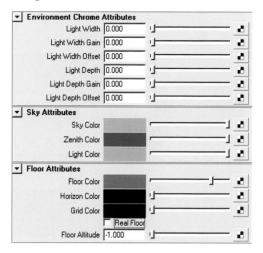

EnvChrome settings

- Also set the **Grid Placement** attributes to **0** as follows:

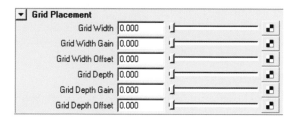

Grid settings

8   Map 3D textures into the chromeEnvironment inputs

The chrome environment map has several inputs for sky and floor color values. You will create a new texture for the floor.

- **Map** the **Floor Color** with a **Rock** texture.

- Set the values to approximate what your ground will look like:

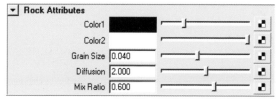

Rock color

Lesson 29

- From the Hypershade window, **MMB-click+drag** the *skyMarble* texture onto the **Horizon Color** input of the *envChrome* node.

Your shading network should look like this:

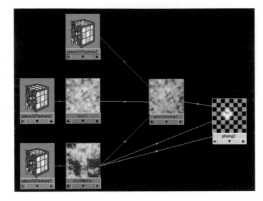

Blobby environment shader network

9 Adjust values

- Experiment with **Radius** and **Threshold** settings for the particles. Also experiment with lighting and texture parameters to see how they affect the look of the render.

10 Render the scene

Add lights and render the scene starting from frame **20**. You should notice that the particles behave with a nice waving effect and react in a similar way to water.

Final water render

11 Save your work

- Save your scene as *29-waterBlob_02.ma*.

Particle cloud shader

The *particleCloud* shader provides tools for many particle rendering effects. This is the most flexible shader mechanism for software particle rendering. The *particleCloud* shader provides volumetric density control and surface material attributes like color, transparency, glow and incandescence. You can create a new *particleCloud* shader in the Hypershade using: **Create → Materials → Volumetric → Particle Cloud**.

This section outlines some of the most important *particleCloud* and particle sampler info node attributes, so you can learn their functions before putting them to work in a practical application.

Note: *The particleCloud material works with cloud and tube particle render types only.*

Density and transparency

Density is closely related to **Transparency** and will interact with the method you choose to drive the particle opacity. The Density attributes allow you to control how a particle will look at its edges and where it overlaps with other particles. Density can be thought of as the volume transparency or as another series of inputs that add greater control over several aspects of shader transparency. It is important to understand how Density works as the Transparency attribute alone will only get you part of the look you may be anticipating. The Transparency attribute will work as the base of particle transparency, whereas the Density attribute applies to the volumetric portion of the shading. The third component is the **Blob Map**, which allows a texture to be added to the internal structure of the particles appearance. Typically, the less Blob Map is applied, the less of the particle surface outline is visible. The Blob Map will also affect how the shapes of the individual clouds are drawn in the render.

Lesson 29
Particle cloud shader

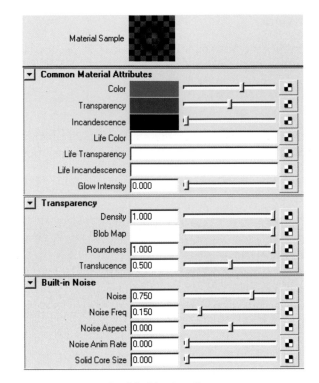

Particle Cloud attributes

Density

This attribute controls how dense the particle shading appears inside the volume. This attribute is also necessary, for example, to increase the shading if there is a lot of noise. If you are using the Transparency attribute to drive the surface shading, you may find that the Density attribute can control the volume portion independently. Typical values between **0** and **1** control slight density but values up to **10** can create interesting internal density for a very transparent particle. Also, keep in mind that the number of overlapping particles is going to affect the range of the Density attribute. If you have a lot of particles overlapping, then density values can be set lower.

Noise

This attribute controls the amount of random noise applied to the modification of the density. **Noise** can give you control of how extreme the density will diffuse across the particle. Typical values range from **0** to **4**, but will also depend on how much density is being used and again, on the number of particles and the specific effect.

Noise Freq

This attribute controls how large or small the spacing of the **Noise** maps across the particle. Typical values can be quite small, around **0.01** to **0.1**, for low frequency noise.

Noise Aspect

This attribute controls at what angle or *shear* the noise will appear to exist in the volume. Typical values of **-1** to **2** will change the noise direction from horizontal to vertical.

Blob Map

This attribute controls the mixture of **surface shading** and **volume shading** independent of the presence of a **Surface Material**. Surface shading is controlled by the **Surface Shading Properties** section in the Attribute Editor, in particular the **Diffuse Coefficient**. **Blob Map** can have a texture applied through it to create a more interesting internal structure to the particle appearance. It will interact with the overall density and transparency. If you turn this value very low you may need to increase the density, noise or transparency to see the particles. A minimum value above **0** for **Blob** Map is necessary for particles being rendered with no surface material shading. Otherwise, they will be invisible. Blob Map is a scaling factor for density. You can think of it as volume transparency. To see how this works, try mapping a **Cloud** texture to the default *particleCloud* shader and then rendering some cloud particles.

Life mapping and particle sampler info node

Life mapping is the process used by the renderer to map attributes from the *particleCloud* shader to the particles with respect to each particle's age.

The **Particle Sampler Info** node is a utility node designed specifically for controlling software rendering of particles. It is an essential part of the life mapping process. In addition, this node lets you use particle attributes, such as ramps and expressions, to drive software shader attributes on a per particle basis. For example, you could use it to make the velocity of a particle affect its transparency or noise value when software rendered. Or, you could make the age of a particle control the color of the particle, similar to what you did with the fountain example with hardware rendered particles.

The following example shows you how life mapping works and introduces you to the particle sampler info node.

Lesson 29

1   Scene file

- Open the scene file called *29-samplerInfo.ma*.

This file contains a simple directional emitter releasing cloud particles with a predefined lifespan.

2   Map a ramp to Color

- Open the **Hypershade**.

- **Map** a **Ramp** to the *newCloud* shader's **Color** attribute.

- Playback to frame **300**.

- Render the scene using the Software Renderer.

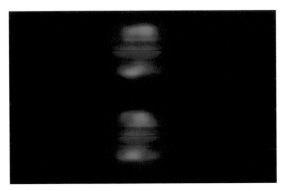

Ramp map to color of newCloud

Notice the ramp pattern is applied across each particle and the mapping begins from the center of the particle. Also, note that there is no relationship between the age of the particles and the mapping in the rendered image at this point.

3   Disconnect the ramp

- Break the connection between the *ramp* and the *newCloud* attribute in the Hypershade by selecting the connection, then pressing the **Delete** key.

- **MMB-click+drag** the *ramp* onto the *newCloud* shader and connect it to **Life Color**.

- Rewind and playback again to frame **300**, then **render** the scene.

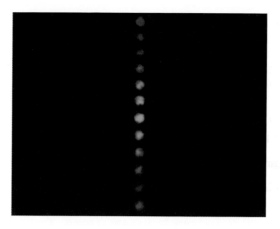

Ramp map to life color of newCloud

When you made the connection to **Life Color**, a *particleSamplerInfo* node was automatically created and connected as an input to the texture placement node of the ramp. This node is what keeps track of how old each particle is and what corresponding color along the **V** direction of the ramp will be assigned to the particle. In this case, and by default, the **Normalized Age** (age/lifespan) is used to look up a value on the ramp.

4 Experiment with the particle sampler info node

Changes you make to the *particleSamplerInfo* node are only visible when you render. Below are some attributes to change and explanations of what they do:

- Switch **Out UV Type** to **Absolute Age**.

When **Absolute Age** is selected, the actual age (not normalized against lifespan), of each particle is used to determine what color on the ramp will be assigned to it. By default, the bottom of the ramp is **0** and the top is **1**. Age is in seconds and is a per particle attribute. Therefore, after a particle has aged one second (24 frames at 24fps), it will have been assigned every color from the bottom to the top of the ramp.

- Set **Normalization Method** to **Oscillate** or **Clamp**.

Normalization Method determines what happens when the age of the particle reaches the top of the ramp.

If **Oscillate** is selected, a wrap around will occur and the particle will continue traveling through the ramp, starting at the bottom again. This wrap around will continue indefinitely until the particle dies.

Lesson 29

If **Clamp** *is selected, no wrap around will occur. Instead, the color at the top of the ramp will remain assigned to the particle after the particle has reached an age of* **1**.

- Adjust the **Normalization Value**.

Perhaps instead of the top of the ramp corresponding to one second of age, you want it corresponding to five seconds of age. In other words, you want the particles to take five seconds to travel through all colors of the ramp. In this case, setting the normalization value to **5** *will accomplish this.*

- Toggle the **Inverse OutUV** option.

This option reverses the direction in which the particles travel through the ramp over age. For example, if the ramp originally goes from red to green to blue, then so will the particles as they age. If **Inverse OutUV** *is enabled, then the particles will be colored from blue to green to red as they age without having to change the original ramp.*

Note: *The particleSamplerInfo node should not be confused with the samplerInfo node, which is commonly used to obtain point on surface shading information with respect to the camera.*

Self-shadowing

Self-shadowing is an important part of getting realistic cloud-like particle rendering. To receive self-shadowing on particles you must:

- Enable **Raytracing** in the **Render Settings**.

- Set the appropriate lights to **Use Raytrace Shadows**.

- Enable the *particleShape* attributes for **Better Illumination**.

- Enable **Casts Shadows** under the **Render Stats** section of the Attribute Editor.

Note: **Better Illumination** *is not required for shadowing, however, it will produce a higher quality image and higher quality shadowing. Better Illumination will increase the number of lighting samples the renderer is using. It is best to leave this option Off until you are at the final tweaking stages of rendering, or if you are ready to do a final render.*

Software particle example

Following is a simple example using software particles.

1 Scene file

- Open the file *29-volcano_01.ma*.

This scene consists of a volcano with particles emitting from the crater. There are three groups of particles: cloud particles, ejecta particles and thick cloud particles.

The separate particle elements have been put on separate layers to facilitate their visibility and selection. Use these layers to operate on only one particle layer at a time. Otherwise, this can be an unmanageable scene due to the large number of particles.

Tip: *Keep track of the Render Settings to keep render times down.*

2 Particle shading samples

- Open the Render Settings window and then open the **Anti-aliasing Quality** section for the Software Renderer.

- In the **Number of Samples** section, set **Particles** to **1**.

- In the **Raytracing Quality** section, enable **Raytracing**.

- Disable **Better Illumination** in the **Render Attributes** section of the Attribute Editor for the *cloudParticleShape* and *thickSmokeShape*.

Raytracing should be done from the beginning because lighting and illumination are considerably different from non-raytraced rendering. For this reason, it is recommended to find as many ways as possible to reduce the load on the renderer, using layers to control visible geometry during testing.

Raytracing provides the best self-shadowing of particles. To speed rendering during testing, use only the most coarse values for shadow quality. The default values currently set in the scene should already be adequate.

3 Position the lights and enable shadows

- Open the Attribute Editor for *backLight* and enable **Use Raytraced Shadows**.

Lesson 29

- Do the same for *keyLight*.

- Select *keyLight* select **Panels** → **Look through Selected**.

- Position *keyLight* to see all of the smoke.

- Do the same for the *frontWideFill* light.

4 Create a cloud material

- In the Hypershade, select **Create** → **Volumetric Materials** → **Particle Cloud**.

- Rename the *particleCloud* material to *cloudShader*.

Note that the shading group of cloudShader contains the **Volume Material** *input that will be used in the next step.*

Note: *To see the shading group in the Hypershade, you must graph the output connections of the new material.*

5 Assign the cloud shader

- Select *cloudParticle*.

- **RMB-click** over the *cloudShader* material in the Hypershade, and select **Assign Material to Selection**.

6 Map solid fractal textures to color and transparency

- **Map** the *cloudShader* **Color** attribute with a **Solid Fractal** texture.

- Rename the texture as *colorFractal*.

7 Adjust the fractal texture

The new solid fractal texture will need its attributes to be set correctly. **Color Gain** attributes on the texture will control much of the strength of the brightness and transparency.

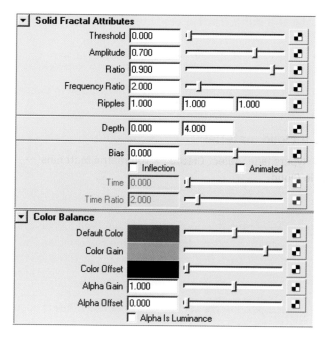

Color fractal settings

8   Adjust cloudShader attributes

Transparency and **Density** are the most important parts of getting a soft voluminous look. Use the values shown here as a starting point:

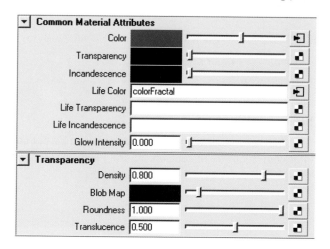

cloudShader attribute settings

9 Duplicate the solid fractal texture

- Select the *colorFractal* texture in the Hypershade.

- Select **Edit** → **Duplicate** → **With Connections to Network**.

This will duplicate the fractal texture with its connection to the placement node.

- Rename the new texture to *transFractal*.

- **MMB-click+drag** *transFractal* onto the *cloudShader* and select **Transparency** from the pop-up menu.

10 Invert the fractal transparency

At this point, the *transFractal* is not transparent the way you would expect. It will create more transparency where the cloud should be and greater opaqueness where it's black. By inverting the *transFractal*, you will get the effect of more luminance and less transparency, like you see in real clouds.

- Select the *transFractal* node and open its Attribute Editor.

- Scroll down to the **Effects** section and enable the **Invert** checkbox.

Note: *You could also use a **Reverse Utility** node instead of using the Invert attribute.*

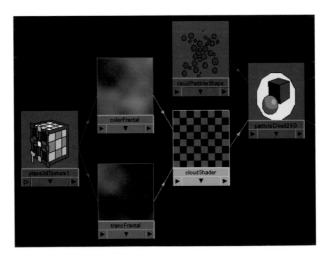

Graph of cloudShader network

11 Create the thickCloud shader

You will create the thick cloud shader from the *cloudShader* you just created. For this shader you will simply modify the attributes to create a thicker and more turbulent look.

- Select *cloudShader* in the Hypershade window.

- Select **Edit** → **Duplicate** → **Shading Network**.

This will duplicate the input nodes and connections.

- Rename these nodes with the *thick* prefix.

- Apply this material to the *thickSmoke* particles.

- Use the following values as guides for setting the fractal textures and material attributes:

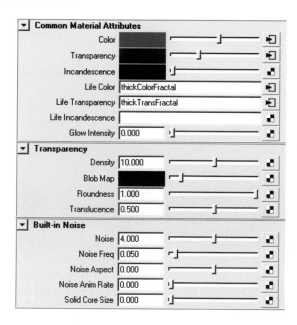

thickCloudShader attribute settings

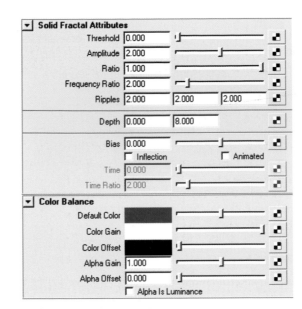

thickColorFractal and thickTransFractal texture attribute settings

12 Create the ejecta shader for the tube particles

For the streaks of red hot rock being ejected from the crater, you will use the **Tube** particle type.

- In the Hypershade window, select **Create → Volumetric Materials → Particle Cloud**.

- Rename this material to *ejectaCloud*.

- Assign this shader to the *ejectaParticle*.

13 Create a life color ramp texture

- Press the **Map** button for **Life Color** for the *ejectaCloud* material.

- Press **Ramp** from the **Create Render Node** window.

Because there is a lifespan attribute associated with the ejecta particles, this ramp texture will now control what the particle color is throughout its life. A particleSamplerInfo node has been created, feeding into the 2D texture placement node. This node will convert the age of the particle into a value that is referenced against the V direction of the ramp texture. The color found at that value is then fed to the color input of the particle cloud material, thus determining the particles' color at that moment.

- Use the following as a guide for setting attributes on the *ejectaCloud* material and the *ejectaLifeColor* ramp.

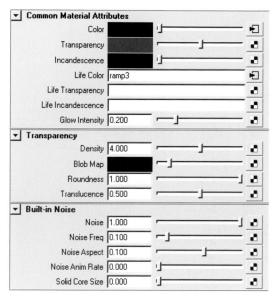

Ejecta particle shader settings

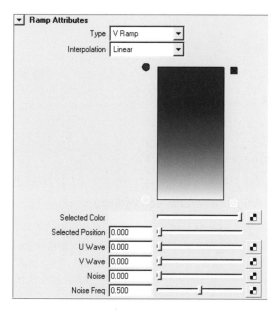

Ejecta life color ramp settings

Lesson 29

14 Playback and test render

- Playback the simulation.

- Render the scene.

- Tweak the shaders and textures as wanted.

Final volcano render

15 Save your work

- Save the scene as *29-volcano_02.ma*.

Tips and traps

- When fading particles out, it is usually a good idea to fade them all the way out before they die, otherwise you will notice popping in your renders. If you are using opacity or transparency to fade them out, move the top handle of the ramp down from the top a little bit. You may want to do the same thing for particles fading in to avoid popping.

- If particles stay opaque throughout their entire life, you might want to increase the **radiusPP** starting from **0** when the particles are born and then diminish the radius to **0** before the particles die. Otherwise, you might notice a pop when the particles show up and die.

- You can control the shading samples rendered for particles by changing the number in the **Particles** field in the Render Settings. This option is listed under **Anti-aliasing Quality → Number of Samples**. Increasing this may increase image quality, but it will also slow your rendering down so only increase it if you cannot get rid of aliasing using other methods.

- Motion blur and IPR are not supported for software rendering of particles.

Project Eight

- The resolution of sphere particles is constant; you cannot change the detail of the sphere. Also, you cannot cause particle collisions to occur at the edge of a sphere particle or at the edges of sprite particles. As shown in the instancing lesson, if you need to change the resolution of the sphere render type, try instancing geometric spheres to point particles as a workaround.

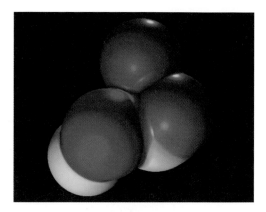

29-blobbyBlended.ma

- Some additional undocumented files related to rendering are *29-blobbyBlended.ma* and *29-blobbyFadeOut.ma*. The first file shows how to mix colors between blobby particles that are intersecting. The second file shows how to fade the transparency of blobby particles with respect to age.

29-blobbyFadeOut.ma

Conclusion

This lesson has introduced you to some ideas and processes involving particle rendering. Now, that you have learned some of the advantages of each method, you may begin to understand the difference between hardware and software rendering. Remember the importance of color, lighting and shadow in your imagery. Often, it is these elements that make the biggest difference.

The upcoming lesson overviews the compositing stage. It will also introduce some other methods for improving the look of your images.

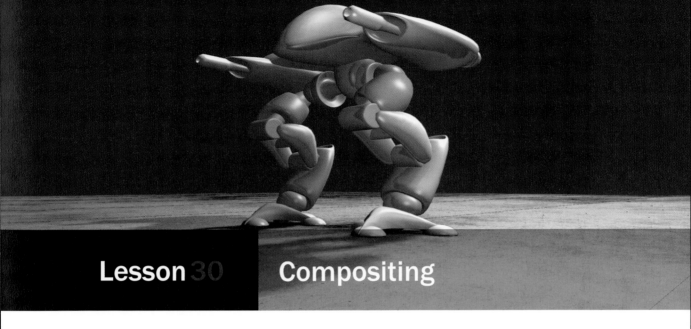

Lesson 30   Compositing

This lesson covers rendering strategies for compositing dynamic effects.

In this lesson you will learn the following:

- Workflow using layers;

- The rendering options for compositing;

- Workflow using the UseBackground shader;

- Workflow using shadow passes;

- Workflow using geometry masking.

Compositing is a timesaver

Compositing is a timesaver

One method of optimizing your production time is to plan and prepare your project around compositing. Compositing has been an integral part of image creation since artists first began committing their images to some form of media. Filmmaking pioneers were quick to grasp the power of combining image elements into a seamless sandwich of layers to produce final projected images that would not be possible otherwise.

Computer graphics is not different and has, in fact, been a prime beneficiary of this process. Separating your image elements into distinct rendered passes has the following advantages:

- Faster render times;

- Flexibility of version injection and artistic control;

- Faster and more precise color matching;

- Sweetening processes and post-process effects;

- Lower resolution demands for inserted elements;

- Hardware particle rendering;v

- Combining software and hardware rendered particles;

- Object and material options for visibility and lighting;

- Integration of shadow and glowing effects;

- Control of timing and editing.

Larger and more elaborate concepts are made possible by compositing. For this reason, all major studios have centered their image creation pipeline around the compositing process. The compositing station is the hub that all elements are fed into.

Maya provides tools to support the process of image creation for compositing:

- Render layer management;

- Shading options for matte opacity, blackHole, useBackground;

- Geometry masking;

- Z-depth and alpha rendering;

- Object visibility;

- Render Passes.

Extensive example

The following scene, called *30-gunbot.ma*, contains an exploding robot. This example utilizes much of what you have learned and applies it to a scene that is in the process of layer creation and manipulation for the compositing process.

In this scene, you have a mechanical biped that is to lose its upper torso in a most violent manner. Although the scene file has been broken down into layers for easy display management, some of the actual rendered layers are derived from set management/rendering flags as well.

Following is a breakdown of the important display layers found in the scene:

gunbotPieces

These are the upper torso pieces that are shattering and flying away. They are rigid bodies that have been animated with various dynamic fields.

ground

This is the ground plane. It is a passive rigid body.

legs

This is the *Gunbot* without the upper torso.

blastWave

This is a sphere that is animated to mimic the initial shock wave and act as a guide for pyro timing.

gunBotBody

This is the upper torso intact. This object will be swapped for the exploding pieces.

gutsLeaders

This is a particle layer that consists of leading particle emitters.

gutsSmoke

This layer is made up of the particles emitted from the *gutsLeaders*. They are software rendered clouds.

chunkSparks

This is a layer of particles that has been emitted from the exploding surface of the *gunbotPieces*.

MattePieces, MatteLegs, MatteGround

These three layers consist of duplicated geometry that is parented to the gunbot and ground surfaces. These objects have useBackground shaders applied to them for use in creating mattes and holdouts of render passes.

Fields and lights

These two layers contain the various fields using dynamics and scene lighting.

Layers breakdown

Now you will learn about the individual rendering passes and how they fit together. Typical effects shots are likely much more complex. The emphasis here is on how the rendering passes were conceived, not on the steps involved in actual compositing.

Note: *All the following renders can be found in the support files.*

Layer1 render: pieces

The *gunbotPieces* are a layer of *rigidBody* NURBS surfaces. They were derived from detached surfaces obtained from the original gunbot body. The guns are included as children of stand-in spheres that make up the actual active rigid bodies.

These pieces were animated using a radial field and gravity. The radial field attributes, as well as the *rigidBodies,* have keyframes on several attributes to add control to the accelerations.

These objects were rendered in software by themselves with the ground visibility turned Off via its layer. The ground still acts as a passive rigid body collision for the *gunbotPieces* when hidden.

These objects are also rendered with **Z-depth** to aid in compositing. But, this is a technique that you do not want to rely on as it can lead to accuracy problems for objects that overlap or are very close. Z-depth is only an 8-bit channel so you don't have a lot of detail to rely on if using Z-depth as a compositing aid.

Layer2 render: ground

This is simply the ground plane software rendered. The ground shadow pass is derived from this layer by applying the useBackground to the ground object, then rendering with primary visibility turned Off on all of the gunbot objects.

Layer3 render: shock

This layer is an animated NURBS sphere. It is software rendered with an X-ray or ghost shader applied. This shader creates the soft edge effect by using the facing ratio of the *SamplerInfo* utility node to drive the transparency of the material. This layer is useful for first timing the rate of explosion and helps to coordinate all the elements of the explosion.

Layer4 render: smoke

These particles are emitted from the guts particles and have only a slight amount of inherited velocity. They also have their own gravity, which is very slight. The intended effect is that they are trailing smoke. These are rendered in software. The geometry of the gunbot and ground are masked by using the *useBackground* shader with **Matte Opacity** set to **blackHole**.

Layer5 render: sparks

This layer of particles is surface emitted from the rigid body pieces. They emit pixie dust, so they sparkle and flash. The sparks collide with the ground and the gunbot. They have a collision event that emits other sparks at the point of collision. They are hardware rendered.

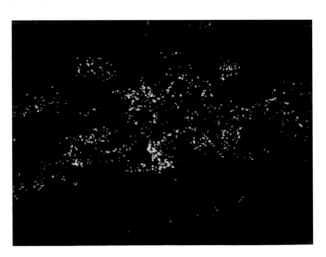

Layer6 render: particles

Stock footage of a
fireball explosion
was inserted into the
composite. Because
these images did
not contain Z-depth
information, the
images were scaled
and positioned inside
the compositing
application. A time
warp was also used to
synch the timing and
duration for this effect.

Layer7 render: shadows

A few different shadow pass sequences were rendered separately, then
composited into the final movie. The shadow pass layers were created using
the useBackground shader on the gunbot and the ground. With their **Primary
Visibility** set **Off**, the geometry acts as shadow catchers. This information is only
visible in the matte channel. To see your matte information when test rendering,
select **Display** → **Alpha Channel** from the Render View. Use a compositor to
manipulate this information further by using it as a mask input channel, thus
recreating the shadows as darker areas on the images. Using this technique,
you can also render the shadows at a lower quality and then blur and add color
to them in compositing. This can significantly shave time off from rendering
large scenes.

Once all these layers
are composited
together in the
compositing software,
you can get a
result similar to
the following:

Final composited image

Lesson 30

Compositing

As the layers or passes are rendered, they should be tested together in a compositing application.

Images that have been rendered should be used in the compositing application as references only. As subsequent improvements or versions are created, it is recommended to keep the different versions and not directly replace referenced images. Doing so will allow you to go back and forth between the different image sequences as needed.

Images can undergo drastic manipulation during compositing with much less rendering time. Lighting effects and manipulation of shadow, color, and intensity as well as softness are prime examples. Rendering shadows separately and with coarse resolution with the intention of softening during composition can be a huge time and effort saver in itself.

Some popular effects achieved during compositing include:

- Color correction and contrast balance;

- Edge anti-aliasing;

- Film grain;

- Camera shake;

- Lighting effects such as glow and lens flare;

- Fake depth of field by blurring certain layers.

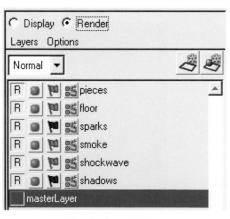

Render Layer Editor

Compositing is also where elements created in other applications are brought together. These packages are also great to bring external plates or video source footage for rotoscoping interaction with image plane or texture elements.

Maya has render layer management that can be used to organize your rendered images into separate color and shadow passes automatically. Render layers can be set up inside the **Render Layers Editor**.

Conclusion

Compositing is an important part of pulling your scene elements together. It is an especially common part of the process for dealing with the look and integration of particle rendering. Hopefully, the movies and descriptions in this lesson have given you a clear idea of what is happening at the compositing stage, as well as showing you how to construct your scenes for this process. Taking advantage of the additional speed and flexibility that compositing offers will expand not only the options you have for affecting the look of your imagery, but will also help you organize and make efficient changes to your work.

Alias *I'm excited about the render pass feature in Maya, and how it automatically*
Tip: *generates all of the images for you, if you want. I can envision that tool becoming an extremely important part of anyone's rendering workflow. With just the five basic render passes and a good compositing tool, you'll save loads of render time, and you'll be able to rapidly experiment with the look of your image.*

Chris Carden | Technical Consultant

Index

Notes

Notes

Notes

Maya™ 7

changing the face of 3D

Alias®

Silver Membership

GET MORE OUT OF MAYA®
with the Maya Silver Membership program!

As award-winning software, Maya® is the most comprehensive 3D and 2D graphics and animation solution on the market. And whether you're using Maya Personal Learning edition to learn more about computer graphics and animation, or you have a full Maya license that you're using to produce professional content, the Maya Silver Membership program helps you take your Maya skill to the next level.

What is Maya Silver Membership?

Your Maya Silver Membership program gives you quick, online access to a wide range of Maya learning resources. These educational tools – in-depth tutorials; real-life, project-based learning materials; the Maya Mentor learning environment plug-in; Weblogs from experienced Maya users – are available for a fixed monthly, or cost-saving annual, subscription fee.

Silver Membership also keeps you abreast of the latest computer graphics industry developments and puts you in touch with other Maya users and industry experts. Plus, you get 30 days of personal help to orient you around the site.

Key Benefits

- Unbeatable Value
- Faster Learning
- Competitive Advantage
- Industry Contacts

For more information visit **www.alias.com/silver**

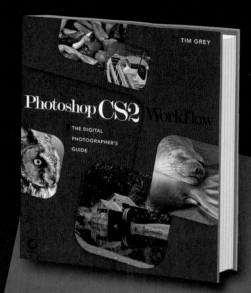

New to 3D
or to **Alias** software?

Break into the industry at your own pace with easy-to-follow books and DVDs aimed at novices and beginners. You'll begin to understand the power of 3D as you familiarize yourself with the Alias software UI and toolset. Get on the road to 3D mastery with titles like *The Art of Maya™, 3rd Edition, Maya Beginner's Guide, Alias MotionBuilder Beginner's Guide®, Learning Maya® 7 | Foundation...*

& more...

◄ **Beginner**

Want to take your skills
to the **next level**?

Improve your skills and find solutions to your production challenges in books and DVDs aimed at the intermediate user. Step-by-step exercises and valuable theoretical discussions ensure you'll understand the tools and workflows available in Alias software. Bring your skills to the next level with titles like *Learning Maya 7 | The Modeling and Animation Handbook, Learning Maya 7 | The Special Effects Handbook, Discover the Game with Alias ...*

& more...

◄ **Intermediate**

Want specific tips &
pointers from industry experts?

Gain insight into a variety of techniques and workflows used by industry experts through the Alias Techniques series. Presented by industry veterans, these DVDs can help you save time, energy, and frustration when trying to solve complex production challenges. Gain industry insight through titles like the *Maya Techniques | Hyper-Realistic series, Maya Techniques | The Making of Ryan, Maya Techniques | Maya Fluid Effects...*

& more...

◄ **Advanced**

Available at www.alias.com/learningtools

ALIAS INDUSTRY SOLUTIONS GUIDE

MaYa™ TECHNIQUES

Hyper-Realistic Production Series

Make your creative fantasy come to life with the Maya Techniques | Hyper-Realistic Production Series. This unique series is authored by a collection of international industry pros, working together to provide you with insight into the entire production process. From modeling to rendering, the Hyper-Real series brings to life a frighteningly realistic, nightmare-inducing beast. Learn how the experts get the results they want, through titles authored by Erick Miller, Sony Pictures Imageworks, Paul Thuriot, EA, Jeff Unay, Weta, Rudy Grossman, Weta, Andy Jones, Sony Pictures Imageworks and more.

 www.alias.com/learningtools

⊙Alias® | Learning Tools

OFFICIAL ALIAS TRAINING GUIDE

LEARNING Maya™ 7

Modeling & Animation Handbook

Alias | Learning Tools